C.A. Fyffe

A History Of Modern Europe

Volume I.

C.A. Fyffe

A History Of Modern Europe
Volume I.

ISBN/EAN: 9783742842671

Manufactured in Europe, USA, Canada, Australia, Japa

Cover: Foto ©Andreas Hilbeck / pixelio.de

Manufactured and distributed by brebook publishing software (www.brebook.com)

C.A. Fyffe

A History Of Modern Europe

E. BLAIR LEIGHTON.   BERTHOLD.

LOUIS XVI. IN THE HALL OF ASSEMBLY.

OF

MODERN EUROPE

BY

C. A. FYFFE M.A.

FELLOW OF UNIVERSITY COLLEGE, OXFORD

VOL. 1.

FROM THE OUTBREAK OF THE REVOLUTIONARY WAR IN 1792
TO THE ACCESSION OF LOUIS XVIII. IN 1814

WITH MAPS

CASSELL AND COMPANY LIMITED
LONDON PARIS & MELBOURNE
1891

PREFACE TO THE FIRST EDITION.

THE object of this work is to show how the States of Europe have gained the form and character which they possess at the present moment. The outbreak of the Revolutionary War in 1792, terminating a period which now appears far removed from us, and setting in motion forces which have in our own day produced a united Germany and a united Italy, forms the natural starting-point of a history of the present century. I have endeavoured to tell a simple story, believing that a narrative in which facts are chosen for their significance, and exhibited in their real connection, may be made to convey as true an impression as a fuller history in which the writer is not forced by the necessity of concentration to exercise the same rigour towards himself and his materials. The second volume of the work will bring the reader down to the year 1848: the third, down to the present time.

London, 1880.

PREFACE TO THE SECOND EDITION.

In revising this volume for the second edition I have occupied myself mainly with two sources of information—the unpublished Records of the English Foreign Office, and the published works which have during recent years resulted from the investigation of the Archives of Vienna. The English Records from 1792 to 1814, for access to which I have to express my thanks to Lord Granville, form a body of first-hand authority of extraordinary richness, compass, and interest. They include the whole correspondence between the representatives of Great Britain at Foreign Courts and the English Foreign Office; a certain number of private communications between Ministers and these representatives; a quantity of reports from consuls, agents, and "informants" of every description; and in addition to these the military reports, often admirably vivid and full of matter, sent by the British officers attached to the head-quarters of our Allies in most of the campaigns from 1792 to 1814. It is impossible that any one person should go through the whole of this material, which it took the Diplomatic Service a quarter of a century to write. I have endeavoured to master the correspondence from each quarter of Europe which, for the time being, had a preponderance in political or military interest, leaving it when its importance became obviously subordinate to that of others; and although I have no doubt left untouched much that would repay investigation, I trust that the narrative has gained in accuracy from a labour which was not a light one, and that the few short extracts which space has permitted me to throw into the notes may serve to bring the reader nearer to events. At some future time I hope to publish a selection from the most important documents of this period. It is strange that our learned Societies, so appreciative of every distant and trivial chronicle of the Middle Ages, should ignore the records of a time of such surpassing interest, and one in which England played so great a part. No just conception can be formed of the difference between English statesmanship and that of the Continental Courts in integrity, truthfulness, and public spirit, until the mass of diplomatic correspondence preserved at London has been studied; nor, until this has been done, can anything like an adequate biography of Pitt be written.

The second and less important group of authorities with which I have busied myself during the work of revision comprises the works of Hüffer, Vivenot, Beer, Helfert, and others, based on Austrian documents, along with the Austrian documents and letters that have been published by Vivenot. The last-named writer is himself a partizan, but the material which he has given to the world is most valuable. The mystery in which the Austrian Government until lately enveloped all its actions caused some of these to be described as worse than they really were; and I believe that in the First Edition I underestimated the bias of Prussian and North-German writers. Where I have seen reasons to alter any statements, I have done so without reserve, as it appears to me childish for any one who attempts to write history to cling to an opinion after the balance of evidence seems to be against it. The publication of the second volume of this work has been delayed by the revision of the first; but I hope that it will appear before many months more. I must express my obligations to Mr. Oscar Browning, a fellow-labourer in the same field, who not only furnished me with various corrections, but placed his own lectures at my disposal; and to Mr. Alfred Kingston, whose unfailing kindness and courtesy make so great a difference to those whose work lies in the department of the Record Office which is under his care.

London, 1883.

CONTENTS.

CHAPTER I.

FRANCE AND GERMANY AT THE OUTBREAK OF THE REVOLUTIONARY WAR.

Outbreak of the Revolutionary War in 1792—Its immediate causes—Declaration of Pillnitz made and withdrawn—Agitation of the Priests and Emigrants—War Policy of the Gironde—Provocations offered to France by the Powers—State of Central Europe in 1792—The Holy Roman Empire—Austria—Rule of the Hapsburgs—The Reforms of Maria Theresa and Joseph II.—Policy of Leopold II.—Government and Foreign Policy of Francis II.—Prussia—Government of Frederick William II.—Social Condition of Prussia—Secondary States of Germany—Ecclesiastical States—Free Cities—Knights—Weakness of Germany 1

CHAPTER II.

THE WAR, DOWN TO THE TREATIES OF BASLE AND THE ESTABLISHMENT OF THE DIRECTORY.

French and Austrian Armies on the Flemish Frontier—Prussia enters the War—Brunswick invades France—His Proclamation—Insurrection of Aug. 10 at Paris—Massacres of September—Character of the War—Brunswick, checked at Valmy, retreats—The War becomes a Crusade of France—Neighbours of France—Custine enters Mainz—Dumouriez conquers the Austrian Netherlands—Nice and Savoy annexed—Decree of the Convention against all Governments—Execution of Louis XVI.—War with England, followed by war with the Mediterranean States—Condition of England—English Parties, how affected by the Revolution—The Gironde and the Mountain—Austria recovers the Netherlands—The Allies invade France—La Vendée—Revolutionary System of 1793—Errors of the Allies—New French Commanders and Democratic Army—Victories of Jourdan, Hoche, and Pichegru—Prussia withdrawing from the War—Polish Affairs—Austria abandons the Netherlands—Treaties of Basle—France in 1795—Insurrection of 13 Vendémiaire—Constitution of 1795—The Directory—Effect of the Revolution on the Spirit of Europe up to 1795 41

CHAPTER III.

ITALIAN CAMPAIGNS: TREATY OF CAMPO FORMIO.

Triple attack on Austria—Moreau, Jourdan—Bonaparte in Italy—Condition of the Italian States—Professions and real intentions of Bonaparte and the Directory—Battle of Montenotte—Armistice with Sardinia—Campaign in Lombardy—Treatment of the Pope, Naples, Tuscany—Siege of Mantua—Castiglione—Moreau and Jourdan in Germany—Their retreat—Secret Treaty with Prussia—Negotiations with England—Cispadane Republic—Rise of the idea of Italian Independence—Battles of Arcola and Rivoli—Peace with the Pope at Tolentino—Venice—Preliminaries of Leoben—The French in Venice—The French take the Ionian Islands and give Venice to Austria—Genoa—Coup d'état of 17 Fructidor in Paris—Treaty of Campo Formio—Victories of England at Sea—Bonaparte's project against Egypt 110

CHAPTER IV.

FROM THE CONGRESS OF RASTADT TO THE ESTABLISHMENT OF THE CONSULATE.

Congress of Rastadt—The Rhenish Provinces ceded—Ecclesiastical States of Germany suppressed—French Intervention in Switzerland—Helvetic Republic—The French invade the Papal States—Roman Republic—Expedition to Egypt—Battle of the Nile—Coalition of 1798—Ferdinand of Naples enters Rome—Mack's defeats—French enter Naples—Parthenopean Republic—War with Austria and Russia—Battle of Stockach—Murder of the French Envoys at Rastadt—Campaign in Lombardy—Reign of Terror at Naples—Austrian designs upon Italy—Suvaroff and the Austrians—Campaign in Switzerland—Campaign in Holland—Bonaparte returns from Egypt—Coup-d'état of 18 Brumaire—Constitution of 1799—System of Bonaparte in France—Its effect on the influence of France abroad 154

CHAPTER V.

FROM MARENGO TO THE RUPTURE OF THE PEACE OF AMIENS.

Overtures of Bonaparte to Austria and England—The War continues—Massena besieged in Genoa—Moreau invades Southern Germany—Bonaparte crosses the St. Bernard, and descends in the rear of the Austrians—Battle of Marengo—Austrians retire behind the Mincio—Treaty between England and Austria—Austria continues the War—Battle of Hohenlinden—Peace of Lunéville—War between England and the Northern Maritime League—Battle of Copenhagen—Murder of Paul—End of the Maritime War—English Army enters Egypt—French defeated at Alexandria—They capitulate at Cairo and Alexandria—Preliminaries of Peace between England and France signed at London, followed by Peace of Amiens—Pitt's Irish Policy and his retirement—

Debates on the Peace—Aggressions of Bonaparte during the Continental Peace—Holland, Italy, Switzerland—Settlement of Germany under French and Russian influence—Suppression of Ecclesiastical States and Free Cities—Its effects—Stein—France under the Consulate—The Civil Code—The Concordat 215

CHAPTER VI.

THE EMPIRE, TO THE PEACE OF PRESBURG.

England claims Malta—War renewed—Bonaparte occupies Hanover, and blockades the Elbe—Remonstrances of Prussia—Cadoudal's Plot—Murder of the Duke of Enghien—Napoleon Emperor—Coalition of 1805—Prussia holds aloof—State of Austria—Failure of Napoleon's Attempt to gain Naval Superiority in the Channel—Campaign in Western Germany—Capitulation of Ulm—Trafalgar—Treaty of Potsdam between Prussia and the Allies—The French enter Vienna—Haugwitz sent to Napoleon with Prussian Ultimatum—Battle of Austerlitz—Haugwitz signs a Treaty of Alliance with Napoleon—Peace—Treaty of Presburg—End of the Holy Roman Empire—Naples given to Joseph Bonaparte—Battle of Maida—The Napoleonic Empire and Dynasty—Federation of the Rhine—State of Germany—Possibility of maintaining the Empire of 1806 266

CHAPTER VII.

DEATH OF PITT, TO THE PEACE OF TILSIT.

Death of Pitt—Ministry of Fox and Grenville—Napoleon forces Prussia into war with England, and then offers Hanover to England—Prussia resolves on war with Napoleon — State of Prussia—Decline of the Army—Southern Germany with Napoleon—Austria neutral—England and Russia about to help Prussia, but not immediately—Campaign of 1806—Battles of Jena and Auerstadt—Ruin of the Prussian Army—Capitulation of Fortresses—Demands of Napoleon—The War continues—Berlin Decree—Exclusion of English goods from the Continent—Russia enters the war—Campaign in Poland and East Prussia—Eylau—Treaty of Bartenstein — Friedland—Interview at Tilsit—Alliance of Napoleon and Alexander—Secret Articles—English expedition to Denmark—The French enter Portugal—Prussia after the Peace of Tilsit—Stein's Edict of Emancipation—The Prussian Peasant—Reform of the Prussian Army, and creation of Municipalities—Stein's other projects of Reform, which are not carried out 309

CHAPTER VIII.

SPAIN, TO THE FALL OF SARAGOSSA.

Spain in 1806—Napoleon uses the quarrel between Ferdinand and Godoy—He affects to be Ferdinand's Protector—Dupont's Army enters Spain—Murat in Spain—Charles abdicates—Ferdinand King—Savary brings

CONTENTS. xi

Ferdinand to Bayonne—Napoleon makes both Charles and Ferdinand resign—Spirit of the Spanish Nation—Contrast with Germany—Rising of all Spain—The Notables at Bayonne—Campaign of 1808—Capitulation of Baylen—Wellesley lands in Portugal—Vimieiro—Convention of Cintra—Effect of the Spanish Rising on Europe—War Party in Prussia—Napoleon and Alexander at Erfurt—Stein resigns, and is proscribed—Napoleon in Spain—Spanish Misgovernment—Campaign on the Ebro—Campaign of Sir John Moore—Corunna—Napoleon leaves Spain—Siege of Saragossa—Successes of the French 367

CHAPTER IX.

WAR OF 1809: THE NAPOLEONIC EMPIRE—SPAIN, TO THE BATTLE OF SALAMANCA.

Austrian preparing for war—The war to be one on behalf of the German Nation—Patriotic movement in Prussia—Expected Insurrection in North Germany—Plans of Campaign—Austrian Manifesto to the Germans—Rising of the Tyrolese—Defeats of the Archduke Charles in Bavaria—French in Vienna—Attempts of Dörnberg and Schill—Battle of Aspern—Second passage of the Danube—Battle of Wagram—Armistice of Znaim—Austria waiting for Events—Wellesley in Spain—He gains the Battle of Talavera, but retreats—Expedition against Antwerp fails—Austria makes Peace—Treaty of Vienna—Real Effects of the War of 1809—Austria after 1809—Metternich—Marriage of Napoleon with Marie Louise—Severance of Napoleon and Alexander—Napoleon annexes the Papal States, Holland, Le Valais, and the North German Coast—The Napoleonic Empire: its benefits and wrongs—The Czar withdraws from Napoleon's Commercial System—War with Russia imminent—Wellington in Portugal; Lines of Torres Vedras; Massena's Campaign of 1810, and retreat—Soult in Andalusia—Wellington's Campaign of 1811—Capture of Ciudad Rodrigo and Badajoz—Salamanca 402

CHAPTER X.

RUSSIAN CAMPAIGN, TO THE TREATY OF KALISCH.

War approaching between France and Russia—Policy of Prussia—Hardenberg's Ministry—Prussia forced into Alliance with Napoleon—Austrian Alliance—Napoleon's Preparations—He enters Russia—Alexander and Bernadotte—Plan of Russians to fight a battle at Drissa frustrated—They retreat on Witepsk—Sufferings of the French—French enter Smolensko—Battle of Borodino—Evacuation of Moscow—Moscow fired—The Retreat from Moscow—French at Smolensko—Advance of Russian Armies from North and South—Battle of Krasnoi—Passage of the Berezina—The French reach the Niemen—York's Convention with the Russians—The Czar and Stein—Russian Army enters Prussia—Stein raises East Prussia—Treaty of Kalisch—Prussia declares War—Enthusiasm of the Nation—Idea of German Unity—The Landwehr. 456

CHAPTER XI.

WAR OF LIBERATION, TO THE PEACE OF PARIS.

The War of Liberation—Blücher crosses the Elbe—Battle of Lützen—The Allies retreat to Silesia—Battle of Bautzen—Armistice—Napoleon intends to intimidate Austria—Mistaken as to the Forces of Austria—Metternich's Policy — Treaty of Reichenbach—Austria offers its Mediation—Congress of Prague—Austria enters the War—Armies and Plans of Napoleon and the Allies—Campaign of August—Battles of Dresden, Grosbeeren, the Katzbach, and Kulm—Effect of these Actions—Battle of Dennewitz—German Policy of Austria favourable to the Princes of the Rhenish Confederacy — Frustrated hopes of German Unity—Battle of Leipzig—The Allies reach the Rhine—Offers of Peace at Frankfort—Plan of Invasion of France—Backwardness of Austria—The Allies enter France—Campaign of 1814—Congress of Châtillon—Napoleon moves to the rear of the Allies—The Allies advance on Paris—Capitulation of Paris—Entry of the Allies—Dethronement of Napoleon—Restoration of the Bourbons—The Charta—Treaty of Paris—Territorial effects of the War, 1792-1814—Every Power except France had gained—France relatively weaker in Europe—Summary of the permanent effects of this period on Europe . . 490

LIST OF ILLUSTRATIONS.

	PAGE
LOUIS XVI. IN THE HALL OF ASSEMBLY	*Frontis.*
ADVANCE OF PICHEGRU'S ARMY	*To face* 95
NAPOLEON AT THE BRIDGE OF LODI	,, 120
NELSON'S RECEPTION AT NAPLES	,, 183
NELSON AT COPENHAGEN	,, 231
MURDER OF THE DUKE OF ENGHIEN	,, 275
THE BATTLE OF TRAFALGAR	,, 290
MURAT ENTERING MADRID	,, 374
DEATH OF MOORE AT CORUNNA	,, 398
NAPOLEON AT MOSCOW	,, 469

MAPS.

EUROPEAN STATES IN 1792	,, 40
CENTRAL EUROPE IN 1812	, 418

MOD. EUR. I.

MODERN EUROPE.

CHAPTER I.

Outbreak of the Revolutionary War in 1792—Its immediate causes—Declaration of Pillnitz made and withdrawn—Agitation of the Priests and Emigrants—War Policy of the Gironde—Provocations offered to France by the Powers—State of Central Europe in 1792—The Holy Roman Empire—Austria—Rule of the Hapsburgs—The Reforms of Maria Theresa and Joseph II.—Policy of Leopold II.—Government and Foreign Policy of Francis II.—Prussia—Government of Frederick William II.—Social condition of Prussia—Secondary States of Germany—Ecclesiastical States—Free Cities—Knights—Weakness of Germany.

ON the morning of the 19th of April, 1792, after weeks of stormy agitation in Paris, the Ministers of Louis XVI. brought down a letter from the King to the Legislative Assembly of France. The letter was brief but significant. It announced that the King intended to appear in the Hall of Assembly at noon on the following day. Though the letter did not disclose the object of the King's visit, it was known that Louis had given way to the pressure of his Ministry and the national cry for war, and that a declaration of war against Austria was the measure which the King was about to propose in person to the Assembly. On the morrow the public thronged the hall; the Assembly broke off its debate at midday in order to be in readiness for the King. Louis entered the hall in the midst of deep silence, and seated himself beside the President in the chair which was now substituted for the throne of France. At the King's bidding General Dumouriez, Minister of Foreign Affairs, read a report to the Assembly upon the relations of France to foreign Powers. The report contained a long series of charges against Austria, and concluded with the recommendation of war. When Dumouriez ceased reading Louis rose, and in a low voice declared that he himself and the whole of the Ministry accepted the report read to the Assembly; that he had used every effort to maintain peace, and in vain; and that he was now come, in accordance with the terms of the Constitution, to propose that the Assembly declare war against the Austrian Sovereign. It was not three months since Louis himself had supplicated the Courts of Europe for armed aid against his own subjects. The words which he now uttered were put in his mouth by men whom he hated, but could not resist: the very outburst of applause that followed them only proved the fatal antagonism that existed between the nation and the King. After the President of the Assembly had made a short answer, Louis retired from the hall. The Assembly itself broke up, to commence its debate on the King's proposal after an interval of some hours. When the House re-assembled in the evening, those few courageous men who argued on grounds of national interest and justice against the passion of the moment could scarcely obtain a hearing. An appeal for a second day's discussion was rejected; the debate abruptly closed;

and the declaration of war was carried against seven dissentient votes. It was a decision big with consequences for France and for the world. From that day began the struggle between Revolutionary France and the established order of Europe. A period opened in which almost every State on the Continent gained some new character from the aggressions of France, from the laws and political changes introduced by the conqueror, or from the awakening of new forces of national life in the crisis of successful resistance or of humiliation. It is my intention to trace the great lines of European history from that time to the present, briefly sketching the condition of some of the principal States at the outbreak of the Revolutionary War, and endeavouring to distinguish, amid scenes of ever-shifting incident, the steps by which the Europe of 1792 has become the Europe of to-day.

The first two years of the Revolution had ended without bringing France into collision with foreign Powers. This was not due to any goodwill that the Courts of Europe bore to the French people, or to want of effort on the part of the French aristocracy to raise the armies of Europe against their own country. The National Assembly, which met in 1789, had cut at the roots of the power of the Crown; it had deprived the nobility of their privileges, and laid its hand upon the revenues of the Church. The brothers of King Louis XVI., with a host of nobles too impatient to pursue a course of steady political opposition at home, quitted France, and wearied

First threats of foreign Courts against France, 1791.

foreign Courts with their appeals for armed assistance. The absolute monarchs of the Continent gave them a warm and even ostentatious welcome; but they confined their support to words and tokens of distinction, and until the summer of 1791 the Revolution was not seriously threatened with the interference of the stranger. The flight of King Louis from Paris in June, 1791, followed by his capture and his strict confinement within the Tuileries, gave rise to the first definite project of foreign intervention.* Louis had fled from his capital and from the National Assembly; he returned, the hostage of a populace already familiar with outrage and bloodshed. For a moment the exasperation of Paris brought the Royal Family into real jeopardy. The Emperor Leopold, brother of Marie Antoinette, trembled for the safety of his unhappy sister, and addressed a letter to the European Courts from Padua, on the 6th of July, proposing that the Powers should unite to preserve the Royal Family of France from popular violence. Six weeks later the Emperor and King Frederick William II. of Prussia met at Pillnitz, in Saxony. A declaration was published by the two Sovereigns, stating that they considered the position of the King of France to be matter of European concern, and that, in the event of all the other great Powers consenting to a joint action, they were prepared to supply an armed force to operate on the French frontier.

Had the National Assembly instantly declared war on

* Ranke, Ursprung und Beginn der Revolutionskriege, p. 90 Vivenot, Quellen zur Geschichte der Kaiserpolitik Oesterreichs, 1, 185, 208.

Leopold and Frederick William, its action would have been justified by every rule of international law. The Assembly did not, however, declare war, and for a good reason. It was known at Paris that the manifesto was no more than a device of the Emperor's to intimidate the enemies of the Royal Family. Leopold, when he pledged himself to join a coalition of all the Powers, was in fact aware that England would be no party to any such coalition. He was determined to do nothing that would force him into war; and it did not occur to him that French politicians would understand the emptiness of his threats as well as he did himself. Yet this turned out to be the case; and whatever indignation the manifesto of Pillnitz excited in the mass of the French people, it was received with more derision than alarm by the men who were cognisant of the affairs of Europe. All the politicians of the National Assembly knew that Prussia and Austria had lately been on the verge of war with one another upon the Eastern question; they even underrated the effect of the French revolution in appeasing the existing enmities of the great Powers. No important party in France regarded the Declaration of Pillnitz as a possible reason for hostilities; and the challenge given to France was soon publicly withdrawn. It was withdrawn when Louis XVI., by accepting the Constitution made by the National Assembly, placed himself, in the sight of Europe, in the position of a free agent. On the 14th September, 1791, the King, by a solemn public oath, identified his

Declaration of Pillnitz withdrawn.

will with that of the nation. It was known in Paris that he had been urged by the emigrants to refuse his assent, and to plunge the nation into civil war by an open breach with the Assembly. The frankness with which Louis pledged himself to the Constitution, the seeming sincerity of his patriotism, again turned the tide of public opinion in his favour. His flight was forgiven; the restrictions placed upon his personal liberty were relaxed. Louis seemed to be once more reconciled with France, and France was relieved from the ban of Europe. The Emperor announced that the circumstances which had provoked the Declaration of Pillnitz no longer existed, and that the Powers, though prepared to revive the League if future occasion should arise, suspended all joint action in reference to the internal affairs of France.

Priests and emigrants keep France in agitation.

The National Assembly, which, in two years, had carried France so far towards the goal of political and social freedom, now declared its work ended. In the mass of the nation there was little desire for further change. The grievances which pressed most heavily upon the common course of men's lives—unfair taxation, exclusion from public employment, monopolies among the townspeople, and the feudal dues which consumed the produce of the peasant,—had been swept away. It was less by any general demand for further reform than by the antagonisms already kindled in the Revolution that France was forced into a new series of violent changes. The King himself was not sincerely at one with the nation; in everything that most keenly touched his conscience he had unwillingly accepted the work of the Assembly. The Church and the noblesse were bent on undoing what had already been done. Without interfering with doctrine or ritual, the National Assembly had re-organised the ecclesiastical system of France, and had enforced that supremacy of the State over the priesthood to which, throughout the eighteenth century, the Governments of Catholic Europe had been steadily tending. The Civil Constitution of the Clergy, which was created by the National Assembly in 1790, transformed the priesthood from a society of landowners into a body of salaried officers of the State, and gave to the laity the election of their bishops and ministers. The change, carried out in this extreme form, threw the whole body of bishops and a great part of the lower clergy into revolt. Their interests were hurt by the sale of the Church lands; their consciences were wounded by the system of popular election, which was condemned by the Pope. In half the pulpits of France the principles of the Revolution were anathematised, and the vengeance of heaven denounced against the purchasers of the secularised Church lands. Beyond the frontier the emigrant nobles, who might have tempered the Revolution by combining with the many liberal men of their order who remained at home, gathered in arms, and sought the help of foreigners against a nation in which they could see nothing but rebellious dependents of their own. The head-quarters of the emigrants were at Coblentz in the dominions of the Elector of Trèves.

They formed themselves into regiments, numbering in all some few thousands, and occupied themselves with extravagant schemes of vengeance against all Frenchmen who had taken part in the destruction of the privileges of their caste.

Had the elections which followed the dissolution of the National Assembly sent to the Legislature a body of men bent only on maintaining the advantages already won, it would have been no easy task to preserve the peace of France in the presence of the secret or open hostility of the Court, the Church, and the emigrants. But the trial was not made. The leading spirits among the new representatives were not men of compromise. In the Legislative Body which met in 1791 there were all the passions of the Assembly of 1789, without any of the experience which that Assembly had gained. A decree, memorable among the achievements of political folly, had prohibited members of the late Chamber from seeking re-election. The new Legislature was composed of men whose political creed had been drawn almost wholly from literary sources; the most dangerous theorists of the former Assembly were released from Parliamentary restraints, and installed, like Robespierre, as the orators of the clubs. Within the Chamber itself the defenders of the Monarchy and of the Constitution which had just been given to France were far outmatched by the party of advance. The most conspicuous of the new deputies formed the group named after the district of the Gironde, where several of their leaders had been elected. The orator Vergniaud, pre-eminent among companions of singular eloquence, the philosopher Condorcet, the veteran journalist Brissot, gave to this party an ascendancy in the Chamber and an influence in the country the more dangerous because it appeared to belong to men elevated above the ordinary regions of political strife. Without the fixed design of turning the monarchy into a republic, the orators of the Gironde sought to carry the revolutionary movement over the barrier erected against it in the Constitution of 1791. From the moment of the opening of the Assembly it was clear that the Girondins intended to precipitate the conflict between the Court and the nation by devoting all the wealth of their eloquence to the subjects which divided France the most. To Brissot and the men who furnished the ideas of the party, it would have seemed a calamity that the Constitution of 1791, with its respect for the prerogative of the Crown and its tolerance of mediæval superstition, should fairly get under way. In spite of Robespierre's prediction that war would give France a strong sovereign in the place of a weak one, the Girondins persuaded themselves that the best means of diminishing or overthrowing monarchical power in France was a war with the sovereigns of Europe; and henceforward they laboured for war with scarcely any disguise.*

War-policy of the Gironde.

Nor were occasions wanting, if war was needful for France. The protection which the Elector of

* Von Sybel, Geschichte der Revolutionszeit, i. 289.

Trèves gave to the emigrant army at Coblentz was so flagrant a violation of international law that the Gironde had the support of the whole nation when they called upon the King to demand the dispersal of the emigrants in the most peremptory form. National feeling was keenly excited by debates in which the military preparations of the emigrants and the encouragement given to them by foreign princes were denounced with all the energy of southern eloquence. On the 13th of December Louis declared to the Electors of Trèves and Mainz that he would treat them as enemies unless the armaments within their territories were dispersed by January 15th; and at the same time he called upon the Emperor Leopold, as head of the Germanic body, to use his influence in bringing the Electors to reason. The demands of France were not resisted. On the 16th January, 1792, Louis informed the Assembly that the emigrants had been expelled from the electorates, and acknowledged the good offices of Leopold in effecting this result. The substantial cause of war seemed to have disappeared; but another had arisen in its place. In a note of December 21st the Austrian minister Kaunitz used expressions which implied that a league of the Powers was still in existence against France. Nothing could have come more opportunely for the war-party in the Assembly. Brissot cried for an immediate declaration of war, and appealed to the French nation to vindicate its honour by an attack both upon the emigrants and

Notes of Kaunitz, Dec. 21, Feb. 17.

upon their imperial protector. The issue depended upon the relative power of the Crown and the Opposition. Leopold saw that war was inevitable unless the Constitutional party, which was still in office, rallied for one last effort, and gained a decisive victory over its antagonists. In the hope of turning public opinion against the Gironde, he permitted Kaunitz to send a despatch to Paris which loaded the leaders of the war-party with abuse, and exhorted the French nation to deliver itself from men who would bring upon it the hostility of Europe. (Feb. 17.)* The despatch gave singular proof of the inability of the cleverest sovereign and the most experienced minister of the age to distinguish between the fears of a timid cabinet and the impulses of an excited nation. Leopold's vituperations might have had the intended effect if they had been addressed to the Margrave of Baden or the Doge of Venice; addressed to the French nation and its popular Assembly in the height of civil conflict, they were as oil poured upon the flames. Leopold ruined the party which he meant to reinforce; he threw the nation into the arms of those whom he attacked. His despatch was received in the Assembly with alternate murmurs and bursts of laughter; in the clubs it excited a wild outburst of rage. The exchange of diplomatic notes continued for a few weeks more; but the real answer of France to Austria was the "Marseillaise," composed at Strasburg almost simultaneously with Kaunitz' attack upon the Jacobins. The sudden death of the Emperor on

* Vivenot, Quellen, i. 372. Buchez et Roux, xiii. 340, xiv. 24.

March 1st produced no pause in the controversy. Delessart, the Foreign Minister of Louis, was thrust from office, and replaced by Dumouriez, the representative of the war-party. Expostulation took a sharper tone; old subjects of complaint were revived; and the armies on each side were already pressing towards the frontier when the unhappy Louis was brought down to the Assembly by his Ministers, and compelled to propose the declaration of war.

War declared, April 20, 1792

It is seldom that the professed grounds correspond with the real motives of a war; nor was this the case in 1792. The ultimatum of the Austrian Government demanded that compensation should be made to certain German nobles whose feudal rights over their peasantry had been abolished in Alsace; that the Pope should be indemnified for Avignon and the Venaissin, which had been taken from him by France; and that a Government should be established at Paris capable of affording the Powers of Europe security against the spread of democratic agitation. No one supposed the first two grievances to be a serious ground for hostilities. The rights of the German nobles in Alsace over their villagers were no doubt protected by the treaties which ceded those districts to France; but every politician in Europe would have laughed at a Government which allowed the feudal system to survive in a corner of its dominions out of respect for a settlement a century and a half old: nor had the Assembly refused to these foreign

Pretended grounds of war.

seigneurs a compensation claimed in vain by King Louis for the nobles of France. As to the annexation of Avignon and the Venaissin, a power which, like Austria, had joined in dismembering Poland, and had just made an unsuccessful attempt to dismember Turkey, could not gravely reproach France for incorporating a district which lay actually within it, and whose inhabitants, or a great portion of them, were anxious to become citizens of France. The third demand, the establishment of such a government as Austria should deem satisfactory, was one which no high-spirited people could be expected to entertain. Nor was this in fact expected by Austria. Leopold had no desire to attack France, but he had used threats, and would not submit to the humiliation of renouncing them. He would not have begun a war for the purpose of delivering the French Crown; but, when he found that he was himself certain to be attacked, he accepted a war with the Revolution without regret. On the other side, when the Gironde denounced the league of the Kings, they exaggerated a far-off danger for the ends of their domestic policy. The Sovereigns of the Continent had indeed made no secret of their hatred to the Revolution. Catherine of Russia had exhorted every Court in Europe to make war; Gustavus of Sweden was surprised by a violent death in the midst of preparations against France; Spain, Naples, and Sardinia were ready to follow leaders stronger than themselves. But the statesmen of the French Assembly

Expectation of foreign attack real among the French people; not real among French politicians.

well understood the interval that separates hostile feeling from actual attack; and the unsubstantial nature of the danger to France, whether from the northern or the southern Powers, was proved by the very fact that Austria, the hereditary enemy of France, and the country of the hated Marie Antoinette, was treated as the main enemy. Nevertheless, the Courts had done enough to excite the anger of millions of French people who knew of their menaces, and not of their hesitations and reserves. The man who composed the "Marseillaise" was no maker of cunningly-devised fables; the crowds who first sang it never doubted the reality of the dangers which the orators of the Assembly denounced. The Courts of Europe had heaped up the fuel; the Girondins applied the torch. The mass of the French nation had little means of appreciating what passed in Europe; they took their facts from their leaders, who considered it no very serious thing to plunge a nation into war for the furtherance of internal liberty. Events were soon to pass their own stern and mocking sentence upon the wisdom of the Girondin statesmanship.

After voting the Declaration of War the French Assembly accepted a manifesto, drawn up by Condorcet, renouncing in the name of the French people all intention of conquest.

Germany follows Austria into the war.

The manifesto expressed what was sincerely felt by men like Condorcet, to whom the Revolution was still too sacred a cause to be stained with the vulgar lust of aggrandisement. But the actual course of the war was determined less by the intentions with which the French began it than by the political condition of the States which bordered upon the French frontier. The war was primarily a war with Austria, but the Sovereign of Austria was also the head of Germany. The German Ecclesiastical Princes who ruled in the Rhenish provinces had been the most zealous protectors of the emigrants; it was impossible that they should now find shelter in neutrality. Prussia had made an alliance with the Emperor against France; other German States followed in the wake of one or other of the great Powers. If France proved stronger than its enemy, there were governments besides that of Austria which would have to take their account with the Revolution. Nor indeed was Austria the power most exposed to violent change. The mass of its territory lay far from France; at the most, it risked the loss of Lombardy and the Netherlands. Germany at large was the real area threatened by the war, and never was a political community less fitted to resist attack than Germany at the end of the eighteenth century. It was in the divisions of the German people, and in the rivalries of the two leading German governments, that France found its surest support throughout the Revolutionary war, and its keenest stimulus to conquest. It will throw light upon the sudden changes that now began to break over Europe if we pause to make a brief survey of the state of Germany at the outbreak of the war, to note the character and policy of its reigning sovereigns, and to cast a glance over the circumstances which had brought the central district of Europe into its actual condition.

State of Germany.

Germany at large still preserved the mediæval name and forms of the Holy Roman Empire. The members of this so-called Empire were, however, a multitude of independent States; and the chief of these States, Austria, combined with its German provinces a large territory which did not even in name form part of the Germanic body. The motley of the Empire was made up by governments of every degree of strength and weakness. Austria and Prussia possessed both political traditions and resources raising them to the rank of great European Powers; but the sovereignties of the second order, such as Saxony and Bavaria, had neither the security of strength nor the free energy often seen in small political communities; whilst in the remaining petty States of Germany, some hundreds in number, all public life had long passed out of mind in a drowsy routine of official benevolence or oppression. In theory there still existed a united Germanic body; in reality Germany was composed of two great monarchies in embittered rivalry with one another, and of a multitude of independent principalities and cities whose membership in the Empire involved little beyond a liability to be dragged into the quarrels of their more powerful neighbours. A German national feeling did not exist, because no combination existed uniting the interests of all Germany. The names and forms of political union had come down from a remote past, and formed a grotesque anachronism amid the realities of the eighteenth century. The head of the Germanic body held office not by hereditary right, but as the elected successor of Charlemagne and the Roman Cæsars. Since the fifteenth century the imperial dignity had rested with the Austrian House of Hapsburg; but, with the exception of Charles V., no sovereign of that House had commanded forces adequate to the creation of a united German state, and the opportunity which then offered itself was allowed to pass away. The Reformation severed Northern Germany from the Catholic monarchy of the south. The Thirty Years' War, terminating in the middle of the seventeenth century, secured the existence of Protestantism on the Continent of Europe, but it secured it at the cost of Germany, which was left exhausted and disintegrated. By the Treaty of Westphalia, A.D. 1648, the independence of every member of the Empire was recognised, and the central authority was henceforth a mere shadow. The Diet of the Empire, where the representatives of the Electors, of the Princes, and of the Free Cities, met in the order of the Middle Ages, sank into a Heralds' College, occupied with questions of title and precedence; affairs of real importance were transacted by envoys from Court to Court. For purposes of war the Empire was divided into Circles, each Circle supplying in theory a contingent of troops; but this military organisation existed only in letter. The greater and the intermediate States regulated their armaments, as they did their policy, without regard to the Diet of Ratisbon; the contingents of the smaller sovereignties and free cities were in every degree of inefficiency,

Since 1648, all the German States independent of the Emperor.

corruption, and disorder; and in spite of the courage of the German soldier, it could make little difference in a European war whether a regiment which had its captain appointed by the city of Gmünd, its lieutenant by the Abbess of Rotenmünster, and its ensign by the Abbot of Gegenbach, did or did not take the field with numbers fifty per cent. below its statutory contingent.* How loose was the connection subsisting between the members of the Empire, how slow and cumbrous its constitutional machinery, was strikingly proved after the first inroads of the French into Germany in 1792, when the Diet deliberated for four weeks before calling out the forces of the Empire, and for five months before declaring war.

The defence of Germany rested in fact with the armies of Austria and Prussia. The Austrian House of

Austria. Hapsburg held the imperial title, and gathered around it the sovereigns of the less progressive German States. While the Protestant communities of Northern Germany identified their interests with those of the rising Prussian Monarchy, religious sympathy and the tradition of ages attached the minor Catholic Courts to the political system of Vienna. Austria gained something by its patronage; it was, however, no real member of the German family. Its interests were not the interests of Germany; its power, great and enduring as it proved, was not based mainly upon German elements, nor used mainly for German

* Häusser, Deutsche Geschichte, i. 88. Vivenot, Herzog Albrecht, i. 78.

ends. The title of the Austrian monarch gave the best idea of the singular variety of races and nationalities which owed their political union only to their submission to a common head. In the shorter form of state the reigning Hapsburg was described as King of Hungary, Bohemia, Croatia, Slavonia, and Galicia; Archduke of Austria; Grand Duke of Transylvania; Duke of Styria, Carinthia, and Carniola; and Princely Count of Hapsburg and Tyrol. At the outbreak of the war of 1792 the dominions of the House of Austria included the Southern Netherlands and the Duchy of Milan, in addition to the great bulk of the territory which it still governs. Eleven distinct languages were spoken in the Austrian monarchy with countless varieties of dialects. Of the elements of the population the Slavic was far the largest, numbering about ten millions, against five million Germans and three million Magyars; but neither numerical strength nor national objects of desire coloured the policy of a family which looked indifferently upon all its subject races as instruments for its own aggrandisement. Milan and the Netherlands had come into the possession of Austria since the beginning of the eighteenth century, but the destiny of the old dominions of the Hapsburg House had been fixed for many generations in the course of the Thirty Years' War. In that struggle, as it affected Austria, the conflict of the ancient and the reformed faith *Catholic policy of the Hapsburgs.* had become a conflict between the Monarchy, allied with the Church, and every element of national life and independence, allied with the Reformation. Protestantism, then dominant in almost all the Hapsburg territories, was not put down without extinguishing the political liberties of Austrian Germany, the national life of Bohemia, the spirit and ambition of the Hungarian nobles. The detestable desire of the Emperor Ferdinand, "Rather a desert than a country full of heretics," was only too well fulfilled in the subsequent history of his dominions. In the German provinces, except the Tyrol, the old Parliaments, and with them all trace of liberty, disappeared; in Bohemia the national Protestant nobility lost their estates, or retained them only at the price of abandoning the religion, the language, and the feelings of their race, until the country of Huss passed out of the sight of civilised Europe, and Bohemia represented no more than a blank, unnoticed mass of tillers of the soil. In Hungary, where the nation was not so completely crushed in the Thirty Years' War, and Protestantism survived, the wholesale executions in 1686, ordered by the Tribunal known as the "Slaughter-house of Eperies," illustrated the traditional policy of the Monarchy towards the spirit of national independence. Two powers alone were allowed to subsist in the Austrian dominions, the power of the Crown and the power of the Priesthood; and, inasmuch as no real national unity could exist among the subject races, the unity of a blind devotion to the Catholic Church was enforced over the greater part of the Monarchy by all the authority of the State.

Under the pressure of this soulless despotism the

mind of man seemed to lose all its finer powers. The seventeenth and eighteenth centuries, in which no decade passed in England and France without the production of some literary masterpiece, some scientific discovery, or some advance in political reasoning, are marked by no single illustrious Austrian name, except that of Haydn the musician. When, after three generations of torpor succeeding the Thirty Years' War, the mind of North Germany awoke again in Winckelmann and Lessing, and a widely-diffused education gave to the middle class some compensation for the absence of all political freedom, no trace of this revival appeared in Austria. The noble hunted and slept; the serf toiled heavily on; where a school existed, the Jesuit taught his schoolboys ecclesiastical Latin, and sent them away unable to read their mother-tongue. To this dull and impenetrable society the beginnings of improvement could only be brought by military disaster. The loss of Silesia in the first years of Maria Theresa disturbed the slumbers of the Government, and reform began. Although the old provincial Assemblies, except in Hungary and the Netherlands, had long lost all real power, the Crown had never attempted to create a uniform system of administration: the collection of taxes, the enlistment of recruits, was still the business of the feudal land-owners of each district. How such an antiquated order was likely to fare in the presence of an energetic enemy was clearly enough shown in the first attack made upon Austria by Frederick the Great. As the basis

Reforms of Maria Theresa. 1740—1780.

of a better military organisation, and in the hope of arousing a stronger national interest among her subjects, Theresa introduced some of the offices of a centralised monarchy, at the same time that she improved the condition of the serf, and substituted a German education and German schoolmasters for those of the Jesuits. The peasant, hitherto in many parts of the monarchy attached to the soil, was now made free to quit his lord's land, and was secured from ejectment so long as he fulfilled his duty of labouring for the lord on a fixed number of days in the year. Beyond this Theresa's reform did not extend. She had no desire to abolish the feudal character of country life; she neither wished to temper the sway of Catholicism, nor to extinguish those provincial forms which gave to the nobles within their own districts a shadow of political independence. Herself conservative in feeling, attached to aristocracy, and personally devout, Theresa consented only to such change as was recommended by her trusted counsellors, and asked no more than she was able to obtain by the charm of her own queenly character.

With the accession of her son Joseph II. in 1780 a new era began for Austria. The work deferred by Theresa was then taken up by a monarch whose conceptions of social and religious reform left little for the boldest innovators of France ten years later to add. There is no doubt that the creation of a great military force for enterprises of foreign conquest was an end always present in Joseph's mind, and that the thirst for uncontrolled despotic power never left

Joseph II. 1780 —1790.

him; but by the side of these coarser elements there was in Joseph's nature something of the true fire of the man who lives for ideas. Passionately desirous of elevating every class of his subjects at the same time that he ignored all their habits and wishes, Joseph attempted to transform the motley and priest-ridden collection of nations over whom he ruled into a single homogeneous body, organised after the model of France and Prussia, worshipping in the spirit of a tolerant and enlightened Christianity, animated in its relations of class to class by the humane philosophy of the eighteenth century. In the first year of his reign Joseph abolished every jurisdiction that did not directly emanate from the Crown, and scattered an army of officials from Ostend to the Dniester to conduct the entire public business of his dominions under the immediate direction of the central authority at Vienna. In succeeding years edict followed edict, dissolving monasteries, forbidding Church festivals and pilgrimages, securing the protection of the State to every form of Christian worship, abolishing the exemption from land-tax and the monopoly of public offices enjoyed by the nobility, transforming the Universities from dens of monkish ignorance into schools of secular learning, converting the peasant's personal service into a rent-charge, and giving him in the officer of the Crown a protector and an arbiter in all his dealings with his lord. Noble and enlightened in his aims, Joseph, like every other reformer of the eighteenth century, underrated the force which the past exerts over the present; he could see nothing but prejudice and unreason in the attachment to provincial custom or time-honoured opinion; he knew nothing of that moral law which limits the success of revolutions by the conditions which precede them. What was worst united with what was best in resistance to his reforms. The bigots of the University of Louvain, who still held out against the discoveries of Newton, excited the mob to insurrection against Joseph, as the enemy of religion; the Magyar landowners in Hungary resisted a system which extinguished the last vestiges of their national independence at the same time that it destroyed the harsh dominion which they themselves exercised over their peasantry. Joseph alternated between concession and the extreme of autocratic violence. At one moment he resolved to sweep away every local right that fettered the exercise of his power; then, after throwing the Netherlands into successful revolt, and forcing Hungary to the verge of armed resistance, he revoked his unconstitutional ordinances (January 28, 1790), and restored all the institutions of the Hungarian monarchy which existed at the date of his accession.

A month later, death removed Joseph from his struggle and his sorrows. His successor, Leopold II., found the monarchy involved as Russia's ally in an attack upon Turkey; threatened by the Northern League of Prussia, England, and Holland; exhausted in finance; weakened by the revolt of the Netherlands; and distracted in every province by the conflict of the ancient and the modern system of government, and the assertion of new social

Leopold II. 1790—1792.

rights that seemed to have been created only in order to be extinguished. The recovery of Belgium and the conclusion of peace with Turkey were effected under circumstances that brought the adroit and guarded statesmanship of Leopold into just credit. His settlement of the conflict between the Crown and the Provinces, between the Church and education, between the noble and the serf, marked the line in which, for better or for worse, Austrian policy was to run for sixty years. Provincial rights, the privileges of orders and corporate bodies, Leopold restored; the personal sovereignty of his house he maintained unimpaired. In the more liberal part of Joseph's legislation, the emancipation of learning from clerical control, the suppression of unjust privilege in taxation, the abolition of the feudal services of the peasant, Leopold was willing to make concessions to the Church and the aristocracy; to the spirit of national independence which his predecessor's aggression had excited in Bohemia as well as in Hungary, he made no concession beyond the restoration of certain cherished forms. An attempt of the Magyar nobles to affix conditions to their acknowledgment of Leopold as King of Hungary was defeated; and, by creating new offices at Vienna for the affairs of Illyria and Transylvania, and making them independent of the Hungarian Diet, Leopold showed that the Crown possessed an instrument against the dominant Magyar race in the Slavic and Romanic elements of the Hungarian Kingdom.* On the other hand, Leopold consented to restore

* Springer, Geschichte Oesterreichs, i., 46.

to the Church its control over the higher education, and to throw back the burden of taxation upon land not occupied by noble owners. He gave new rigour to the censorship of the press; but the gain was not to the Church, to which the censorship had formerly belonged, but to the Government, which now employed it as an instrument of State. In the great question of the emancipation of the serf Leopold was confronted by a more resolute and powerful body of nobility in Hungary than existed in any other province. The right of the lord to fetter the peasant to the soil and to control his marriage Leopold refused to restore in any part of his dominions; but, while in parts of Bohemia he succeeded in maintaining the right given by Joseph to the peasant to commute his personal service for a money payment, in Hungary he was compelled to fall back upon the system of Theresa, and to leave the final settlement of the question to the Diet. Twenty years later the statesman who emancipated the peasants of Prussia observed that Hungary was the only part of the Austrian dominions in which the peasant was not in a better condition than his fellows in North Germany;* and so torpid was the humanity of the Diet that until the year 1835 the prison and the flogging-board continued to form a part of every Hungarian manor.

Of the self-sacrificing ardour of Joseph there was no trace in Leopold's character; yet his political aims were not low. During twenty-four years' government of Tuscany he had proved himself almost an ideal ruler

* Pertz, Leben Stein, ii., 402. Paget, Travels in Hungary, I. 131.

in the pursuit of peace, of religious enlightenment, and of the material improvement of his little sovereignty. Raised to the Austrian throne, the compromise which he effected with the Church and the aristocracy resulted more from a supposed political necessity than from his own inclination. So long as Leopold lived Austria would not have wanted an intelligence capable of surveying the entire field of public business, nor a will capable of imposing unity of action upon the servants of State. To the misfortune of Europe no less than of his own dominions, Leopold was carried off by sickness at the moment when the Revolutionary War broke out. An uneasy reaction against Joseph's reforms and a well-grounded dread of the national movements in Hungary and the Netherlands were already the principal forces in the official world at Vienna; in addition to these came the new terror of the armed proselytism of the Revolution. The successor of Leopold, Francis II., was a sickly prince, in whose homely and unimaginative mind the great enterprises of Joseph, amidst which he had been brought up, excited only aversion. Amongst the men who surrounded him, routine and the dread of change made an end of the higher forms of public life. The Government openly declared that all change should cease so long as the war lasted; even the pressing question of the peasant's relation to his lord was allowed to remain unsettled by the Hungarian Diet, lest the spirit of national independence should find expression in its debates. Over the whole internal

Death of Leopold, March 1, 1792.

Francis II., 1792.

administration of Austria the torpor of the days before Theresa seemed to be returning. Its foreign policy, however, bore no trace of this timorous, conservative spirit. Joseph, as restless abroad as at home, had shared the ambition of the Russian Empress Catherine, and troubled Europe with his designs upon Turkey, Venice, and Bavaria. These and similar schemes of territorial extension continued to fill the minds of Austrian courtiers and ambassadors. Shortly after the outbreak of war with France the aged minister Kaunitz, who had been at the head of the Foreign Office during three reigns, retired from power. In spite of the first partition of Poland, made in combination with Russia and Prussia in 1772, and in spite of subsequent attempts of Joseph against Turkey and Bavaria, the policy of Kaunitz had not been one of mere adventure and shifting attack. He had on the whole remained true to the principle of alliance with France and antagonism to Prussia; and when the revolution brought war within sight, he desired to limit the object of the war to the restoration of monarchical government in France. The conditions under which the young Emperor and the King of Prussia agreed to turn the war to purposes of territorial aggrandisement caused Kaunitz, with a true sense of the fatal import of this policy, to surrender the power which he had held for forty years. It was secretly agreed between the two courts that Prussia should recoup itself for its expenses against France by seizing part of Poland. On behalf of Austria it was demanded that the Emperor should annex Bavaria, giving Belgium to the elector as compensation. Both these schemes violated what Kaunitz held to be sound policy. He believed that the interests of Austria required the consolidation rather than the destruction of Poland; and he declared the exchange of the Netherlands for Bavaria to be, in the actual state of affairs, impracticable.* Had the coalition of 1792 been framed on the principles advocated by Kaunitz, though Austria might not have effected the restoration of monarchical power in France, the alliance would not have disgracefully shattered on the crimes and infamies attending the second partition of Poland.

From the moment when Kaunitz retired from office, territorial extension became the great object of the Austrian Court. To prudent statesmen the scattered provinces and varied population of the Austrian State would have suggested that Austria had more to lose than any European Power; to the men of 1792 it appeared that she had more to gain. The Netherlands might be increased with a strip of French Flanders; Bavaria, Poland, and Italy were all weak neighbours, who might be made to enrich Austria in their turn. A sort of magical virtue was attached to the acquisition of territory. If so many square miles and so many head of population were gained, whether of alien or kindred race, mutinous or friendly, the end of all statesmanship was realised, and the heaviest sacrifice of life and industry repaid. Austria affected

---

* Ranke, Ursprung und Beginn, p. 256. Vivenot, Quellen, i., 133, 165. The acquisition of Bavaria was declared by the Austrian Cabinet to be the *summum bonum* of the monarchy.

to act as the centre of a defensive alliance, and to fight for the common purpose of giving a Government to France which would respect the rights of its neighbours. In reality, its own military operations were too often controlled, and an effective common warfare frustrated, at one moment by a design upon French Flanders, at another by the course of Polish or Bavarian intrigue, at another by the hope of conquests in Italy. Of all the interests which centred in the head of the House of Hapsburg, the least befriended at Vienna was the interest of the Empire and of Germany.

Nor, if Austria was found wanting, had Germany any permanent safeguard in the rival Protestant State. Prussia, the second great German Power and the ancient enemy of Austria, had been raised to an influence in Europe quite out of proportion to its scanty resources by the genius of Frederick the Great and the earlier Princes of the House of Hohenzollern. Its population was not one-third of that of France or Austria; its wealth was perhaps not superior to that of the Republic of Venice. That a State so poor in men and money should play the part of one of the great Powers of Europe was possible only so long as an energetic ruler watched every movement of that complicated machinery which formed both army and nation after the prince's own type. Frederick gave his subjects a just administration of the law; he taught them productive industries; he sought to bring education to their doors*; but he required that

Prussia.

* Biedermann, Deutschland im Achtzehnten Jahrhundert, iv. 1144.

the citizen should account himself before all the servant of the State. Every Prussian either worked in the great official hierarchy or looked up to it as the providence which was to direct all his actions and supply all his judgments. The burden of taxation imposed by the support of an army relatively three times as great as that of any other Power was wonderfully lightened by Frederick's economy: far more serious than the tobacco-monopoly and the forage-requisitions, at which Frederick's subjects grumbled during his lifetime, was the danger that a nation which had only attained political greatness by its obedience to a rigorous administration should fall into political helplessness, when the clear purpose and all-controlling care of its ruler no longer animated a system which, without him, was only a pedantic routine. What in England we are accustomed to consider as the very substance of national life,—the mass of political interest and opinion, diffused in some degree amongst all classes, at once the support and the judge of the servants of the State, —had in Prussia no existence. Frederick's subjects obeyed and trusted their Monarch; there were probably not five hundred persons outside the public service who had any political opinions of their own. Prussia did not possess even the form of a national representation; and, although certain provincial assemblies continued to meet, they met only to receive the instructions of the Crown-officers of their district. In the absence of all public criticism, the old age of Frederick must in itself have endangered the efficiency of the military system which had raised Prussia to its sudden eminence.* The impulse of Frederick's successor was sufficient to reverse the whole system of Prussian foreign policy, and to plunge the country in alliance with Austria into a speculative and unnecessary war.

On the death of Frederick in 1786, the crown passed to Frederick William II., his nephew. Frederick William was a man of common type, showy and pleasure-loving, interested in public affairs, but incapable of acting on any fixed principle. His mistresses gave the tone to political society. A knot of courtiers intrigued against one another for the management of the King; and the policy of Prussia veered from point to point as one unsteady impulse gave place to another. In countries less dependent than Prussia upon the personal activity of the monarch, Frederick William's faults might have been neutralised by able Ministers; in Prussia the weakness of the King was the decline of the State. The whole fabric of national greatness had been built up by the royal power; the quality of the public service, apart from which the nation was politically non-existent, was the quality of its head. When in the palace profusion and intrigue took the place of Frederick the Great's unflagging labour, the old uprightness, industry, and precision which had been the pride of Prussian administration fell out of fashion everywhere. Yet the frivolity of the Court, was a less active cause of military decline than the,

Frederick William II., 1786.

---

* Carlyle, Friedrich, vi. 667.

abandonment of the first principles of Prussian policy.* If any political sentiment existed in the nation, it was the sentiment of antagonism to Austria. The patriotism of the army, with all the traditions of the great King, turned wholly in this direction. When, out of sympathy with the Bourbon family and the emigrant French nobles, Frederick William allied himself with Austria (Feb. 1792), and threw himself into the arms of his ancient enemy in order to attack a nation which had not wronged him, he made an end of all zealous obedience amongst his servants. Brunswick, the Prussian Commander-in-Chief, hated the French emigrants as much as he did the Revolution; and even the generals who did not originally share Brunswick's dislike to the war recovered their old jealousy of Austria after the first defeat, and exerted themselves only to get quit of the war at the first moment that Prussia could retire from it without disgrace. The very enterprise in which Austria had consented that the Court of Berlin should seek its reward —the seizure of a part of Poland—proved fatal to the coalition. The Empress Catherine was already laying her hand for the second time upon this unfortunate country. It was easy for the opponents of the Austrian alliance who surrounded King Frederick William to contrast the barren effort of a war against France with the cheap and certain advantages to be won by annexation, in concert with Russia, of Polish territory. To pursue one of these objects with vigour it was necessary to relinquish

marginal note: Alliance with Austria against France. Feb. 1792.

* Häusser, i. 197. Hardenberg (Ranke), i. 139. Von Sybel, i. 272.

D

the other. Prussia was not rich enough to maintain armies both on the Vistula and the Rhine. Nor, in the opinion of its rulers, was it rich enough to be very tender of its honour or very loyal towards its allies.*

<small>Social system of Prussia.</small> In the institutions of Prussia two opposite systems existed side by side, exhibiting in the strongest form a contrast which in a less degree was present in most Continental States. The political independence of the nobility had long been crushed; the King's Government busied itself with every detail of town and village administration; yet along with this rigorous development of the modern doctrine of the unity and the authority of the State there existed a social order more truly archaic than that of the Middle Ages at their better epochs. The inhabitants of Prussia were divided into the three classes of nobles, burghers, and peasants, each confined to its own stated occupations, and not marrying outside its own order. The soil of the country bore the same

* "The connection with the House of Austria and the present undertaking continue to be very unpopular. It is openly said that one half of the treasure was uselessly spent at Reichenbach, and that the other half will be spent on the present occasion, and that the sovereign will be reduced to his former level of Margrave of Brandenburg." Eden, from Berlin; June 19, 1792. Records: Prussia, vol. 151. "He (Möllendorf) reprobated the alliance with Austria, condemning the present interference in the affairs of France as ruinous, and censuring as undignified and contrary to the most important interests of this country the leaving Russia sole arbitress of the fate of Poland. He, however, said, what every Prussian without any exception of party will say, that this country can never acquiesce in the establishment of a good government in Poland, since in a short time it would rise to a very decided superiority." *Id.*, July 17. Mr. Cobden's theory that the partition of Poland was effected in the interest of good government must have caused some surprise at Berlin.

distinction; peasant's land could not be owned by a burgher; burgher's land could not be owned by a noble. No occupation was lawful for the noble, who was usually no more than a poor gentleman, but the service of the Crown; the peasant, even where free, might not practise the handicraft of a burgher. But the mass of the peasantry in the country east of the Elbe were serfs attached to the soil; and the noble, who was not permitted to exercise the slightest influence upon the government of his country, inherited along with his manor a jurisdiction and police-control over all who were settled within it. Frederick had allowed serfage to continue because it gave him in each manorial lord a task-master whom he could employ in his own service. System and obedience were the sources of his power; and if there existed among his subjects one class trained to command and another trained to obey, it was so much the easier for him to force the country into the habits of industry which he required of it. In the same spirit, Frederick officered his army only with men of the noble caste. They brought with them the habit of command ready-formed; the peasants who ploughed and threshed at their orders were not likely to disobey them in the presence of the enemy. It was possible that such a system should produce great results so long as Frederick was there to guard against its abuses; Frederick gone, the degradation of servitude, the insolence of caste, was what remained. When the army of France, led by men who had worked with their fathers in the fields, hunted a King of Prussia amidst his capitulating grandees from the centre to the verge of his dominions, it was seen what was the permanent value of a system which recognised in the nature of the poor no capacity but one for hereditary subjection. The French peasant, plundered as he was by the State, and vexed as he was with feudal services, knew no such bondage as that of the Prussian serf, who might not leave the spot where he was born; only in scattered districts in the border-provinces had serfage survived in France. It is significant of the difference in self-respect existing in the peasantry of the two countries that the custom of striking the common soldier, universal in Germany, was in France no more than an abuse, practised by the admirers of Frederick, and condemned by the better officers themselves.

In all the secondary States of Germany the government was an absolute monarchy; though, here and there, as in Würtemberg, the shadow of the old Assembly of the Estates survived; and in Hanover the absence of the Elector, King George III., placed power in the hands of a group of nobles who ruled in his name. Society everywhere rested on a sharp division of classes similar in kind to that of Prussia; the condition of the peasant ranging from one of serfage, as it existed in Mecklenburg,* to one of comparative freedom and

Minor States of Germany.

* The condition of Mecklenburg is thus described in a letter written by Stein during a journey in 1802 :—" I found the aspect of the country as cheerless as its misty northern sky ; great estates, much of them in pasture or fallow; an extremely thin population ; the entire labouring class under the yoke of serfage; stretches of land attached to solitary ill-built farm-

comfort in parts of the southern and western States. The sovereigns differed widely in the enlightenment or selfishness of their rule; but, on the whole, the character of government had changed for the better of late years; and, especially in the Protestant States, efforts to improve the condition of the people were not wanting. Frederick the Great had in fact created a new standard of monarchy in Germany. Forty years earlier, Versailles, with its unfeeling splendours, its glorification of the personal indulgence of the monarch, had been the ideal which, with a due sense of their own inferiority, the German princes had done their best to imitate. To be a sovereign was to cover acres of ground with state apartments, to lavish the revenues of the country upon a troop of mistresses and adventurers, to patronise the arts, to collect with the same complacency the masterpieces of ancient painting that adorn the Dresden Gallery, or an array of valuables scarcely more interesting than the chests of treasure that were paid for them. In the ecclesiastical States, headed by the Electorates of Mainz, Trèves, and Cologne, the affection of a distinctively Christian or spiritual character had long been abandoned. The prince-bishop and canons, who were nobles appointed from some other province, lived after the

<small>houses; in short, a monotony, a dead stillness, spreading over the whole country, an absence of life and activity that quite overcame my spirits. The home of the Mecklenburg noble, who weighs like a load on his peasants instead of improving their condition, gives me the idea of the den of some wild beast, who devastates everything about him, and surrounds himself with the silence of the grave" Pertz, Leben Stein, I., 192. For a more cheerful description of Münster, see *id.*, I., 241.</small>

gay fashion of the time, at the expense of a land in which they had no interest extending beyond their own lifetime. The only feature distinguishing the ecclesiastical residence from that of one of the minor secular princes was that the parade of state was performed by monks in the cathedral instead of by soldiers on the drill-ground, and that even the pretence of married life was wanting among the flaunting harpies who frequented a celibate Court. Yet even on the Rhine and on the Moselle the influence of the great King of Prussia had begun to make itself felt. The intense and penetrating industry of Frederick was not within the reach of every petty sovereign who might envy its results; but the better spirit of the time was seen under some of the ecclesiastical princes in the encouragement of schools, the improvement of the roads, and a retrenchment in courtly expenditure. That deeply-seated moral disease which resulted from centuries of priestly rule was not to be so lightly shaken off. In a district where Nature most bountifully rewards the industry of man, twenty-four out of every hundred of the population were monks, nuns, or beggars.*

Petty States. Free Cities. Knights. Two hundred petty principalities, amongst which Weimar, the home of Goethe, stood out in the brightest relief from the level of princely routine and self-indulgence; fifty imperial cities, in most of which the once vigorous organism of civic life had shrivelled to the type of the English rotten borough, did not exhaust the

* Perthes, Staatsleben, p. 116. Rigby, Letters from France, p. 215.

divisions of Germany. Several hundred Knights of the Empire, owing no allegiance except to the Emperor, exercised, each over a domain averaging from three to four hundred inhabitants, all the rights of sovereignty, with the exception of the right to make war and treaties. The districts in which this order survived were scattered over the Catholic States of the south-west of Germany, where the knights maintained their prerogatives by federations among themselves and by the support of the Emperor, to whom they granted sums of money. There were instances in which this union of the rights of the sovereign and the landlord was turned to good account; but the knight's land was usually the scene of such poverty and degradation that the traveller needed no guide to inform him when he entered it. Its wretched tracks interrupted the great lines of communication between the Rhine and further Germany; its hovels were the refuge of all the criminals and vagabonds of the surrounding country; for no police existed but the bailiffs of the knight, and the only jurisdiction was that of the lawyer whom the knight brought over from the nearest town. Nor was the disadvantage only on the side of those who were thus governed. The knight himself, even if he cherished some traditional reverence for the shadow of the Empire, was in the position of a man who belongs to no real country. If his sons desired any more active career than that of annuitants upon the family domains, they could obtain it only by seeking employment at one or other of the greater Courts, and by identifying themselves with the interests of a land which they entered as strangers.

Such was in outline the condition of Germany at the moment when it was brought into collision with the new and unknown forces of the French Revolution. A system of small States, which in the past of Greece and Italy had produced the finest types of energy and genius, had in Germany resulted in the extinction of all vigorous life, and in the ascendancy of all that was stagnant, little, and corrupt. If political disorganisation, the decay of public spirit, and the absence of a national idea, are the signs of impending downfall, Germany was ripe for foreign conquest. The obsolete and dilapidated fabric of the Empire had for a century past been sustained only by the European tradition of the Balance of Power, or by the absence of serious attack from without. Austria once overpowered, the Empire was ready to fall to pieces by itself: and where, among the princes or the people of Germany, were the elements that gave hope of its renovation in any better form of national life?

CHAPTER II.

French and Austrian armies on the Flemish frontier—Prussia enters the war—Brunswick invades France—His Proclamation—Insurrection of Aug. 10 at Paris—Massacres of September—Character of the war—Brunswick, checked at Valmy, retreats—The War becomes a Crusade of France—Neighbours of France—Custine enters Mainz—Dumouriez conquers the Austrian Netherlands—Nice and Savoy annexed—Decree of the Convention against all Governments—Execution of Louis XVI.—War with England, followed by war with the Mediterranean States—Condition of England—English Parties, how affected by the Revolution—The Gironde and the Mountain—Austria recovers the Netherlands—The Allies invade France—La Vendée—Revolutionary System of 1793—Errors of the Allies—New French Commanders and Democratic Army—Victories of Jourdan, Hoche, and Pichegru—Prussia withdrawing from the war—Polish Affairs—Austria abandons the Netherlands—Treaties of Basle—France in 1795—Insurrection of 13 Vendémiaire—Constitution of 1795—The Directory—Effect of the Revolution on the spirit of Europe up to 1795.

THE war between France and Austria opened in April, 1792, on the Flemish frontier. The first encounters were discreditable to the French soldiery, who took to flight and murdered one of their generals. *Fighting on Flemish frontier. April, 1792.* The discouragement with which the nation heard of these reverses deepened into sullen indignation against the Court, as weeks and months passed by, and the forces lay idle on the frontier or met the enemy only in trifling skirmishes which left both sides where they were before. If at this crisis of the Revolution, with all the patriotism, all the bravery, all the military genius of France burning for service, the Government conducted the war with results scarcely distinguishable from those of a parade, the suggestion of treason on the part of the Court was only too likely to be entertained. The internal difficulties of the country were increasing. The Assembly had determined to banish from France the priests who rejected the new ecclesiastical system, and the King had placed his veto upon their decree. He had refused to permit the formation of a camp of volunteers in the neighbourhood of Paris. He had dismissed the popular Ministry forced upon him by the Gironde. A tumult on the 20th of June, in which the mob forced their way into the Tuileries, showed the nature of the attack impending upon the monarchy if Louis continued to oppose himself to the demands of the nation; but the lesson was lost upon the King. Louis was as little able to nerve himself for an armed conflict with the populace as to reconcile his conscience to the Ecclesiastical Decrees, and he surrendered himself to a pious inertia at a moment when the alarm of foreign invasion doubled revolutionary passion all over France. Prussia, in pursuance of a treaty made in February, united its forces to those of Austria. Forty thousand Prussian troops, under the Duke of Brunswick, the best of Frederick's surviving generals, advanced along the Moselle. From Belgium and the upper Rhine two Austrian armies converged upon the line of invasion; and the emigrant nobles were given their place among the forces of the Allies.

Prussian army invades France, July, 1792. Proclamation.

On the 25th of July the Duke of Brunswick, in the name of the Emperor and the King of Prussia, issued a proclamation to the French people, which, but for the difference between violent words and violent deeds, would have left little to be complained of in the cruelties that henceforward stained the popular cause. In this manifesto, after declaring that the Allies entered France in order to deliver Louis from captivity, and that members of the National Guard fighting against the invaders would be punished as rebels against their king, the Sovereigns addressed themselves to the city of Paris and to the representatives of the French nation:—" The city of Paris and its inhabitants are warned to submit without delay to their King; to set that Prince at entire liberty, and to show to him and to all the Royal Family the inviolability and respect which the law of nature and of nations imposes on subjects towards their Sovereigns. Their Imperial and Royal Majesties will hold all the members of the National Assembly, of the Municipality, and of the National Guard of Paris responsible for all events with their heads, before military tribunals, without hope of pardon. They further declare that, if the Tuileries be forced or insulted, or the least violence offered to the King, the Queen, or the Royal Family, and if provision be not at once made for their safety and liberty, they will inflict a memorable vengeance, by delivering up the city of Paris to military execution and total overthrow, and the rebels guilty of such crimes to the punishment they have merited." *

* Buchez et Roux, xvi., 279. One of the originals of this declaration, handed to the British ambassador, is in the London Records: Prussia, vol. 151.

This challenge was not necessary to determine the fate of Louis. Since the capture of the Bastille in the first days of the Revolution the National Government had with difficulty supported itself against the populace of the capital; and, even before the foreigner threatened Paris with fire and sword, Paris had learnt to look for the will of France within itself. As the columns of Brunswick advanced across the north-eastern frontier, Danton and the leaders of the city-democracy marshalled their army of the poor and the desperate to overthrow that monarchy whose cause the invader had made his own. The Republic which had floated so long in the thoughts of the Girondins was won in a single day by the populace of Paris, amid the roar of cannons and the flash of bayonets. On the 10th of August Danton let loose the armed mob upon the Tuileries.

Insurrection, August 10, 1792. Louis quitted the Palace without giving orders to the guard either to fight or to retire; but the guard were ignorant that their master desired them to offer no resistance, and one hundred and sixty of the mob were shot down before an order reached the troops to abandon the Palace. The cruelties which followed the victory of the people indicated the fate in store for those whom the invader came to protect. It is doubtful whether the foreign Courts would have made any serious attempt to undo the social changes effected by the Revolution in France; but no one supposed that those thousands of self-exiled nobles who now returned behind the guns of Brunswick had returned in order to take their places peacefully in the new social order. In their own imagination, as much as in that of the people, they returned with fire and sword to repossess themselves of rights of which they had been despoiled, and to take vengeance upon the men who were responsible for the changes made in France since 1789.* In the midst of a panic little justified by the real military situation, Danton inflamed the nation with his own passionate courage and resolution; he unhappily also thought it necessary to a successful national defence that the reactionary party at Paris should be paralysed by a terrible example. The prisons were filled with persons suspected of hostility to the national cause, and in the first days of September many

_{Massacres in Paris, Sept. 2-5.}

* The accounts of the emigrants sent to England by Lord Elgin, envoy at Brussels, and Sir J. Murray, our military attaché with Brunswick's army (in Records: Flanders, vol. 221) are instructive: "The conduct of the army under the Princes of France is universally reprobated. Their appearance in dress, in attendants, in preparations, is ridiculous. As an instance, however trivial, it may be mentioned that on one of the waggons was written *Toilette de Monsieur*. The spirit of vengeance, however, which they discover on every occasion is far more serious. Wherever they have passed, they have exercised acts of cruelty, in banishing and severely punishing those persons who, though probably culpable, had yet been left untouched by the Prussian commanders. To such an extent has this been carried that the commander at Verdun would not suffer any Frenchman (emigrant) to pass a night in the town without a special permission." Sept. 21. After the failure of the campaign, Elgin writes of the emigrants: "They everywhere added to the cruelties for some of which several hussars had been executed: carried to its extent the vengeance threatened in the Duke of Brunswick's Declaration, in burning whole villages where a shot was fired on them: and on the other hand by their self-sufficiency, want of subordination and personal disrespect, have drawn upon themselves the contempt of the combined armies." Oct. 6. So late as 1796, the exile Louis XVIII. declared his intention to restore the "property and rights" (*i.e.*, tithes, feudal dues, &c.) of the nobles and clergy, and to punish the men who had "committed offences." See Letter to Pichegru, May 4, 1796, in Manuscrit Inédit de Louis XVIII., p. 464.

hundreds of these unfortunate persons were massacred by gangs of assassins paid by a committee of the Municipality. Danton did not disguise his approval of the act. He had made up his mind that the work of the Revolution could only be saved by striking terror into its enemies, and by preventing the Royalists from co-operating with the invader. But the multitudes who flocked to the standards of 1792 carried with them the patriotism of Danton unstained by his guilt. Right or wrong in its origin, the war was now unquestionably a just one on the part of France, a war against a privileged class attempting to recover by force the unjust advantages that they had not been able to maintain, a war against the foreigner in defence of the right of the nation to deal with its own government.

The war now a war of defence.

Since the great religious wars there had been no cause so rooted in the hearts, so close to the lives of those who fought for it. Every soldier who joined the armies of France in 1792 joined of his own free will. No conscription dragged the peasant to the frontier. Men left their homes in order that the fruit of the poor man's labour should be his own, in order that the children of France should inherit some better birthright than exaction and want, in order that the late-won sense of human right should not be swept from the earth by the arms of privilege and caste. It was a time of high-wrought hope, of generous and pathetic self-sacrifice; a time that left a deep and indelible impression upon those who judged it as eye-witnesses. Years afterwards the poet Wordsworth, then alienated from France and cold in the cause of liberty, could not recall without tears the memories of 1792.*

The defence of France rested on General Dumouriez. The fortresses of Longwy and Verdun, covering the passage of the Meuse, had fallen after the briefest resistance; the troops that could be collected before Brunswick's approach were too few to meet the enemy in the open field. Happily for France the slow advance of the Prussian general permitted Dumouriez to occupy the difficult country of the Argonne, where, while waiting for his reinforcements, he was able for some time to hold the invaders in check. At length Brunswick made his way past the defile which Dumouriez had chosen for his first line of defence; but it was only to find the French posted in such strength on his flank that any further advance would imperil his own army. If the advance was to be continued, Dumouriez must be dislodged. Accordingly, on the 20th of September, Brunswick directed his artillery against the hills of Valmy, where the French left was encamped. The cannonade continued for some hours, but it was followed by no general attack. The firmness of the French under Brunswick's fire made it clear that they would not be displaced without an obstinate battle; and, disappointed of victory, the King of Prussia began to listen to proposals of peace sent to him by Dumouriez.† A week spent in negotiation served

_{Brunswick checked at Valmy, Sept. 20.}

* Wordsworth, Prelude, Book IX.
† The correspondence is in Ranke, Ursprung und Beginn, p. 371. Such was the famine in the Prussian camp that Dumouriez sent the King

only to strengthen the French and to aggravate the scarcity and sickness within the German camp. Dissensions broke out between the Prussian and Austrian commanders; a retreat was ordered; and to the astonishment of Europe the veteran forces of Brunswick fell back before the mutinous soldiery and unknown generals of the Revolution, powerless to delay for a single month the evacuation of France and the restoration of the fortresses which they had captured.

Retreat of Brunswick.

In the meantime the Legislative Assembly had decreed its own dissolution in consequence of the overthrow of the monarchy on August 10th, and had ordered the election of representatives to frame a constitution for France. The elections were held in the crisis of invasion, in the height of national indignation against the alliance of the aristocracy with the foreigner, and, in some districts, under the influence of men who had not shrunk from ordering the massacres in the prisons. At such a moment a Constitutional Royalist had scarcely more chance of election than a detected spy from the enemy's camp. The Girondins, who had been the party of extremes in the Legislative Assembly, were the party of moderation and order in the Convention. By their side there were returned men whose whole being seemed to be compounded out of the forces of conflict, men who, sometimes without conscious depravity, carried into

The Convention meets. Proclaims Republic, Sept. 21.

of Prussia twelve loaves, twelve pounds of coffee, and twelve pounds of sugar. The official account of the campaign is in the *Berlinische Zeitung* of Oct. 11, 1792.

political and social struggles that direct, unquestioning employment of force which has ordinarily been reserved for war or for the diffusion of religious doctrines. The moral differences that separated this party from the Gironde were at once conspicuous: the political creed of the two parties appeared at first to be much the same. Monarchy was abolished, and France declared a Republic. (Sept. 21.) Office continued in the hands of the Gironde; but the vehement, uncompromising spirit of their rivals, the so-called party of the Mountain, quickly made itself felt in all the relations of France to foreign Powers. The intention of conquest might still be disavowed as it had been five months before; but were the converts to liberty to be denied the right of uniting themselves to the French people by their own free will? When the armies of the Republic had swept its assailants from the border-provinces that gave them entrance into France, were those provinces to be handed back to a government of priests and nobles? The scruples which had condemned all annexation of territory vanished in that orgy of patriotism which followed the expulsion of the invader and the discovery that the Revolution was already a power in other lands than France. The nation that had to fight the battle of European freedom must appeal to the spirit of freedom wherever it would answer the call: the conflict with sovereigns must be maintained by arming their subjects against them in every land. In this conception of the universal alliance of the nations, the Governments with

The war becomes a crusade of democracy.

which France was not yet at war were scarcely distinguished from those which had pronounced against her. The frontier-lines traced by an obsolete diplomacy, the artificial guarantees of treaties, were of little account against the living and inalienable sovereignty of the people. To men inflamed with the passions of 1792 an argument of international law scarcely conveyed more meaning than to Peter the Hermit. Among the statesmen of other lands, who had no intention of abandoning all the principles recognised as the public right of Europe, the language now used by France could only be understood as the avowal of indiscriminate aggression.

The Revolution had displayed itself in France as a force of union as well as of division. It had driven the nobles across the frontier; it had torn the clergy from their altars; but it had reconciled sullen Corsica; and by abolishing feudal rights it had made France the real fatherland of the Teutonic peasant in Alsace and Lorraine. It was now about to prove its attractive power in foreign lands. At the close of the last century the nationalities of Europe were far less consolidated than they are at present; only on the Spanish and the Swiss frontier had France a neighbour that could be called a nation. On the north, what is now the kingdom of Belgium was in 1792 a collection of provinces subject to the House of Austria. The German population both of the districts west of the Rhine and of those opposite to Alsace was parcelled out among a number of petty principalities. Savoy,

The neighbours of France.

though west of the chain of the Alps and French in speech, formed part of the kingdom of Piedmont, which was itself severed by history and by national character from the other States of Northern Italy. Along the entire frontier, from Dunkirk to the Maritime Alps, France nowhere touched a strong, united, and independent people; and along this entire frontier, except in the country opposite Alsace, the armed proselytism of the French Revolution proved a greater force than the influences on which the existing order of things depended. In the Low Countries, in the Principalities of the Rhine, in Switzerland, in Savoy, in Piedmont itself, the doctrines of the Revolution were welcomed by a more or less numerous class, and the armies of France appeared, though but for a moment, as the missionaries of liberty and right rather than as an invading enemy.

No sooner had Brunswick been brought to a stand by Dumouriez at Valmy than a French division under Custine crossed the Alsatian frontier and advanced upon Spires, where Brunswick had left large stores of war. *Custine enters Mainz, Oct. 20.* The garrison was defeated in an encounter outside the town; Spires and Worms surrendered to Custine. In the neighbouring fortress of Mainz, the key to western Germany, Custine's advance was watched by a republican party among the inhabitants, from whom the French general learnt that he had only to appear before the city to become its master. Brunswick had indeed apprehended the failure of his invasion of France, but he had never given a thought to the defence of Germany; and, although the

King of Prussia had been warned of the defenceless state of Mainz, no steps had been taken beyond the payment of a sum of money for the repair of the fortifications, which money the Archbishop expended in the purchase of a wood belonging to himself and the erection of a timber patchwork. On news arriving of the capture of Spires, the Archbishop fled, leaving the administration to the Dean, the Chancellor, and the Commandant. The Chancellor made a speech, calling upon his "beloved brethren" the citizens to defend themselves to the last extremity, and daily announced the overthrow of Dumouriez and the approaching entry of the Allies into Paris, until Custine's soldiers actually came into sight.* Then a council of war declared the city to be untenable; and before Custine had brought up a single siege-gun the garrison capitulated, and the French were welcomed into Mainz by the partisans of the Republic (Oct. 20). With the French arms came the French organisation of liberty. A club was formed on the model of the Jacobin Club of Paris; existing officers and distinctions of rank were abolished; and although the mass of the inhabitants held aloof, a Republic was finally proclaimed, and incorporated with the Republic of France.

Dumouriez invades the Netherlands. The success of Custine's raid into Germany did not divert the Convention from the design of attacking Austria in the Netherlands, which Dumouriez had from the first pressed upon the Government. It was not three years since the Netherlands had been in revolt against

* Forster, Werke, vi., 386.

the Emperor Joseph. In its origin the revolt was a reactionary movement of the clerical party against Joseph's reforms; but there soon sprang up ambitions and hopes at variance with the first impulses of the insurrection; and by the side of monks and monopolists a national party came into existence, proclaiming the sovereignty of the people, and imitating all the movements of the French Revolution. During the brief suspension of Austrian rule the popular and the reactionary parties attacked one another; and on the restoration of Leopold's authority in 1791 the democratic leaders, with a large body of their followers, took refuge beyond the frontier, looking forward to the outbreak of war between Austria and France. Their partisans formed a French connection in the interior of the country; and, by some strange illusion, the priests themselves and the close corporations which had been attacked by Joseph supposed that their interests would be respected by Revolutionary France.* Thus the ground was everywhere prepared for a French invasion. Dumouriez crossed the frontier. The border fortresses no longer existed; and after a single battle won by

<small>Battle of Jemappes, Nov. 6.</small>

---

* "The very night the news of the late Emperor's (Leopold's) death arrived here (Brussels), inflammatory advertisements and invitations to arm were distributed." One culprit "belonged to the Choir of St. Gudule: he chose the middle of the day, and in the presence of many people posted up a paper in the church, exhorting to a general insurrection. The remainder of this strange production was the description of a vision he pretended to have seen, representing the soul of the late emperor on its way to join that of Joseph, already suffering in the other world." Col. Gardiner, March 20, 1792. Records: Flanders, vol. 220.

the French at Jemappes on the 6th of November,* the Austrians, finding the population universally hostile, abandoned the Netherlands without a struggle.

The victory of Jemappes, the first pitched battle won by the Republic, excited an outburst of revolutionary fervour in the Convention which deeply affected the relations of France to Great Britain, hitherto a neutral spectator of the war. A manifesto was published declaring that the French nation offered its alliance to all peoples who wished to recover their freedom, and charging the generals of the Republic to give their protection to all persons who might suffer in the cause of liberty. (Nov. 19.) A week later Savoy and Nice were annexed to France, the population of Savoy having declared in favour of France on the outbreak of war between France and Sardinia. On the 15th of December the Convention proclaimed that social and political revolution was henceforth to accompany every movement of its armies on foreign soil. "In every country that shall be occupied by the armies of the French Republic"—such was the sub-

Nice and Savoy annexed.

* Elgin, from Brussels, Nov. 6. "A brisk cannonade has been heard this whole forenoon in the direction of Mons. It is at this moment somewhat diminished, though not at an end." Nov. 7. "Several messengers have arrived from camp in the course of the night, but all the Ministers (I have seen them all) deny having received one word of detail. . . . Couriers have been sent this night in every direction to call in all the detachments on the frontiers. . . . The Government is making every arrangement for quitting Brussels: their papers are already prepared, their carriages ready." . . . Then a PS. "A cannonade is distinctly heard again. . . . All the emigrants now here are removing with the utmost haste." Nov. 9. "The confusion throughout the country is extreme. The roads are covered with emigrants, and persons of those provinces flying from the French armies." Records: Flanders, vol. 222.

stance of the Decree of December 15th—"the generals shall announce the abolition of all existing authorities; of nobility, of serfage, of every feudal right and every monopoly; they shall proclaim the sovereignty of the people, and convoke the inhabitants in assemblies to form a provisional Government, to which no officer of a former Government, no noble, nor any member of the former privileged corporations shall be eligible. They shall place under the charge of the French Republic all property belonging to the Sovereign or his adherents, and the property of every civil or religious corporation. The French nation will treat as enemies any people which, refusing liberty and equality, desires to preserve its prince and privileged castes, or to make any accommodation with them." *Decree of Dec. 15.*

This singular announcement of a new crusade caused the Government of Great Britain to arm. Although the decree of the Convention related only to States with which France was at war, the Convention had in fact formed connections with the English revolutionary societies; and the French Minister of Marine informed his sailors that they were about to carry fifty thousand caps of liberty to their English brethren. No prudent statesman would treat a mere series of threats against all existing authorities as ground for war; but the acts of the French Government showed that it intended to carry into effect the violent interference in the affairs of other nations announced in its manifestos. Its agents were stirring up dissatisfaction in every State; *England arms.*

and although the annexation of Savoy and the occupation of the Netherlands might be treated as incidental to the conflict with Austria and Sardinia, in which Great Britain had pledged itself to neutrality, other acts of the Convention were certainly infringements of the rights of allies of England. A series of European treaties, oppressive according to our own ideas, but in keeping with the ideas of that age, prohibited the navigation of the River Schelde, on which Antwerp is situated, in order that the commerce of the North Sea might flow exclusively into Dutch ports. On the conquest of Belgium the French Government gave orders to Dumouriez to send a flotilla down the river, and to declare Antwerp an open port in right of the law of nature, which treaties cannot abrogate. Whatever the folly of commercial restraints, the navigation of the Schelde was a question between the Antwerpers and the Dutch, and one in which France had no direct concern. The incident, though trivial, was viewed in England as one among many proofs of the intention of the French to interfere with the affairs of neighbouring States at their pleasure. In ordinary times it would not have been easy to excite much interest in England on behalf of a Dutch monopoly; but the feeling of this country towards the French Revolution had been converted into a passionate hatred by the massacres of September, and by the open alliance between the Convention and the Revolutionary societies in England itself. Pitt indeed, whom the Parisians imagined to

The Schelde.

be their most malignant enemy, laboured against the swelling national passion, and hoped against all hope for peace. Not only was Pitt guiltless of the desire to add this country to the enemies of France, but he earnestly desired to reconcile France with Austria, in order that the Western States, whose embroilment left Eastern Europe at the mercy of Catherine of Russia, might unite to save both Poland and Turkey from falling into the hands of a Power whose steady aggression threatened Europe more seriously than all the noisy and outspoken excitement of the French Convention. Pitt, moreover, viewed with deep disapproval the secret designs of Austria and Prussia.* If the French

---

* In Nov. 1792, Grenville ordered the English envoys at Vienna and Berlin to discover, if possible, the real designs of aggrandisement held by those Courts. Mr. Straton, at Vienna, got wind of the agreement against Poland. "I requested Count Philip Cobenzl" (the Austrian Minister) "that he would have the goodness to open himself confidentially to me on the precise object which the two allied Courts might have in contemplation. This, however, the Count was by no means disposed to do; on the contrary, he went round the compass of evasion in order to avoid a direct answer. But determined as I was to push the Austrian Minister, I heaped question on question, until I forced him to say, blushing, and with evident signs of embarrassment, 'Count Stadion' (Ambassador at London) 'will be able to satisfy the curiosity of the British Minister, to whatever point it may be directed.'" Jan. 20, 1793. Records: Austria, vol. 32. Stadion accordingly informed Lord Grenville of the Polish and Bavarian plans. Grenville expressed his concern and regret at the aggression on Poland, and gave reasons against the Bavarian exchange. To our envoy with the King of Prussia Grenville wrote: "It may possibly be the intention of the Courts to adopt a plan of indemnifying themselves for the expense of the war by fresh acquisitions in Poland, and carrying into execution a new partition of that country. You will not fail to explain in the most distinct and pointed manner his Majesty's entire disapprobation of such a plan, and his determination on no account to concur in any measures which may tend to the completion of a design so unjust in itself." Jan. 4, 1793. Records: Army in Germany, vol. 437. At Vienna Cobenzl declared, Feb. 9, that Austria could not now

executive would have given any assurance that the Netherlands should not be annexed, or if the French ambassador, Chauvelin, who was connected with English plotters, had been superseded by a trustworthy negotiator, it is probable that peace might have been preserved. But when, on the execution of King Louis (Jan, 21, 1793), Chauvelin was expelled from England as a suspected alien, war became a question of days.*

<small>Execution of Louis XVI., Jan. 21, 1793</small>

Points of technical right figured in the complaints of both sides; but the real ground of war was perfectly understood. France considered itself entitled to advance the Revolution and the Rights of Man wherever its own arms or popular insurrection gave it the command. England denied the right of any Power to annul the political system of Europe at its pleasure, No more serious, no more sufficient, ground of war ever existed between two nations; yet the event proved that, with the highest justification for war, the highest wisdom would yet have chosen peace. England's entry into the war converted it from an affair of two or three campaigns into a struggle of twenty years, resulting in more violent convulsions, more widespread misery, and more atrocious crimes, than in all probability would

---

" even manifest a wish to oppose the projects of Prussia in Poland, as in that case his Prussian Majesty would probably withdraw his assistance from the French war; nay, perhaps even enter into an alliance with that nation and invade Bohemia." Records: Austria, vol. 32.

* Auckland, ii. 464. Papers presented to Parliament, 1793. Mr. Oscar Browning, in *Fortnightly Review*, Feb. 1883.

have resulted even from the temporary triumph of the revolutionary cause in 1793. But in both nations political passion welcomed impending calamity; and the declaration of war by the Convention on February 1st only anticipated the desire of the English people. Great Britain once committed to the struggle, Pitt spared neither money nor intimidation in his efforts to unite all Europe against France. Holland was included with England in the French declaration of war: the Mediterranean States felt that the navy of England was nearer to them than the armies of Austria and Prussia; and before the end of the summer of 1793, Spain, Portugal, Naples, Tuscany, and the Papal States had joined the Coalition. *(War with England, Feb. 1st, 1793. Holland and Mediterranean States enter the war.)*

The Jacobins of Paris had formed a wrong estimate of the political condition of England. At the outbreak of the war they believed that England itself was on the verge of revolution. They mistook the undoubted discontent of a portion of the middle and lower classes, which showed itself in the cry for parliamentary reform, for a general sentiment of hatred towards existing institutions, like that which in France had swept away the old order at a single blow. The Convention received the addresses of English Radical societies, and imagined that the abuses of the parliamentary system under George III. had alienated the whole nation. What they had found in Belgium and in Savoy— *(French wrongly think England inclined to revolution.)*

a people thankful to receive the Rights of Man from the soldiers of the Revolution—they expected to find among the dissenting congregations of London and the factory-hands of Sheffield. The singular attraction exercised by each class in England upon the one below it, as well as the indifference of the nation generally to all ideals, was little understood in France, although the Revolutions of the two countries bore this contrast on their face. A month after the fall of the Bastille the whole system of class-privilege and monopoly had vanished from French law; fifteen years of the English Commonwealth had left the structure of English society what it had been at the beginning. But political observation vanished in the delirium of 1793; and the French only discovered when it was too late that in Great Britain the Revolution had fallen upon an enemy of unparalleled stubbornness and inexhaustible strength.

In the first Assembly of the Revolution it was usual to speak of the English as free men whom the French ought to imitate; in the Convention it was usual to speak of them as slaves whom the French ought to deliver. The institutions of England bore in fact a very different aspect when compared with the absolute monarchy of the Bourbons and when compared with the democracy of 1793. Frenchmen who had lived under the government of a Court which made laws by edict and possessed the right to imprison by letters-patent looked with respect upon the Parliament of

Political condition of England.

England, its trial by jury, and its freedom of the press. The men who had sent a king to prison and confiscated the estates of a great part of the aristocracy could only feel compassion for a land where three-fourths of the national representatives were nominees of the Crown or of wealthy peers. Nor, in spite of the personal sympathy of Fox with the French revolutionary movement, was there any real affinity between the English Whig party and that which now ruled in the Convention. The event which fixed the character of English liberty during the eighteenth century, the Revolution of 1688, had nothing democratic in its nature. *The Whigs not democratic.* That revolution was directed against a system of Roman Catholic despotism; it gave political power not to the mass of the nation, which had no desire and no capacity to exercise it, but to a group of noble families and their retainers, who, during the reigns of the first two Georges, added all the patronage and influence of the Crown to their social and constitutional weight in the country. The domestic history of England since the accession of George III. had turned chiefly upon the obstinate struggle of this monarch to deliver himself from all dependence upon party. The divisions of the Whigs, their jealousies, but, above all, their real alienation from the mass of the people whose rights they professed to defend, ultimately gave the King the victory, when, after twenty years of errors, he found in the younger Pitt a Minister capable of uniting the interests of the Crown with the ablest and most patriotic liberal statesmanship. Bribes, threats, and every species of base influence had been employed by King George to break up the great Coalition of 1783, which united all sections of the Whigs against him under the Ministry of Fox and North; but the real support of Pitt, whom the King placed in office with a minority in the House of Commons, was the temper of the nation itself, wearied with the exclusiveness, the corruption, and the party-spirit of the Whigs, and willing to believe that a popular Minister, even if he had entered upon power unconstitutionally, might do more for the country than the constitutional proprietors of the rotten boroughs.

From 1783 down to the outbreak of the French Revolution, Pitt, as a Tory Minister confronted by a Whig Opposition, governed England on more liberal principles than any statesman who had held power during the eighteenth century. These years were the last of the party-system of England in its original form. The French Revolution made an end of that old distinction in which the Tory was known as the upholder of Crown-prerogative and the Whig as the supporter of a constitutional oligarchy of great families. It created that new political antagonism in which, whether under the names of Whig and Tory, or of Liberal and Conservative, two great parties have contended, one for a series of beneficial changes, the other for the preservation of the existing order. The convulsions of France and the dread of revolutionary agitation in England trans-

Pitt Minister, 1783.

formed both Pitt and the Whigs by whom he was opposed. Pitt sacrificed his schemes of peaceful progress to foreign war and domestic repression, and set his face against the reform of Parliament which he had once himself proposed. The Whigs broke up into two sections, led respectively by Burke and by Fox, the one denouncing the violence of the Revolution, and ultimately uniting itself with Pitt; the other friendly to the Revolution, in spite of its excesses, as the cause of civil and religious liberty, and identifying itself, under the healthy influence of parliamentary defeat and disappointment, with the defence of popular rights in England and the advocacy of enlightened reform. *[Effect of French Revolution on English Parties.]*

The obliteration of the old dividing-line in English politics may be said to date from the day when the ancient friendship of Burke and Fox was bitterly severed by the former in the House of Commons. (May 6, 1791.) The charter of the modern Conservative party was that appeal to the nation which Burke had already published, in the autumn of 1790, under the title of " Reflections on the French Revolution."

In this survey of the political forces which he saw in action around him, the great Whig writer, who in past times had so passionately defended the liberties of America and the constitutional tradition of the English Parliament against the aggression of George III., attacked the Revolution as a system of violence and caprice more formidable to freedom than the tyranny of any Crown. He proved that the *[Burke's "Reflections," Oct., 1790.]*

politicians and societies of England who had given it their sympathy had given their sympathy to measures and to theories opposed to every principle of 1688. Above all, he laid bare that agency of riot and destructiveness which, even within the first few months of the Revolution, filled him with presentiment of the calamities about to fall upon France. Burke's treatise was no dispassionate inquiry into the condition of a neighbouring state : it was a denunciation of Jacobinism as fierce and as little qualified by political charity as were the maledictions of the Hebrew prophets upon their idolatrous neighbours ; and it was intended, like these, to excite his own countrymen against innovations among themselves. It completely succeeded. It expressed, and it heightened, the alarm arising among the Liberal section of the propertied class, at first well inclined to the Revolution : and, although the Whigs of the House of Commons pronounced in favour of Fox upon his first rupture with Burke, the tide of public feeling, rising higher with every new outrage of the Revolution, soon invaded the legislature, and carried the bulk of the Whig party to the side of the Minister, leaving to Fox and his few faithful adherents the task of maintaining an unheeded protest against the blind passions of war, and the increasing rigour with which Pitt repressed every symptom of popular disaffection.

Most of the Whigs support Pitt against France.

The character of violence which Burke traced and condemned in the earliest acts of the Revolution displayed itself in a much stronger light after the overthrow of the Monarchy by the insurrection of August 10th. That event was the work of men who commanded the Parisian democracy, not the work of orators and party-leaders in the Assembly. The Girondins had not hesitated to treat the victory as their own, by placing the great offices of State, with one exception, in the hands of their leaders; they instantly found that the real sovereignty lay elsewhere. The Council of the Commune, or Municipality, of Paris, whose members had seized their post at the moment of the insurrection, was the only administrative body that possessed the power to enforce its commands; in the Ministries of State one will alone made itself felt, that of Danton, whom the Girondins had unwillingly admitted to office along with themselves. The massacres of September threw into full light the powerlessness of the expiring Assembly. For five successive days it was unable to check the massacres; it was unable to bring to justice the men who had planned them, and who called upon the rest of France to follow their example. With the meeting of the Convention, however, the Girondins, who now regarded themselves as the legitimate government, and forgot that they owed office to an insurrection, expected to reduce the capital to submission. They commanded an overwhelming majority in the new chamber; they were supported by the middle class in all the great cities of France. The party of the Mountain embraced at first only the deputies of Paris, and a group of determined men who admitted no

marginal note: The Gironde and the Commune of Paris.

criticism on the measures which the democracy of Paris had thought necessary for the Revolution. *The Gironde and the Mountain in the Convention.* In the Convention they were the assailed, not the assailants. Without waiting to secure themselves by an armed force, the orators of the Gironde attempted to crush both the Municipality and the deputies who ruled at the Clubs. They reproached the Municipality with the murders of September; they accused Robespierre of aiming at the Dictatorship. It was under the pressure of these attacks that the party of the Mountain gathered its strength within the Convention, and that the populace of Paris transferred to the Gironde the passionate hatred which it had hitherto borne to the King and the aristocracy. The gulf that lay between the people and those who had imagined themselves to be its leaders burst into view. The Girondins saw with dismay that the thousands of hungry workmen whose victory had placed them in power had fought for something more tangible than Republican phrases from Tacitus and Plutarch. On one side was a handful of orators and writers, steeped in the rhetoric and the commonplace of ancient Rome, and totally strange to the real duties of government; on the other side the populace of Paris, such as centuries of despotism, privilege, and priestcraft had made it: sanguinary, unjust, vindictive; convulsed since the outbreak of the Revolution with every passion that sways men in the mass; taught no conception of progress but the overthrow of authority, and acquainted with no title to power but that which was bestowed by itself. If the

Girondins were to remain in power, they could do so only by drawing an army from the departments, or by identifying themselves with the multitude. They declined to take either course. Their audience was in the Assembly alone; their support in the distant provinces. Paris, daily more violent, listened to men of another stamp. The Municipality defied the Government; the Mountain answered the threats and invectives of the majority in the Assembly by displays of popular menace and tumult. In the eyes of the common people, who after so many changes of government found themselves more famished and more destitute than ever, the Gironde was now but the last of a succession of tyrannies; its statesmen but impostors who stood between the people and the enjoyment of their liberty.

Among the leaders of the Mountain, Danton aimed at the creation of a central Revolutionary Government, armed with absolute powers for the prosecution of the war; and he attacked the Girondins only when they themselves had rejected his support. Robespierre, himself the author of little beyond destruction, was the idol of those whom Rousseau's writings had filled with the idea of a direct exercise of sovereignty by the people. It was in the trial of the King that the Gironde first confessed its submission to the democracy of Paris. The Girondins in their hearts desired to save the King; they voted for his death with the hope of maintaining their influence in Paris, and of clearing themselves from the charge of lukewarmness in the cause of the Revolution. But the sacrifice was as vain as it was dishonourable. The populace and the party of the Mountain took the act in its true character, as an acknowledgment of their own victory. A series of measures was brought forward providing for the poorer classes at the expense of the wealthy. The Gironde, now forced to become the defenders of property, encountered the fatal charge of deserting the cause of the people; and from this time nothing but successful foreign warfare could have saved their party from ruin.

Instead of success came inaction, disaster, and treason. The army of Flanders lay idle during January and February for want of provisions and materials of war; and no sooner had Dumouriez opened the campaign against Holland than he was recalled by intelligence that the Austrians had fallen upon his lieutenant, Miranda, at Maestricht, and driven the French army before them. Dumouriez returned, in order to fight a pitched battle before Brussels. He attacked the Austrians at Neerwinden (March 18), and suffered a repulse inconsiderable in itself, but sufficient to demoralise an army composed in great part of recruits and National Guards.* His defeat laid Flanders open to the

<small>Defeat and treason of Dumouriez, March, 1793.</small>

* Von Sybel, ii., 259. Thugut, Vertrauliche Briefe, i., 17. Letters from Brussels, 23rd March in Records: Flanders, vol. 222. "The Huzars are in motion all round, so that we hope to have them here tomorrow. Most of the French troops who arrived last, and which are mostly peasants armed with pikes, are returning home, besides a great number of their volunteers." 24th March. "At this moment we hear the cannon. The French have just had it cry'd in the town that all the tailors who are making coats for the army must bring them made or unmade, and be paid directly. . . . . They beat the drums to drown the report of the cannon. . . . . You have not a conception of the confusion in the town.

Austrians; but Dumouriez intended that it should inflict upon the Republic a far heavier blow. Since the execution of the King, he had been at open enmity with the Jacobins. He now proposed to the Austrian commander to unite with him in an attack upon the Convention, and in re-establishing monarchy in France. The first pledge of Dumouriez's treason was the surrender of three commissioners sent by the Convention to his camp; the second was to have been the surrender of the fortress of Condé. But Dumouriez had overrated his influence with the army. Plainer minds than his own knew how to deal with a general who intrigues with the foreigner. Dumouriez's orders were disregarded; his movements watched; and he fled to the Austrian lines under the fire of his own soldiers. About thirty officers and eight hundred men passed with him to the enemy.

The defeat and treason of Dumouriez brought the army of Austria over the northern frontier. Almost at the same moment Custine was overpowered in the Palatinate; and the conquests of the previous autumn, with the exception of Mainz, were lost as rapidly as they had been won. Custine fell back upon the lines of Weissenburg, leaving the defence of Mainz to a garrison of 17,000 men, which, alone among the Republican armies, now maintained its reputation. In France itself civil war

Defeats on the North and East. Revolt of La Vendée, March, 1793.

.... This moment passed four Austrians with their heads cut to pieces, and one with his eye poked out. The French are retiring by the Porte d'Anderlecht." Ostend, April 4th. "This day, before two of the clock, twenty-five Austrian huzars enter'd the town while the inhabitants were employed burning the tree of liberty."

broke out. The peasants of La Vendée, a district destitute of large towns, and scarcely touched either by the evils which had produced the Revolution or by the hopes which animated the rest of France, had seen with anger the expulsion of the parish priests who refused to take the oath to the Constitution. A levy of 300,000 men, which was ordered by the Convention in February, 1793, threw into revolt the simple Vendeans, who cared for nothing outside their own parishes, and preferred to fight against their countrymen rather than to quit their homes. The priests and the Royalists fanned these village outbreaks into a religious war of the most serious character. Though poorly armed, and accustomed to return to their homes as soon as fighting was over, the Vendean peasantry proved themselves a formidable soldiery in the moment of attack, and cut to pieces the half-disciplined battalions which the Government sent against them. On the north, France was now assailed by the English as well as by the Austrians. The Allies laid siege to Condé and Valenciennes, and drove the French army back in disorder at Famars. Each defeat was a blow dealt to the Government of the Gironde at Paris. With foreign and civil war adding disaster to disaster, with the general to whom the Gironde had entrusted the defence of the Republic openly betraying it to its enemies, the fury of the capital was easily excited against the party charged with all the misfortunes of France. A threatening movement of the middle classes in resistance to a forced loan precipitated the struggle. The Girondins were accused of arresting the armies of the Republic in the midst of their conquests, of throwing the frontier open to the foreigner, and of kindling the civil war of La Vendée. On the 31st of May a raging mob invaded the Convention. Two days later the representatives of France were surrounded by the armed forces of the Commune; the twenty-four leading members of the Gironde were placed under arrest, and the victory of the Mountain was completed.* *The Commune crushes the Gironde, June 2*

The situation of France, which was serious before, now became desperate; for the Girondins, escaping from their arrest, called the departments to arms against Paris. *Civil War. The Committee of Public Safety.*
Normandy, Bordeaux, Marseilles, Lyons, rose in insurrection against the tyranny of the Mountain, and the Royalists of the south and west threw themselves into a civil war which they hoped to turn to their own advantage. But a form of government had now arisen in France well fitted to cope with extraordinary perils. It was a form of government in which there was little trace of the constitutional tendencies of 1789, one that had come into being as the stress of conflict threw into the background the earlier hopes and efforts of the Revolution. In the two earlier Assemblies it had been a fixed principle that the representatives of the people were to control the Government, but were not to assume executive powers themselves. After the overthrow of Monarchy on the 10th

* Mortimer-Ternaux, vii., 412.

August, the Ministers, though still nominally possessed of powers distinct from the representative body, began to be checked by Committees of the Convention appointed for various branches of the public service; and in March, 1793, in order to meet the increasing difficulties of the war, a Committee of Public Safety was appointed, charged with the duty of exercising a general surveillance over the administration. In this Committee, however, as in all the others, the Gironde were in the majority; and the twenty-four members who composed it were too numerous a body to act with effect. The growing ascendancy of the Mountain produced that concentration of force which the times required. The Committee was reduced in April to nine members, and in this form it ultimately became the supreme central power. It was not until after the revolt of Lyons that the Committee, exchanging Danton's influence for that of Robespierre, adopted the principle of Terror which has made the memory of their rule one of the most sinister in history.

Their authority steadily increased. The members divided among themselves the great branches of government. One directed the army, another the navy, another foreign affairs; the signature of three members practically gave to any measure the force of law, for the Convention accepted and voted their reports as a matter of course. Whilst the Com-
Commissioners of the Convention.
mittee gave orders as the supreme executive, eighty of the most energetic of the Mountain spread themselves over France, in parties of

two and three, with the title of Commissioners of the Convention, and with powers over-riding those of all the local authorities. They were originally appointed for the purpose of hastening on the levy ordered by the Convention in March, but their powers were gradually extended over the whole range of administration. Their will was absolute, their authority supreme. Where the councillors of the Departments or the municipal officers were good Jacobins, the Commissioners availed themselves of local machinery; where they suspected their principles, they sent them to the scaffold, and enforced their own orders by whatever means were readiest. They censured and dismissed the generals; one of them even directed the movements of a fleet at sea. What was lost by waste and confusion and by the interference of the Commissioners in military movements was more than counterbalanced by the vigour which they threw into all the preparations of war, and by the unity of purpose which, at the price of unsparing bloodshed, they communicated to every group where Frenchmen met together.

But no individual energy could have sustained these dictatorships without the support of a popular organisation. All over France a system of revolutionary government sprang up, which superseded all existing institutions just as the authority of the Commissioners of the Convention superseded all existing local powers. The local revolutionary administration consisted of a Committee, a Club, and a Tribunal.* In each of 21,000 communes

Local revolutionary system of 1793.

---
* Berriat-St-Prix, La Justice Révolutionnaire, introd.

a committee of twelve was elected by the people, and entrusted by the Convention, as the Terror gained ground, with boundless powers of arrest and imprisonment. Popular excitement was sustained by clubs, where the peasants and labourers assembled at the close of their day's work, and applauded the victories or denounced the enemies of the Revolution. A Tribunal with swift procedure and powers of life and death sat in each of the largest towns, and judged the prisoners who were sent to it by the committees of the neighbouring district. Such was the government of 1793—an executive of uncontrolled power drawn from the members of a single Assembly, and itself brought into immediate contact with the poorest of the people in their assemblies and clubs. The balance of interests which creates a constitutional system, the security of life, liberty, and property, which is the essence of every recognised social order, did not now exist in France. One public purpose, the defence of the Revolution, became the law before which all others lost their force. Treating all France like a town in a state of siege, the Government took upon itself the duty of providing support for the poorest classes by enactments controlling the sale and possession of the necessaries of life. The price of corn and other necessaries was fixed; and, when the traders and producers consequently ceased to bring their goods to market, the Commissioners of the Convention were empowered to make requisition of a certain quantity of corn for every acre of ground. Property was thus placed at the disposal of

Law of the Maximum.

the men who already exercised absolute political power. "The state of France," said Burke, "is perfectly simple. It consists of but two descriptions, the oppressors and the oppressed." It is in vain that the attempt has been made to extenuate the atrocious and senseless cruelties of this time by extolling the great legislative projects of the Convention, or pleading the dire necessity of a land attacked on every side by the foreigner, and rent with civil war. The more that is known of the Reign of Terror, the more hateful, the meaner and more disgusting is the picture unveiled. France was saved not by the brutalities, but by the energy, of the faction that ruled it. It is scarcely too much to say that the cause of European progress would have been less injured by the military overthrow of the Republic, by the severance of the border provinces from France and the restoration of some shadow of the ancient régime, than by the traditions of horror which for the next fifty years were inseparably associated in men's minds with the victory of the people over established power.

The Revolutionary organisation did not reach its full vigour till the autumn of 1793, when the prospects of France were at their worst. Custine, who was brought up from Alsace to take command of the Army of the North, found it so demoralised that he was unable to attempt the relief of the fortresses which were now besieged by the Allies. Condé surrendered to the Austrians on the 10th of July; Valenciennes capitulated to the Duke of York a fortnight later. In the

French disasters, March—Sept., 1793.

east the fortune of war was no better. An attack made on the Prussian army besieging Mainz totally failed; and on the 23rd of July this great fortress, which had been besieged since the middle of April, passed back into the hands of the Germans. On every side the Republic seemed to be sinking before its enemies. Its frontier defences had fallen before the victorious Austrians and English; Brunswick was ready to advance upon Alsace from conquered Mainz; Lyons and Toulon were in revolt; La Vendée had proved the grave of the forces sent to subdue it. It was in this crisis of misfortune that the Convention placed the entire male population of France between the ages of eighteen and twenty-five at the disposal of the Government, and turned the whole country into one great camp and arsenal of war. Nor was there wanting a mind equal to the task of giving order to this vast material. The appointment of Carnot, an officer of engineers, to a seat on the Committee of Public Safety placed the military administration of France in the hands of a man who, as an organiser, if not as a strategist, was soon to prove himself without equal in Europe.

Nevertheless, it was to the dissensions and to the bad policy of the Allies more than to the energy of its own Government that France owed its safety. The object for which the Allies professed to be carrying on the war, the establishment of a pacific Government in France, was subordinated to schemes of aggrandisement, known as the acquisition of just indemnities. While Prussia, bent

The Allies seek each their separate ends.

chiefly on preventing the Emperor from gaining Bavaria in exchange for Belgium, kept its own army inactive on the Rhine,* Austria, with the full approval of Pitt's Cabinet, claimed annexations in Northern France, as well as Alsace, and treated the conquered town of Condé as Austrian territory.† Henceforward all the operations of the northern army were directed to the acquisition of frontier territory, not to the pursuit and overthrow of the Republican forces. The war was

---

* "The King of Prussia has been educated in the persuasion that the execution of that exchange involves the ruin of his family, and he is the more sore about it that by the qualified consent which he has given to its taking place he has precluded himself from opposing it by arms. Accordingly, every idle story which arrives from Munich which tends to revive this apprehension makes an impression which I am unable, at the first moment, to efface." Lord Yarmouth, from the Prussian camp, Aug. 12, 1793, Records: Army in Germany, 437. "Marquis Lucchesini, the effectual director, is desirous of avoiding every expense and every exertion of the troops; of leaving the whole burden of the war on Austria and the other combined Powers; and of seeing difficulties multiply in the arrangements which the Court of Vienna may wish to form. I do not perceive any object beyond this; no desire of diminishing the power of France; no system or feeling for crushing the opinions, the doctrines, of that country." Elgin, May 17. Records: Flanders, vol. 223.

† Auckland, iii., 24. Thugut, Vertrauliche Briefe i., 18. Grenville to Eden, Sept. 7th, 1793, Records: Austria, vol. 34: a most important historical document, setting out the principles of alliance between England and Austria. Austria, if it will abandon the Bavarian exchange, may claim annexations on the border of the Netherlands, in Alsace and Lorraine, and in the intermediate parts of the frontier of France. England's indemnity "must be looked for in the foreign settlements and colonies of France. : . . His Majesty has an interest in seeing the House of Austria strengthen itself by acquisitions on the French frontier. The Emperor must see with pleasure the relative increase of the naval and commercial resources of this country beyond those of France." In the face of this paper, it cannot be maintained that the war of 1793 was, after the first few months, purely defensive on England's part; though no doubt Pitt's notion of an indemnity was fair and modest in comparison with the schemes and acts of his enemy.

openly converted from a war of defence into a war of spoliation. It was a change which mocked the disinterested professions with which the Allies had taken up arms; in its military results it was absolutely ruinous. In face of the immense levies which promised the French certain victory in a long war, the only hope for the Allies lay in a rapid march to Paris; they preferred the extreme of division and delay. No sooner had the advance of their united armies driven Custine from his stronghold at Famars, than the English commander led off his forces to besiege Dunkirk, while the Austrians, under Prince Coburg, proceeded to invest Cambray and Le Quesnoy. The line of the invaders thus extended from the Channel to Brunswick's posts at Landau, on the border of Alsace; the main armies were out of reach of one another, and their strength was diminished by the corps detached to keep up their communications. The French held the inner circle; and the advantage which this gave them was well understood by Carnot, who now inspired the measures of the Committee. In steadiness and precision the French recruits were no match for the trained armies of Germany; but the supply of them was inexhaustible, and Carnot knew that when they were thrown in sufficient masses upon the enemy their courage and enthusiasm would make amends for their inexperience. The successes of the Allies, unbroken from February to August, now began to alternate with defeats; the flood of invasion was first slowly and obstinately repelled, then swept away before a victorious advance.

It was on the British commander that the first blow was struck. The forces that could be detached from the French Northern army were not sufficient to drive York from before Dunkirk; but on the Moselle there were troops engaged in watching an enemy who was not likely to advance; and the Committee did not hesitate to leave this side of France open to the Prussians in order to deal a decisive stroke in the north. Before the movement was noticed by the enemy, Carnot had transported 30,000 men from Metz to the English Channel; and in the first week of September the German corps covering York was assailed by General Houchard with numbers double its own. *York driven from Dunkirk, Sept. 8.* The Germans were driven back upon Dunkirk; York only saved his own army from destruction by hastily raising the siege and abandoning his heavy artillery. The victory of the French, however, was ill followed up. Houchard was sent before the Revolutionary Tribunal, and he paid with his life for his mistakes. Custine had already perished, unjustly condemned for the loss of Mainz and Valenciennes.

It was no unimportant change for France when the successors of Custine and Houchard received their commands from the Committee of Public Safety. *Commands given to men of the people.* The levelling principle of the Reign of Terror left its effect on France through its operation in the army, and through this almost alone. Its executions produced only horror and reaction; its confiscations were soon reversed; but the creation of a thoroughly democratic army, the work of the men who overthrew the Gironde, gave the most powerful and abiding impulse to social equality in France. The first generals of the Revolution had been officers of the old army, men, with a few exceptions, of noble birth, who, like Custine, had enrolled themselves on the popular side when most of their companions quitted the country. These generals were connected with the politicians of the Gironde, and were involved in its fall. The victory of the Mountain brought men of another type into command. Almost all the leaders appointed by the Committee of Public Safety were soldiers who had served in the ranks. In the levies of 1792 and 1793 the officers of the newly-formed battalions were chosen by the recruits themselves. Patriotism, energy of character, acquaintance with warfare, instantly brought men into prominence. Soldiers of the old army, like Massena, who had reached middle life with their knapsacks on their backs; lawyers, like the Breton Moreau; waiters at inns, like Murat, found themselves at the head of their battalions, and knew that Carnot was ever watching for genius and ability to call it to the highest commands. With a million of men under arms, there were many in whom great natural gifts supplied the want of professional training. It was also inevitable that at the outset command should sometimes fall into the hands of mere busy politicians; but the character of the generals steadily rose as the Committee gained the ascendancy over a knot of demagogues who held the War Ministry during the summer of 1793; and by the end of the year there was scarcely one officer in high command who had not proved himself worthy of his post. In the investigation into Houchard's conduct at Dunkirk, Carnot learnt that the victory had in fact been won by Jourdan, one of the generals of division. Jourdan had begun life as a common soldier fifteen years before. Discharged at the end of the American War, he had set up a draper's shop in Limoges, his native town. He joined the army a second time on the outbreak of the Revolutionary War, and the men of his battalion elected him captain. His ability was noticed; he was made successively general of brigade and general of division; and, upon the dismissal of Houchard, Carnot summoned him to the command of the Army of the North. The Austrians were now engaged in the investment of Maubeuge. On the 15th of October Jourdan attacked and defeated their covering army at Wattignies. His victory forced the Austrians to raise the siege, and brought the campaign to an end for the winter. <small>Jourdan's victory at Wattignies, Oct. 15.</small>

Thus successful on the northern frontier, the Republic carried on war against its internal enemies without pause and without mercy. Lyons surrendered in October; its citizens were slaughtered by hundreds in cold blood. Toulon had thrown itself into the hands of the English, and proclaimed King Louis XVII. It was besieged by land; but the operations produced no effect until Napoleon Bonaparte, captain of artillery, planned the capture of a ridge from which the cannon of the besiegers would command the English fleet in the <small>Lyons, Toulon, La Vendée, conquered, Oct.—Dec. 1793.</small>

G

harbour. Hood, the British admiral, now found his position hopeless. He took several thousands of the inhabitants on board his ships, and put out to sea, blowing up the French ships which he left in the harbour. Hood had received the fleet from the Royalists in trust for their King; its destruction gave England command of the Mediterranean and freed Naples from fear of attack; and Hood thought too little of the consequences which his act would bring down upon those of the inhabitants of Toulon whom he left behind.* The horrors that followed the entry of the Republican army into the city did not prevent Pitt from including among the subjects of congratulation in the King's Speech of 1794 " the circumstances attending the evacuation of Toulon." It was perhaps fortunate for the Royalists in other parts of France that they

* The first mention of Bonaparte's name in any British document occurs in an account of the army of Toulon sent to London in Dec. 1793 by a spy. " Les capitaines d'artillérie, élévés dans cet état, connoissent leur service et ont tous du talens. Ils préféroient l'employer pour une meilleure cause... Le sixième, nommé Bonaparte, très republicain, a été tué sous les murs de Toulon." Records: France, vol. 599. Austria undertook to send 5,000 troops from Lombardy to defend Toulon, but broke its engagement. "You will wait on M. Thugut (the Austrian Minister) and claim in the most peremptory terms the performance of this engagement. It would be very offensive to his Majesty that a request made so repeatedly on his part should be neglected; but it is infinitely more so to see that, when this country is straining every nerve for the common cause, a body of troops for the want of which Toulon may possibly at this moment be lost, have remained inactive at Milan. You will admit of no further excuses." Grenville to Eden, Nov. 24, 1793. Thugut's written answer was, " The Emperor gave the order of march at a moment when the town of Toulon had no garrison. Its preservation then seemed matter of pressing necessity, but now all inquietude on this score has happily disappeared. The troops of different nations already assembled at Toulon put the place out of all danger." Records: Austria, vol. 35.

failed to receive the assistance of England. Help was promised to the Vendeans, but it arrived too late. The appearance of Kleber at the head of the army which had defended Mainz had already turned the scale. Brave as they were, the Vendeans could not long resist trained armies. The war of pitched battles ended on the Loire with the year 1793. It was succeeded by a war of merciless and systematic destruction on the one side, and of ambush and surprises on the other.

At home the foes of the Republic were sinking; its invaders were too much at discord with one another to threaten it any longer with serious danger. Prussia was in fact withdrawing from the war. It has been seen that when King Frederick William and the Emperor concerted the autumn campaign of 1792, the understanding was formed that Prussia, in return for its efforts against France, should be allowed to seize part of western Poland, if the Empress Catherine should give her consent. With this prospect before it, the thoughts of the Prussian Government had been from the first busied more with Poland, where it hoped to enter into possession, than with France, where it had only to fight Austria's battles. Negotiations on the Polish question had been actively carried on between Berlin and St. Petersburg during the first months of the war; and in January, 1793, the Empress Catherine had concluded a Treaty of Partition with King Frederick William, in virtue of which a Prussian army under General Möllendorf immediately entered western Poland. It was thought good

Prussia withdrawing from the war on account of Polish affairs.

policy to keep the terms of this treaty secret from Austria, as it granted a much larger portion of Poland to Prussia than Austria was willing that it should receive. Two months passed before the Austrian Sovereign learnt how he had been treated by his ally. He then denounced the treaty, and assumed so threatening an attitude that the Prussians thought it necessary to fortify the territory that they had seized.* The Ministers who had been outwitted by the Court of Berlin were dismissed; Baron Thugut, who from the first had prophesied nothing but evil of the Prussian alliance, was called to power. The history of this statesman, who for the next eight years directed the war-policy of Austria, and filled a part in Europe subordinate only to those of Pitt and Bonaparte, has until a recent date been drawn chiefly from the representations of his enemies. Humbly born, scornful and inaccessible, Thugut was detested by the Viennese aristocracy; the French emigrants hated and maligned him on account of his indifference to their cause; the public opinion of Austria held him responsible for unparalleled military disasters; Prussian generals and ambassadors, whose reports have formed the basis of Prussian histories, pictured him as a Satanic antagonist. It was long believed of Thugut that while ambassador at Constantinople he had sold the Austrian cypher to the French;

* Häusser, i., 482. "La Prusse," wrote Thugut at this time, "parviendra au moyen de son alliance à nous faire plus de mal qu'elle ne nous a fait par les guerres les plus sanglantes." Briefe i., 12, 15. Thugut even proposed that England should encourage the Poles to resist. Eden, April 15; Records : Austria, vol. 33.

that in 1794 he prevented his master's armies from winning victories because he had speculated in the French funds; and that in 1799 he occasioned the murder of the French envoys at Rastadt, in order to recover documents incriminating himself. Better sources of information are now opened, and a statesman, jealous, bitter, and over-reaching, but not without great qualities of character, stands in the place of the legendary criminal. It is indeed clear that Thugut's hatred of Prussia amounted almost to mania; it is also clear that his designs of aggression, formed in the school of the Emperor Joseph, were fatally in conflict with the defensive principles which Europe ought to have opposed to the aggressions of France. Evidence exists that during the eight years of Thugut's ministry he entertained, together or successively, projects for the annexation of French Flanders, Bavaria, Alsace, part of Poland, Venice and Dalmatia, Salzburg, the Papal Legations, the Republic of Genoa, Piedmont, and Bosnia; and to this list Tuscany and Savoy ought probably to be added. But the charges brought against Thugut of underhand dealings with France, and of the willing abandonment of German interests in return for compensation to Austria in Italy, rest on insufficient ground. Though, like every other politician at Vienna and Berlin, he viewed German affairs not as a matter of nationality but in subordination to the general interests of his own Court, Thugut appears to have been, of all the Continental statesmen of that time, the steadiest enemy of French aggression, and to have offered the longest resistance to a peace that was purchased by the cession of German soil.*

Nevertheless, from the moment when Thugut was called to power the alliance between Austria and Prussia was doomed. Others might perhaps have averted a rupture; Thugut made no attempt to do so. The siege of Mainz was the last serious operation of war which the Prussian army performed. The mission of an Austrian envoy, Lehrbach, to the Prussian camp in August, 1793, and his negotiations on the Polish and the Bavarian questions, only widened the breach between the two Courts. It was known that the Austrians were encouraging the Polish Diet to refuse the cession of the provinces occupied by Prussia; and the advisers of King Frederick William in consequence recommended him to quit the Rhine, and to place himself at the head of an army in Poland. At the head-quarters of the Allies, between Mainz and the Alsatian frontier, all was dissension and intrigue. The impetuosity of the Austrian general, Wurmser, who advanced upon Alsace without consulting the King, was construed as a studied insult. On the 29th of September, after informing the allied Courts that Prussia would henceforth take only a subordinate part in the war, King Frederick William

* The English Government found that Thugut was from the first indifferent to their own aim, the restoration of the Bourbons, or establishment of some orderly government in France. In so far as he concerned himself with the internal affairs of France, he hoped rather for continued dissension, as facilitating the annexation of French territory by Austria. " Qu'on profite de ce conflit des partis en France pour tâcher de se rendre maître des forteresses, afin de faire la loi au parti qui aura prévalu, et l'obliger d'acheter la paix et la protection de l'empereur, en lui cedant telle partie de ses conquêtes que S. M. jugera de sa convenance." Briefe, i., 13.

quitted the army, leaving orders with the Duke of Brunswick to fight no great battle. It was in vain that Wurmser stormed the lines of Weissenburg (Oct. 13), and victoriously pushed forward into Alsace. The hopes of a Royalist insurrection in Strasburg proved illusory. The German sympathies shown by a portion of the upper and middle classes of Alsace only brought down upon them a bloody vengeance at the hands of St. Just, commissioner of the Convention. The peasantry, partly from hatred of the feudal burdens of the old régime, partly from fear of St. Just and the guillotine, thronged to the French camp. In place of the beaten generals came Hoche and Pichegru: Hoche, lately a common soldier in the Guards, earning by a humble industry little sums for the purchase of books, now, at the age of twenty-six, a commander more than a match for the wrangling veterans of Germany; Pichegru, six years older, also a man sprung from the people, once a teacher in the military school of Brienne, afterwards a private of artillery in the American War. A series of harassing encounters took place during December. At length, with St. Just cheering on the Alsatian peasants in the hottest of the fire, these generals victoriously carried the Austrian positions at Wörth and at Weissenburg (Dec. 23, 26). The Austrian commander declared his army to be utterly ruined; and Brunswick, who had abstained from rendering his ally any real assistance, found himself a second time back upon the Rhine.*

Victories of Hoche and Pichegru at Wörth and Weissenburg, Dec. 23, 26.

---

* The despatches of Lord Yarmouth from the Prussian and Austrian

The virtual retirement of Prussia from the Coalition was no secret to the French Government: amongst the Allies it was viewed in various lights. The Empress Catherine, who had counted on seeing her troublesome Prussian friend engaged with her detested French enemy, taunted the King of Prussia with the loss of his personal honour. Austria, conscious of the antagonism between Prussian and Austrian interests and of the hollow character of the Coalition, would concede nothing to keep Prussia in arms. Pitt alone was willing to make a sacrifice, in order to prevent the rupture of the alliance. The King of Prussia was ready to continue the struggle with France if his expenses were paid, but not otherwise. Accordingly, after Austria had refused to contribute the small sum which Pitt asked, a bargain was struck between Lord Malmesbury and the Prussian Minister Haugwitz, by which Great Britain undertook to furnish a subsidy, provided that 60,000 Prussian troops, under General Möllendorf, were placed at the disposal of the Maritime Powers.* It was Pitt's intention that the troops which he subsidised should be massed with Austrian and English forces for

Marginal note: Pitt's bargain with Prussia, April, 1794.

---

head-quarters, from July 17 to Nov. 22, 1793, give a lively picture both of the military operations and of the political intrigues of this period. They are accompanied by the MS. journal of the Austrian army from Sept. 15 to Dec. 14, each copy apparently with Wurmser's autograph, and by the original letter of the Prussian Minister, Lucchesini, to Lord Yarmouth, announcing the withdrawal of Prussia from the war. "M. de Lucchesini read it to me very hastily, and seemed almost ashamed of a part of its contents." Records: Army in Germany, vols. 437, 438, 439.

* Hardenberg (Ranke), i., 181. Vivenot, Herzog Albrecht, i., 10.

the defence of Belgium: the Prussian Ministry, availing themselves of an ambiguous expression in the treaty, insisted on keeping them inactive upon the Upper Rhine. Möllendorf wished to guard Mainz: other men of influence longed to abandon the alliance with Austria, and to employ the whole of Prussia's force in Poland. At the moment when Haugwitz was contracting to place Möllendorf's army at Pitt's disposal, Poland had risen in revolt under Kosciusko, and the Russian garrison which occupied Warsaw had been overpowered and cut to pieces. Catherine called upon the King of Prussia for assistance; but it was not so much a desire to rescue the Empress from a momentary danger that excited the Prussian Cabinet as the belief that her vengeance would now make an absolute end of what remained of the Polish kingdom. The prey was doomed; the wisdom of Prussia was to be the first to seize and drag it to the ground. So large a prospect offered itself to the Power that should crush Poland during the brief paralysis of the Russian arms, that, on the first news of the outbreak, the King's advisers urged him instantly to make peace with France and to throw his whole strength into the Polish struggle. Frederick William could not reconcile himself to making peace with the Jacobins; but he ordered an army to march upon Warsaw, and shortly afterwards placed himself at its head. (May, 1794.) When the King, who was the only politician in Prussia who took an interest in the French war, thus publicly acknowledged the higher importance of the Polish

Revolt of Kosciusko, April, 1794.

campaign, his generals upon the Rhine made it their only object to do nothing which it was possible to leave undone without actually forfeiting the British subsidy. Instead of fighting, Möllendorf spent his time in urging other people to make peace. It was in vain that Malmesbury argued that the very object of Pitt's bargain was to keep the French out of the Netherlands: Möllendorf had made up his mind that the army should not be committed to the orders of Pitt and the Austrians. He continued in the Palatinate, alleging that any movement of the Prussian army towards the north would give the French admittance to southern Germany. Pitt's hope of defending the Netherlands now rested on the energy and on the sincerity of the Austrian Cabinet, and on this alone.

Möllendorf refuses to help in Flanders.

After breaking up from winter quarters in the spring of 1794, the Austrian and English allied forces had successfully laid siege to Landrecies, and defeated the enemy in its neighbourhood.*

Battles on the Sambre, May—June, 1794.

Their advance, however, was checked by a movement of the French Army of the North, now com-

---

* Elgin reports after this engagement, May 1st, 1794—" The French army appears to continue much what it has hitherto been, vigorous and persevering where (as in villages and woods) the local advantages are of a nature to supply the defects of military science; weak and helpless beyond belief where cavalry can act, and manœuvres are possible. . . . The magazines of the army are stored, and the provisions regularly given out to the troops, and good in quality. Indeed, it is singular to observe in all the villages where we have been forward forage, &c., in plenty, and all the country cultivated as usual. The inhabitants, however, have retired with the French army; and to that degree that the tract we have lately taken possession of is absolutely deserted. . . . The execution of Danton

manded by Pichegru, towards the Flemish coast. York and the English troops were exposed to the attack, and suffered a defeat at Turcoing. The decision of the campaign lay, however, not in the west of Flanders, but at the other end of the Allies' position, at Charleroi on the Sambre, where a French victory would either force the Austrians to fall back eastwards, leaving York to his fate, or sever their communications with Germany. This became evident to the French Government; and in May the Commissioners of the Convention forced the generals on the Sambre to fight a series of battles, in which the French repeatedly succeeded in crossing the Sambre, and were repeatedly driven back again. The fate of the Netherlands depended, however, on something beside victory or defeat on the Sambre. The Emperor had come with Baron Thugut to Belgium in the hope of imparting greater unity and energy to the allied forces, but his presence proved useless. Among the Austrian generals and diplomatists there were several who desired to withdraw from the contest in the Netherlands, and to follow the example of Prussia in Poland. The action of the army was paralysed by intrigues. "Every one," wrote Thugut, "does exactly as he pleases:

has produced no greater effect in the army than other executions, and we have found many papers on those who fell in the late actions treating it with ridicule, and as a source of joy." Records: Flanders, 226. "I am in hopes to hear from you on the subject of the French prisoners, as to where I am to apply for the money I advance for their subsistence. They are a great number of them almost naked, some entirely so. It is absolutely shocking to humanity to see them. I would purchase some coarse clothing for those that are in the worst state, but know not how far I should be authorised. They are mostly old men and boys." Consul Harward, at Ostend, March 4th, *id.*

there is absolute anarchy and disorder."* At the beginning of June the Emperor quitted the army; the combats on the Sambre were taken up by Jourdan and 50,000 fresh troops brought from the army of the Moselle; and on the 26th of June the French defeated Coburg at Fleurus, as he advanced to the relief of Charleroi, unconscious that Charleroi had surrendered on the day before. Even now the defence of Belgium was not hopeless; but after one council of war had declared in favour of fighting, a second determined on a retreat. It was in vain that the representatives of England appealed to the good faith and military honour of Austria. Namur and Louvain were abandoned; the French pressed onwards; and before the end of July the Austrian army had fallen back behind the Meuse. York, forsaken by his allies, retired northwards before the superior forces of Pichegru, who entered

<small>Austria abandons the Netherlands, July, 1794.</small>

---

* These events are the subject of controversy. See Huffer, Oestreich und Preussen, p. 62. Von Sybel, iii., 138. Vivenot, Clorfayt, p. 38. The old belief, defended by Von Sybel, was that Thugut himself had determined upon the evacuation of Belgium, and treacherously deprived Coburg of forces for its defence. But, apart from other evidence, the tone of exasperation that runs through Thugut's private letters is irreconcilable with this theory. Lord Elgin, whose reports are used by Von Sybel, no doubt believed that Thugut was playing false; but he was a bad judge, being in the hands of Thugut's opponents, especially General Mack, whom he glorifies in the most absurd way. The other English envoy in Belgium, Lord Yarmouth, reported in favour of Thugut's good faith in this matter, and against military intriguers. Records: Army in Germany, vol. 440. A letter of Prince Waldeck's in Thugut, i., 387, and a conversation between Mack and Sir Morton Eden, on Feb. 3rd, 1797, reported by the latter in Records: Austria, vol. 48, appear to fix the responsibility for the evacuation of Belgium on these two generals, Waldeck and Mack, and on the Emperor's confidential military adviser, Rollin.

Antwerp and made himself master of the whole of the Netherlands up to the Dutch frontier.*

Such was the result of Great Britain's well-meant effort to assist the two great military Powers to defend Europe against the Revolution. To the aim of the English Minister, the defence of existing rights against democratic aggression, most of the public men alike of Austria and Prussia were now absolutely indifferent. They were willing to let the French seize and revolutionise any territory they pleased, provided that they themselves obtained their equivalent in Poland. England was in fact in the position of a man who sets out to attack a highway robber, and offers each of his arms to a pickpocket. The motives and conduct of these politicians were justly enough described by the English statesmen and generals who were brought into closest contact with them. In the councils of Prussia, Malmesbury declared

_{England disappointed by the Allies.}

---

* "Should the French come they will find this town perfectly empty. Except my own, I do not think there are three houses in Ostend with a bed in them. So general a panic I never witnessed." June 30th.—" To remain here alone would be a wanton sacrifice. God knows 'tis an awful stroke to me to leave a place just as I began to be comfortably settled." Consul Harward; Records: Army in Germany, vol. 440. "All the English are arrested in Ostend: the men are confined in the Capuchin convent, and the women in the Convent des Sœurs Blancs. All the Flamands from the age of 17 to 32 are forced to go for soldiers. At Bruges the French issued an order for 800 men to present themselves. Thirty only came, in consequence of which they rang a bell on the Grand Place, and the inhabitants thinking that it was some ordinance, quitted their houses to hear it, when they were surrounded by the French soldiers, and upwards of 1,000 men secured, gentle and simple, who were all immediately set to work on the canals." Mr. W. Poppleton, Flushing, Sept. 4. Records: Flanders, vol. 227.

that he could find no quality but "great and shabby art and cunning; ill will, jealousy, and every sort of dirty passion." From the head-quarters of Möllendorf he wrote to a member of Pitt's Cabinet: "Here I have to do with knavery and dotage. . . . If we listened only to our feelings, it would be difficult to keep any measure with Prussia. We must consider it an alliance with the Algerians, whom it is no disgrace to pay, or any impeachment of good sense to be cheated by." To the Austrian commander the Duke of York addressed himself with royal plainness: "Your Serene Highness, the British nation, whose public opinion is not to be despised, will consider that it has been bought and sold."*

The sorry concert lasted for a few months longer. Coburg, the Austrian commander, was dismissed at the peremptory demand of Great Britain; his successor, Clerfayt, after losing a battle on the Ourthe, offered no further resistance to the advance of the Republican army, and the campaign ended in the capture of Cologne by the French, and the disappearance of the Austrians behind the Rhine. The Prussian subsidies granted by England resulted in some useless engagements between Möllendorf's corps in the Palatinate and a French army double its size, followed by the retreat of the Prussians into Mainz. It only remained for Great Britain to attempt to keep the French out of Hol-

<small>French reach the Rhine, Oct., 1794.</small>

---

* Malmesbury, ii., 125. Von Sybel, iii., 168. Grenville made Coburg's dismissal a *sine quâ non* of the continuance of English co-operation. Instructions to Lord Spencer, July 19, 1794. Records: Austria, 36. But for the Austrian complaints against the English, see Vivenot, Clerfayt, p. 30.

ADVANCE OF PICHEGRU'S ARMY.

land. The defence of the Dutch, after everything south of the river Waal had been lost, Pitt determined to entrust to abler hands than those of the Duke of York; but the presence of one high-born blunderer more or less made little difference in a series of operations conceived in indifference and perversity. Clerfayt would not, or could not, obey the Emperor's orders and succour his ally. City after city in Holland welcomed the French. The very elements seemed to declare for the Republic. Pichegru's army marched in safety over the frozen rivers; and, when the conquest of the land was completed, his cavalry crowned the campaign by the capture of the Dutch fleet in the midst of the ice-bound waters of the Texel.

<small>Pichegru conquers Holland, Dec., 1794.</small>

The British regiments, cut off from home, made their way eastward through the snow towards the Hanoverian frontier, in a state of prostrate misery which is compared by an eye-witness of both events to that of the French on their retreat in 1813 after the battle of Leipzig.*

The first act of the struggle between France and the Monarchies of Europe was concluded. The result of three years of war was that Belgium, Nice, and Savoy had been added to the territory of the Republic, and that French armies were in possession of Holland, and the whole of Germany west of the Rhine. In Spain and in Piedmont the mountain-passes and some extent of country had been won. Even on the seas, in spite of the destruction of the fleet at Toulon, and of a heavy

---

* Schlosser, xv., 203 : borne out by the Narrative of an Officer, printed in Annual Register, 1795, p. 143.

defeat by Lord Howe off Ushant on the 1st of June, 1794, the strength of France was still formidable; and the losses which she inflicted on the commercial marine of her enemies exceeded those which she herself sustained. England, which had captured most of the French West Indian Islands, was the only Power that had wrested anything from the Republic. The dream of suppressing the Revolution by force of arms had vanished away; and the States which had entered upon the contest in levity, in fanaticism, or at the bidding of more powerful allies, found it necessary to make peace upon such terms as they could obtain. Holland, in which a strong Republican party had always maintained connection with France, abolished the rule of its Stadtholder, and placed its resources at the disposal of its conquerors. Sardinia entered upon abortive negotiations. Spain, in return for peace, ceded to the Republic the Spanish half of St. Domingo (July 22, 1795). Prussia concluded a Treaty at Basle (April 5), which marked and perpetuated the division of Germany by providing that, although the Empire as a body was still at war with France, the benefit of Prussia's neutrality should extend to all German States north of a certain line. A secret article stipulated that, upon the conclusion of a general peace, if the Empire should cede to France the principalities west of the Rhine, Prussia should cede its own territory lying in that district, and receive compensation elsewhere.*

<small>Treaties of Basle with Prussia, April 5, and Spain, July 22, 1795.</small>

* Vivenot, Herzog Albrecht, iii., 59, 512. Martens, Recueil des Traités, vi., 45, 52. Hardenberg, i., 287. Vivenot, Clerfayt, p. 32. "Le Roi de

Humiliating such a peace certainly was; yet it would probably have been the happiest issue for Europe had every Power been forced to accept its conditions. The territory gained by France was not much more than the very principle of the Balance of Power would have entitled it to demand, at a moment when Russia, victorious over the Polish rebellion, was proceeding to make the final partition of Poland among the three Eastern Monarchies; and, with all its faults, the France of 1795 would have offered to Europe the example of a great free State, such as the growth of the military spirit made impossible after the first of Napoleon's campaigns. But the dark future was withdrawn from the view of those British statesmen who most keenly felt the evils of the present; and England, resolutely set against the course of French aggression, still found in Austria an ally willing to continue the struggle. The financial help of Great Britain, the Russian offer of a large share in the spoils of Poland, stimulated the flagging energy of the Emperor's government. Orders were sent to Clerfayt to advance from the Rhine at whatever risk, in order to withdraw the troops of the Republic from the west of France, where England was about to land a body of Royalists. Clerfayt, however, disobeyed his instructions, and remained inactive till the autumn. He then defeated a French army pushing beyond the

Austria and England continue the war, 1795.

Prusse," wrote the Empress Catherine, " est une méchante bête et un grand cochon." Prussia made no attempt to deliver the unhappy son of Louis XVI. from his captivity.

H

Rhine, and drove back the besiegers of Mainz; but the British expedition had already failed, and the time was passed when Clerfayt's successes might have produced a decisive result.*

<small>France in 1795.</small>
A new Government was now entering upon power in France. The Reign of Terror had ended in July, 1794, with the life of Robespierre. The men by whom Robespierre was overthrown were Terrorists more cruel and less earnest than himself, who attacked him only in order to save their own lives, and without the least intention of restoring a constitutional Government to France. An overwhelming national reaction forced them, however, to represent themselves as the party of clemency. The reaction was indeed a simple outburst of human feeling rather than a change in political opinion. Among the victims of the Terror

---

* The British Government had formed the most sanguine estimate of the strength of the Royalist movement in France. "I cannot let your servant return without troubling you with those few lines to conjure you to use every possible effort to give life and vigour to the Austrian Government at this critical moment. Strongly as I have spoken in my despatch of the present state of France, I have said much less than my information, drawn from various quarters, and applying to almost every part of France, would fairly warrant. We can never hope that the circumstances, as far as they regard the state of France, can be more favourable than they now are. For God's sake enforce these points with all the earnestness which I am sure you will feel upon them." Grenville to Eden, April 17, 1795; Records: Austria, vol. 41. After the failure of the expedition, the British Government made the grave charge against Thugut that while he was officially sending Clerfayt pressing orders to advance, he secretly told him to do nothing. "It is in vain to reason with the Austrian Ministers on the folly and ill faith of a system which they have been under the necessity of concealing from you, and which they will probably endeavour to disguise." Grenville to Eden, Oct., 1795; *id.*, vol. 43. This charge, repeated by historians, is disproved by Thugut's private letters. Briefe, i., 221, *seq*. No one more bitterly resented Clerfayt's inaction.

the great majority had been men of the lower or middle class, who, except in La Vendée and Brittany, were as little friendly to the old *régime* as their executioners. Every class in France, with the exception of the starving city mobs, longed for security, and the quiet routine of life. After the disorders of the Republic a monarchical government naturally seemed to many the best guarantee of peace; but the monarchy so contemplated was the liberal monarchy of 1791, not the ancient Court, with its accessories of a landed Church and privileged noblesse. Religion was still a power in France; but the peasant, with all his superstition and all his desire for order, was perfectly free from any delusions about the good old times. He liked to see his children baptised; but he had no desire to see the priest's tithe-collector back in his barn: he shuddered at the summary marketing of Conventional Commissioners; but he had no wish to resume his labours on the fields of his late seigneur. To be a Monarchist in 1795, among the shopkeepers of Paris or the farmers of Normandy, meant no more than to wish for a political system capable of subsisting for twelve months together, and resting on some other basis than forced loans and compulsory sales of property. But among the men of the Convention, who had abolished monarchy and passed sentence of death upon the King, the restoration of the Crown seemed the bitterest condemnation of all that the Convention had done for France, and a sentence of outlawry against themselves. If the will of the nation was for the moment in favour of a restored monarchy, the Convention determined that its will must be overpowered by force or thwarted by constitutional forms. Threatened alternately by the Jacobin mob of Paris and by the Royalist middle class, the Government played off one enemy against the other, until an ill-timed effort of the emigrant noblesse gave to the Convention the prestige of a decisive victory over Royalists and foreigners combined. On the 27th of June, 1795, an English fleet landed the flower of the old nobility of France at the Bay of Quiberon in southern Brittany. It was only to give one last fatal proof of their incapacity that these unhappy men appeared once more on French soil. Within three weeks after their landing, in a region where for years together the peasantry, led by their landlords, baffled the best generals of the Republic, this invading army of the nobles, supported by the fleet, the arms, and the money of England, was brought to utter ruin by the discord of its own leaders. Before the nobles had settled who was to command and who was to obey, General Hoche surprised their fort, beat them back to the edge of the peninsula where they had landed, and captured all who were not killed fighting or rescued by English boats. (July 20.) The Commissioner Tallien, in order to purge himself from the just suspicion of Royalist intrigues, caused six hundred prisoners to be shot in cold blood.*

Landing at Quiberon, June 27, 1795.

At the moment when the emigrant army reached

---

* The documents relating to the expedition to Quiberon, with several letters of D'Artois, Charette, and the Vendean leaders, are in Records: France, vol. 600.

France, the Convention was engaged in discussing the political system which was to succeed its own rule. A week earlier, the Committee appointed to draw up a new constitution for France had presented its report. Project of Constitution, 1795. The main object of the new constitution in its original form was to secure France against a recurrence of those evils which it had suffered since 1792. The calamities of the last three years were ascribed to the sovereignty of a single Assembly. A vote of the Convention had established the Revolutionary Tribunal, proscribed the Girondins, and placed France at the mercy of eighty individuals selected by the Convention from itself. The legislators of 1795 desired a guarantee that no party, however determined, should thus destroy its enemies by a single law, and unite supreme legislative and executive power in its own hands. With the object of dividing authority, the executive was, in the new draft-constitution, made independent of the legislature, and the legislature itself was broken up into two chambers. A Directory of five members, chosen by the Assemblies, but not responsible except under actual impeachment, was to conduct the administration, without the right of proposing laws; a Chamber of five hundred was to submit laws to the approval of a Council of two hundred and fifty Ancients, or men of middle life; but neither of these bodies was to exercise any influence upon the actual government. One director and a third part of each of the legislative bodies were to retire every year.*

* Von Sybel, iii. 537. Buchez et Roux, xxxvi., 485.

The project thus outlined met with general approval, and gained even that of the Royalists, who believed that a popular election would place them in a majority in the two new Assemblies. Such an event was, however, in the eyes of the Convention, the one fatal possibility that must be averted at every cost. In the midst of the debates upon the draft-constitution there arrived the news of Hoche's victory at Quiberon. The Convention gained courage to add a clause providing that two-thirds of the new deputies should be appointed from among its own members, thus rendering a Royalist majority in the Chambers impossible. With this condition attached to it, the Constitution was laid before the country. The provinces accepted it; the Royalist middle class of Paris rose in insurrection, and marched against the Convention in the Tuileries. Their revolt was foreseen; the defence of the Convention was entrusted to General Bonaparte, who met the attack of the Parisians in a style unknown in the warfare of the capital. Bonaparte's command of trained artillery secured him victory; but the struggle of the 4th of October (13 Vendémiaire) was the severest that took place in Paris during the Revolution, and the loss of life in fighting greater than on the day that overthrew the Monarchy.

Constitution of 1795. Insurrection of Vendémiaire, Oct. 4.

The new Government of France now entered into power. Members of the Convention formed two-thirds of the new legislative bodies; the one-third which the country was permitted to elect consisted chiefly of men of moderate or Royalist opinions.

The Directory, Oct., 1795.

The five persons who were chosen Directors were all Conventionalists who had voted for the death of the King; Carnot, however, who had won the victories without sharing in the cruelties of the Reign of Terror, was the only member of the late Committee of Public Safety who was placed in power. In spite of the striking homage paid to the great act of regicide in the election of the five Directors, the establishment of the Directory was accepted by Europe as the close of revolutionary disorder. The return of constitutional rule in France was marked by a declaration on the part of the King of England of his willingness to treat for peace. A gentler spirit seemed to have arisen in the Republic. Although the laws against the emigrants and non-juring priests were still unrepealed, the exiles began to return unmolested to their homes. Life resumed something of its old aspect in the capital. The rich and the gay consoled themselves with costlier luxury for all the austerities of the Reign of Terror. The labouring classes, now harmless and disarmed, were sharply taught that they must be content with such improvement in their lot as the progress of society might bring.

At the close of this first period of the Revolutionary War we may pause to make an estimate of the new influences which the French Revolution had brought into Europe, and of the effects which had thus far resulted from them. The opinion current among the French people themselves, that the Revolution gave birth to the modern life not of France only but of the Western Continent generally, is

What was new to Europe in the Revolution.

true of one great set of facts; it is untrue of another. There were conceptions in France in 1789 which made France a real contrast to most of the Continental monarchies; there were others which it shared in common with them. The ideas of social, legal, and ecclesiastical reform which were realised in 1789 were not peculiar to France; what was peculiar to France was the idea that these reforms were to be effected by the nation itself. In other countries reforms had been initiated by Governments, and forced upon an unwilling people. Innovation sprang from the Crown; its agents were the servants of the State. A distinct class of improvements, many of them identical with the changes made by the Revolution in France, attracted the attention in a greater or less degree of almost all the Western Courts of the eighteenth century.

Absolute governments of 18th century engaged in reforms.

The creation of a simple and regular administrative system; the reform of the clergy; the emancipation of the Church from the jurisdiction of the Pope, and of all orders in the State from the jurisdiction of the Church; the amelioration of the lot of the peasant; the introduction of codes of law abolishing both the cruelties and the confusion of ancient practice,—all these were purposes more or less familiar to the absolute sovereigns of the eighteenth century, whom the French so summarily described as benighted tyrants. It was in Austria, Prussia, and Tuscany that the civilising energy of the Crown had been seen in its strongest form, but even the Governments of Naples and Spain had caught the spirit of change. The religious tolerance which Joseph gave to Austria, the rejection of Papal authority and the abolition of the punishment of death which Leopold effected in Tuscany, were bolder efforts of the same political rationalism which in Spain minimised the powers of the Inquisition and in Naples attempted to found a system of public education. In all this, however, there was no trace of the action of the people, or of any sense that a nation ought to raise itself above a state of tutelage. Men of ideas called upon Governments to impose better institutions upon the people, not upon the people to wrest them from the Governments.

In France alone a view of public affairs had grown up which impelled the nation to create its reforms for itself. If the substance of many of the French revolutionary changes coincided with the objects of Austrian or of Tuscan reform, there was nothing similar in their method. In other countries reform sprang from the command of an enlightened ruler; in France it started with the Declaration of the Rights of Man, and aimed at the creation of local authority to be exercised by the citizens themselves. The source of this difference lay partly in the influence of England and America upon French opinion, but much more in the existence within France of a numerous and energetic middle class, enriched by commerce, and keenly interested in all the speculation and literary activity of the age. This was a class that both understood the wrongs which the other classes inflicted or suffered, and felt itself capable of redressing them. For the flogged and over-driven peasant in Naples or

In France the nation itself acted.

Hungary no ally existed but the Crown. In most of those poor and backward States which made up monarchical Europe, the fraction of the inhabitants which neither enjoyed privilege nor stood in bondage to it was too small to think of forcing itself into power. The nobles sought to preserve their feudal rights: the Crown sought to reduce them; the nation, elsewhere than in France, did not intervene and lay hands upon power for itself, because the nation was nothing but the four mutually exclusive classes of the landlords who commanded, the peasants who served, the priests who idled, and the soldiers who fought. France differed from all the other monarchies of the Continent in possessing a public which blended all classes and was dominated by none; a public comprehending thousands of men who were familiar with the great interests of society, and who, whether noble or not noble, possessed the wealth and the intelligence that made them rightly desire a share in power.

Liberty, the right of the nation to govern itself, seemed at the outset to be the great principle of the Revolution. The French people themselves believed the question at issue to be mainly between authority and popular right; the rest of Europe saw the Revolution under the same aspect. Hence, in those countries where the example of France produced political movements, the effect was in the first instance to excite agitation against the Government, whatever might be the form of the latter. In England the agitation was one of the middle class

Movements against governments outside France.

against the aristocratic parliamentary system; in Hungary, it was an agitation of the nobles against the Crown; on the Rhine it was an agitation of the commercial classes against ecclesiastical rule. But in every case in which the reforming movement was not supported by the presence of French armies, the terrors which succeeded the first sanguine hopes of the Revolution struck the leaders of these movements with revulsion and despair, and converted even the better Governments into engines of reaction. In France itself it was seen that the desire for liberty among an enlightened class could not suddenly transform the habits of a nation accustomed to accept everything from authority. Privilege was destroyed, equality was advanced; but instead of self-government the Revolution brought France the most absolute rule it had ever known. It was not that the Revolution had swept by, leaving things where they were before: it had in fact accomplished most of those great changes which lay the foundation of a sound social life: but the faculty of self-government, the first condition of any lasting political liberty, remained to be slowly won.

Outside France reaction set in without the benefit of previous change. At London, Vienna, Naples, and Madrid, Governments gave up all other objects in order to devote themselves to the suppression of Jacobinism. Pitt, whose noble aims had been the extinction of the slave-trade, the reform of Parliament, and the advance of national intercourse by free trade, surrendered himself to men whose thoughts centred upon informers, Gagging Acts, and constructive

Reaction.

treasons, and who opposed all legislation upon the slave-trade because slaves had been freed by the Jacobins of the Convention. State trials and imprisonments became the order of the day; but the reaction in England at least stopped short of the scaffold. At Vienna and Naples fear was more cruel. The men who either were, or affected to be, in such fear of revolution that they discovered a Jacobinical allegory in Mozart's last opera,* did not spare life when the threads of anything like a real conspiracy were placed in their hands. At Vienna terror was employed to crush the constitutional opposition of Hungary to the Austrian Court. In Naples a long reign of cruelty and oppression began with the creation of a secret tribunal to investigate charges of conspiracy made by informers. In Mainz, the Archbishop occupied the last years of his government, after his restoration in 1793, with a series of brutal punishments and tyrannical precautions.

These were but instances of the effect which the first epoch of the Revolution produced upon the old European States. After a momentary stimulus to freedom it threw the nations themselves into reaction and apathy; it totally changed the spirit of the better governments, attaching to all liberal ideas the stigma of Revolution, and identifying the work of authority with resistance to every kind of reform. There were States in which this change, the first effect of the Revolution, was also its only one; States whose history, as in the

* For the police interpretation of the *Zauberflöte*, see Springer, Geschichte Oesterreichs, vol. i., p. 49.

case of England, is for a whole generation the history of political progress unnaturally checked and thrown out of its course. There were others, and these the more numerous, where the first stimulus and the first reaction were soon forgotten in new and penetrating changes produced by the successive victories of France. The nature of these changes, even more than the warfare which introduced them, gives its interest to the period on which we are about to enter.

CHAPTER III.

Triple attack on Austria—Moreau, Jourdan—Bonaparte in Italy—Condition of the Italian States—Professions and real intentions of Bonaparte and the Directory—Battle of Montenotte—Armistice with Sardinia—Campaign in Lombardy—Treatment of the Pope, Naples, Tuscany—Siege of Mantua—Castiglione—Moreau and Jourdan in Germany—Their retreat—Secret Treaty with Prussia—Negotiations with England—Cispadane Republic—Rise of the idea of Italian Independence—Battles of Arcola and Rivoli—Peace with the Pope at Tolentino—Venice—Preliminaries of Leoben—The French in Venice—The French take the Ionian Islands and give Venice to Austria—Genoa—Coup d'état of 17 Fructidor in Paris—Treaty of Campo Formio—Victories of England at sea—Bonaparte's project against Egypt.

WITH the opening of the year 1796 the leading interest of European history passes to a new scene. Hitherto the progress of French victory had been in the direction of the Rhine: the advance of the army of the Pyrenees had been cut short by the conclusion of peace with Spain; the army of Italy had achieved little beyond some obscure successes in the mountains. It was the appointment of Napoleon Bonaparte to the command of the latter force, in the spring of 1796, that first centred the fortunes of the Republic in the land beyond the Alps. Freed from Prussia by the Treaty of Basle, the Directory was now able to withdraw its attention from Holland and from the Lower Rhine, and to throw its whole force into the struggle with Austria. By the advice of Bonaparte a threefold movement was undertaken against Vienna, by

Armies of Italy, the Danube, and the Main, 1796.

way of Lombardy, by the valley of the Danube, and by the valley of the Main. General Jourdan, in command of the army that had conquered the Netherlands, was ordered to enter Germany by Frankfort; Moreau crossed the Rhine at Strasburg: Bonaparte himself, drawing his scanty supplies along the coast-road from Nice, faced the allied forces of Austria and Sardinia upon the slopes of the Maritime Apennines, forty miles to the west of Genoa. The country in which he was about to operate was familiar to Bonaparte from service there in 1794; his own descent and language gave him singular advantages in any enterprise undertaken in Italy. Bonaparte was no Italian at heart; but he knew at least enough of the Italian nature to work upon its better impulses, and to attach its hopes, so long as he needed the support of Italian opinion, to his own career of victory.

Three centuries separated the Italy of that day from the bright and vigorous Italy which, in the glow of its Republican freedom, had given so much to Northern Europe in art, in letters, and in the charm of life. A long epoch of subjection to despotic or foreign rule, of commercial inaction, of decline in mind and character, had made the Italians of no account among the political forces of Europe. Down to the peace of Aix-la-Chapelle in 1748 their provinces were bartered between the Bourbons and the Hapsburgs; and although the settlement of that date left no part of Italy, except the Duchy of Milan, incorporated in a foreign empire, yet the crown of Naples was vested in a younger branch of the Spanish Bourbons, and the mar-

Condition of Italy.

riage of Maria Theresa with the Archduke Francis made Tuscany an appanage of the House of Austria. Venice and Genoa retained their independence and their republican government, but little of their ancient spirit. At the outbreak of the Revolutionary War, Austrian influence was dominant throughout the peninsula, Marie Caroline, the Queen and the ruler of Ferdinand of Naples, being the sister of the Emperor Leopold and Marie Antoinette. With the exception of Piedmont, which preserved a strong military sentiment and the tradition of an active and patriotic policy, the Italian States were either, like Venice and Genoa, anxious to keep themselves out of danger by seeming to hear and see nothing that passed around them, or governed by families in the closest connection with the great reigning Houses of the Continent. Neither in Italy itself, nor in the general course of European affairs during the Napoleonic period, was anything determined by the sentiment of the Italian people. The peasantry at times fought against the French with energy; but no strong impulse, like that of the Spaniards, enlisted the upper class of Italians either on the side of Napoleon or on that of his enemies. Acquiescence and submission had become the habit of the race; the sense of national unity and worth, the personal pride which makes the absence of liberty an intolerable wrong, only entered the Italian character at a later date.

Yet in spite of its political nullity, Italy was not in a state of decline. Its worst days had ended before the middle of the eighteenth century. The fifty years preceding the French Revolution, if they had brought nothing of the spirit of liberty, had in all other respects been years of progress and revival. In Lombardy the government of Maria Theresa and Joseph awoke life and motion after ages of Spanish torpor and misrule. Traditions of local activity revived; the communes were encouraged in their works of irrigation and rural improvement; a singular liberality towards opinion and the press made the Austrian possessions the centre of the intellectual movement of Italy. In the south, progress began on the day when the last foreign Viceroy disappeared from Naples (1735), and King Charles III., though a member of the Spanish House, entered upon the government of the two Sicilies as an independent kingdom. Venice and the Papal States alone seemed to be untouched by the spirit of material and social improvement, so active in the rest of Italy before the interest in political life had come into being.

Revival after 1740.

Nor was the age without its intellectual distinction. If the literature of Italy in the second half of the eighteenth century had little that recalled the inspiration of its splendid youth, it showed at least a return to seriousness and an interest in important things. The political economists of Lombardy were scarcely behind those of England; the work of the Milanese Beccaria on "Crimes and Punishments" stimulated the reform of criminal law in every country in Europe; an intelligent and increasing attention to problems of agriculture, commerce, and education took the place of the fatuous gallantries and insipid criticism which had hitherto made up the life of Italians of birth and culture. One man of genius, Vittorio Alfieri, the creator of Italian tragedy, idealised both in prose and verse a type of rugged independence and resistance to tyrannical power. Alfieri was neither a man of political judgment himself nor the representative of any real political current in Italy; but the lesson which he taught to the Italians, the lesson of respect for themselves and their country, was the one which Italy most of all required to learn; and the appearance of this manly and energetic spirit in its literature gave hope that the Italian nation would not long be content to remain without political being.

Italy, to the outside world, meant little more than the ruins of the Roman Forum, the galleries of Florence, the paradise of Capri and the Neapolitan coast; the singular variety in its local conditions of life gained little attention from the foreigner. There were districts in Italy where the social order was almost of a Polish type of barbarism; there were others where the rich and the poor lived perhaps under a happier relation than in any other country in Europe. The difference depended chiefly upon the extent to which municipal life had in past time superseded the feudal order under which the territorial lord was the judge and the ruler of his own domain. In Tuscany the city had done the most in absorbing the landed nobility; in Naples and Sicily it had done the least. When, during the middle ages, the Republic of Florence forced the feudal lords who surrounded it to enter its walls as citizens, in some cases it deprived

Social condition.

Tuscany.

them of all authority, in others it permitted them to retain a jurisdiction over their peasants; but even in these instances the sovereignty of the city deprived the feudal relation of most of its harshness and force. After the loss of Florentine liberty, the Medici, aping the custom of older monarchies, conferred the title of marquis and count upon men who preferred servitude to freedom, and accompanied the grant of rank with one of hereditary local authority; but the new institutions took no deep hold on country life, and the legislation of the first Archduke of the House of Lorraine (1749) left the landed aristocracy in the position of mere country gentlemen.* Estates were not very large: the prevalent agricultural system was, as it still is, that of the *mezzeria*, a partnership between the landlord and tenant; the tenant holding by custom in perpetuity, and sharing the produce with the landlord, who supplied a part of the stock and materials for farming. In Tuscany the conditions of the *mezzeria* were extremely favourable to the tenant; and if a cheerful country life under a mild and enlightened government were all that a State need desire, Tuscany enjoyed rare happiness.

Far different was the condition of Sicily and Naples. Here the growth of city life had never affected the rough sovereignty which the barons exercised over great tracts of country withdrawn from the civilised world. When Charles III. ascended the throne in 1735, he found whole provinces in which there was absolutely no administration of justice on the

Naples and Sicily.

---

* Zobi, Storia Civile della Toscana, i., 284.

part of the State. The feudal rights of the nobility were in the last degree oppressive, the barbarism of the people was in many districts extreme. Out of two thousand six hundred towns and villages in the kingdom, there were only fifty that were not subject to feudal authority. In the manor of San Gennaro di Palma, fifteen miles from Naples, even down to the year 1786 the officers of the baron were the only persons who lived in houses; the peasants, two thousand in number, slept among the corn-ricks.* Charles, during his tenure of the Neapolitan crown, from 1735 to 1759, and the Ministers Tanucci and Caraccioli under his feeble successor Ferdinand IV., enforced the authority of the State in justice and administration, and abolished some of the most oppressive feudal rights of the nobility; but their legislation, though bold and even revolutionary according to an English standard, could not in the course of two generations transform a social system based upon centuries of misgovernment and disorder. At the outbreak of the French Revolution the Kingdom of the Two Sicilies was, as it still in a less degree is, a land of extreme inequalities of wealth and poverty, a land where great estates wasted in the hands of oppressive or

* Galanti, Descrizione delle Sicilie, 1786, i., 279. He adds, "The Samnites and the Lucanians could not have shown so horrible a spectacle, because they had no feudal laws." Galanti's book gives perhaps the best idea of the immense task faced by monarchy in the eighteenth century in its struggle against what he justly calls " gli orrori del governo feudale." Nothing but a study of these details of actual life described by eye-witnesses can convey an adequate impression of the completeness and the misery of the feudal order in the more backward countries of Europe till far down in the eighteenth century. There is a good anonymous account of Sicily in 1810 in Castlereagh, S. 217.

indolent owners, and the peasantry, untrained either by remunerative industry or by a just and regular enforcement of the law, found no better guide than a savage and fanatical priesthood. Over the rest of Italy the conditions of life varied through all degrees between the Tuscan and the Neapolitan type. Piedmont, in military spirit and patriotism far superior to the other Italian States, was socially one of the most backward of all. It was a land of priests, nobles, and soldiers, where a gloomy routine and the repression of all originality of thought and character drove the most gifted of its children, like the poet Alfieri, to seek a home on some more liberal soil.

<small>Piedmont.</small>

During the first years of the Revolution, an attempt had been made by French enthusiasts to extend the Revolution into Italy by means of associations in the principal towns; but it met with no great success. A certain liberal movement arose among the young men of the upper classes at Naples, where, under the influence of Queen Marie Caroline, the Government had now become reactionary; and in Turin and several of the Lombard cities the French were not without partisans; but no general disaffection like that of Savoy existed east of the Alps. The agitation of 1789 and 1792 had passed by without bringing either liberty or national independence to the Italians. When Bonaparte received his command, that fervour of Republican passion which, in the midst of violence and wrong, had seldom been wanting in the first leaders of the Revolutionary War, had died out in

<small>Professions and real intentions of the Directory and Bonaparte, 1796.</small>

France. The politicians who survived the Reign of Terror and gained office in the Directory repeated the old phrases about the Rights of Man and the Liberation of the Peoples only as a mode of cajolery. Bonaparte entered Italy proclaiming himself the restorer of Italian freedom, but with the deliberate purpose of using Italy as a means of recruiting the exhausted treasury of France. His correspondence with the Directory exposes with brazen frankness this well-considered system of pillage and deceit, in which the general and the Government were cordially at one. On the further question, how France should dispose of any territory that might be conquered in Northern Italy, Bonaparte and the Directory had formed no understanding, and their purposes were in fact at variance. The Directory wished to conquer Lombardy in order to hand it back to Austria in return for the Netherlands; Bonaparte had at least formed the conception that an Italian State was possible, and he intended to convert either Austrian Lombardy itself, or some other portion of Northern Italy, into a Republic, serving as a military outwork for France.

The campaign of 1796 commenced in April, in the mountains above the coast-road connecting Nice and Genoa. Bonaparte's own army numbered 40,000 men; the force opposed to it consisted of 38,000 Austrians, under Beaulieu, and a smaller Sardinian army, so placed upon the Piedmontese Apennines as to block the passes from the coast-road into Piedmont, and to threaten the rear of the French if they advanced eastward against Genoa.

Bonaparte separates the Austrian and Sardinian Armies, April 1796.

The Piedmontese army drew its supplies from Turin, the Austrian from Mantua; to sever the two armies was to force them on to lines of retreat conducting them farther and farther apart from one another. Bonaparte foresaw the effect which such a separation of the two armies would produce upon the Sardinian Government. For four days he reiterated his attacks at Montenotte and Millesimo, until he had forced his own army into a position in the centre of the Allies; then, leaving a small force to watch the Austrians, he threw the mass of his troops upon the Piedmontese, and drove them back to within thirty miles of Turin. The terror-stricken Government, anticipating an outbreak in the capital itself, accepted an armistice from Bonaparte at Cherasco (April 28), and handed over to the French the fortresses of Coni, Ceva, and Tortona, which command the entrances of Italy. It was an unworthy capitulation, for Turin could not have been taken before the Austrians returned in force; but Bonaparte had justly calculated the effect of his victory; and the armistice, which was soon followed by a treaty of peace between France and Sardinia, ceding Savoy to the Republic, left him free to follow the Austrians, untroubled by the existence of some of the strongest fortresses of Europe behind him.

Armistice and peace with Sardinia.

In the negotiations with Sardinia Bonaparte demanded the surrender of the town of Valenza, as necessary to secure his passage over the river Po. Having thus led the Austrian Beaulieu to concentrate his forces at this point, he suddenly moved eastward along the southern bank of the river, and crossed at Piacenza, fifty miles below the spot where Beaulieu was awaiting him. It was an admirable movement. The Austrian general, with the enemy threatening his communications, had to abandon Milan and all the country west of it, and to fall back upon the line of the Adda. Bonaparte followed, and on the 10th of May attacked the Austrians at Lodi. He himself stormed the bridge of Lodi at the head of his Grenadiers. The battle was so disastrous to the Austrians that they could risk no second engagement, and retired upon Mantua and the line of the Mincio.*

<small>Bridge of Lodi, May 10.</small>

Bonaparte now made his triumphal entry into Milan (May 15). The splendour of his victories and his warm expressions of friendship for Italy excited the enthusiasm of a population not hitherto hostile to Austrian rule. A new political movement began. With the French army there came all the partisans of the French Republic who had been expelled from other parts of Italy. Uniting with the small

<small>Bonaparte in Milan. Extortions.</small>

---

* Correspondance de Napoleon, i., 260. Botta, lib. vi. Despatches of Col. Graham, British attaché with the Austrian army, in Records: Italian States, vol. 57. These most interesting letters, which begin on May 19, show the discord and suspicion prevalent from the first in the Austrian army. "Beaulieu has not met with cordial co-operation from his own generals, still less from the Piedmontese. He accuses them of having chosen to be beat in order to bring about a peace promised in January last." "Beaulieu was more violent than ever against his generals who have occasioned the failure of his plans. He said nine of them were cowards. I believe some of them are ill-affected to the cause." June 15.—"Many of the officers comfort themselves with thinking that defeat must force peace, and others express themselves in terms of despair." July 25.—Beaulieu told Graham that if Bonaparte had pushed on after the battle of Lodi, he might have gone straight into Mantua. The preparations for defence were made later.

NAPOLEON AT THE BRIDGE OF LODI

(p. 120).

revolutionary element already existing in Milan, they began to form a new public opinion by means of journals and patriotic meetings. It was of the utmost importance to Bonaparte that a Republican party should be organised among the better classes in the towns of Lombardy; for the depredations of the French army exasperated the peasants, and Bonaparte's own measures were by no means of a character to win him unmixed goodwill. The instructions which he received from the Directory were extremely simple. "Leave nothing in Italy," they wrote to him on the day of his entry into Milan, "which will be useful to us, and which the political situation will allow you to remove." If Bonaparte had felt any doubt as to the meaning of such an order, the pillage of works of art in Belgium and Holland in preceding years would have shown him that it was meant to be literally interpreted. Accordingly, in return for the gift of liberty, the Milanese were invited to offer to their deliverers twenty million francs, and a selection from the paintings in their churches and galleries. The Dukes of Parma and Modena, in return for an armistice, were required to hand over forty of their best pictures, and a sum of money proportioned to their revenues. The Dukes and the townspeople paid their contributions with good grace: the peasantry of Lombardy, whose cattle were seized in order to supply an army that marched without any stores of its own, rose in arms, and threw themselves into Pavia, killing all the French soldiers who fell in their way. The revolt was instantly suppressed, and the town of Pavia given up to pillage. In deference to the Liberal party of Italy, the movement was described as a conspiracy of priests and nobles. The way into Central Italy now lay open before Bonaparte. Rome and Naples were in no condition to offer resistance; but with true military judgment the French general declined to move against this feeble prey until the army of Austria, already crippled, was completely driven out of the field. Instead of crossing the Apennines, Bonaparte advanced against the Austrian positions upon the Mincio. It suited him to violate the neutrality of the adjacent Venetian territory by seizing the town of Brescia. His example was followed by Beaulieu, who occupied Peschiera, at the foot of the Lake of Garda, and thus held the Mincio along its whole course from the lake to Mantua. A battle was fought and lost by the Austrians half-way between the lake and the fortress. Beaulieu's strength was exhausted; he could meet the enemy no more in the field, and led his army out of Italy into the Tyrol, leaving Mantua to be invested by the French. The first care of the conqueror was to make Venice pay for the crime of possessing territory intervening between the eastern and western extremes of the Austrian district. Bonaparte affected to believe that the Venetians had permitted Beaulieu to occupy Peschiera before he seized upon Brescia himself. He uttered terrifying threats to the envoys who came from Venice to excuse an imaginary crime. He was determined to extort money from the Venetian Republic; he also needed a pretext

Battle on the Mincio, May 20.

for occupying Verona, and for any future wrongs. "I have purposely devised this rupture," he wrote to the Directory (June 7th), "in case you should wish to obtain five or six millions of francs from Venice. If you have more decided intentions, I think it would be well to keep up the quarrel." The intention referred to was the disgraceful project of sacrificing Venice to Austria in return for the cession of the Netherlands, a measure based on plans familiar to Thugut as early as the year 1793.*

<small>Venice.</small>

The Austrians were fairly driven out of Lombardy, and Bonaparte was now free to deal with southern Italy. He advanced into the States of the Church, and expelled the Papal Legate from Bologna. Ferdinand of Naples, who had lately called heaven and earth to witness the fury of his zeal against an accursed horde of regicides, thought it prudent to stay Bonaparte's hand, at least until the Austrians were in a condition to renew the war in Lombardy. He asked for a suspension of hostilities against his own kingdom. The fleet and the sea-board of Naples gave it importance in the struggle between France and England, and Bonaparte granted the king an armistice on easy terms. The Pope, in order to gain a

<small>Armistice with Naples, June 6.</small>

<small>Armistice with the Pope, June 23.</small>

---

* Thugut. Briefe, i., 107. A correspondence on this subject was carried on in cypher between Thugut and Ludwig Cobenzl, Austrian Ambassador at St. Petersburg in 1793-4. During Thugut's absence in Belgium, June, 1794, Cobenzl sent a duplicate despatch, not in cypher, to Vienna. Old Prince Kaunitz, the ex-minister, heard that a courier had arrived from St. Petersburg, and demanded the despatch at the Foreign Office "like a dictator." It was given to him. "Ainsi," says Thugut, "adieu au secret qui depuis un an a été conservé avec tant de soins!"

few months' truce, had to permit the occupation of Ferrara, Ravenna, and Ancona, and to recognise the necessities, the learning, the taste, and the virtue of his conquerors by a gift of twenty million francs, five hundred manuscripts, a hundred pictures, and the busts of Marcus and Lucius Brutus. The rule of the Pope was unpopular in Bologna, and a Senate which Bonaparte placed in power, pending the formation of a popular Government, gladly took the oath of fidelity to the French Republic. Tuscany was the only State that remained to be dealt with. Tuscany had indeed made peace with the Republic a year before, but the ships and cargoes of the English merchants at Leghorn were surely fair prey; and, with the pretence of punishing insults offered by the English to the French flag, Bonaparte descended upon Leghorn, and seized upon everything that was not removed before his approach. Once established in Leghorn, the French declined to quit it. By way of adjusting the relations of the Grand Duke, the English seized his harbour of Porto Ferraio, in the island of Elba.

Mantua was meanwhile invested, and thither, after his brief incursion into Central Italy, Bonaparte returned.

Battles of Lonato and Gustaglione, July, Aug., 1796. Towards the end of July an Austrian relieving army, nearly double the strength of Bonaparte's, descended from the Tyrol. It was divided into three corps: one, under Quosdanovich, advanced by the road on the west of Lake Garda; the others, under Wurmser, the commander-in-chief, by the roads between the lake and the river Adige.

The peril of the French was extreme; their outlying divisions were defeated and driven in; Bonaparte could only hope to save himself by collecting all his forces at the foot of the lake, and striking at one or other of the Austrian armies before they effected their junction on the Mincio. He instantly broke up the siege of Mantua, and withdrew from every position east of the river. On the 30th of July, Quosdanovich was attacked and checked at Lonato, on the west of the Lake of Garda. Wurmser, unaware of his colleague's repulse, entered Mantua in triumph, and then set out, expecting to envelop Bonaparte between two fires. But the French were ready for his approach. Wurmser was stopped and defeated at Castiglione, while the western Austrian divisions were still held in check at Lonato. The junction of the Austrian armies had become impossible. In five days the skill of Bonaparte and the unsparing exertions of his soldiery had more than retrieved all that appeared to have been lost.* The Austrians retired into

* Wurmser's reports are in Vivenot, Olorfayt, p. 477. Graham's daily despatches from the Austrian head-quarters give a vivid picture of these operations, and of the sudden change from exultation to despair. Aug. 1.—" I have the honour to inform your lordship that the siege of Mantua is raised, the French having retreated last night with the utmost precipitation." Aug. 2.—" The Austrians are in possession of all the French mortars and cannon, amounting to about 140, with 190,000 shells and bombs; the loss of the Imperial army is inconsiderable." Aug. 5.—" The rout of this day has sadly changed the state of affairs. There are no accounts of General Quosdanovich." Aug. 9.—" Our loss in men and cannon was much greater than was imagined. I had no idea of the possibility of the extent of such misfortunes as have overwhelmed us." Aug. 17.—" It is scarcely possible to describe the state of disorder and discouragement that prevails in the army. Were I free from apprehensions about the fate of my letter " (he had lost his baggage and his cypher in it), " I should despair of finding language adequate to convey a just idea of the discontent of the

the Tyrol, beaten and dispirited, and leaving 15,000 prisoners in the hands of the enemy.

Bonaparte now prepared to force his way into Germany by the Adige, in fulfilment of the original plan of the campaign. In the first days of September he again routed the Austrians, and gained possession of Roveredo and Trent. Wurmser hereupon attempted to shut the French up in the mountains by a movement southwards; but, while he operated with insufficient forces between the Brenta and the Adige, he was cut off from Germany, and only escaped capture by throwing himself into Mantua with the shattered remnant of his army. The road into Germany through the Tyrol now lay open; but in the midst of his victories Bonaparte learnt that the northern armies of Moreau and Jourdan, with which he had intended to co-operate in an attack upon Vienna, were in full retreat.

Moreau's advance into the valley of the Danube had, during the months of July and August, been attended with unbroken military and political success. The Archduke Charles,

Invasion of Germany by Moreau and Jourdan, June—Oct.,1706.

officers with General Wurmser. From generals to subalterns the universal language is 'qu'il faut faire la paix, car nous ne savons pas faire la guerre.'" Aug. 18.—"Not only the commander-in-chief, but the greatest number of the generals are objects of contempt and ridicule." Aug. 27. —"I do not exaggerate when I say that I have met with instances of downright dotage." "It was in general orders that wine should be distributed to the men previous to the attack of the 29th. There was some difficulty in getting it up to Monte Baldo. General Bayolitzy observed that 'it did not signify, for the men might get the value in money afterwards.' The men marched at six in the evening without it, to attack at daybreak, and received four kreutzers afterwards. This is a fact I can attest. In action I saw officers sent on urgent messages going at a foot's pace: they say that their horses are half starved, and that they cannot afford to kill them."

who was entrusted with the defence of the Empire, found himself unable to bring two armies into the field capable of resisting those of Moreau and Jourdan separately, and he therefore determined to fall back before Moreau towards Nuremberg, ordering Wartensleben, who commanded the troops facing Jourdan on the Main, to retreat in the same direction, in order that the two armies might throw their collected force upon Jourdan while still at some distance north of Moreau.* The design of the Archduke succeeded in the end, but it opened Germany to the French for six weeks, and showed how worthless was the military constitution of the Empire, and how little the Germans had to expect from one another. After every skirmish won by Moreau some neighbouring State abandoned the common defence and hastened to make its terms with the invader. On the 17th of July the Duke of Würtemberg purchased an armistice at the price of four million francs; a week later Baden gained the French general's protection in return for immense supplies of food and stores. The troops of the Swabian Circle of the Empire, who were ridiculed as "harlequins" by the more martial Austrians, dispersed to their homes; and no sooner had Moreau entered Bavaria than the Bavarian contingent in its turn withdrew from the Archduke. Some consideration was shown by Moreau's soldiery to those districts which had paid tribute to their general; but in the region of the Main, Jourdan's army plundered without distinction

---

* Grundsätze (Archduke Charles), ii. 202. Bulletins in Wiener Zeitung, June—Oct. 1796.

and without mercy. They sacked the churches, they maltreated the children, they robbed the very beggars of their pence. Before the Archduke Charles was ready to strike, the peasantry of this country, whom their governments were afraid to arm, had begun effective reprisals of their own. At length the retreating movement of the Austrians stopped. Leaving 30,000 men on the Lech to disguise his motions from Moreau, Charles turned suddenly northwards from Neuburg on the 17th August, met Wartensleben at Amberg, and attacked Jourdan at this place with greatly superior numbers. Jourdan was defeated and driven back in confusion towards the Rhine. The issue of the campaign was decided before Moreau heard of his colleague's danger. It only remained for him to save his own army by a skilful retreat. Jourdan's soldiers, returning through districts which they had devastated, suffered heavier losses from the vengeance of the peasantry than from the army that pursued them. By the autumn of 1796 no Frenchman remained beyond the Rhine. The campaign had restored the military spirit of Austria; it had given Germany a general in whom soldiers could trust; but it had also shown how willing were the Governments of the minor States to become the vassals of a foreigner, how little was wanting to convert the western half of the Empire into a dependency of France.

The Archduke Charles overpowers Jourdan

With each change in the fortunes of the campaign of 1796 the diplomacy of the Continent had changed its tone. When Moreau won his first victories, the Court of Prussia, yielding

Secret Treaty with Prussia, Aug. 5.

to the pressure of the Directory, substituted for the conditional clauses of the Treaty of Basle a definite agreement to the cession of the left bank of the Rhine, and a stipulation that Prussia should be compensated for her own loss by the annexation of the Bishopric of Münster. Prussia could not itself cede provinces of the Empire : it could only agree to their cession. In this treaty, however, Prussia definitely renounced the integrity of the Empire, and accepted the system known as the Secularisation of Ecclesiastical States, the first step towards an entire reconstruction of Germany.* The engagement was kept secret both from the Emperor and from the ecclesiastical princes. In their negotiations with Austria the Directory were less successful. Although the long series of Austrian disasters had raised a general outcry against Thugut's persistence in the war, the resolute spirit of the Minister never bent; and the ultimate victory of the Archduke Charles more than restored his influence over the Emperor. Austria refused to enter into any negotiation not conducted in common with England, and the Directory were for the present foiled in their attempts to isolate England from the Continental Powers. It was not that Thugut either hoped or cared for that restoration of Austrian rule in the Netherlands which was the first object of England's Continental policy. The abandonment of the Netherlands by France was, however, in his opinion necessary for Austria, as a step towards the acquisition of Bavaria, which was still the

* Martens, vi., 59.

cherished hope of the Viennese Government. It was in vain that the Directory suggested that Austria should annex Bavaria without offering Belgium or any other compensation to its ruler. Thugut could hardly be induced to listen to the French overtures. He had received the promise of immediate help from the Empress Catherine; he was convinced that the Republic, already anxious for peace, might by one sustained effort be forced to abandon all its conquests; and this was the object for which, in the winter of 1796, army after army was hurled against the positions where Bonaparte kept his guard on the north of the still unconquered Mantua.*

In England itself the victory of the Archduke Charles raised expectations of peace. The war had become unpopular through the loss of trade with France, Spain, and Holland, and petitions for peace daily reached Parliament. Pitt so far yielded to the prevalent feeling as to enter into negotiations with the Directory, and despatched Lord Malmesbury to Paris;

Malmesbury sent to Paris, Oct., 1796.

but the condition upon which Pitt insisted, the restoration of the Netherlands to Austria, rendered agreement hopeless; and as soon as

---

* This seems to me to be the probable truth about Austria's policy in 1796, of which opposite views will be found in Häusser, vol. ii.. ch. 1—3 and in Hüffer, Oestreich und Preussen, p. 142. Thugut professed in 1793 to have given up the project of the Bavarian exchange in deference to England. He admitted, however, soon afterwards, that he had again been pressing the King of Prussia to consent to it, but said that this was a ruse, intended to make Prussia consent to Austria's annexing a large piece of France instead. Eden, Sept., 1793; Records: Austria, vol. 34. The incident shows the difficulty of getting at the truth in diplomacy.

Pitt's terms were known to the Directory, Malmesbury was ordered to leave Paris. Nevertheless, the negotiation was not a mere feint on Pitt's part. He was possessed by a fixed idea that the resources of France were exhausted, and that, in spite of the conquest of Lombardy and the Rhine, the Republic must feel itself too weak to continue the war. Amid the disorders of Revolutionary finance, and exaggerated reports of suffering and distress, Pitt failed to recognise the enormous increase of production resulting from the changes which had given the peasant full property in his land and labour, and thrown vast quantities of half-waste domain into the busy hands of middling and small proprietors.* Whatever were the resources of France before the Revolution, they were now probably more than doubled. Pitt's belief in the economic ruin of France, the only ground on which he could imagine that the Directory

* Yet the Government had had warning of this in a series of striking reports sent by one of Lord Elgin's spies during the Reign of Terror. "Jamais la France ne fut cultivée comme elle l'est. Il n'y a pas un arpent qui ne soit ensemencé, sauf dans les lieux où opèrent les armées belligérantes. Cette culture universelle a été forcée par les Directrices là où on ne la faisait pas volontairement." June 8, 1794; Records: Flanders, vol. 226. Elgin had established a line of spies from Paris to the Belgian frontier. Every one of these persons was arrested by the Revolutionary authorities. Elgin then fell in with the writer of the above, whose name is concealed, and placed him on the Swiss frontier. He was evidently a person thoroughly familiar with both civil and military administration. He appears to have talked to every Frenchman who entered Switzerland; and his reports contain far the best information that reached England during the Reign of Terror, contradicting the Royalists, who said that the war was only kept up by terrorism. He warned the English Government that the French nation in a mass was on the side of the Revolution, and declared that the downfall of Robespierre and the terrorists would make no difference in the prosecution of the war. The Government seems to have paid no attention to his reports, if indeed they were ever read.

would give up Belgium without fighting for it, was wholly erroneous, and the French Government would have acted strangely if they had listened to his demand.

Nevertheless, though the Directory would not hear of surrendering Belgium, they were anxious to conclude peace with Austria, and unwilling to enter into any engagements in the conquered provinces of Italy which might render peace with Austria more difficult. They had instructed Bonaparte to stir up the Italians against their Governments, but this was done with the object of paralysing the Governments, not of emancipating the peoples. They looked with dislike upon any scheme of Italian reconstruction which should bind France to the support of newly-formed Italian States. Here, however, the scruples of the Directory and the ambition of Bonaparte were in direct conflict. Bonaparte intended to create a political system in Italy which should bear the stamp of his own mind and require his own strong hand to support it. In one of his despatches to the Directory he suggested the formation of a client Republic out of the Duchy of Modena, where revolutionary movements had broken out. Before it was possible for the Government to answer him, he published a decree, declaring the population of Modena and Reggio under the protection of the French army, and deposing all the officers of the Duke (Oct. 4). When, some days later, the answer of the Directory arrived, it cautioned Bonaparte against disturbing the existing order of the Italian States. Bonaparte replied by uniting to Modena the Papal

Bonaparte creates a Cispadane Republic, Oct., 1796.

provinces of Bologna and Ferrara, and by giving to the State which he had thus created the title of the Cispadane Republic.*

The event was no insignificant one. It is from this time that the idea of Italian independence, though foreign to the great mass of the nation, may be said to have taken birth as one of those political hopes which wane and recede, but do not again leave the world. A class of men who had turned with dislike from the earlier agitation of French Republicans in Italy rightly judged the continued victories of Bonaparte over the Austrians to be the beginning of a series of great changes, and now joined the revolutionary movement in the hope of winning from the overthrow of the old Powers some real form of national independence. In its origin the French party may have been composed of hirelings and enthusiasts. This ceased to be the case when, after the passage of the Mincio, Bonaparte entered the Papal States. Among the citizens of Bologna in particular there were men of weight and intelligence who aimed at free constitutional government, and checked in some degree the more numerous popular party which merely repeated the phrases of French democracy. Bonaparte's own language and action excited the brightest hopes. At Modena he

margin note: Idea of free Italy.

---

* Correspondance de Napoleon, ii. 28. Thugut, about this time, formed the plan of annexing Bologna and Ferrara to Austria, and said that if this result could be achieved, the French attack upon the Papal States would be no bad matter. See the instructions to Allvintzy, in Vivenot, Clerfayt, 'p. 511, which also contain the first Austrian orders to imprison Italian innovators, the beginning of Austria's later Italian policy.

harangued the citizens upon the mischief of Italy's divisions, and exhorted them to unite with their brethren whom he had freed from the Pope. A Congress was held at Modena on the 16th of October. The representatives of Modena, Reggio, Bologna, and Ferrara declared themselves united in a Republic under the protection of France. They abolished feudal nobility, decreed a national levy, and summoned a General Assembly to meet at Reggio two months later, in order to create the Constitution of the new Cispadane Republic. It was in the Congress of Modena, and in the subsequent Assembly of Reggio (Dec. 25), that the idea of Italian unity and independence first awoke the enthusiasm of any considerable body of men. With what degree of sincerity Bonaparte himself acted may be judged from the circumstance that, while he harangued the Cispadanes on the necessity of Italian union, he imprisoned the Milanese who attempted to excite a popular movement for the purpose of extending this union to themselves. Peace was not yet made with Austria, and it was uncertain to what account Milan might best be turned.

Mantua still held out, and in November the relieving operations of the Austrians were renewed. Two armies, commanded by Allvintzy and Davidovich, descended the valleys of the Adige and the Piave, offering to Bonaparte, whose centre was at Verona, a new opportunity of crushing his enemy in detail. Allvintzy, coming from the Piave, brought the French into extreme danger in a three days' battle at Arcola, but was at last forced to retreat

<small>Arcola, Nov. 15 —17.</small>

with heavy loss. Davidovich, who had been successful on the Adige, retired on learning the overthrow of his colleague. Two months more passed, and the Austrians for the third time appeared on the Adige. A feint made below Verona nearly succeeded in drawing Bonaparte away from Rivoli, between the Adige and Lake Garda, where Allvintzy and his main army were about to make the assault; but the strength of Allvintzy's force was discovered before it was too late, and by throwing his divisions from point to point with extraordinary rapidity, Bonaparte at length overwhelmed the Austrians in every quarter of the battle-field. This was their last effort. The surrender of Mantua on the 2nd February, 1797, completed the French conquest of Austrian Lombardy.* *Rivoli, Jan. 14, 15, 1797.*

The Pope now found himself left to settle his account with the invaders, against whom, even after the armistice, he had never ceased to intrigue.† His despatches to Vienna fell into the hands of Bonaparte, who declared *Peace of Tolentino, Feb. 19, 1797.*

---

* Wurmser had orders to break out southwards into the Papal States. "These orders he (Thugut) knew had reached the Marshal, but they were also known to the enemy, as a cadet of Strasoldo's regiment, who was carrying the duplicate, had been taken prisoner, and having been seen to swallow a ball of wax, in which the order was wrapped up, he was immediately put to death and the paper taken out of his stomach." Eden, Jan., 1797; Records: Austria, vol. 48. Colonel Graham, who had been shut up in Mantua since Sept. 10, escaped on Dec. 17, and restored communication between Wurmser and Allvintzy. He was present at the battle of Rivoli, which is described in his despatches.

† "We expect every hour to hear of the entry of the Neapolitan troops and the declaration of a religious war. Every preparation has been made for such an event." Graves to Lord Grenville, Oct. 1, 1796; Records: Rome, vol. 56.

the truce broken, and a second time invaded the Papal territory. A show of resistance was made by the Roman troops; but the country was in fact at the mercy of Bonaparte, who advanced as far as Tolentino, thirty miles south of Ancona. Here the Pope tendered his submission. If the Roman Court had never appeared to be in a more desperate condition, it had never found a more moderate or a more politic conqueror. Bonaparte was as free from any sentiment of Christian piety as Nero or Diocletian; but he respected the power of the Papacy over men's minds, and he understood the immense advantage which any Government of France supported by the priesthood would possess over those who had to struggle with its hostility. In his negotiations with the Papal envoys he deplored the violence of the French Executive, and consoled the Church with the promise of his own protection and sympathy. The terms of peace which he granted, although they greatly diminished the ecclesiastical territory, were in fact more favourable than the Pope had any right to expect. Bologna, Ferrara, and the Romagna, which had been occupied in virtue of the armistice, were now ceded by the Papacy. But conditions affecting the exercise of the spiritual power which had been proposed by the Directory were withdrawn; and, beyond a provision for certain payments in money, nothing of importance was added to the stipulations of the armistice.

The last days of the Venetian Republic were now at hand. It was in vain that Venice had maintained its neutrality when all the rest of Italy joined the enemies of France; its refusal of a French alliance was made an unpardonable crime. So long as the war with Austria lasted, Bonaparte exhausted the Venetian territory with requisitions: when peace came within view, it was necessary that he should have some pretext for seizing it or handing it over to the enemy. In fulfilment of his own design of keeping a quarrel open, he had subjected the Government to every insult and wrong likely to goad it into an act of war. When at length Venice armed for the purpose of protecting its neutrality, the organs of the invader called upon the inhabitants of the Venetian mainland to rise against the oligarchy, and to throw in their lot with the liberated province of Milan. A French alliance was once more urged upon Venice by Bonaparte: it was refused, and the outbreak which the French had prepared instantly followed. Bergamo and Brescia, where French garrisons deprived the Venetian Government of all power of defence, rose in revolt, and renounced all connection with Venice. The Senate begged Bonaparte to withdraw the French garrisons; its entreaties drew nothing from him but repeated demands for the acceptance of the French alliance, which was only another name for subjection. Little as the Venetians suspected it, the only doubt now present to Bonaparte was whether he should add the provinces of Venetia to his own Cispadane Republic or hand them over to Austria in exchange for other cessions which France required.

Austria could defend itself in Italy no longer. Before the end of March the mountain-passes into

Carinthia were carried by Bonaparte. His army drove the enemy before it along the road to Vienna, until both pursuers and pursued were within eighty miles of the capital. At Leoben, on the 7th of April, the Austrian commander asked for a suspension of arms. It was granted, and negotiations for peace commenced.* Bonaparte offered the Venetian provinces, but not the city of Venice, to the Emperor. On the 18th of April preliminaries of peace were signed at Leoben, by which, in return for the Netherlands and for Lombardy west of the river Oglio, Bonaparte secretly agreed to hand over to Austria the whole of the territory of Venice upon the mainland east of the Oglio, in addition to its Adriatic provinces of Istria and Dalmatia. To disguise the act

<small>Preliminaries of Leoben, April 18.</small>

---

* "The clamours for peace have become loud and importunate. His Imperial Majesty is constantly assailed by all his Ministers, M. de Thugut alone excepted, and by all who approach his person. Attempts are even made to alarm him with a dread of insurrection. In the midst of these calamities M. de Thugut retains his firmness of mind, and continues to struggle against the united voice of the nobility and the numerous and trying adversities that press upon him." Eden, April 1. "The confusion at the army exceeds the bounds of belief. Had Bonaparte continued his progress hither (Vienna), no doubt is entertained that he might have entered the place without opposition. That, instead of risking this enterprise, he should have stopped and given the Austrians six days to recover from their alarm and to prepare for defence, is a circumstance which it is impossible to account for." April 12. "He" (Mack) "said that when this place was threatened by the enemy, Her Imperial Majesty broke in upon the Emperor while in conference with his Minister, and, throwing herself and her children at his feet, determined His Majesty to open the negotiation which terminated in the shameful desertion of his ally." Aug. 16; Records: Austria, vols. 49, 50. Thugut subsequently told Lord Minto that if he could have laid his hand upon £500,000 in cash to stop the run on the Bank of Vienna, the war would have been continued, in which case he believed he would have surrounded Bonaparte's army.

of spoliation, it was pretended that Bologna and Ferrara should be offered to Venice in return.*

But worse was yet to come. While Bonaparte was in conference at Leoben, an outbreak took place at Verona, and three hundred French soldiers, including the sick in the hospital, perished by popular violence. The Venetian Senate despatched envoys to Bonaparte to express their grief and to offer satisfaction; in the midst of the negotiations intelligence arrived that the commander of a Venetian fort had fired upon a French vessel and killed some of the crew. Bonaparte drove the envoys from his presence, declaring that he could not treat with men whose hands were dripping with French blood. A declaration of war was published, charging the Senate with the design of repeating the Sicilian Vespers, and the panic which it was Bonaparte's object to inspire instantly followed. The Government threw themselves upon his mercy. Bonaparte pretended that he desired no more than to establish a popular government in Venice in the place of the oligarchy. His terms were accepted. The Senate consented to abrogate the ancient Constitution of the Republic, and to introduce a French garrison into Venice. On the 12th of May the Grand Council voted its own dissolution. Peace was concluded. The public articles of the treaty declared that there should be friendship between the French and the Venetian Republics; that the sovereignty

French enter Venice.

---

* The cession of the Rhenish Provinces was not, as usually stated, contained in the Preliminaries. Corr. de Napoleon, 2, 497; Hüffer, p. 259, where the details of the subsequent negotiations will be found.

of Venice should reside in the body of the citizens; and that the French garrison should retire so soon as the new Government announced that it had no further need of its support. Secret articles stipulated for a money-payment, and for the usual surrender of works of art; an indefinite expression relating to an exchange of territory was intended to cover the surrender of the Venetian mainland, and the union of Bologna and Ferrara with what remained of Venice. The friendship and alliance of France, which Bonaparte had been so anxious to bestow on Venice, were now to bear their fruit. "I shall do everything in my power," he wrote to the new Government of Venice, " to give you proof of the great desire I have to see your liberty take root, and to see this unhappy Italy, freed from the rule of the stranger, at length take its place with glory on the scene of the world, and resume, among the great nations, the rank to which nature, destiny, and its own position call it." This was for Venice; for the French Directory Bonaparte had a very different tale. "I had several motives," he wrote (May 19), "in concluding the treaty:—to enter the city without difficulty; to have the arsenal and all else in our possession, in order to take from it whatever we needed, under pretext of the secret articles; . . . to evade the odium attaching to the Preliminaries of Leoben; to furnish pretexts for them, and to facilitate their execution."

French seize Ionian Islands. As the firstfruits of the Venetian alliance, Bonaparte seized upon Corfu and the other Ionian Islands. "You will start," he wrote to

General Gentili, "as quickly and as secretly as possible, and take possession of all the Venetian establishments in the Levant. . . If the inhabitants should be inclined for independence, you should flatter their tastes, and in all your proclamations you should not fail to allude to Greece, Athens, and Sparta." This was to be the French share in the spoil. Yet even now, though stripped of its islands, its coasts, and its ancient Italian territory, Venice might still have remained a prominent city in Italy. It was sacrificed in order to gain the Rhenish Provinces for France. Bonaparte had returned to the neighbourhood of Milan, and received the Austrian envoy, De Gallo, at the villa of Montebello. Wresting a forced meaning from the Preliminaries of Leoben, Bonaparte claimed the frontier of the Rhine, offering to Austria not only the territory of Venice upon the mainland, but the city of Venice itself. De Gallo yielded. Whatever causes subsequently prolonged the negotiation, no trace of honour or pity in Bonaparte led him even to feign a reluctance to betray Venice. "We have to-day had our first conference on the definitive treaty," he wrote to the Directory, on the night of the 26th of May, "and have agreed to present the following propositions: the line of the Rhine for France; Salzburg, Passau for the Emperor; . . . the maintenance of the Germanic Body; . . . Venice for the Emperor. Venice," he continued, "which has been in decadence since the discovery of the Cape of Good Hope and the rise of Trieste and Ancona, can scarcely survive the blows we

Venice to be given to Austria.

have just struck. With a cowardly and helpless population in no way fit for liberty, without territory and without rivers, it is but natural that she should go to those to whom we give the mainland." Thus was Italy to be freed from foreign intervention; and thus was Venice to be regenerated by the friendship of France!

In comparison with the fate preparing for Venice, the sister-republic of Genoa met with generous treatment. A revolutionary movement, long prepared by the French envoy, overthrew the ancient oligarchical Government; but democratic opinion and French sympathies did not extend below the middle classes of the population; and, after the Government had abandoned its own cause, the charcoal-burners and dock-labourers rose in its defence, and attacked the French party with the cry of "Viva Maria," and with figures of the Virgin fastened to their hats, in the place where their opponents wore the French tricolour. Religious fanaticism won the day; the old Government was restored, and a number of Frenchmen who had taken part in the conflict were thrown into prison. The imprisonment of the Frenchmen gave Bonaparte a pretext for intervention. He disclaimed all desire to alter the Government, and demanded only the liberation of his countrymen and the arrest of the enemies of France. But the overthrow of the oligarchy had been long arranged with Faypoult, the French envoy; and Genoa received a democratic constitution which placed the friends of France in power (June 5).

While Bonaparte, holding Court in the Villa of Montebello, continued to negotiate with Austria upon the basis of the Preliminaries of Leoben, events took place in France which offered him an opportunity of interfering directly in the government of the Republic. The elections which were to replace one-third of the members of the Legislature took place in the spring of 1797. The feeling of the country was now much the same as it had been in 1795, when a large Royalist element was returned for those seats in the Councils which the Convention had not reserved for its own members. France desired a more equitable and a more tolerant rule. The Directory had indeed allowed the sanguinary laws against non-juring priests and returning emigrants to remain unenforced; but the spirit and traditions of official Jacobinism were still active in the Government. The Directors themselves were all regicides; the execution of the King was still celebrated by a national *fête*; offices, great and small, were held by men who had risen in the Revolution; the whole of the old gentry of France was excluded from participation in public life. It was against this revolutionary class-rule, against a system which placed the country as much at the mercy of a few directors and generals as it had been at the mercy of the Conventional Committee, that the elections of 1797 were a protest. Along with certain Bourbonist conspirators, a large majority of men were returned who, though described as Royalists, were in fact moderate Constitutionalists, and desired only to undo that part of the Revolution which excluded whole classes of the nation from public life.*

Opposition to the Directory.
Such a party in the legislative body naturally took the character of an Opposition to the more violent section of the Directory. The Director retiring in 1797 was replaced by the Constitutionalist Barthélemy, negotiator of the treaty of Basle; Carnot, who continued in office, took part with the Opposition, justly fearing that the rule of the Directory would soon amount to nothing more than the rule of Bonaparte himself. The first debates in the new Chamber arose upon the laws relating to emigrants; the next, upon Bonaparte's usurpation of sovereign power in Italy. On the 23rd of June a motion for information on the affairs of Venice and Genoa was brought forward in the Council of Five Hundred. Dumolard, the mover, complained of the secrecy of Bonaparte's action, of the contempt shown by him to the Assembly, of his tyrannical and un-republican interference with the institutions of friendly States. No resolution was adopted by the Assembly; but the mere fact that the Assembly had listened to a hostile criticism of his own actions was sufficient ground in Bonaparte's eyes to charge it with Royalism and with treason. Three of the Directors, Barras, Rewbell, and Laréveillère, had already formed the project of overpowering the Assembly by force. Bonaparte's own interests led him to offer them his support. If the Constitutional party gained power, there

* Gohier, Mémoires i. Carnot, Réponse a Bailleul. Correspondance de Napoleon, ii. 188. Miot de Melito, ch. vi.

was an end to his own unshackled rule in Italy; if the Bourbonists succeeded, a different class of men would hold all the honours of the State. However feeble the Government of the Directory, its continuance secured his own present ascendancy, and left him the hope of gaining supreme power when the public could tolerate the Directory no longer.

The fate of the Assembly was sealed. On the anniversary of the capture of the Bastille, Bonaparte issued a proclamation to his army declaring the Republic to be threatened by Royalist intrigues. A banquet was held, and the officers and soldiers of every division signed addresses to the Directory full of threats and fury against conspiring aristocrats. "Indignation is at its height in the army," wrote Bonaparte to the Government; "the soldiers are asking with loud cries whether they are to be rewarded by assassination on their return home, as it appears all patriots are to be so dealt with. The peril is increasing every day, and I think, citizen Directors, you must decide to act one way or other." The Directors had no difficulty in deciding after such an exhortation as this; but, as soon as Bonaparte had worked up their courage, he withdrew into the background, and sent General Augereau, a blustering Jacobin, to Paris, to risk the failure or bear the odium of the crime. Augereau received the military command of the capital; the air was filled with rumours of an impending blow; but neither the majority in the Councils nor the two threatened Directors, Carnot and Barthélemy, knew how to take measures of

Coup d'état, 17 Fructidor (Sept. 3).

defence. On the night of the 3rd September (17 Fructidor) the troops of Augereau surrounded the Tuileries. Barthélemy was seized at the Luxembourg; Carnot fled for his life; the members of the Councils, marching in procession to the Tuileries early the next morning, were arrested or dispersed by the soldiers. Later in the day a minority of the Councils was assembled to ratify the measures determined upon by Augereau and the three Directors. Fifty members of the Legislature, and the writers, proprietors, and editors of forty-two journals, were sentenced to exile; the elections of forty-eight departments were annulled; the laws against priests and emigrants were renewed; and the Directory was empowered to suppress all journals at its pleasure. This coup d'état was described as the suppression of a Royalist conspiracy. It was this, but it was something more. It was the suppression of all Constitutional government, and all but the last step to the despotism of the chief of the army.

The effect of the movement was instantly felt in the negotiations with Austria and with England. Lord Malmesbury was now again in France, treating for peace with fair hopes of success, since the Preliminaries of Leoben had removed England's opposition to the cession of the Netherlands. The discomfiture of the moderate party in the Councils brought his mission to an abrupt end. Austria, on the other hand, had prolonged its negotiations because Bonaparte claimed Mantua and the Rhenish Provinces in addition to the cessions agreed upon at Leoben. Count

Peace signed with Austria, Oct. 17.

Ludwig Cobenzl, Austrian ambassador at St. Petersburg, who had protected his master's interests only too well in the last partition of Poland, was now at the head of the plenipotentiaries in Italy, endeavouring to bring Bonaparte back to the terms fixed in the Preliminaries, or to gain additional territory for Austria in Italy. The Jacobin victory at Paris depressed the Austrians as much as it elated the French leader. Bonaparte was resolved on concluding a peace that should be all his own, and this was only possible by anticipating an invasion of Germany, about to be undertaken by Augereau at the head of the Army of the Rhine. It was to this personal ambition of Bonaparte that Venice was sacrificed. The Directors were willing that Austria should receive part of the Venetian territory: they forbade the proposed cession of Venice itself. Within a few weeks more, the advance of the Army of the Rhine would have enabled France to dictate its own terms; but no consideration either for France or for Italy could induce Bonaparte to share the glory of the Peace with another. On the 17th of October he signed the final treaty of Campo Formio, which gave France the frontier of the Rhine, and made both the Venetian territory beyond the Adige and Venice itself the property of the Emperor. For a moment it seemed that the Treaty might be repudiated at Vienna as well as at Paris. Thugut protested against it, because it surrendered Mantua and the Rhenish Provinces without gaining for Austria the Papal Legations; and he drew up the ratification only at the absolute command of the Emperor. The Directory, on the other hand, condemned the cession of Venice. But their fear of Bonaparte and their own bad conscience left them impotent accessories of his treachery; and the French nation at large was too delighted with the peace to resent its baser conditions.*

By the public articles of the Treaty of Campo Formio, the Emperor ceded to France the Austrian possessions in Lombardy and in the Netherlands, and agreed to the establishment of a Cisalpine Republic, formed out of Austrian Lombardy, the Venetian territory west of the Adige, and the districts hitherto composing the new Cispadane State. France took the Ionian Islands, Austria the City of Venice, with Istria and Dalmatia, and the Venetian mainland east of the Adige. For the conclusion of peace between France and the Holy Roman Empire, it was agreed that a Congress should meet at Rastadt; but a secret article

Treaty of Campo Formio, Oct. 17.

---

* Martens, Traités, vi., 420; Thugut, Briefe ii., 64. These letters breathe a fire and passion rare among German statesmen of that day, and show the fine side of Thugut's character. The well-known story of the destruction of Cobenzl's vase by Bonaparte at the last sitting, with the words, "Thus will I dash the Austrian Monarchy to pieces," is mythical. Cobenzl's own account of the scene is as follows:—" Bonaparte, excited by not having slept for two nights, emptied glass after glass of punch. When I explained with the greatest composure, ... Bonaparte started up in a violent rage, and poured out a flood of abuse, at the same time scratching his name illegibly at the foot of the statement which he had handed in as protocol. Then without waiting for our signatures, he put on his hat in the conference-room itself, and left us. Until he was in the street he continued to vociferate in a manner that could only be ascribed to intoxication, though Clarke and the rest of his suite, who were waiting in the hall, did their best to restrain him." "He behaved as if he had escaped from a lunatic asylum. His own people are all agreed about this." Hüffer, Oestreich und Preussen, p. 453.

provided that the Emperor should use his efforts to gain for France the whole left bank of the Rhine, except a tract including the Prussian Duchies of Cleve and Guelders. With humorous duplicity the French Government, which had promised Prussia the Bishopric of Münster in return for this very district, now pledged itself to Austria that Prussia should receive no extension whatever, and affected to exclude the Prussian Duchies from the Rhenish territory which was to be made over to France. Austria was promised the independent Bishopric of Salzburg, and that portion of Bavaria which lies between the Inn and the Salza. The secular princes dispossessed in the Rhenish Provinces were to be compensated in the interior of the Empire by a scheme framed in concert with France.

The immense advantages which the Treaty of Campo Formio gave to France—its extension over the Netherlands and the Rhenish Provinces, *Austria sacrifices Germany.* and the virtual annexation of Lombardy, Modena, and the Papal Legations under the form of a client-republic —were not out of proportion to its splendid military successes. Far otherwise was it with Austria. With the exception of the Archduke's campaign of 1796, the warfare of the last three years had brought Austria nothing but a series of disasters; yet Austria gained by the Treaty of Campo Formio as much as it lost. In the place of the distant Netherlands and of Milan it gained, in Venice and Dalmatia, a territory touching its own, nearly equal to the Netherlands and Milan together in population, and so situated as to enable Austria to become one of the naval Powers of the Mediterranean. The price which Austria paid was the abandonment of Germany, a matter which, in spite of Thugut's protests, disturbed the Court of Vienna as little as the betrayal of Venice disturbed Bonaparte. The Rhenish Provinces were surrendered to the stranger; German districts were to be handed over to compensate the ejected Sovereigns of Holland and of Modena; the internal condition and order of the Empire were to be superseded by one framed not for the purpose of benefiting Germany, but for the purpose of extending the influence of France.

As defenders of Germany, both Prussia and Austria had been found wanting. The latter Power seemed to have reaped in Italy the reward of its firmness in prolonging the war. Bonaparte ridiculed the men who, in the earlier spirit of the Revolution, desired to found a freer political system in Europe upon the ruins of Austria's power. "I have not drawn my support in Italy," he wrote to Talleyrand (Oct. 7), "from the love of the peoples for liberty and equality, or at least but a very feeble support. The real support of the army of Italy has been its own discipline, . . . above all, our promptitude in repressing malcontents and punishing those who declared against us. This is history; what I say in my proclamations and speeches is a romance. . . . If we return to the foreign policy of 1793, we shall do so knowing that a different policy has brought us success, and that we have no longer the great masses of 1793 to enrol in our armies, nor the support of an enthusiasm which has its day and does

Policy of Bonaparte.

not return." Austria might well, for the present, be left in some strength, and France was fortunate to have so dangerous an enemy off her hands. England required the whole forces of the Republic. "The present situation," wrote Bonaparte, after the Peace of Campo Formio, "offers us a good chance. We must set all our strength upon the sea; we must destroy England; and the Continent is at our feet."

It had been the natural hope of the earlier Republicans that the Spanish and the Dutch navies, if they could be brought to the side of France, would make France superior to Great Britain as a maritime Power. *Battles of St. Vincent, Feb. 14, 1797, and Camperdown, Oct. 6.* The conquest of Holland had been planned by Carnot as the first step towards an invasion of England. For a while these plans seemed to be approaching their fulfilment. Holland was won; Spain first made peace, and then entered into alliance with the Directory (Aug. 1796). But each increase in the naval forces of the Republic only gave the admirals of Great Britain new material to destroy. The Spanish fleet was beaten by Jarvis off St. Vincent; even the mutiny of the British squadrons at Spithead and the Nore, in the spring and summer of 1797, caused no change in the naval situation in the North Sea. Duncan, who was blockading the Dutch fleet in the Texel when his own squadron joined the mutineers, continued the blockade with one ship beside his own, signalling all the while as if the whole fleet were at his back; until the misused seamen, who had lately turned their guns upon the Thames, returned to the admiral, and earned his forgiveness by destroying the Dutch at Camperdown as soon as they ventured out of shelter.

It is doubtful whether at any time after his return from Italy Bonaparte seriously entertained the project of invading England. The plan was at any rate soon abandoned, and the preparations, which caused great alarm in the English coast-towns, were continued only for the purpose of disguising Bonaparte's real design of an attack upon Egypt. From the beginning of his career Bonaparte's thoughts had turned towards the vast and undefended East. While still little known, he had asked the French Government to send him to Constantinople to organise the Turkish army; as soon as Venice fell into his hands, he had seized the Ionian Islands as the base for a future conquest of the Levant. Every engagement that confirmed the superiority of England upon the western seas gave additional reason for attacking her where her power was most precarious, in the East. Bonaparte knew that Alexander had conquered the country of the Indus by a land-march from the Mediterranean, and this was perhaps all the information which he possessed regarding the approaches to India; but it was enough to fix his mind upon the conquest of Egypt and Syria, as the first step towards the destruction of the Asiatic Empire of England. Mingled with the design upon India was a dream of overthrowing the Mohammedan Government of Turkey, and attacking Austria from the East with an army drawn from the liberated Christian races of the Ottoman Empire. The very vagueness of a scheme of

Bonaparte about to invade Egypt.

Eastern conquest made it the more attractive to Bonaparte's genius and ambition. Nor was there any inclination on the part of the Government to detain the general at home. The Directory, little concerned with the real merits or dangers of the enterprise, consented to Bonaparte's project of an attack upon Egypt, thankful for any opportunity of loosening the grasp which was now closing so firmly upon themselves.

CHAPTER IV.

Congress of Rastadt—The Rhenish Provinces ceded—Ecclesiastical States of Germany suppressed—French intervention in Switzerland—Helvetic Republic—The French invade the Papal States—Roman Republic—Expedition to Egypt—Battle of the Nile—Coalition of 1798—Ferdinand of Naples enters Rome—Mack's defeats—French enter Naples—Parthenopean Republic—War with Austria and Russia—Battle of Stockach—Murder of the French Envoys at Rastadt—Campaign in Lombardy—Reign of Terror at Naples—Austrian designs upon Italy—Suvaroff and the Austrians—Campaign in Switzerland—Campaign in Holland—Bonaparte returns from Egypt—Coup-d'état of 18 Brumaire—Constitution of 1799—System of Bonaparte in France—Its effect on the influence of France abroad.

THE public articles of the Treaty of Campo Formio contained only the terms which had been agreed upon by France and Austria in relation to Italy and the Netherlands: the conditions of peace between France and the Germanic Body, which had been secretly arranged between France and the two leading Powers, were referred by a diplomatic fiction to a Congress that was to assemble at Rastadt. Accordingly, after Prussia and Austria had each signed an agreement abandoning the Rhenish Provinces, the Congress was duly summoned. As if in mockery of his helpless countrymen, the Emperor informed the members of the Diet that "in unshaken fidelity to the great principle of the unity and indivisibility of the German Empire, they were to maintain the common interests of the Fatherland with noble conscientiousness and German steadfastness; and so, united with their imperial head, to promote a just and lasting peace, founded upon the basis of the

Congress of Rastadt, Nov. 1797.

integrity of the Empire and of its Constitution."* Thus the Congress was convoked upon the pretence of preserving what the two greater States had determined to sacrifice; while its real object, the suppression of the ecclesiastical principalities and the curtailment of Bavaria, was studiously put out of sight.

The Congress was composed of two French envoys, of the representatives of Prussia and Austria, and of a committee, numbering with their secretaries seventy-four persons, appointed by the Diet of Ratisbon. *Rivalry of the Germans.* But the recognised negotiators formed only a small part of the diplomatists who flocked to Rastadt in the hope of picking up something from the wreck of the Empire. Every petty German sovereign, even communities which possessed no political rights at all, thought it necessary to have an agent on the spot, in order to filch, if possible, some trifling advantage from a neighbour, or to catch the first rumour of a proposed annexation. It was the saturnalia of the whole tribe of busybodies and intriguers who passed in Germany for men of state. They spied upon one another; they bribed the secretaries and doorkeepers, they bribed the very cooks and coachmen, of the two omnipotent French envoys. Of the national humiliation of Germany, of the dishonour attaching to the loss of entire provinces and the reorganisation of what remained at the bidding of the stranger, there seems to have been

---

* Häusser, Deutsche Geschichte, 2, 147. Vivenot, Rastadter Congress, p. 17. Von Lang, Memoiren, i. 33. It is alleged that the official who drew up this document had not been made acquainted with the secret clauses.

no sense in the political circles of the day. The collapse of the Empire was viewed rather as a subject of merriment. A gaiety of life and language prevailed, impossible among men who did not consider themselves as the spectators of a comedy. Cobenzl, the chief Austrian plenipotentiary, took his travels in a fly, because his mistress, the *citoyenne* Hyacinthe, had decamped with all his carriages and horses. A witty but profane pamphlet was circulated, in which the impending sacrifice of the Empire was described in language borrowed from the Gospel narrative, Prussia taking the part of Judas Iscariot, Austria that of Pontius Pilate, the Congress itself being the chief priests and Pharisees assembling that they may take the Holy Roman Empire by craft, while the army of the Empire figures as the "multitude who smote upon their breasts and departed." In the utter absence of any German pride or patriotism the French envoys not only obtained the territory that they required, but successfully embroiled the two leading Powers with one another, and accustomed the minor States to look to France for their own promotion at the cost of their neighbours. The contradictory pledges which the French Government had given to Austria and to Prussia caused it no embarrassment. To deceive one of the two powers was to win the gratitude of the other; and the Directory determined to fulfil its engagement to Prussia at the expense of the bishoprics, and to ignore what it had promised to Austria at the expense of Bavaria.

A momentary difficulty arose upon the opening of the Congress, when it appeared that, misled by the

Emperor's protestations, the Diet had only empowered its Committee to treat upon the basis of the integrity of the Empire (Dec. 9). The French declined to negotiate until the Committee had procured full powers: and the prospects of the integrity of the Empire were made clear enough a few days later by the entry of the French into Mainz, and the formal organisation of the Rhenish Provinces as four French Departments. In due course a decree of the Diet arrived, empowering the Committee to negotiate at their discretion: and for some weeks after the inhabitants of the Rhenish Provinces had been subjected to the laws, the magistracy, and the taxation of France, the Committee deliberated upon the proposal for their cession with as much minuteness and as much impartiality as if it had been a point of speculative philosophy. At length the French put an end to the tedious trifling, and proceeded to the question of compensation for the dispossessed lay Princes. This they proposed to effect by means of the disestablishment, or secularisation, of ecclesiastical States in the interior of Germany. Prussia eagerly supported the French proposal, both with a view to the annexation of the great Bishopric of Münster, and from ancient hostility to the ecclesiastical States as instruments and allies of Catholic Austria. The Emperor opposed the destruction of his faithful dependents; the ecclesiastical princes themselves raised a bitter outcry, and demonstrated that the fall of their order would unloose the keystone of the political system

Rhenish Provinces.

Ecclesiastical States suppressed.

of Europe; but they found few friends. If Prussia coveted the great spoils of Münster, the minor sovereigns, as a rule, were just as eager for the convents and abbeys that broke the continuity of their own territories: only the feeblest of all the members of the Empire, the counts, the knights, and the cities, felt a respectful sympathy for their ecclesiastical neighbours, and foresaw that in a system of annexation their own turn would come next. The principle of secularisation was accepted by the Congress without much difficulty, all the energy of debate being reserved for the discussion of details: arrangements which were to transfer a few miles of ground and half a dozen custom-houses from some bankrupt ecclesiastic to some French-bought duke excited more interest in Germany than the loss of the Rhenish provinces, and the subjection of a tenth part of the German nation to a foreign rule.

One more question was unexpectedly presented to the Congress. After proclaiming for six years that the Rhine was the natural boundary of France, the French Government discovered that a river cannot be a military frontier at all. Of what service, urged the French plenipotentiaries, were Strasburg and Mainz, so long as they were commanded by the guns on the opposite bank? If the Rhine was to be of any use to France, France must be put in possession of the fortresses of Kehl and Castel upon the German side. Outrageous as such a demand appears, it found supporters among the venal politicians of the smaller Courts, and furnished the Committee with material for arguments that extended over four months. But the policy of Austria was now taking a direction that rendered the resolutions of the Congress of very little importance. It had become clear that France was inclining to an alliance with Prussia, and that the Bavarian annexations promised to Austria by the secret articles of Campo Formio were to be withheld. Once convinced, by the failure of a private negotiation in Alsace, that the French would neither be content with their gains of 1797, nor permit Austria to extend its territory in Italy, Thugut determined upon a renewal of the war.* In spite of a powerful opposition at Court, Thugut's stubborn will still controlled the fortune of Austria: and the aggressions of the French Republic in Switzerland and the Papal States, at the moment when it was dictating terms of peace to the Empire, gave only too much cause for the formation of a new European league.

<small>Austria determines on war, 1798.</small>

At the close of the last century there was no country where the spirit of Republican freedom was so strong, or where the conditions of life were so level, as in Switzerland; its inhabitants, however, were far from enjoying complete political equality. There were districts which stood in the relation of subject dependencies to one or other of the ruling cantons: the Pays de Vaud was governed by an officer from Berne; the valley of the Ticino belonged

<small>French intervention in Switzerland.</small>

---

* "Tout annonce qu'il sera de toute impossibilité de finir avec ces gueux de Français autrement que par moyens de fermeté." Thugut, ii., 105. For the negotiation at Seltz, see Historische Zeitschrift, xxiii., 27.

to Uri; and in most of the sovereign cantons themselves authority was vested in a close circle of patrician families. Thus, although Switzerland was free from the more oppressive distinctions of caste, and the Governments, even where not democratic, were usually just and temperate, a sufficiently large class was excluded from political rights to give scope to an agitation which received its impulse from Paris. It was indeed among communities advanced in comfort and intelligence, and divided from those who governed them by no great barrier of wealth and prestige, that the doctrines of the Revolution found a circulation which they could never gain among the hereditary serfs of Prussia or the priest-ridden peasantry of the Roman States. As early as the year 1792 a French army had entered the territory of Geneva, in order to co-operate with the democratic party in the city. The movement was, however, checked by the resolute action of the Bernese Senate; and the relations of France to the Federal Government had subsequently been kept upon a friendly footing by the good sense of Barthélemy, the French ambassador at Berne, and the discretion with which the Swiss Government avoided every occasion of offence. On the conquest of Northern Italy, Bonaparte was brought into direct connection with Swiss affairs by a reference of certain points in dispute to his authority as arbitrator. Bonaparte solved the difficulty by annexing the district of the Valteline to the Cisalpine Republic; and from that time he continued in communication with the Swiss democratic leaders on the subject of a French intervention in Switzerland, the real purpose of which was to secure the treasure of Berne, and to organise a government, like that of Holland and the Cisalpine Republic, in immediate dependence upon France.

At length the moment for armed interference arrived. On the 15th December, 1797, a French force entered the Bishopric of Basle, and gave the signal for insurrection in the Pays de Vaud. *War between France and Swiss Federation, June, 1798.* The Senate of Berne summoned the Diet of the Confederacy to provide for the common defence: the oath of federation was renewed, and a decree was passed calling out the Federal army. It was now announced by the French that they would support the Vaudois revolutionary party, if attacked. The Bernese troops, however, advanced; and the bearer of a flag of truce having been accidentally killed, war was declared between the French Republic and the Government of Berne. Democratic movements immediately followed in the northern and western cantons; the Bernese Government attempted to negotiate with the French invaders, but discovered that no terms would be accepted short of the entire destruction of the existing Federal Constitution. Hostilities commenced; and the Bernese troops, supported by contingents from most of the other cantons, offered a brave but ineffectual resistance to the advance of the French, who entered the Federal capital on the 6th of March, 1798. The treasure of Berne, amounting to about £800,000, accumulated by ages of thrift and good management, was seized in order to provide for Bonaparte's next campaign, and for a host of voracious soldiers and contractors. A system of robbery and extortion, more shameless even than that practised in Italy, was put in force against the cantonal governments, against the monasteries, and against private individuals. In compensation for the material losses inflicted upon the country, the new Helvetic Republic, one and indivisible, was proclaimed at Aarau. It conferred an equality of political rights upon all natives of Switzerland, and substituted for the ancient varieties of cantonal sovereignty a single national government, composed, like that of France, of a Directory and two Councils of Legislature.

<small>Helvetic Republic, April 12.</small>

The towns and districts which had been hitherto excluded from a share in government welcomed a change which seemed to place them on a level with their former superiors: the mountain-cantons fought with traditional heroism in defence of the liberties which they had inherited from their fathers; but they were compelled, one after another, to submit to the overwhelming force of France, and to accept the new constitution. Yet, even now, when peace seemed to have been restored, and the whole purpose of France attained, the tyranny and violence of the invaders exhausted the endurance of a spirited people. The magistrates of the Republic were expelled from office at the word of a French Commission; hostages were seized; at length an oath of allegiance to the new order was required as a condition for the evacuation of Switzerland by the French army. Revolt broke out in Unterwalden, and a handful of peasants met the French army at the village of Stanz, near the eastern shore of the Lake of Lucerne (Sept. 8). There for three days they fought with unyielding courage. Their resistance inflamed the French to a cruel vengeance: slaughtered families and burning villages renewed, in this so-called crusade of liberty, the savagery of ancient war.

Intrigues at Rome paved the way for a French intervention in the affairs of the Papal States, coincident in time with the invasion of Switzerland. The residence of the French ambassador at Rome, Joseph Bonaparte, was the centre of a democratic agitation. The men who moved about him were in great part strangers from the north of Italy, but they found adherents in the middle and professional classes in Rome itself, although the mass of the poor people, as well as the numerous body whose salaries or profits depended upon ecclesiastical expenditure, were devoted to the priests and the Papacy. In anticipation of disturbances, the Government ordered companies of soldiers to patrol the city. A collision occurred on the 28th December, 1797, between the patrols and a band of revolutionists, who, being roughly handled by the populace as well as by the soldiers, made their way for protection to the courtyard of the Palazzo Corsini, where Joseph Bonaparte resided. Here, in the midst of a confused struggle, General Duphot, a member of the Embassy, was shot by a Papal soldier.*

The French had now the pretext against the Papal

---

* Botta, lib. xiii. Letters of Mr. J. Denham and others in Records; Sicily, vol. 44.

Government which they desired. Joseph Bonaparte instantly left the city, and orders were sent to Berthier, chief of the staff in northern Italy, to march upon Rome. Berthier advanced amid the accla-

Berthier enters Rome, Feb. 10, 1798

mations of the towns and the curses of the peasantry, and entered Rome on the 10th of February, 1798. Events had produced in the capital a much stronger inclination towards change than existed on the approach of Bonaparte a year before. The treaty of Tolentino had shaken the prestige of Papal authority; the loss of so many well-known works of art, the imposition of new and unpopular taxes, had excited as much hatred against the defeated government as against the extortionate conquerors; even among the clergy and their retainers the sale of a portion of the Church-lands and the curtailment of the old Papal splendours had produced alienation and discontent. There existed too within the Italian Church itself a reforming party, lately headed by Ricci, bishop of Pistoia, which claimed a higher degree of independence for the clergy, and condemned the assumption of universal authority by the Roman See. The ill-judged exercise of the Pope's temporal power during the last six years had gained many converts to the opinion that the head of the Church would best perform his office if emancipated from a worldly sovereignty, and restored to his original position of the first among the bishops. Thus, on its approach to Rome, the Republican army found the city ripe for revolution. On the 15th of February an excited multitude assembled in the Forum, and, after planting the tree of liberty in front of the Capitol, renounced the authority of the Pope, and declared that the Roman people constituted itself a free Republic. The resolution was conveyed to Berthier, who recognised the Roman Commonwealth, and made a procession through the city with the solemnity of an ancient triumph. The Pope shut himself up in the Vatican. His Swiss guard was removed, and replaced by one composed of French soldiers, at whose hands the Pontiff, now in his eighty-first year, suffered unworthy insults. He was then required to renounce his temporal power, and, upon his refusal, was removed to Tuscany, and afterwards beyond the Alps to Valence, where in 1799 he died, attended by a solitary ecclesiastic.

<small>Roman Republic, Feb. 15, 1798.</small>

In the liberated capital a course of spoliation began, more thorough and systematic than any that the French had yet effected. The riches of Rome brought all the brokers and contractors of Paris to the spot. The museums, the Papal residence, and the palaces of many of the nobility were robbed of every article that could be moved; the very fixtures were cut away, when worth the carriage. On the first meeting of the National Institute in the Vatican it was found that the doors had lost their locks; and when, by order of the French, masses were celebrated in the churches in expiation of the death of Duphot, the patrols who were placed at the gates to preserve order rushed in and seized the sacred vessels. Yet the general robbery was far less the work of the army than of the agents and contractors sent by the Government. In the midst of endless peculation the soldiers were in want of their pay and their food. A sense of the dishonour done to France arose at length in the subordinate ranks of the army; and General Massena, who succeeded Berthier, was forced to quit his command in consequence of the protests of the soldiery against a system to which Massena had conspicuously given his personal sanction. It remained to embody the recovered liberties of Rome in a Republican Constitution, which was, as a matter of course, a reproduction of the French Directory and Councils of Legislature, under the practical control of the French general in command. What Rome had given to the Revolution in the fashion of classical expressions was now more than repaid. The Directors were styled Consuls; the divisions of the Legislature were known as the Senate and the Tribunate; the Prætorship and the Quæstorship were recalled to life in the Courts of Justice. That the new era might not want its classical memorial, a medal was struck, with the image and superscription of Roman heroism, to "Berthier, the restorer of the city," and to "Gaul, the salvation of the human race."

Expedition to Egypt, May, 1798.

It was in the midst of these enterprises in Switzerland and Central Italy that the Directory assembled the forces which Bonaparte was to lead to the East. The port of embarkation was Toulon; and there, on the 9th of May, 1798, Bonaparte took the command of the most formidable armament that had ever left the French shores. Great Britain was still but feebly represented in the

Mediterranean, a detachment from St. Vincent's fleet at Cadiz, placed under the command of Nelson, being the sole British force in these waters. Heavy reinforcements were at hand; but in the meantime Nelson had been driven by stress of weather from his watch upon Toulon. On the 19th of May the French armament put out to sea, its destination being still kept secret from the soldiers themselves. It appeared before Malta on the 16th of June. By the treachery of the knights Bonaparte was put in possession of this stronghold, which he could not even have attempted to besiege. After a short delay the voyage was resumed, and the fleet reached Alexandria without having fallen in with the English, who had now received their reinforcements. The landing was safely effected, and Alexandria fell at the first assault. After five days the army advanced upon Cairo. At the foot of the Pyramids the Mameluke cavalry vainly threw themselves upon Bonaparte's soldiers. They were repulsed with enormous loss on their own side and scarcely any on that of the French. Their camp was stormed; Cairo was occupied; and there no longer existed a force in Egypt capable of offering any serious resistance to the invaders.

But the fortune which had brought Bonaparte's army safe into the Egyptian capital was destined to be purchased by the utter destruction of his fleet. Nelson had passed the French in the night, when, after much perplexity, he decided on sailing in the direction of Egypt. Arriving at Alexandria before his prey, he had hurried off in an imaginary pursuit to Rhodes and Crete. At length he received information which led him to visit Alexandria a second time. He found the French fleet, numbering thirteen ships of the line and four frigates, at anchor in Aboukir Bay.* His own fleet was slightly inferior in men and guns, but he entered battle with a presentiment of the completeness of his victory. Other naval battles have been fought with larger forces; no destruction was ever so complete as that of the Battle of the Nile (August 1). Two ships of the line and two frigates, out of the seventeen sail that met Nelson, alone escaped from his hands. Of eleven thousand officers and men, nine thousand were taken prisoners, or perished in the engagement. The army of Bonaparte was cut off from all hope of support or return; the Republic was deprived of communication with its best troops and its greatest general.

<small>Battle of the Nile, Aug. 1.</small>

A coalition was now gathering against France superior to that of 1793 in the support of Russia and the Ottoman Empire, although Spain was now on the side of the Republic, and Prussia, in spite of the warnings of the last two years, refused to stir from its neutrality. The death of the Empress Catherine, and the accession of Paul, had caused a most serious change in the prospects of Europe. Hitherto the policy of the Russian Court had been to embroil the Western Powers with one another, and to confine its efforts against the French Republic to promises and assurances; with Paul, after an interval of total reaction,

<small>Coalition of 1798.</small>

* Nelson Despatches, iii. 48.

the professions became realities.* No monarch entered so cordially into Pitt's schemes for a renewal of the European league; no ally had joined the English minister with a sincerity so like his own. On the part of the Ottoman Government, the pretences of friendship with which Bonaparte disguised the occupation of Egypt were taken at their real worth. War was declared by the Porte; and a series of negotiations, carried on during the autumn of 1798, united Russia, England, Turkey, and Naples in engagements of mutual support against the French Republic.

A Russian army set out on its long march towards the Adriatic: the levies of Austria prepared for a campaign in the spring of 1799; but to the English Government every moment that elapsed before actual hostilities was so much time given to uncertainties; and the man who had won the Battle of the Nile ridiculed the precaution which had hitherto suffered the French to spread their intrigues through Italy, and closed the ports of Sicily and Naples to his own most urgent needs. Towards the end of September, Nelson appeared in the Bay of Naples, and was received with a delirium that recalled the most effusive scenes in the French Revolution.† In the city of Naples, as in the kingdom

<small>Nelson at Naples, Sept., 1798.</small>

---

* Bernhardi, Geschichte Russlands, ii., 2, 382.

† "Quel bonheur, quelle gloire, quelle consolation pour cette grande et illustre nation! Que je vous suis obligée, reconnaissante! J'ai plouré et embrassé mes enfans, mon mari. Si jamais on fait un portrait du brave Nelson je le veux avoir dans ma chambre. Hip, Hip, Hip. Ma chère Miladi je suis folle de joye." Queen of Naples to Lady Hamilton, Sept. 4, 1798; Records: Sicily, vol. 44. The news of the overwhelming victory of the Nile seems literally to have driven people out of their senses at

generally, the poorest classes were the fiercest enemies of reform, and the steady allies of the Queen and the priesthood against that section of the better-educated classes which had begun to hope for liberty. The system of espionage and persecution with which the sister of Marie Antoinette avenged upon her own subjects the sufferings of her kindred had grown more oppressive with every new victory of the Revolution. In the summer of 1798 there were men languishing for the fifth year in prison, whose offences had never been investigated, and whose relatives were not allowed to know whether they were dead or alive. A mode of expression, a fashion of dress, the word of an informer, consigned innocent persons to the dungeon, with the possibility of torture. In the midst of this tyranny of suspicion, in the midst of a corruption which made the naval and military forces of the kingdom worse than useless, King Ferdinand and his satellites were unwearied in their theatrical invocations of the Virgin and St. Januarius against the assailants of divine right and the conquerors of Rome. A Court cowardly almost beyond the example of Courts, a police that had trained every Neapolitan to look upon his neighbour as a traitor, an

---

Naples. "Lady Hamilton fell apparently dead, and is not yet (Sept. 25) perfectly recovered from her severe bruises." Nelson Despatches, 3, 130. On Nelson's arrival, "up flew her ladyship, and exclaiming, ' O God, is it possible?' she fell into my arms more dead than alive." It has been urged in extenuation of Nelson's subsequent cruelties that the contagion of this frenzy, following the effects of a severe wound in the head, had deprived his mind of its balance. "My head is ready to split, and I am always so sick." Aug. 10. "It required all the kindness of my friends to set me up." Sept. 25.

administration that had turned one of the hardiest races in Europe into soldiers of notorious and disgraceful cowardice—such were the allies whom Nelson, ill-fitted for politics by his sailor-like inexperience and facile vanity, heroic in his tenderness and fidelity, in an evil hour encouraged to believe themselves invincible because they possessed his own support. On the 14th of November, 1798, King Ferdinand published a proclamation, which, without declaring war on the French, announced that the King intended to occupy the Papal States and restore the Papal government. The manifesto disclaimed all intention of conquest, and offered a free pardon to all compromised persons. Ten days later the Neapolitan army crossed the frontier, led by the Austrian general, Mack, who passed among his admirers for the greatest soldier in Europe.*

The mass of the French troops, about twelve thousand in number, lay in the neighbourhood of Ancona; Rome and the intermediate stations were held

* Sir W. Hamilton's despatch, Nov. 28, in Records: Sicily, vol. 44, where there are originals of most of the Neapolitan proclamations, &c., of this time. Mack had been a famous character since the campaign of 1793. Elgin's letters to Lord Grenville from the Netherlands, private as well as public, are full of extravagant praise of him. In July, 1796, Graham writes from the Italian army: "In the opinion of all here, the greatest general in Europe is the Quartermaster Mack, who was in England in 1793. Would to God he was marching, and here now." Mack, on the other hand, did not grudge flattery to the English:—" Je perdrais partout espoir et patience si je n'avais pas vu pour mon bonheur et ma consolation l'adorable Triumvirat" (Pitt, Grenville, Dundas) "qui surveille à Londres nos affaires. Soyez, mon cher ami, l'organe de ma profonde vénération envers ces Ministres incomparables." Mack to Elgin, 23 Feb. 1794. The British Government was constantly pressing Thugut to make Mack commander-in-chief. Thugut, who had formed a shrewd notion of Mack's real quality, gained much obloquy by his steady refusal.

by small detachments. Had Mack pushed forward towards the Upper Tiber, his inroad, even if it failed to crush the separated wings of the French army, must have forced them to retreat; but, instead of moving with all his strength through Central Italy, Mack led the bulk of his army upon Rome, where there was no French force capable of making a stand, and sent weak isolated columns towards the east of the peninsula, where the French were strong enough to make a good defence. On the approach of the Neapolitans to Rome, Championnet, the French commander, evacuated the city, leaving a garrison in the Castle of St. Angelo, and fell back on Civita Castellana, thirty miles north of the capital. The King of Naples entered Rome on the 29th November. The res-

Ferdinand enters Rome, Nov. 29.

toration of religion was celebrated by the erection of an immense cross in the place of the tree of liberty, by the immersion of several Jews in the Tiber, by the execution of a number of compromised persons whose pardon the King had promised, and by a threat to shoot one of the sick French soldiers in the hospital for every shot fired by the guns of St. Angelo.* Intelligence was despatched to the exiled Pontiff of the discomfiture of his enemies. "By help of the divine grace," wrote King Ferdinand, " and of the most miraculous St. Januarius, we have to-day with our army entered the sacred city of Rome, so lately profaned by the impious, who now fly terror-stricken at the sight of the Cross

---

* Signed by Mack. Colletta, p. 176. Mack's own account of the campaign is in Vivenot, Rastadter Congress, p. 83.

and of my arms. Leave then, your Holiness, your too
modest abode, and on the wings of cherubim, like the
virgin of Loreto, come and descend upon the Vatican,
to purify it by your sacred presence." A letter to the
King of Piedmont, who had already been exhorted by
Ferdinand to encourage his peasants to assassinate French
soldiers, informed him that "the Neapolitans, guided by
General Mack, had sounded the hour of death to the
French, and proclaimed to Europe, from the summit of
the Capitol, that the time of the Kings had come."

The despatches to Piedmont fell into the hands of
the enemy, and the usual modes of locomotion would
scarcely have brought Pope Pius to Rome in time to
witness the exit of his deliverer. Ferdinand's rhapsodies
were cut short by the news that his columns advancing
into the centre and east of the Papal States had all been
beaten or captured. Mack, at the head of the main
army, now advanced to avenge the defeat upon the
French at Civita Castellana and Terni. But
his dispositions were as unskilful as ever: *Mack defeated by Championnet, Dec. 6—13.*
wherever his troops encountered the enemy
they were put to the rout; and, as he had neglected
to fortify or secure a single position upon his line of
march, his defeat by a handful of French soldiers on the
north of Rome involved the loss of the country almost
up to the gates of Naples. On the first rumour of
Mack's reverses the Republican party at Rome declared
for France. King Ferdinand fled; Championnet re-
entered Rome, and, after a few days' delay, advanced
into Neapolitan territory. Here, however, he found

himself attacked by an enemy more formidable than the army which had been organised to expel the French from Italy. The Neapolitan peasantry, who, in soldiers' uniform and under the orders of Mack, could scarcely be brought within sight of the French, fought with courage when an appeal to their religious passions collected them in brigand-like bands under leaders of their own. Divisions of Championnet's army sustained severe losses; they succeeded, however, in effecting their junction upon the Volturno; and the stronghold of Gaeta, being defended by regular soldiers and not by brigands, surrendered to the French at the first summons.

Mack was now concentrating his troops in an entrenched camp before Capua. The whole country was rising against the invaders; and, in spite of lost battles and abandoned fortresses, the Neapolitan Government, if it had possessed a spark of courage, might still have overthrown the French army, which numbered only 18,000 men. But the panic and suspicion which the Government had fostered among its subjects were now avenged upon itself. The cry of treachery was raised on every side. The Court dreaded a Republican rising; the priests and the populace accused the Court of conspiracy with the French; Mack protested that the soldiers were resolved to be beaten; the soldiers swore that they were betrayed by Mack. On the night of the 21st of December the Royal Family secretly went on board Nelson's ship the *Vanguard*, and after a short interval they set sail for Palermo, leaving the capital in charge of Prince Pignatelli, a courtier whom no one was willing to obey.* Order was, however, maintained by a civic guard enrolled by the Municipality, until it became known that Mack and Pignatelli had concluded an armistice with the French, and surrendered Capua and the neighbouring towns. Then the populace broke into wild uproar. The prisons were thrown open; and with the arms taken from the arsenal the lazzaroni formed themselves into a tumultuous army, along with thousands of desperate men let loose from the gaols and the galleys. The priests, hearing that negotiations for peace were opened, raised the cry of treason anew; and, with the watchword of the Queen, "All the gentlemen are Jacobins; only the people are faithful," they hounded on the mob to riot and murder. On the morning of January 15th hordes of lazzaroni issued from the gates to throw themselves upon the French, who were now about nine miles from the city; others dragged the guns down from the forts to defend the streets. The Republican party, however, and that considerable body among the upper class which was made Republican by

* Nelson, iii., 210; Hamilton's despatch, Dec. 28, 1798, in Records: Sicily, vol. 44. "It was impossible to prevent a suspicion getting abroad of the intention of the Royal Family to make their escape. However, the secret was so well kept that we contrived to get their Majesties' treasure in jewels and money, to a very considerable extent, on board of H.M. ship the *Vanguard* the 20th of December, and Lord Nelson went on the next night by a secret passage into the Palace, and brought off in his boats their Sicilian Majesties and all the Royal Family. It was not discovered at Naples, until very late at night, that the Royal Family had escaped. ... On the morning of Christmas Day, some hours before we got into Palermo, Prince Albert, one of their Majesties' sons, six years of age, was, either from fright or fatigue, taken with violent convulsions, and died in the arms of Lady Hamilton, the Queen, the Princesses, and women attendants being in such confusion as to be incapable of affording any assistance."

the chaos into which the Court, with its allies, the priests, and the populace, had thrown Naples, kept up communication with Championnet, and looked forward to the entrance of the French as the only means of averting destruction and massacre. By a stratagem carried out on the night of the 20th they gained possession of the fort of St. Elmo, while the French were already engaged in a bloody assault upon the suburbs. On the 23rd Championnet ordered the attack to be renewed. The conspirators within St. Elmo hoisted the French flag and turned their guns upon the populace; the fortress of the Carmine was stormed by the French; and, before the last struggle for life and death commenced in the centre of the city, the leaders of the lazzaroni listened to words of friendship which Championnet addressed to them in their own language, and, with the incoherence of a half-savage race, escorted his soldiers with cries of joy to the Church of St. Januarius, which Championnet promised to respect and protect.

French enter Naples, Jan. 23, 1799.

Championnet used his victory with a discretion and forbearance rare amongst French conquerors. He humoured the superstition of the populace; he encouraged the political hopes of the enlightened. A vehement revulsion of feeling against the fugitive Court and in favour of Republican government followed the creation of a National Council by the French general, and his ironical homage to the patron saint.

Parthenopean Republic.

The Kingdom of Naples was converted into the Parthenopean Republic. New laws, new institutions, discussed in a representative assembly, excited hopes and interests unknown in Naples before. But the inevitable incidents of a French occupation, extortion and impoverishment, with all their bitter effects on the mind of the people, were not long delayed. In every country district the priests were exciting insurrection. The agents of the new Government, men with no experience in public affairs, carried confusion wherever they went. Civil war broke out in fifty different places; and the barbarity of native leaders of insurrection, like Fra Diavolo, was only too well requited by the French columns which traversed the districts in revolt.

The time was ill chosen by the French Government for an extension of the area of combat to southern Italy. Already the first division of the Russian army, led by Suvaroff, had reached Moravia, and the Court of Vienna was only awaiting its own moment for declaring war. So far were the newly-established Governments in Rome and Naples from being able to assist the French upon the Adige, that the French had to send troops to Rome and Naples to support the new Governments. The force which the French could place upon the frontier was inferior to that which two years of preparation had given to Austria: the Russians, who were expected to arrive in Lombardy in April, approached with the confidence of men who had given to the French none of their recent triumphs. Nor among the leaders was personal superiority any longer markedly on the side

War with Austria and Russia, March, 1799.

M

of the French, as in the war of the First Coalition. Suvaroff and the Archduke Charles were a fair match for any of the Republican generals, except Bonaparte, who was absent in Egypt. The executive of France had deeply declined. Carnot was in exile; the work of organisation which he had pursued with such energy and disinterestedness flagged under his mediocre and corrupt successors. Skilful generals and brave soldiers were never wanting to the Republic; but no single controlling will, no storm of national passion, inspired the Government with the force which it had possessed under the Convention, and which returned to it under Napoleon.

A new character was given to the war now breaking out by the inclusion of Switzerland in the area of combat. In the war of the first Coalition, Switzerland had been neutral territory; but the events of 1798 had left the French in possession of all Switzerland west of the Rhine, and an Austrian force subsequently occupied the Grisons. The line separating the combatants now ran without a break from Mainz to the Adriatic. The French armies were in continuous communication with one another, and the movements of each could be modified according to the requirements of the rest. On the other hand, a disaster sustained at any one point of the line endangered every other point; for no neutral territory intervened, as in 1796, to check a lateral movement of the enemy, and to protect the communications of a French army in Lombardy from a victorious Austrian force in southern Germany. The importance of the Swiss passes in this relation was understood and even overrated by the French Government; and an energy was thrown into their mountain warfare which might have produced greater results upon the plains.

Three armies formed the order of battle on either side. Jourdan held the French command upon the Rhine; Massena in Switzerland; Scherer, the least capable of the Republican generals, on the Adige. On the side of the Allies the Archduke Charles commanded in southern Germany; in Lombardy the Austrians were led by Kray, pending the arrival of Suvaroff and his corps; in Switzerland the command was given to Hotze, a Swiss officer who had gained some distinction in foreign service. It was the design of the French to push their centre under Massena through the mountains into the Tyrol, and by a combined attack of the central and the southern army to destroy the Austrians upon the upper Adige, while Jourdan, also in communication with the centre, drove the Archduke down the Danube upon Vienna. Early in March the campaign opened. Massena assailed the Austrian positions east of the head-waters of the Rhine, and forced back the enemy into the heart of the Grisons. Jourdan crossed the Rhine at Strasburg, and passed the Black Forest with 40,000 men. His orders were to attack the Archduke Charles, whatever the Archduke's superiority of force. The French and the Austrian armies met at Stockach, near the head of the Lake of Constance. (March 25.) Overwhelming numbers gave the Archduke a complete victory. Jourdan was not only stopped in his advance, but forced to

The Archduke Charles defeats Jourdan at Stockach, March 25.

retreat beyond the Rhine. Whatever might be the fortune of the armies of Switzerland and Italy, all hope of an advance upon Vienna by the Danube was at an end.

Freed from the invader's presence, the Austrians now spread themselves over Baden, up to the gates of Rastadt, where, in spite of the war between France and Austria, the envoys of the minor German States still continued their conferences with the French agents. On the 28th of April the French envoys, now three in number, were required by the Austrians to depart within twenty-four hours. An escort, for which they applied, was refused. Scarcely had their carriages passed through the city gates when they were attacked by a squadron of Austrian hussars. Two of the French envoys were murdered; the third left for dead. Whether this frightful violation of international law was the mere outrage of a drunken soldiery, as it was represented to be by the Austrian Government; whether it was to any extent occasioned by superior civil orders, or connected with French emigrants living in the neighbourhood, remains unknown. Investigations begun by the Archduke Charles were stopped by the Cabinet, in order that a more public inquiry might be held by the Diet. This inquiry, however, never took place. In the year 1804 all papers relating to the Archduke's investigation were removed by the Government from the military archives. They have never since been discovered.*

Murder of the French envoys at Rastadt, April 28.

* See Helfert, Der Rastatter Gesandtenmord, and Sybel's article thereon, in Hist. Zeitschrift, vol. 32.

The outburst of wrath with which the French people learnt the fate of their envoys would have cost Austria dear if Austria had now been the losing party in the war; but, for the present, everything seemed to turn against the Republic. Jourdan had scarcely been overthrown in Germany before a ruinous defeat at Magnano, on the Adige, drove back the army of Italy to within a few miles of Milan; while Massena, deprived of the fruit of his own victories by the disasters of his colleagues, had to abandon the eastern half of Switzerland, and to retire upon the line of the river Limnat, Lucerne, and the Gothard. Charles now moved from Germany into Switzerland. Massena fixed his centre at Zürich, and awaited the Archduke's assault. For five weeks Charles remained inactive: at length, on the 4th of June, he gave battle. After two days' struggle against greatly superior forces, Massena was compelled to evacuate Zürich. He retreated, however, no farther than to the ridge of the Uetliberg, a few miles west of the city; and here, fortifying his new position, he held obstinately on, while the Austrians established themselves in the central passes of Switzerland, and disaster after disaster seemed to be annihilating the French arms in Italy. *[margin: Battle of Magnano, April 5.]*

Suvaroff, at the head of 17,000 Russians, had arrived in Lombardy in the middle of April. His first battle was fought, and his first victory won, at the passage of the Adda on the 25th of April. It was followed by the surrender of Milan and the dissolution of the Cisalpine Republic. *[margin: Suvaroff's Campaign in Lombardy, April–June.]*

Moreau, who now held the French command, fell back upon Alessandria, intending to cover both Genoa and Turin; but a sudden movement of Suvaroff brought the Russians into the Sardinian capital before it was even known to be in jeopardy. The French general, cut off from the roads over the Alps, threw himself upon the Apennines above Genoa, and waited for the army which had occupied Naples, and which, under the command of Macdonald, was now hurrying to his support, gathering with it on its march the troops that lay scattered on the south of the Po. Macdonald moved swiftly through central Italy, and crossed the Apennines above Pistoia in the beginning of June. His arrival at Modena with 20,000 men threatened to turn the balance in favour of the French. Suvaroff, aware of his danger, collected all the troops within reach with the utmost despatch, and pushed eastwards to meet Macdonald on the Trebbia. Moreau descended from the Apennines in the same direction; but he had underrated the swiftness of the Russian general; and, before he had advanced over half the distance, Macdonald was attacked by Suvaroff on the Trebbia, and overthrown in three days of the most desperate fighting that had been seen in the war. (June 18.)*

All southern Italy now rose against the Governments established by the French. Cardinal Ruffo, with a band of fanatical peasants, known as the Army of the Faith, made himself master of Apulia and Calabria

* Danilevsky-Miliutin, ii. 214. Despatch of Lord W. Bentinck from the allied head-quarters at Piacenza, June 23, in Records: Italian States, vol. 58. Bentinck arrived a few days before this battle: **his despatches cover the whole North-Italian campaign from this time.**

amid scenes of savage cruelty, and appeared before Naples, where the lazzaroni were ready to unite with the hordes of the Faithful in murder and pillage. Confident of support within the city, and assisted by some English and Russian vessels in the harbour, Ruffo attacked the suburbs of Naples on the morning of the 13th of June. Massacre and outrage continued within and without the city for five days. On the morning of the 19th, the Cardinal proposed a suspension of arms. It was accepted by the Republicans, who were in possession of the forts. Negotiations followed. On the 23rd conditions of peace were signed by Ruffo on behalf of the King of Naples, and by the representatives of Great Britain and of Russia in guarantee for their faithful execution. It was agreed that the Republican garrison should march out with the honours of war; that their persons and property should be respected; that those who might prefer to leave the country should be conveyed to Toulon on neutral vessels; and that all who remained at home should be free from molestation.

The garrison did not leave the forts that night. On the following morning, while they were embarking on board the polaccas which were to take them to Toulon, Nelson's fleet appeared in the Bay of Naples. Nelson declared that in treating with rebels Cardinal Ruffo had disobeyed the King's orders, and he pronounced the capitulation null and void. The polaccas, with the Republicans crowded on board, were attached to the sterns of the English ships, pending the arrival of King Ferdinand. On the 29th of June, Admiral Caracciolo, who had taken office under the new Government, and on its fall had attempted to escape in disguise, was brought a captive before Nelson. Nelson ordered him to be tried by a Neapolitan court-martial, and, in spite of his old age, his rank, and his long service to the State, caused him to be hanged from a Neapolitan ship's yard-arm, and his body to be thrown into the sea. Some days later King Ferdinand arrived from Palermo, and Nelson now handed over all his prisoners to the Bourbon authorities. A reign of terror followed. Innumerable persons were thrown into prison. Courts-martial, or commissions administering any law that pleased themselves, sent the flower of the Neapolitan nation to the scaffold. Above a hundred sentences of death were carried out in Naples itself: confiscation, exile, and imprisonment struck down thousands of families. It was peculiar to the Neapolitan proscriptions that a Government with the names of religion and right incessantly upon its lips selected for extermination both among men and women those who were most distinguished in character, in science, and in letters, whilst it chose for promotion and enrichment those who were known for deeds of savage violence. The part borne by Nelson in this work of death has left a stain on his glory which time cannot efface.*

Reign of Terror.

* Nelson Despatches, iii., 447; Sir W. Hamilton's Despatch of July 14, in Records : Sicily, vol. 45. Helfert, Königin Karolina, p. 38. Details of the proscription in Colletta, v., 6. According to Hamilton, some of the Republicans in the forts had actually gone to their homes before Nelson pronounced the capitulation void. " When we anchored in the Bay, the 24th of June, the capitulation of the castles had in some measure taken place. Fourteen large polacks had taken on board out of the castles

It was on the advance of the Army of Naples under Macdonald that the French rested their last hope of recovering Lombardy. The battle of the Trebbia scattered this hope to the winds, and left it only too doubtful whether France could be saved from invasion. Suvaroff himself was eager to fall upon Moreau before Macdonald could rally from his defeat, and to drive him westwards along the coast-road into France. It was a moment when the fortune of the Republic hung in the scales. Had Suvaroff been permitted to follow his own counsels, France would probably have seen the remnant of her Italian armies totally destroyed, and the Russians advancing upon Lyons or Marseilles. The Republic was saved, as it had been in 1793, by the dissensions of its enemies. It was not only for the purpose of resisting French aggression that Austria had renewed the war, but for the purpose of extending its own dominion in Italy. These designs were con- *Austrian designs in Italy.* cealed from Russia; they were partially made known by

the most conspicuous and criminal of the Neapolitan rebels that had chosen to go to Toulon; the others had already been permitted to return to their homes." If this is so, Nelson's pretext that the capitulation had not been executed was a mere afterthought. Helfort is mistaken in calling the letter or proclamation of July 8th repudiating the treaty a forgery. It is perfectly genuine. It was published by Nelson in the King's name, and is enclosed in Hamilton's despatch. Hamilton's exultations about himself and his wife, and their share in these events, are sorry reading. "In short, Lord Nelson and I, with Emma, have carried affairs to this happy crisis. Emma is really the Queen's bosom friend. . . You may imagine, when we three agree, what real business is done. . . At least I shall end my diplomatical career gloriously, as you will see by what the King of Naples writes from this ship to his Minister in London, owing the recovery of his kingdom to the King's fleet, and Lord Nelson and me." (Aug. 4, *id.*) Hamilton states the number of persons in prison at Naples on Sept. 12 to be above eight thousand.

Thugut to the British ambassador, under the most stringent obligation to secrecy. On the 17th of August, 1799, Lord Minto acquainted his Government with the intentions of the Austrian Court. "The Emperor proposes to retain Piedmont, and to take all that part of Savoy which is important in a military view. I have no doubt of his intention to keep Nice also, if he gets it, which will make the Var his boundary with France. The whole territory of the Genoese Republic seems to be an object of serious speculation. . . The Papal Legations will, I am persuaded, be retained by the Emperor . . I am not yet master of the designs on Tuscany."* This was the sense in which Austria understood the phrase of defending the rights of Europe against French aggression. It was not, however, for this that the Czar had sent his army from beyond the Carpathians. Since the opening of the campaign Suvaroff had been in perpetual conflict with the military Council of Vienna.† Suvaroff was bent upon a ceaseless

---

* Castlereagh, iv.; Records: Austria, 56. Lord Minto had just succeeded Sir Morton Eden as ambassador. The English Government was willing to grant the House of Hapsburg almost anything for the sake "of strengthening that barrier which the military means and resources of Vienna can alone oppose against the future enterprises of France." Grenville to Minto, May 13, 1800. Though they felt some regard for the rights of the King of Piedmont, Pitt and Grenville were just as ready to hand over the Republic of Genoa to the Hapsburgs as Bonaparte had been to hand over Venice; in fact, they looked forward to the destruction of the Genoese State with avowed pleasure, because it easily fell under the influence of France. Their principal anxiety was that if Austria "should retain Venice and Genoa and possibly acquire Leghorn," it should grant England an advantageous commercial treaty. Grenville to Minto, Feb. 8, 1800; Castlereagh, v. 3—11.

† Lord Mulgrave to Grenville, Sept. 12, 1799; Records: Army of Switzerland, vol. 80. "Suvaroff opened himself to me in the most unre-

pursuit of the enemy; the Austrian Council insisted upon the reduction of fortresses. What at first appeared as a mere difference of military opinion appeared in its true political character when the allied troops entered Piedmont. The Czar desired with his whole soul to crush the men of the Revolution, and to restore the governments which France had overthrown. As soon as his troops entered Turin, Suvaroff proclaimed the restoration of the House of Savoy, and summoned all Sardinian officers to fight for their King. He was interrupted by a letter from Vienna requiring him to leave political affairs in the hands of the Viennese Ministry.* The Russians had already done as much in

served manner. He began by stating that he had been called at a very advanced period of life from his retirement, where his ample fortune and honours placed him beyond the allurement of any motives of interest. Attachment to his sovereign and zeal for his God inspired him with the hope and the expectation of conquests. He now found himself under very different circumstances. He found himself surrounded by the parasites or spies of Thugut, men at his devotion, creatures of his power: an army bigoted to a defensive system, afraid even to pursue their successes when that system had permitted them to obtain any; he had to encounter the further check of a Government at Vienna averse to enterprise, &c.

* Miliutin, 2. 20, 3. 186; Minto, Aug. 10, 1799; Records: Austria, vol. 56. "I had no sooner mentioned this topic (Piedmont) than I perceived I had touched a very delicate point. M. de Thugut's manner changed instantly from that of coolness and civility to a great show of warmth attended with some sharpness. He became immediately loud and animated, and expressed chagrin at the invitation sent to the King of Sardinia. . . He considers the conquest of Piedmont as one made by Austria of an enemy's country. He denies that the King of Sardinia can be considered as an ally or as a friend, or even as a neuter; and, besides imputing a thousand instances of ill-faith to that Court, relies on the actual alliance made by it with the French Republic by which the King of Sardinia had appropriated to himself part of the Emperor's dominions in Lombardy, an offence which, I perceive, will not be easily forgotten. . . I mention these circumstances to show the degree of passion which the Court of Vienna mixes with this discussion." Minto answered Thugut's invective

Italy as the Austrian Cabinet desired them to do, and the first wish of Thugut was now to free himself from his troublesome ally. Suvaroff raged against the Austrian Government in every despatch, and tendered his resignation. His complaints inclined the Czar to accept a new military scheme, which was supported by the English Government in the hope of terminating the contention between Suvaroff and the Austrian Council. It was agreed at St. Petersburg that, as soon as the French armies were destroyed, the reduction of the Italian fortresses should be left exclusively to the Austrians; and that Suvaroff, uniting with a new Russian army now not far distant, should complete the conquest of Switzerland, and then invade France by the Jura, supported on his right by the Archduke Charles. An attack was to be made at the same time upon Holland by a combined British and Russian force.

<small>New Plan of the War.</small>

If executed in its original form, this design would have thrown a formidable army upon France at the side of Franche Comté, where it is least protected by fortresses. But at the last moment an alteration in the plan was made at Vienna. The prospect of an Anglo-

with the odd remark " that perhaps in the present extraordinary period the most rational object of this war was to restore the integrity of the moral principle both in civil and political life, and that this principle of justice should take the lead in his mind of those considerations of temporary convenience which in ordinary times might not have escaped his notice." Thugut then said " that the Emperor of Russia had desisted from his measure of the King of Sardinia's immediate recall, leaving the time of that return to the Emperor." On the margin of the despatch, against this sentence, is written in pencil, in Lord Grenville's handwriting, " I am persuaded this is not true."

Russian victory in Holland again fixed the thoughts of the Austrian Minister upon Belgium, which had been so lightly abandoned five years before, and which Thugut now hoped to re-occupy and to barter for Bavaria or some other territory. "The Emperor," he wrote, "cannot turn a deaf ear to the appeal of his subjects. He cannot consent that the Netherlands shall be disposed of without his own concurrence."* The effect of this perverse and mischievous resolution was that the Archduke Charles received orders to send the greater part of his army from Switzerland to the Lower Rhine, and to leave only 25,000 men to support the new Russian division which, under General Korsakoff, was approaching from the north to meet Suvaroff. The Archduke, as soon as the new instructions reached him, was filled with the presentiment of disaster, and warned his Government that in the general displacement of forces an opportunity would be given to Massena, who was still above Zürich, to strike a fatal blow. Every despatch that passed between Vienna and St. Petersburg now increased the Czar's suspicion of Austria. The Pope and the King of Naples were convinced that Thugut had the same design upon their own territories which had been shown in his treatment of Piedmont.†

* Miliutin, 3. 117. And so almost verbatim in a conversation described in Eden's despatch, Aug. 3; Records: Austria, vol. 55. "M. de Thugut's answer was evidently dictated by a suspicion rankling in his mind that the Netherlands might be made a means of aggrandisement for Prussia. His jealousy and aversion to that Power are at this moment more inveterate than I have before seen them. It is probable that he may have some idea of establishing there the Great Duke of Tuscany."

† Thugut's territorial policy did actually make him propose to abolish the Papacy not only as a temporal Power, but as a religious institution. "Baron Thugut argued strongly on the possibility of doing without a Pope,

They appealed to the Czar for protection. The Czar proposed a European Congress, at which the Powers might learn one another's real intentions. The proposal was not accepted by Austria; but, while disclaiming all desire to despoil the King of Sardinia, the Pope, or the King of Naples, Thugut admitted that Austria claimed an improvement of its Italian frontier, in other words, the annexation of a portion of Piedmont, and of the northern part of the Roman States. The Czar replied that he had taken up arms in order to check one aggressive Government, and that he should not permit another to take its place.

For the moment, however, the allied forces continued to co-operate in Italy against the French army on the Apennines covering Genoa. This army had received reinforcements, and was now placed under the command

and of each sovereign taking on himself the function of head of the National Church, as in England. I said that, as a Protestant, I could not be supposed to think the authority of the Bishop of Rome necessary; but that in the present state of religious opinion, and considering the only alternative in those matters, viz., the subsistence of the Roman Catholic faith or the extinction of Christianity itself, I preferred, though a Protestant, the Pope to the Goddess of Reason. However, the mind of Baron Thugut is not open to any reasoning of a general nature when it is put in competition with conquest or acquisition of territory." Minto to Grenville, Oct. 22, 1799; Records: Austria, vol. 57. The suspicions of Austria current at the Neapolitan Court are curiously shown in the Nelson Correspondence. Nelson writes to Minto (Aug. 20) at Vienna: "For the sake of the civilised world, let us work together, and as the best act of our lives manage to hang Thugut. . . As you are with Thugut, your penetrating mind will discover the villain in all his actions. . . . That Thugut is caballing . . . Pray keep an eye upon the rascal, and you will soon find what I say is true. Let us hang these three miscreants, and all will go smooth." Suvaroff was not more complimentary. "How can that desk-worm, that night-owl, direct an army from his dusky nest, even if he had the sword of Scanderbeg?" (Sept. 3.)

of Joubert, one of the youngest and most spirited of the Republican generals. Joubert determined to attack the Russians before the fall of Mantua should add the besieging army to Suvaroff's forces in the field. But the information which he received from Lombardy misled him. In the second week of August he was still unaware that Mantua had fallen a fortnight before. He descended from the mountains to attack Suvaroff at Tortona, with a force about equal to Suvaroff's own. On reaching Novi he learnt that the army of Mantua was also before him. (Aug. 15.) It was too late to retreat; Joubert could only give to his men the example of Republican spirit and devotion. Suvaroff himself, with Kray, the conqueror of Mantua, began the attack: the onset of a second Austrian corps, at the moment when the strength of the Russians was failing, decided the day. Joubert did not live to witness the close of a defeat which cost France eleven thousand men.*

Battle of Novi, Aug. 15.

The allied Governments had so framed their plans that the most overwhelming victory could produce no result. Instead of entering France, Suvaroff was compelled to turn back into Switzerland, while the Austrians continued to besiege the fortresses of Piedmont. In Switzerland Suvaroff had to meet an enemy who was forewarned of his approach, and who

Suvaroff goes into Switzerland.

---

* Miliutin, iii. 37; Bentinck, Aug. 16, from the battle-field; Records: Italian States, vol. 58. His letter ends: "I must apologise to your Lordship for the appearance of this despatch" (it is on thin Italian paper and almost illegible): "we" (*i.e.*, Suvaroff's staff) "have had the misfortune to have had our baggage plundered by the Cossacks."

had employed every resource of military skill and daring to prevent the union of the two Russian armies now advancing from the south and the north. Before Suvaroff could leave Italy, a series of admirably-planned attacks had given Massena the whole network of the central Alpine passes, and closed every avenue of communication between Suvaroff and the army with which he hoped to co-operate. The folly of the Austrian Cabinet seconded the French general's exertions. No sooner had Korsakoff and the new Russian division reached Schaffhausen than the Archduke Charles, forced by his orders from Vienna, turned northwards (Sept. 3), leaving the Russians with no support but Hotze's corps, which was scattered over six cantons.* Korsakoff advanced to Zürich; Massena remained in his old position on the Uetliberg. It was now that Suvaroff began his march into the Alps, sorely harassed and delayed by the want of the mountain-teams which the Austrians had promised him, and filled with the apprehension that Korsakoff would suffer some irreparable disaster before his own arrival.

* Every capable soldier saw the ruinous mischief of the Archduke's withdrawal. "Not only are all prospects of our making any progress in Switzerland at an end, but the chance of maintaining the position now occupied is extremely precarious. The jealousy and mistrust that exists between the Austrians and Russians is inconceivable. I shall not pretend to offer an opinion on what might be the most advantageous arrangement for the army of Switzerland, but it is certain that none can be so bad as that which at present exists." Colonel Crauford, English military envoy, Sept. 5, 1799; Records: Army of Switzerland, vol. 79. The subsequent operations of Korsakoff are described in despatches of Colonel Ramsay and Lord Mulgrave, id. vol. 80, 81. Conversations with the Archduke Charles in those of Mr. Wickham, id. vol. 77.

Two roads lead from the Italian lakes to central Switzerland; one, starting from the head of Lago Maggiore and crossing the Gothard, ends on the shore of Lake Lucerne; the other, crossing the Splügen, runs from the Lake of Como to Reichenau, in the valley of the Rhine. The Gothard in 1799 was not practicable for cannon; it was chosen by Suvaroff, however, for his own advance, with the object of falling upon Massena's rear with the utmost possible speed. He left Bellinzona on the 21st of September, fought his way in a desperate fashion through the French outposts that guarded the defiles of the Gothard, and arrived at Altorf near the Lake of Lucerne. Here it was discovered that the westward road by which Suvaroff meant to strike upon the enemy's communications had no existence. Abandoning this design, Suvaroff made straight for the district where his colleague was encamped, by a shepherd's path leading north-eastwards across heights of 7,000 feet to the valley of the Muotta. Over this desolate region the Russians made their way; and the resolution which brought them as far as the Muotta would have brought them past every other obstacle to the spot where they were to meet their countrymen. But the hour was past. While Suvaroff was still struggling in the mountains, Massena advanced against Zürich, put Korsakoff's army to total rout, <small>Second Battle of Zürich, Sept. 20.</small> and drove it, with the loss of all its baggage and of a great part of its artillery, outside the area of hostilities.

The first rumours of the catastrophe reached Suvaroff on the Muotta; he still pushed on eastwards, and, though almost without ammunition, overthrew a corps commanded by Massena in person, and cleared the road over the Pragel at the point of the bayonet, arriving in Glarus on the 1st of October. Here the full extent of Korsakoff's disaster was made known to him. To advance or to fall back was ruin. It only remained for Suvaroff's army to make its escape across a wild and snow-covered mountain-tract into the valley of the Rhine, where the river flows below the northern heights of the Grisons. This exploit crowned a campaign which filled Europe with astonishment. The Alpine traveller of to-day turns with some distrust from narratives which characterise with every epithet of horror and dismay scenes which are the delight of our age ; but the retreat of Suvaroff's army, a starving, footsore multitude, over what was then an untrodden wilderness of rock, and through fresh-fallen autumn snow two feet deep, had little in common with the boldest feats of Alpine hardihood.* It was achieved with loss and suffering;

Retreat of Suvaroff.

* The despatches of Colonel Clinton, English attaché with Suvaroff, are in singular contrast to the highly-coloured accounts of this retreat common in histories. Of the most critical part he only says: " On the 6th the army passed the Panix mountain, which the snow that had fallen during the last week had rendered dangerous, and several horses and mules were lost on the march." He expresses the poorest opinion of Suvaroff and his officers: " The Marshal is entirely worn out and incapable of any exertion: he will not suffer the subject of the indiscipline of his army to be mentioned to him. He is popular with his army because he puts no check whatever on its licentiousness. His honesty is now his only remaining good quality." Records: Army of Switzerland, vol. 80. The elaborate plan for Suvaroff's and Korsakoff's combined movements, made as if Switzerland had been an open country and Massena's army a flock of sheep, was constructed by the Austrian colonel Weyrother, the same person who subsequently planned the battle of Austerlitz. On learning the plan from Suvaroff, Lord Mulgrave, who was no great genius, wrote to London demonstrating it brought the army from a position of the utmost danger into one of security; but it was followed by no renewed attack. Proposals for a combination between Suvaroff and the Archduke Charles resulted only in mutual taunts and menaces. The co-operation of Russia in the war was at an end. The French remained masters of the whole of the Swiss territory that they had lost since the beginning of the campaign.

In the summer months of 1799 the Czar had relieved his irritation against Austria by framing in concert with the British Cabinet the plan for a joint expedition against Holland. It was agreed that 25,000 English and 17,000 Russian troops, brought from the Baltic in British ships, should attack the French in the Batavian Republic, and raise an insurrection on behalf of the exiled Stadtholder. Throughout July the Kentish coast-towns were alive with the bustle of war; and on the 13th of August the first English division, numbering 12,000 men, set sail from Deal under the command of Sir Ralph Abercromby. After tossing off the Dutch coast for a fortnight, the troops landed at the promontory of the Helder. A Dutch corps was defeated on the sand-hills, and the English captured the fort of the Helder, commanding the Texel anchorage. Immediately afterwards a movement in favour of the Stadtholder broke out among the officers of the Dutch fleet. The captains hoisted the Orange flag, and brought their ships over to the English.

British and Russian expedition against Holland, Aug., 1799

its certain failure, and predicting almost exactly the events that took place.

This was the first and the last result of the expedition. The Russian contingent and a second English division reached Holland in the middle of September, and with them came the Duke of York, who now took the command out of the hands of Abercromby. On the other side reinforcements daily arrived from France, until the enemy's troops, led by General Brune, were equal in strength to the invaders. A battle fought at Alkmaar on the 19th of September gave the Allies some partial successes and no permanent advantage; and on the 3rd of October the Duke of York gained one of those so-called victories which result in the retreat of the conquerors. Never were there so many good reasons for a bad conclusion. The Russians moved too fast or too slow; the ditches set at nought the rules of strategy; it was discovered that the climate of Holland was unfavourable to health, and that the Dutch had not the slightest inclination to get back their Stadtholder. The result of a series of mischances, every one of which would have been foreseen by an average midshipman in Nelson's fleet, or an average sergeant in Massena's army, was that York had to purchase a retreat for the allied forces at a price equivalent to an unconditional surrender. He was allowed to re-embark on consideration that Great Britain restored to the French 8,000 French and Dutch prisoners, and handed over in perfect repair all the military works which our own soldiers had erected at the Helder. Bitter complaints were raised among the Russian officers against York's conduct of the expedition. He was accused of sacrificing the Russian regiments in battle, and of courting a general defeat in order not to expose his own men. The accusation was groundless. Where York was, treachery or bad faith was superfluous. York in command, the feeblest enemy became invincible. Incompetence among the hereditary chiefs of the English army had become part of the order of nature. The Ministry, when taxed with failure, obstinately shut their eyes to the true cause of the disaster. Parliament was reminded that defeat was the most probable conclusion of any military operations that we might undertake, and that England ought not to expect success when Prussia and Austria had so long met only with misfortune. Under the command of Nelson, English sailors were indeed manifesting that kind of superiority to the seamen of other nations which the hunter possesses over his prey; yet this gave no reason why foresight and daring should count for anything ashore. If the nation wished to see its soldiers undefeated, it must keep them at home to defend their country. Even among the Opposition no voice was raised to protest against the system which sacrificed English life and military honour to the dignity of the Royal Family. The collapse of the Anglo-Russian expedition was viewed with more equanimity in England than in Russia. The Czar dismissed his unfortunate generals. York returned home, to run horses at Newmarket, to job commissions with his mistress, and to earn his column at St. James's Park.

It was at this moment, when the tide of military success was already turning in favour of the Republic, that the revolution took place which made Bonaparte absolute ruler of France. Since the attack of the Government upon the Royalists in Fructidor, 1797, the Directory and the factions had come no nearer to a system of mutual concession, or to a peaceful acquiescence in the will of a parliamentary majority. The Directory, assailed both by the extreme Jacobins and by the Constitutionalists, was still strong enough to crush each party in its turn. The elections of 1798, which strengthened the Jacobins, were annulled with as little scruple as the Royalist elections in the preceding year; it was only when defeat in Germany and Italy had brought the Government into universal discredit that the Constitutionalist party, fortified by the return of a large majority in the elections of 1799, dared to turn the attack upon the Directors themselves. The excitement of foreign conquest had hitherto shielded the abuses of Government from criticism; but when Italy was lost, when generals and soldiers found themselves without pay, without clothes, without reinforcements, one general outcry arose against the Directory, and the nation resolved to have done with a Government whose outrages and extortions had led to nothing but military ruin. The disasters of France in the spring of 1799, which resulted from the failure of the Government to raise the armies to their proper strength, were not in reality connected with the defects of the Constitution. They were caused in part by the shameless jobbery of individual members of the Administration, in part by the absence of any agency, like that of the Conventional

Unpopularity of the Directory.

Commissioners of 1793, to enforce the control of the central Government over the local authorities, left isolated and independent by the changes of 1789. Faults enough belonged, however, to the existing political order; and the Constitutionalists, who now for the second time found themselves with a majority in the Councils, were not disposed to prolong a system which from the first had turned their majorities into derision. A party grew up around the Abbé Siéyès intent upon some change which should give France a government really representing its best elements. What the change was to be few could say; but it was known that Siéyès, who had taken a leading part in 1789, and had condemned the Constitution of 1795 from the moment when it was sketched, had elaborated a scheme which he considered exempt from every error that had vitiated its predecessors. As the first step to reform, Siéyès himself was elected to a Directorship then falling vacant. Barras attached himself to Siéyès; the three remaining Directors, who were Jacobins and popular in Paris, were forced to surrender their seats. Siéyès now only needed a soldier to carry out his plans. His first thought had turned on Joubert, but Joubert was killed at Novi. Moreau scrupled to raise his hand against the law; Bernadotte, a general distinguished both in war and in administration, declined to play a secondary part. Nor in fact was the support of Siéyès indispensable to any popular and ambitious soldier who was prepared to attack the Government. Siéyès and his friends offered the alliance of a party weighty in

Plans of Siéyès, 1799.

character and antecedents; but there were other well-known names and powerful interests at the command of an enterprising leader, and all France awaited the downfall of a Government whose action had resulted only in disorder at home and defeat abroad.

Such was the political situation when, in the summer of 1799, Bonaparte, baffled in an attack upon the Syrian fortress of St. Jean d'Acre, returned to Egypt, and received the first tidings from Europe which had reached him since the outbreak of the war. He saw that his opportunity had arrived. He determined to leave his army, whose ultimate failure was inevitable, and to offer to France in his own person that sovereignty of genius and strength for which the whole nation was longing. On the 7th of October a despatch from Bonaparte was read in the Council of Five Hundred, announcing a victory over the Turks at Aboukir. It brought the first news that had been received for many months from the army of Egypt; it excited an outburst of joyous enthusiasm for the general and the army whom a hated Government was believed to have sent into exile; it recalled that succession of victories which had been unchecked by a single defeat, and that Peace which had given France a dominion wider than any that her Kings had won. While every thought was turned upon Bonaparte, the French nation suddenly heard that Bonaparte himself had landed on the coast of Provence. "I was sitting that day," says Béranger in his autobiography, "in our reading-room with thirty or forty other persons. Suddenly the news was brought in that Bonaparte had returned from

Egypt. At the words, every man in the room started to his feet and burst into one long shout of joy." The emotion portrayed by Béranger was that of the whole of France. Almost everything that now darkens the early fame of Bonaparte was then unknown. *Bonaparte returns from Egypt, Oct., 1799.* His falsities, his cold, unpitying heart were familiar only to accomplices and distant sufferers; even his most flagrant wrongs, such as the destruction of Venice, were excused by a political necessity, or disguised as acts of righteous chastisement. The hopes, the imagination of France saw in Bonaparte the young, unsullied, irresistible hero of the Republic. His fame had risen throughout a crisis which had destroyed all confidence in others. The stale placemen of the factions sank into insignificance by his side; even sincere Republicans, who feared the rule of a soldier, confessed that it is not always given to a nation to choose the mode of its own deliverance. From the moment that Bonaparte landed at Fréjus, he was master of France.

Siéyès saw that Bonaparte, and no one else, was the man through whom he could overthrow the existing Constitution.* So little sympathy existed, however, between Siéyès and the soldier to whom he now offered his support, that Bonaparte only accepted Siéyès' project after satisfying himself that neither Barras nor Bernadotte would help him to supreme power. Once convinced of this, Bonaparte closed with Siéyès' offers. It was agreed that Siéyès and his friend Ducos should resign their

Conspiracy of Siéyès and Bonaparte.

* Miot de Melito, ch. ix. Lucien Bonaparte, Révolution de Brumaire, p. 31.

Directorships, and that the three remaining Directors should be driven from office. The Assemblies, or any part of them favourable to the plot, were to appoint a Triumvirate composed of Bonaparte, Siéyès, and Ducos, for the purpose of drawing up a new Constitution. In the new Constitution it was understood, though without any definite arrangement, that Bonaparte and Siéyès were to be the leading figures. The Council of Ancients was in great part in league with the conspirators: the only obstacle likely to hinder the success of the plot was a rising of the Parisian populace. As a precaution against attack, it was determined to transfer the meeting of the Councils to St. Cloud. Bonaparte had secured the support of almost all the generals and troops in Paris. His brother Lucien, now President of the Council of Five Hundred, hoped to paralyse the action of his own Assembly, in which the conspirators were in the minority.

Early on the morning of the 9th of November (18 Brumaire), a crowd of generals and officers met before Bonaparte's house. At the same moment a portion of the Council of Ancients assembled, and passed a decree which adjourned the session to St. Cloud, and conferred on Bonaparte the command over all the troops in Paris. The decree was carried to Bonaparte's house and read to the military throng, who acknowledged it by brandishing their swords. Bonaparte then ordered the troops to their posts, received the resignation of Barras, and arrested the two remaining Directors in the Luxembourg. During the

Coup d'état, 18 Brumaire (Nov. 9), 1799.

night there was great agitation in Paris. The arrest of the two Directors and the display of military force revealed the true nature of the conspiracy, and excited men to resistance who had hitherto seen no great cause for alarm. The Councils met at St. Cloud at two on the next day. The Ancients were ready for what was coming; the Five Hundred refused to listen to Bonaparte's accomplices, and took the oath of fidelity to the Constitution. Bonaparte himself entered the Council of Ancients, and in violent, confused language declared that he had come to save the Republic from unseen dangers. He then left the Assembly, and entered the Chamber of the Five Hundred, escorted by armed grenadiers. A roar of indignation greeted the appearance of the bayonets. The members rushed in a mass upon Bonaparte, and drove him out of the hall. His brother now left the President's chair and joined the soldiers outside, whom he harangued in the character of President of the Assembly. The soldiers, hitherto wavering, were assured by Lucien's civil authority and his treacherous eloquence. The drums beat; the word of command was given; and the last free representatives of France struggled through doorways and windows before the levelled and advancing bayonets.

The Constitution which Siéyès hoped now to impose upon France had been elaborated by its author at the close of the Reign of Terror. Designed at that epoch, it bore the trace of all those apprehensions which gave shape to the Constitution of 1795. The statutory outrages of 1793, the Royalist reaction

Siéyès' plan of Constitution.

shown in the events of Vendémiaire, were the perils from which both Siéyès and the legislators of 1795 endeavoured to guard the future of France. It had become clear that a popular election might at any moment return a royalist majority to the Assembly: the Constitution of 1795 averted this danger by prolonging the power of the Conventionalists; Siéyès overcame it by extinguishing popular election altogether. He gave to the nation no right but that of selecting half a million persons who should be eligible to offices in the Communes, and who should themselves elect a smaller body of fifty thousand, eligible to offices in the Departments. The fifty thousand were in their turn to choose five thousand, who should be eligible to places in the Government and the Legislature. The actual appointments were to be made, however, not by the electors, but by the Executive. With the irrational multitude thus deprived of the power to bring back its old oppressors, priests, royalists, and nobles might safely do their worst. By way of still further precaution, Siéyès proposed that every Frenchman who had been elected to the Legislature since 1789 should be inscribed for ten years among the privileged five thousand.

Such were the safeguards provided against a Bourbonist reaction. To guard against a recurrence of those evils which France had suffered from the precipitate votes of a single Assembly, Siéyès broke up the legislature into as many chambers as there are stages in the passing of a law. The first chamber, or Council of State, was to give shape to measures suggested by the

Executive; a second chamber, known as the Tribunate, was to discuss the measures so framed, and ascertain the objections to which they were liable; the third chamber, known as the Legislative Body, was to decide in silence for or against the measures, after hearing an argument between representatives of the Council and of the Tribunate. As a last impregnable bulwark against Jacobins and Bourbonists alike, Siéyès created a Senate whose members should hold office for life, and be empowered to annul every law in which the Chambers might infringe upon the Constitution.

It only remained to invent an Executive. In the other parts of his Constitution, Siéyès had borrowed from Rome, from Greece, and from Venice; in his Executive he improved upon the political theories of Great Britain. He proposed that the Government should consist of two Consuls and a Great Elector; the Elector, like an English king, appointing and dismissing the Consuls, but taking no active part in the administration himself. The Consuls were to be respectively restricted to the affairs of peace and of war. Grotesque under every aspect, the Constitution of Siéyès was really calculated to effect in all points but one the end which he had in view. His object was to terminate the convulsions of France by depriving every element in the State of the power to create sudden change. The members of his body politic, a Council that could only draft, a Tribunate that could only discuss, a Legislature that could only vote, Yes or No, were impotent for mischief; and the nation itself ceased to have a political existence as soon as it had selected its half-million notables.

<small>Siéyès and Bonaparte.</small> So far, nothing could have better suited the views of Bonaparte; and up to this point Bonaparte quietly accepted Siéyès' plan. But the general had his own scheme for what was to follow. Siéyès might apportion the act of deliberation among debating societies and dumb juries to the full extent of his own ingenuity; but the moment that he applied his disintegrating method to the Executive, Bonaparte swept away the flimsy reasoner, and set in the midst of his edifice of shadows the reality of an absolute personal rule. The phantom Elector, and the Consuls who were to be the Elector's tenants-at-will, corresponded very little to the power which France desired to see at its head. "Was there ever anything so ridiculous?" cried Bonaparte. "What man of spirit could accept such a post?" It was in vain that Siéyès had so nicely set the balance. His theories gave to France only the pageants which disguised the extinction of the nation beneath a single will: the frame of executive government which the country received in 1799 was that which Bonaparte deduced from the conception of an absolute central power. The First Consul summed up all executive authority in his own person. By his side there were set two colleagues whose only function was to advise. A Council of State placed the highest skill and experience in France at the disposal of the chief magistrate, without infringing upon his sovereignty. All offices, both in the Ministries of State and in the provinces,

were filled by the nominees of the First Consul. No law could be proposed but at his desire.

The institutions given to France by the National Assembly of 1789 and those given to it in the Consulate exhibited a direct contrast seldom found outside the region of abstract terms. Local customs, survivals of earlier law, such as soften the difference between England and the various democracies of the United States, had no place in the sharp-cut types in which the political order of France was recast in 1791 and 1799. The Constituent Assembly had cleared the field before it began to reconstruct. Its reconstruction was based upon the Rights of Man, identified with the principle of local self-government by popular election. It deduced a system of communal administration so completely independent that France was described by foreign critics as partitioned into 40,000 republics; and the criticism was justified when, in 1793, it was found necessary to create a new central Government, and to send commissioners from the capital into the provinces. In the Constitution of 1791, judges, bishops, officers of the National Guard, were all alike subjected to popular election; the Minister of War could scarcely move a regiment from one village to another without the leave of the mayor of the commune. In the Constitution of 1799 all authority was derived from the head of the State. A system of centralisation came into force with which France under her kings had nothing to compare. All that had once served as a check upon monarchical power, the legal

Contrast of the Institutions of 1791 and 1799.

Centralisation of 1799.

Parliaments, the Provincial Estates of Brittany and Languedoc, the rights of lay and ecclesiastical corporations, had vanished away. In the place of the motley of privileges that had tempered the Bourbon monarchy, in the place of the popular Assemblies of the Revolution, there sprang up a series of magistracies as regular and as absolute as the orders of military rank.* Where, under the Constitution of 1791, a body of local representatives had met to conduct the business of the Department, there was now a Préfet, appointed by the First Consul, absolute, like the First Consul himself, and assisted only by the advice of a nominated council, which met for one fortnight in the year. In subordination to the Préfet, an officer and similar council transacted the local business of the Arrondissement. Even the 40,000 Maires with their communal councils were all appointed directly or indirectly by the Chief of the State. There existed in France no authority that could repair a village bridge, or light the streets of a town, but such as owed its appointment to the central Government. Nor was the power of the First Consul limited to the administration. With the exception of the lowest and the highest members of the judicature, he nominated all judges, and transferred them at his pleasure to inferior or superior posts.

Such was the system which, based to a great extent upon the preferences of the French people, fixed even more deeply in the national character the willingness to depend upon an omnipresent, all-

* Law of Feb. 17, 1800 (28 Pluviôse, viii.).

directing power. Through its rational order, its regularity, its command of the highest science and experience, this system of government could not fail to confer great and rapid benefits upon the country. It has usually been viewed by the French themselves as one of the finest creations of political wisdom. In comparison with the self-government which then and long afterwards existed in England, the centralisation of France had all the superiority of progress and intelligence over torpor and self-contradiction. Yet a heavy, an incalculable price is paid by every nation which for the sake of administrative efficiency abandons its local liberties, and all that is bound up with their enjoyment. No practice in the exercise of public right armed a later generation of Frenchmen against the audacity of a common usurper: no immortality of youth secured the institutions framed by Napoleon against the weakness and corruption which at some period undermine all despotisms. The historian who has exhausted every term of praise upon the political system of the Consulate lived to declare, as Chief of the State himself, that the first need of France was the decentralisation of power.*

After ten years of disquiet, it was impossible that any Government could be more welcome to the French nation than one which proclaimed itself the representative, not of party or of opinion, but of France itself. No section of the nation had won a triumph in the establishment of the Consulate; no section had suffered a defeat. In his own elevation

State policy of Bonaparte.

* M. Thiers, Feb. 21, 1872.

Bonaparte announced the close of civil conflict. A Government had arisen which summoned all to its service; which would employ all, reward all, reconcile all. The earliest measures of the First Consul exhibited the policy of reconciliation by which he hoped to rally the whole of France to his side. The law of hostages, under which hundreds of families were confined in retaliation for local Royalist disturbances, was repealed, and Bonaparte himself went to announce their liberty to the prisoners in the Temple. Great numbers of names were struck off the list of the emigrants, and the road to pardon was subsequently opened to all who had not actually served against their country. In the selection of his officers of State, Bonaparte showed the same desire to win men of all parties. Cambacérès, a regicide, was made Second Consul; Lebrun, an old official of Louis XVI., became his colleague. In the Ministries, in the Senate, and in the Council of State the nation saw men of proved ability chosen from all callings in life and from all political ranks. No Government of France had counted among its members so many names eminent for capacity and experience. One quality alone was indispensable, a readiness to serve and to obey. In that intellectual greatness which made the combination of all the forces of France a familiar thought in Bonaparte's mind, there was none of the moral generosity which could pardon opposition to himself, or tolerate energy acting under other auspices than his own. He desired to see authority in the best hands; he sought talent and promoted it, but on the understanding that it took its direction from himself. Outside this limit ability was his enemy, not his friend; and what could not be caressed or promoted was treated with tyrannical injustice. While Bonaparte boasted of the career that he had thrown open to talent, he suppressed the whole of the independent journalism of Paris, and banished Mme. de Stael, whose guests continued to converse, when they might not write, about liberty. Equally partial, equally calculated, was Bonaparte's indulgence towards the ancient enemies of the Revolution, the Royalists and the priests. He felt nothing of the old hatred of Paris towards the Vendean noble and the superstitious Breton; he offered his friendship to the stubborn Breton race, whose loyalty and piety he appreciated as good qualities in subjects; but failing their submission, he instructed his generals in the west of France to burn down their villages, and to set a price upon the heads of their chiefs. Justice, tolerance, good faith, were things which had no being for Bonaparte outside the circle of his instruments and allies.

In the foreign relations of France it was not possible for the most unscrupulous will to carry aggression farther than it had been already carried; yet the elevation of Bonaparte deeply affected the fortunes of all those States whose lot depended upon France. It was not only that a mind accustomed to regard all human things as objects for its own disposal now directed an irresistible military force, but from the day when France submitted to Bonaparte, the political changes accompanying the advance of the

Effect of Bonaparte's autocracy outside France.

French armies took a different character. Belgium and Holland, the Rhine Provinces, the Cisalpine, the Roman, and the Parthenopean Republics, had all received, under whatever circumstances of wrong, at least the forms of popular sovereignty. The reality of power may have belonged to French generals and commissioners; but, however insincerely uttered, the call to freedom excited hopes and aspirations which were not insincere themselves. The Italian festivals of emancipation, the trees of liberty, the rhetoric of patriotic assemblies, had betrayed little enough of the instinct for self-government; but they marked a separation from the past; and the period between the years 1796 and 1799 was in fact the birth-time of those hopes which have since been realised in the freedom and the unity of Italy. So long as France had her own tumultuous assemblies, her elections in the village and in the county-town, it was impossible for her to form republics beyond the Alps without introducing at least some germ of republican organisation and spirit. But when all power was concentrated in a single man, when the spoken and the written word became an offence against the State, when the commotion of the old municipalities was succeeded by the silence and the discipline of a body of clerks working round their chief, then the advance of French influence ceased to mean the support of popular forces against the Governments. The form which Bonaparte had given to France was the form which he intended for the clients of France. Hence in those communities which

<small>France ceases to excite democracy abroad, but promotes equality under monarchical systems.</small>

directly received the impress of the Consulate, as in Bavaria and the minor German States, authority, instead of being overthrown, was greatly strengthened. Bonaparte carried beyond the Rhine that portion of the spirit of the Revolution which he accepted at home, the suppression of privilege, the extinction of feudal rights, the reduction of all ranks to equality before the law, and the admission of all to the public service. But this levelling of the social order in the client-states of France, and the establishment of system and unity in the place of obsolete privilege, cleared the way not for the supremacy of the people, but for the supremacy of the Crown. The power which was taken away from corporations, from knights, and from ecclesiastics, was given, not to a popular Representative, but to Cabinet Ministers and officials ranged after the model of the official hierarchy of France. What the French had in the first epoch of their Revolution endeavoured to impart to Europe—the spirit of liberty and self-government—they had now renounced themselves. The belief in popular right, which made the difference between the changes of 1789 and those attempted by the Emperor Joseph, sank in the storms of the Revolution.

Yet the statesmanship of Bonaparte, if it repelled the liberal and disinterested sentiment of 1789, was no mere cunning of a Corsican soldier, or exploit of mediæval genius born outside its age. Subject to the fullest gratification of his own most despotic or most malignant impulse, Bonaparte carried into his creations the ideas upon which the greatest European innovators before the

French Revolution had based their work. What Frederick and Joseph had accomplished, or failed to accomplish, was realised in Western Germany when its Sovereigns became the clients of the First Consul. Bonaparte was no child of the French Revolution; he was the last and the greatest of the autocratic legislators who worked in an unfree age. Under his rule France lost what had seemed to be most its own; it most powerfully advanced the forms of progress common to itself and the rest of Europe. Bonaparte raised no population to liberty; yet in extinguishing privilege and abolishing the legal distinctions of birth, in levelling all personal and corporate authority beneath the single rule of the State, he prepared the way for a rational freedom, when, at a later day, the Government of the State should itself become the representative of the nation's will.

Marginal note: Bonaparte legislates in the spirit of the reforming monarchs of the 18th century.

CHAPTER V.

Overtures of Bonaparte to Austria and England—The War continues—Massena besieged in Genoa—Moreau invades Southern Germany—Bonaparte crosses the St. Bernard, and descends in the rear of the Austrians—Battle of Marengo—Austrians retire behind the Mincio—Treaty between England and Austria—Austria continues the War—Battle of Hohenlinden—Peace of Lunéville—War between England and the Northern Maritime League—Battle of Copenhagen—Murder of Paul—End of the Maritime War—English Army enters Egypt—French defeated at Alexandria—They capitulate at Cairo and Alexandria—Preliminaries of Peace between England and France signed at London, followed by Peace of Amiens—Pitt's Irish Policy and his retirement—Debates on the Peace—Aggressions of Bonaparte during the Continental Peace—Holland, Italy, Switzerland—Settlement of Germany under French and Russian influence—Suppression of Ecclesiastical States and Free Cities—Its effects—Stein—France under the Consulate—The Civil Code—The Concordat.

THE establishment of the Consulate gave France peace from the strife of parties. Peace from foreign warfare was not less desired by the nation; and although the First Consul himself was restlessly planning the next campaign, it belonged to his policy to represent himself as the mediator between France and Europe. Discarding the usual diplomatic forms, Bonaparte addressed letters in his own name to the Emperor Francis and to King George III., deploring the miseries inflicted by war upon nations naturally allied, and declaring his personal anxiety to enter upon negotiations for peace. The reply of Austria, which was courteously worded, produced an offer on the part of Bonaparte to treat for peace upon

Overtures of Bonaparte to Austria and to England 1799.

the basis of the Treaty of Campo Formio. Such a proposal was the best evidence of Bonaparte's real intentions. Austria had re-conquered Lombardy, and driven the armies of the Republic from the Adige to within a few miles of Nice. To propose a peace which should merely restore the situation existing at the beginning of the war was pure irony. The Austrian Government accordingly declared itself unable to treat without the concurrence of its allies. The answer of England to the overtures of the First Consul was rough and defiant. It recounted the causes of war and distrust which precluded England from negotiating with a revolutionary Government; and, though not insisting on the restoration of the Bourbons as a condition of peace, it stated that no guarantee for the sincerity and good behaviour of France would be so acceptable to Great Britain as the recall of the ancient family.*

Few State papers have been distinguished by worse faults of judgment than this English manifesto. It was intended to recommend the Bourbons to France as a means of procuring peace: it enabled Bonaparte to represent England as violently interfering with the rights of the French people, and the Bourbons as seeking their restoration at the hand of the enemy of their country. The answer made to Pitt's Government from Paris was such as one high-spirited nation which had recently expelled its rulers might address to another that had expelled its rulers a century before. France, it was said, had as good a right to dismiss an incapable dynasty

* Parl. Hist. xxxiv. 1198. Thugut, Briefe, ii., 445.

as Great Britain. If Talleyrand's reply failed to convince King George that before restoring the Bourbons he ought to surrender his own throne to the Stuarts, it succeeded in transferring attention from the wrongs inflicted by France to the pretensions advanced by England. That it affected the actual course of events there is no reason to believe. The French Government was well acquainted with the real grounds of war possessed by England, in spite of the errors by which the British Cabinet weakened the statement of its cause. What the mass of the French people now thought, or did not think, had become a matter of very little importance.

The war continued. Winter and the early spring of 1800 passed in France amidst vigorous but concealed preparations for the campaign *Situation of the armies.* which was to drive the Austrians from Italy. In Piedmont the Austrians spent months in inaction, which might have given them Genoa and completed the conquest of Italy before Bonaparte's army could take the field. It was not until the beginning of April that Melas, their general, assailed the French positions on the Genoese Apennines; a fortnight more was spent in mountain warfare before Massena, who now held the French command, found himself shut up in Genoa and blockaded by land and sea. The army which Bonaparte was about to lead into Italy lay in between Dijon and Geneva, awaiting the arrival of the First Consul. On the Rhine, from Strasburg to Schaffhausen, a force of 100,000 men was ready to cross into Germany under the command of

Moreau, who was charged with the task of pushing the Austrians back from the Upper Danube, and so rendering any attack through Switzerland upon the communications of Bonaparte's Italian force impossible.

Moreau invades South Germany, April, 1800. Moreau's army was the first to move. An Austrian force, not inferior to Moreau's own, lay within the bend of the Rhine that covers Baden and Würtemberg. Moreau crossed the Rhine at various points, and by a succession of ingenious manœuvres led his adversary, Kray, to occupy all the roads through the Black Forest except those by which the northern divisions of the French were actually passing. A series of engagements, conspicuous for the skill of the French general and the courage of the defeated Austrians, gave Moreau possession of the country south of the Danube as far as Ulm, where Kray took refuge in his entrenched camp. Beyond this point Moreau's instructions forbade him to advance. His task was fulfilled by the severance of the Austrian army from the roads into Italy.

Bonaparte's own army was now in motion. Its destination was still secret; its very existence *Bonaparte crosses the Alps, May, 1800.* was doubted by the Austrian generals. On the 8th of May the First Consul himself arrived at Geneva, and assumed the command. The campaign upon which this army was now entering was designed by Bonaparte to surpass everything that Europe had hitherto seen most striking in war. The feats of Massena and Suvaroff in the Alps had filled his imagination with mountain warfare. A victory over nature more imposing than theirs might, in the present position of the Austrian forces in Lombardy, be made the prelude to a victory in the field without a parallel in its effects upon the enemy. Instead of relieving Genoa by an advance along the coast-road, Bonaparte intended to march across the Alps and to descend in the rear of the Austrians. A single defeat would then cut the Austrians off from their communications with Mantua, and result either in the capitulation of their army or in the evacuation of the whole of the country that they had won. Bonaparte led his army into the mountains. The pass of the Great St. Bernard, though not a carriage-road, offered little difficulty to a commander supplied with every resource of engineering material and skill; and by this road the army crossed the Alps. The cannons were taken from their carriages and dragged up the mountain in hollowed trees; thousands of mules transported the ammunition and supplies; workshops for repairs were established on either slope of the mountain; and in the Monastery of St. Bernard there were stores collected sufficient to feed the soldiers as they reached the summit during six successive days (May 15—20). The passage of the St. Bernard was a triumph of organisation, foresight, and good management; as a military exploit it involved none of the danger, none of the suffering, none of the hazard, which gave such interest to the campaign of Massena and Suvaroff.

Bonaparte had rightly calculated upon the unreadiness of his enemy. The advanced guard of the French army poured down the valley of the Dora-Baltea upon the scanty Austrian detachments at Ivrea and Chiusella, before Melas, who had in vain been warned of the departure of the French from Geneva, arrived with a few thousand men at Turin to dispute the entrance into Italy. Melas himself, on the opening of the campaign, had followed a French division to Nice, leaving General Ott in charge of the army investing Genoa. On reaching Turin he discovered the full extent of his peril, and sent orders to Ott to raise the siege of Genoa and to join him with every regiment that he could collect. Ott, however, was unwilling to abandon the prey at this moment falling into his grasp. He remained stationary till the 5th of June, when Massena, reduced to the most cruel extremities by famine, was forced to surrender Genoa to the besiegers. But his obstinate endurance had the full effect of a battle won. Ott's delay rendered Melas powerless to hinder the movements of Bonaparte, when, instead of marching upon Genoa, as both French and Austrians expected him to do, he turned eastward, and thrust his army between the Austrians and their own fortresses. Bonaparte himself entered Milan (June 2); Lannes and Murat were sent to seize the bridges over the Po and the Adda. The Austrian detachment guarding Piacenza was overpowered; the communications of Melas with the country north of the Po were completely severed. Nothing remained for the Austrian commander but to break through the French or to make his escape to Genoa.

Bonaparte cuts off the Austrian army from Eastern Lombardy.

The French centre was now at Stradella, half-way between Piacenza and Alessandria. Melas was at length joined by Ott at Alessandria, but so scattered were the Austrian forces, that out of 80,000 men Melas had not more than 33,000 at his command. Bonaparte's forces were equal in number; his only fear was that Melas might use his last line of retreat, and escape to Genoa without an engagement. The Austrian general, however, who had shared with Suvaroff the triumph over Joubert at Novi, resolved to stake everything upon a pitched battle. He awaited Bonaparte's approach at Alessandria. On the 12th of June Bonaparte advanced westward from Stradella. His anxiety lest Melas might be escaping from his hands increased with every hour of the march that brought him no tidings of the enemy; and on the 13th, when his advanced guard had come almost up to the walls of Alessandria without seeing an enemy, he could bear the suspense no longer, and ordered Desaix to march southward towards Novi and hold the road to Genoa. Desaix led off his division. Early the next morning the whole army of Melas issued from Alessandria, and threw itself upon the weakened line of the French at Marengo. The attack carried everything before it: at the end of seven hours' fighting, Melas, exhausted by his personal exertions, returned into Alessandria, and sent out tidings of a complete victory. It was at this moment that Desaix, who had turned at the sound of the cannon, appeared on the field, and declared that, although one battle had been lost, another might be won. A sudden cavalry-charge struck panic into the Austrians, who believed the battle ended and the foe

Battle of Marengo, June 14, 1800.

overthrown. Whole brigades threw down their arms and fled; and ere the day closed a mass of fugitives, cavalry and infantry, thronging over the marshes of the Bormida, was all that remained of the victorious Austrian centre. The suddenness of the disaster, the desperate position of the army, cut off from its communications, overthrew the mind of Melas, and he agreed to an armistice more fatal than an unconditional surrender. The Austrians retired behind the Mincio, and abandoned to the French every fortress in Northern Italy that lay west of that river. A single battle had produced the result of a campaign of victories and sieges. Marengo was the most brilliant in conception of all Bonaparte's triumphs. If in its execution the genius of the great commander had for a moment failed him, no mention of the long hours of peril and confusion was allowed to obscure the splendour of Bonaparte's victory. Every document was altered or suppressed which contained a report of the real facts of the battle. The descriptions given to the French nation claimed only new homage to the First Consul's invincible genius and power.*

Conditions of Armistice.

At Vienna the military situation was viewed more calmly than in Melas' camp. The conditions of the armistice were generally condemned, and any sudden change in the policy of Austria was prevented by a treaty with England, binding Austria, in return for British subsidies, and for a secret

Austria continues the war.

* Mémorial du Dépôt de la Guerre, 1826, iv., 268. Bentinck's despatch, June 16; Records: Italian States, vol. 59.

promise of part of Piedmont, to make no separate peace with France before the end of February, 1801. This treaty was signed a few hours before the arrival of the news of Marengo. It was the work of Thugut, who still maintained his influence over the Emperor, in spite of growing unpopularity and almost universal opposition. Public opinion, however, forced the Emperor at least to take steps for ascertaining the French terms of peace. An envoy was sent to Paris; and, as there could be no peace without the consent of England, conferences were held with the object of establishing a naval armistice between England and France. England, however, refused the concessions demanded by the First Consul; and the negotiations were broken off in September. But this interval of three months had weakened the authority of the Minister and stimulated the intrigues which at every great crisis paralysed the action of Austria. At length, while Thugut was receiving the subsidies of Great Britain and arranging for the most vigorous prosecution of the war, the Emperor, concealing the transaction from his Minister, purchased a new armistice by the surrender of the fortresses of Ulm and Ingolstadt to Moreau's army.*

* Thugut, Briefe ii. 227, 281, 393; Minto's despatch, Sept. 24, 1800; Records: Austria, vol. 60. "The Emperor was in the act of receiving a considerable subsidy for a vigorous prosecution of the war at the very moment when he was clandestinely and in person making the most abject submission to the common enemy. Baron Thugut was all yesterday under the greatest uneasiness concerning the event which he had reason to apprehend, but which was not yet certain. He still retained, however, a slight hope, from the apparent impossibility of any one's committing such an act of infamy and folly. I never saw him or any other man so affected as he was when he communicated this transaction to me to-day. I said

A letter written by Thugut after a council held on the 25th of September gives some indication of the stormy scene which then passed in the Emperor's presence. Thugut tendered his resignation, which was accepted; and Lehrbach, the author of the new armistice, was placed in office. But the reproaches of the British ambassador forced the weak Emperor to rescind this appointment on the day after it had been published to the world. There was no one in Vienna capable of filling the vacant post; and after a short interval the old Minister resumed the duties of his office, without, however, openly resuming the title. The remainder of the armistice was employed in strengthening the force opposed to Moreau, who now received orders to advance upon Vienna. The Archduke John, a royal strategist of eighteen, was furnished with a plan for surrounding the French army and cutting it off from its communications. Moreau lay upon the Isar; the Austrians held the line

that these fortresses being demanded as pledges of sincerity, the Emperor should have given on the same principle the arms and ammunition of the army. Baron Thugut added that after giving up the soldiers' muskets, the clothes would be required off their backs, and that if the Emperor took pains to acquaint the world that he would not defend his crown, there would not be wanting those who would take it from his head, and perhaps his head with it. He became so strongly affected that, in laying hold of my hand to express the strong concern he felt at the notion of having committed me and abused the confidence I had reposed in his counsels, he burst into tears and literally wept. I mention these details because they confirm the assurance that every part of these feeble measures has either been adopted against his opinion or executed surreptitiously and contrary to the directions he had given." After the final collapse of Austria, Minto writes of Thugut: "He never for a moment lost his presence of mind or his courage, nor ever bent to weak and unbecoming counsels. And perhaps this can be said of him alone in this whole empire." Jan. 3, 1801, *id.*

of the Inn. On the termination of the armistice the Austrians advanced and made some devious marches in pursuance of the Archduke's enterprise, until a general confusion, attributed to the weather, caused them to abandon their manœuvres and move straight against the enemy. On the 3rd of December the Austrians plunged into the snow-blocked roads of the Forest of Hohenlinden, believing that they had nothing near them but the rear-guard of a retiring French division. Moreau waited until they had reached the heart of the forest, and then fell upon them with his whole force in front, in flank, and in the rear. The defeat of the Austrians was overwhelming. What remained of the war was rather a chase than a struggle. Moreau successively crossed the Inn, the Salza, and the Traun; and on the 25th of December the Emperor, seeing that no effort of Pitt could keep Moreau out of Vienna, accepted an armistice at Steyer, and agreed to treat for peace without reference to Great Britain.

Battle of Hohenlinden, Dec. 3, 1800.

Defeats on the Mincio, announced during the following days, increased the necessity for peace. Thugut was finally removed from power. Some resistance was offered to the conditions proposed by Bonaparte, but these were directed more to the establishment of French influence in Germany than to the humiliation of the House of Hapsburg. Little was taken from Austria but what she had surrendered at Campo Formio. It was not by the cession of Italian or Slavonic provinces that the Government of Vienna paid for Marengo and Hohenlinden, but at the cost of that

P

divided German race whose misfortune it was to have for its head a sovereign whose interests in the Empire and in Germany were among the least of all his interests.

Peace of Lunéville, Feb. 9, 1801.

The Peace of Lunéville,* concluded between France and the Emperor on the 9th of February, 1801, without even a reference to the Diet of the Empire, placed the minor States of Germany at the mercy of the French Republic. It left to the House of Hapsburg the Venetian territory which it had gained in 1797; it required no reduction of the Hapsburg influence in Italy beyond the abdication of the Grand Duke of Tuscany; but it ceded to France, without the disguises of 1797, the German provinces west of the Rhine, and it formally bound the Empire to compensate the dispossessed lay Sovereigns in such a manner as should be approved by France. The French Republic was thus made arbiter, as a matter of right, in the rearrangement of the maimed and shattered Empire. Even the Grand Duke of Tuscany, like his predecessor in ejection, the Duke of Modena, was to receive some portion of the German race for his subjects, in compensation for the Italians taken from him. To such a pass had political disunion brought a nation which at that time could show the greatest names in Europe in letters, in science, and in art.

Peace with Naples.

Austria having succumbed, the Court of Naples, which had been the first of the Allies to declare war, was left at the mercy of Bonaparte. Its cruelties and tyranny called for severe

* Martens, vii., 296.

punishment; but the intercession of the Czar kept the Bourbons upon the throne, and Naples received peace upon no harder condition than the exclusion of English vessels from its ports. England was now left alone in its struggle with the French Republic. Nor was it any longer to be a struggle only against France and its dependencies. The rigour with which the English Government had used its superiority at sea, combined with the folly which it had shown in the Anglo-Russian attack upon Holland, raised against it a Maritime League under the leadership of a Power which England had offended as a neutral and exasperated as an ally. Since the pitiful Dutch campaign, the Czar had transferred to Great Britain the hatred which he had hitherto borne to France. The occasion was skilfully used by Bonaparte, to whom, as a soldier, the Czar felt less repugnance than to the Government of advocates and contractors which he had attacked in 1799. The First Consul restored without ransom several thousands of Russian prisoners, for whom the Austrians and the English had refused to give up Frenchmen in exchange, and followed up this advance by proposing that the guardianship of Malta, which was now blockaded by the English, should be given to the Czar. Paul had caused himself to be made Grand Master of the Maltese Order of St. John of Jerusalem. His vanity was touched by Bonaparte's proposal, and a friendly relation was established between the French and Russian Governments. England, on the other hand, refused to place Malta under Russian guardianship, either before or after

Russia turns against England.

its surrender. This completed the breach between the Courts of London and St. Petersburg. The Czar seized all the English vessels in his ports and imprisoned their crews (Sept. 9). A difference of long standing existed between England and the Northern Maritime Powers, which was capable at any moment of being made a cause of war. The rights exercised over neutral vessels by English ships in time of hostilities, though good in international law, were so oppressive that, at the time of the American rebellion, the Northern Powers had formed a league, known as the Armed Neutrality, for the purpose of resisting by force the interference of the English with neutral merchantmen upon the high seas. Since the outbreak of war with France, English vessels had again pushed the rights of belligerents to extremes. The Armed Neutrality of 1780 was accordingly revived under the auspices of the Czar. The League

<small>Northern Maritime League, Dec., 1800.</small> was signed on the 16th of December, 1800, by Russia, Sweden, and Denmark. Some days later Prussia gave in its adhesion.*

The points at issue between Great Britain and the Neutrals were such as arise between a great <small>* Points at issue.</small> naval Power intent upon ruining its adversary and that larger part of the world which remains at peace and desires to carry on its trade with as little obstruction as possible. It was admitted on all sides that a belligerent may search a neutral vessel in order to ascertain that it is not conveying contraband of war,

---

* Koch und Schoell. Histoire des Traités, vi., 6. Nelson Despatches, iv., 299.

and that a neutral vessel, attempting to enter a blockaded port, renders itself liable to forfeiture; but beyond these two points everything was in dispute. A Danish ship conveys a cargo of wine from a Bordeaux merchant to his agent in New York. Is the wine liable to be seized in the mid-Atlantic by an English cruiser, to the destruction of the Danish carrying-trade, or is the Danish flag to protect French property from a Power whose naval superiority makes capture upon the high seas its principal means of offence? England announces that a French port is in a state of blockade. Is a Swedish vessel, stopped while making for the port in question, to be considered a lawful prize, when, if it had reached the port, it would as a matter of fact have found no real blockade in existence? A Russian cargo of hemp, pitch, and timber is intercepted by an English vessel on its way to an open port in France. Is the staple produce of the Russian Empire to lose its market as contraband of war? or is an English man-of-war to allow material to pass into France, without which the repair of French vessels of war would be impossible?

These were the questions raised as often as a firm of shipowners in a neutral country saw their vessel come back into port cleared of its cargo, or heard that it was lying in the Thames awaiting the judgment of the Admiralty Court. Great Britain claimed the right to seize all French property, in whatever vessel it might be sailing, and to confiscate, as contraband of war, not only muskets, gunpowder, and cannon, but wheat, on which the provisioning of armies depended, and hemp, pitch, iron, and timber, out of which the navies of her adversary were formed. The Neutrals, on the other hand, demanded that a neutral flag should give safe passage to all goods on board, not being contraband of war; that the presence of a vessel of State as convoy should exempt merchantmen from search; that no port should be considered in a state of blockade unless a competent blockading force was actually in front of it; and that contraband of war should include no other stores than those directly available for battle. Considerations of reason and equity may be urged in support of every possible theory of the rights of belligerents and neutrals; but the theory of every nation has, as a matter of fact, been that which at the time accorded with its own interests. When a long era of peace had familiarised Great Britain with the idea that in the future struggles of Europe it was more likely to be a spectator than a belligerent, Great Britain accepted the Neutrals' theory of international law at the Congress of Paris in 1856; but in 1801, when the lot of England seemed to be eternal warfare, any limitation of the rights of a belligerent appeared to every English jurist to contradict the first principles of reason. Better to add a general maritime war to the existing difficulties of the country than to abandon the exercise of its naval superiority in crippling the commerce of an adversary. The Declaration of armed Neutrality, announcing the intention of the Allied Powers to resist the seizure of French goods on

War between England and the Northern Maritime Powers, Jan., 1801.

NELSON AT COPENHAGEN.

(p. 231

board their own merchantmen, was treated in this country as a declaration of war. The Government laid an embargo upon all vessels of the allied neutrals lying in English ports (Jan. 14th, 1801), and issued a swarm of privateers against the trading ships making for the Baltic. Negotiations failed to lower the demands of either side, and England prepared to deal with the navies of Russia, Denmark, Sweden, and Prussia.

At the moment, the concentrated naval strength of England made it more than a match for its adversaries. A fleet of seventeen ships of the line sailed from Yarmouth on the 12th of March, under the command of Parker and Nelson, with orders to coerce the Danes and to prevent the junction of the confederate navies. The fleet reached the Sound. The Swedish batteries commanding the Sound failed to open fire. Nelson kept to the eastern side of the channel, and brought his ships safely past the storm of shot poured upon them from the Danish guns at Elsinore. He appeared before Copenhagen at mid-day on the 30th of March. Preparations for resistance were *Battle of Copenhagen, April 2, 1801.* made by the Danes with extraordinary spirit and resolution. The whole population of Copenhagen volunteered for service on the ships, the forts, and the floating batteries. Two days were spent by the English in exploring the shallows of the channel; on the morning of the 2nd of April Nelson led his ships into action in front of the harbour. Three ran aground; the Danish fire from land and sea was so violent that after some hours Admiral Parker, who watched the engagement from the mid-channel, gave the signal of recall. Nelson laughed at the signal, and continued the battle. In another hour the six Danish men-of-war and the whole of the floating batteries were disabled or sunk. The English themselves had suffered most severely from a resistance more skilful and more determined than anything that they had experienced from the French, and Nelson gladly offered a truce as soon as his own victory was assured. The truce was followed by negotiation, and the negotiation by an armistice for fourteen weeks, a term which Nelson considered sufficient to enable him to visit and to overthrow the navies of Sweden and Russia.

But an event had already occurred more momentous in its bearing upon the Northern Confederacy than the battle of Copenhagen itself. On the night of the 23rd of March the Czar of Russia was assassinated in his palace. Paul's tyrannical violence, and his caprice verging upon insanity, had exhausted the patience of a court acquainted with no mode of remonstrance but homicide. Blood-stained hands brought to the Grand Duke Alexander the crown which he had consented to receive after a pacific abdication. Alexander immediately reversed the policy of his father, and sent friendly communications both to the Government at London and to the commander of the British fleet in the Baltic. The maintenance of commerce with England was in fact more important to Russia than the protection of its carrying trade. Nelson's attack was averted. A compromise was made between the two Governments, which saved Russia's interests without

Murder of Paul, March 23.

depriving England of its chief rights against France. The principles of the Armed Neutrality were abandoned by the Government of St. Petersburg in so far as they related to the protection of an enemy's goods by the neutral flag. Great Britain continued to seize French merchandise on board whatever craft it might be found; but it was stipulated that the presence of a ship of war should exempt neutral vessels from search by privateers, and that no port should be considered as in a state of blockade unless a reasonable blockading force was actually in front of it. The articles condemned as contraband were so limited as not to include the flax, hemp, and timber, on whose export the commerce of Russia depended. With these concessions the Czar was easily brought to declare Russia again neutral. The minor Powers of the Baltic followed the example of St. Petersburg; and the naval confederacy which had threatened to turn the balance in the conflict between England and the French Republic left its only trace in the undeserved suffering of Denmark.

Peace between England and the Northern Powers.

Eight years of warfare had left France unassailable in Western Europe, and England in command of every sea. No Continental armies could any longer be raised by British subsidies: the navies of the Baltic, with which Bonaparte had hoped to meet England on the seas, lay at peace in their ports. Egypt was now the only arena remaining where French and English combatants could meet, and the dissolution of the Northern Confederacy had determined

Affairs in Egypt.

the fate of Egypt by leaving England in undisputed command of the approach to Egypt by sea. The French army, vainly expecting reinforcements, and attacked by the Turks from the east, was caught in a trap. Soon after the departure of Bonaparte from Alexandria, his successor, General Kleber, had addressed a report to the Directory, describing the miserable condition of the force which Bonaparte had chosen to abandon. The report was intercepted by the English, and the Government immediately determined to accept no capitulation which did not surrender the whole of the French army as prisoners of war. An order to this effect was sent to the Mediterranean. Before, however, the order reached Sir Sidney Smith, the English admiral co-operating with the Turks, an agreement had been already signed by him at El Arish, granting Kleber's army a free return to France. (Feb. 24, 1800.) After Kleber, in fulfilment of the conditions of the treaty, had withdrawn his troops from certain positions, Sir Sidney Smith found himself compelled to inform the French General that in the negotiations of El Arish he had exceeded his powers, and that the British Government insisted upon the surrender of the French forces. Kleber replied by instantly giving battle to the Turks at Heliopolis, and putting to the rout an army six times as numerous as his own. The position of the French seemed to be growing stronger in Egypt, and the prospect of a Turkish re-conquest more doubtful, when the dagger of a fanatic robbed the French of their able chief, and transferred the command to General Menou, one of the very few French officers of marked incapacity who held command at any time during the war. The British Government, as soon as it learnt what had taken place between Kleber and Sir Sidney Smith, declared itself willing to be bound by the convention of El Arish. The offer was, however, rejected by the French. It was clear that the Turks could never end the war by themselves; and the British Ministry at last came to understand that Egypt must be re-conquered by English arms.

On the 8th of March, 1801, a corps of 17,000 men, led by Sir Ralph Abercromby, landed at Aboukir Bay. According to the plan of the British Government, Abercromby's attack was to be supported by a Turkish corps from Syria, and by an Anglo-Indian division brought from Ceylon to Kosseir, on the Red Sea. The Turks and the Indian troops were, however, behind their time, and Abercromby opened the campaign alone. Menou had still 27,000 troops at his disposal. Had he moved up with the whole of his army from Cairo, he might have destroyed the English immediately after their landing. Instead of doing so, he allowed weak isolated detachments of the French to sink before superior numbers. The English had already gained confidence of victory when Menou advanced in some force in order to give battle in front of Alexandria. The decisive engagement took place on the 21st of March. The French were completely defeated. Menou, however, still refused to concentrate his forces; and in the course of a few weeks 13,000 French troops which had been left behind at

English army lands in Egypt, March, 1801.

Cairo were cut off from communication with the rest of the army. A series of attempts made by Admiral Ganteaume to land reinforcements from France ended fruitlessly. Towards the end of June the arrival of a Turkish force enabled the English to surround the French in Cairo. The circuit of the works was too large to be successfully defended; on the other hand, the English were without the heavy artillery necessary for a siege. Under these circumstances the terms which had originally been offered at El Arish were again proposed to General Belliard for himself and the army of Cairo. They were accepted, and Cairo was surrendered to the English on condition that the garrison should be conveyed back to France (June 27). Soon after the capitulation General Baird reached Lower Egypt with an Anglo-Indian division. Menou with the remainder of the French army was now shut up in Alexandria. His forts and outworks were successively carried; his flotilla was destroyed; and when all hope of support from France had been abandoned, the army of Alexandria, which formed the remnant of the troops with which Bonaparte had won his earliest victories in Italy, found itself compelled to surrender the last stronghold of the French in Egypt (Aug. 30). It was the first important success which had been gained by English soldiers over the troops of the Republic; the first campaign in which English generalship had permitted the army to show itself in its true quality.

French capitulate at Cairo, June 27, 1801.

And at Alexandria, Aug 30.

Peace was now at hand. Soon after the Treaty of

Lunéville had withdrawn Austria from the war, unofficial negotiations had begun between the Governments of Great Britain and France. *Negotiations for peace.* The object with which Pitt had entered upon the war, the maintenance of the old European system against the aggression of France, was now seen to be one which England must abandon. England had borne its share in the defence of the Continent. If the Continental Powers could no longer resist the ascendancy of a single State, England could not struggle for the Balance of Power alone. The negotiations of 1801 had little in common with those of 1796. Belgium, which had been the burden of all Pitt's earlier despatches, no longer figured as an object of contention. The frontier of the Rhine, with the virtual possession of Holland and Northern Italy, under the title of the Batavian, Ligurian, and Cisalpine Republics, was tacitly conceded to France. In place of the restoration of the Netherlands, the negotiators of 1801 argued about the disposal of Egypt, of Malta, and of the colonies which Great Britain had conquered from France and its allies. Events decided the fate of Egypt. The restoration of Malta to the Knights of St. John was strenuously demanded by France, and not refused by England. It was in relation to the colonial claims of France that the two Governments found it most difficult to agree. Great Britain, which had lost no territory itself, had conquered nearly all the Asiatic and Atlantic colonies of the French Republic and of its Dutch and Spanish allies. In return for the restoration of Ceylon, the Cape of Good Hope,

Guiana, Trinidad, and various East and West Indian settlements, France had nothing to offer to Great Britain but peace. If peace, however, was to be made, the only possible settlement was by means of a compromise; and it was finally agreed that England should retain Ceylon and Trinidad, and restore the rest of the colonies which it had taken from France, Spain, and Holland. Preliminaries of peace embodying these conditions were signed at London on the 1st of October, 1801. Hostilities ceased; but an interval of several months between the preliminary agreement and the conclusion of the final treaty was employed by Bonaparte in new usurpations upon the Continent, to which he forced the British Government to lend a kind of sanction in the continuance of the negotiations. The Government, though discontented, was unwilling to treat these acts as new occasions of war. The conferences were at length brought to a close, and the definitive treaty between France and Great Britain was signed at Amiens on the 27th of March, 1802.*

Preliminaries of London, Oct 1, 1801.

Peace of Amiens, March 27, 1802.

The Minister who, since the first outbreak of war, had so resolutely struggled for the freedom of Europe, was no longer in power when Great Britain entered into negotiations with the First Consul. In the same week that Austria signed the Peace of Lunéville, Pitt had retired from office. The catastrophe which dissolved his last Continental alliance may possibly have disposed Pitt to make way for men

Pitt's retirement. Its cause.

---

* De Clercq, Traités de la France, i., 484.

who could treat for peace with a better grace than himself, but the immediate cause of his retirement was an affair of internal policy. Among the few important domestic measures which Pitt had not sacrificed to foreign warfare, was a project for the Legislative Union of Great Britain and Ireland. Ireland had up to this time possessed a Parliament nominally independent of that of Great Britain. Its population, however, was too much divided to create a really national government; and, even if the internal conditions of the country had been better, the practical sovereignty of Great Britain must at that time have prevented the Parliament of Dublin from being more than an agency of ministerial corruption. It was the desire of Pitt to give to Ireland, in the place of a fictitious independence, that real participation in the political life of Great Britain which had more than recompensed Scotland and Wales for the loss of separate nationality. As an earnest of legislative justice, Pitt gave hopes to the leaders of the Irish Catholic party that the disabilities which excluded Roman Catholics from the House of Commons and from many offices in the public service would be no longer maintained. On this understanding the Catholics of Ireland abstained from offering to Pitt's project a resistance which would probably have led to its failure. A majority of members in the Protestant Parliament of Dublin accepted the price which the Ministry offered for their votes. A series of resolutions in favour of the Legislative Union of the two countries was transmitted to England in the

Union of Ireland and Great Britain, 1800.

spring of 1800; the English Parliament passed the Act of Union in the same summer; and the first United Parliament of Great Britain and Ireland assembled at London at the beginning of the year 1801.

Pitt desires to emancipate the Catholics. Pitt now prepared to fulfil his virtual promise to the Irish Catholics. A measure obliterating the ancient lines of civil and religious enmity, and calling to public life a class hitherto treated as alien and hostile to the State, would have been in true consonance with all that was best in Pitt's own statesmanship. But the ignorant bigotry of King George III. was excited against him by men who hated every act of justice or tolerance to Roman Catholics; and it proved of greater force than the genius of the Minister. The old threat of the King's personal enmity was publicly addressed to Pitt's colleague, Dundas, when the proposal for Catholic emancipation was under discussion in the Cabinet; and, with a just regard for his own dignity, Pitt withdrew from office (Feb. 5, 1801), unable to influence a Sovereign who believed his soul to be staked on the letter of the Coronation Oath. The ablest members of Pitt's Government, Grenville, Dundas, and Windham, retired with their leader. Addington, Speaker of the House of Commons, became Prime Minister, with colleagues as undistinguished as himself. It was under the Government of Addington that the negotiations were begun which resulted in the signature of Preliminaries of Peace in October, 1801.

Pitt resigns, Feb. 1801.

Addington Minister.

Pitt himself supported the new Ministry in their

policy of peace; Grenville, lately Pitt's Foreign Minister, unsparingly condemned both the cession of the conquered colonies and the policy of granting France peace on any terms whatever. Viewed by the light of our own knowledge of events, the Peace of 1801 appears no more than an unprofitable break in an inevitable war; and perhaps even then the signs of Bonaparte's ambition justified those who, like Grenville, urged the nation to give no truce to France, and to trust to Bonaparte's own injustice to raise us up allies upon the Continent. But, for the moment, peace seemed at least worth a trial. The modes of prosecuting a war of offence were exhausted; the cost of the national defence remained the same. There were no more navies to destroy, no more colonies to seize; the sole means of injuring the enemy was by blockading his ports, and depriving him of his maritime commerce. On the other hand, the possibility of a French invasion required the maintenance of an enormous army and militia in England, and prevented any great reduction in the expenses of the war, which had already added two hundred millions to the National Debt. Nothing was lost by making peace, except certain colonies and military positions which few were anxious to retain. The argument that England could at any moment recover what she now surrendered was indeed a far sounder one than most of those which went to prove that the positions in question were of no real service. Yet even on the latter point there was no want of high authority. It was Nelson himself who assured the House of Lords

The Peace of 1801.

that neither Malta nor the Cape of Good Hope could ever be of importance to Great Britain.* In the face of such testimony, the men who lamented that England should allow the adversary to recover any lost ground in the midst of a struggle for life or death, passed for obstinate fanatics. The Legislature reflected the general feeling of the nation; and the policy of the Government was confirmed in the Lords and the Commons by majorities of ten to one.

Although the Ministry of Addington had acted with energy both in Egypt and in the Baltic, it was generally felt that Pitt's retirement marked the surrender of that resolute policy which had guided England since 1793. When once the Preliminaries of Peace had been signed in London, Bonaparte rightly judged that Addington would waive many just causes of complaint, rather than break off the negotiations which were to convert the Preliminaries into a definitive treaty. Accordingly, in his instructions to Joseph Bonaparte, who represented France at the conferences held at Amiens, the First Consul wrote through Talleyrand as follows:—"You are forbidden to entertain any proposition relating to the King of Sardinia, or to the Stadtholder, or to the internal affairs of Batavia, of Helvetia, or the Republic of Italy. None of these subjects have anything to do with the discussions of England." The list of subjects excluded from the consideration of England was the list of aggressions by which Bonaparte intended to fill up the interval of Con-

Aggressions of Bonaparte during the Continental peace.

* Parl. Hist. Nov. 3, 1801.

tinental peace. In the Treaty of Lunéville, the independence of the newly-established republics in Holland, Switzerland, and Italy had been recognised by France. The restoration of Piedmont to the House of Savoy had been the condition on which the Czar made peace. But on every one of these points the engagements of France were made only to be broken. So far from bringing independence to the client-republics of France, the peace of Lunéville was but the introduction to a series of changes which brought these States directly into the hands of the First Consul. The establishment of absolute government in France itself entailed a corresponding change in each of its dependencies, and the creation of an executive which should accept the First Consul's orders with as little question as the Prefect of a French department. Holland received its new constitution while France was still at war with England. *Holland, Sept., 1801.* The existing Government and Legislature of the Batavian Republic were dissolved (Sept., 1801), and replaced by a council of twelve persons, each holding the office of President in turn for a period of three months, and by a legislature of thirty-five, which met only for a few days in the year. The power given to the new President during his office was enough, and not more than enough, to make him an effective servant: a three-months' Minister and an Assembly that met and parted at the word of command were not likely to enter into serious rivalry with the First Consul. The Dutch peaceably accepted the constitution thus forced upon them; they possessed no means of resistance, and their affairs excited but little interest upon the Continent.

Far more striking was the revolution next effected by the First Consul. In obedience to orders sent from Paris to the Legislature of the Cisalpine Republic, a body of four hundred and fifty Italian representatives crossed the Alps in the middle of winter in order to meet the First Consul at Lyons, and to deliberate upon a constitution for the Cisalpine Republic.

Bonaparte made President of the Italian Republic, Jan., 1802.

The constitution had, as a matter of fact, been drawn up by Talleyrand, and sent to the Legislature at Milan some months before. But it was not for the sake of Italy that its representatives were collected at Lyons, in the presence of the First Consul, with every circumstance of national solemnity. It was the most striking homage which Bonaparte could exact from a foreign race in the face of all France; it was the testimony that other lands besides France desired Bonaparte to be their sovereign. When all the minor offices in the new Cisalpine Constitution had been filled, the Italians learnt that the real object of the convocation was to place the sceptre in Bonaparte's hands. They accepted the part which they found themselves forced to play, and offered to the First Consul the presidency of the Cisalpine State (Jan. 25, 1802). Unlike the French Consulate, the chief magistracy in the new Cisalpine Constitution might be prolonged beyond the term of ten years. Bonaparte had practically won the Crown of Lombardy; and he had given to France the example of a submission more unqualified than its own. A single phrase rewarded the people who had thus placed themselves in his hands. The Cisalpine Republic was allowed to assume the name of Italian Republic. The new title indicated the national hopes which had sprung up in Italy during the past ten years; it indicated no real desire on the part of Bonaparte to form either a free or a united Italian nation. In the Cisalpine State itself, although a good administration and the extinction of feudal privileges made Bonaparte's government acceptable, patriots who asked for freedom ran the risk of exile or imprisonment. What further influence was exercised by France upon Italian soil was not employed for the consolidation of Italy. Tuscany was bestowed by Bonaparte upon the Spanish Prince of Parma, and controlled by agents of the First Consul. Piedmont, which had long been governed by French generals, was at length definitely annexed to France.

Piedmont annexed to France, Sept., 1802.

Switzerland had not, like the Cisalpine Republic, derived its liberty from the victories of French armies, nor could Bonaparte claim the presidency of the Helvetic State under the title of its founder. The struggles of the Swiss parties, however, placed the country at the mercy of France. Since the expulsion of the Austrians by Massena in 1799, the antagonism between the Democrats of the town and the Federalists of the Forest Cantons had broken out afresh. A French army still occupied Switzerland; the Minister of the First Consul received instructions to interfere with all parties and consolidate none. In the autumn of

Intervention in Switzerland.

1801, the Federalists were permitted to dissolve the central Helvetic Government, which had been created by the Directory in 1798. One change followed another, until, on the 19th of May, 1802, a second Constitution was proclaimed, based, like that of 179S, on centralising and democratic principles, and almost extinguishing the old local independence of the members of the Swiss League. No sooner had French partisans created this Constitution, which could only be maintained by force against the hostility of Berne and the Forest Cantons, than the French army quitted Switzerland. Civil war instantly broke out, and in the course of a few weeks the Government established by the French had lost all Switzerland except the Pays de Vaud. This was the crisis for which Bonaparte had been waiting. On the 4th of October a proclamation appeared at Lausanne, announcing that the First Consul had accepted the office of Mediator of the Helvetic League. A French army entered Switzerland. Fifty-six deputies from the cantons were summoned to Paris; and, in the beginning of 1803, a new Constitution, which left the central Government powerless in the hands of France and reduced the national sovereignty to cantonal self-administration, placed Switzerland on a level with the Batavian and the Cisalpine dependencies of Bonaparte. The Rhone Valley, with the mountains crossed by the new road over the Simplon, was converted into a separate republic under the title of La Valais. The new chief magistrate of the Helvetic Confederacy entered

Bonaparte Mediator of the Helvetic League, Oct. 4, 1802.

upon his office with a pension paid out of Bonaparte's secret police fund.

Such was the nature of the independence which the Peace of Lunéville gave to Holland, to Northern Italy, and to Switzerland. The re-organisation of Germany, which was provided for by the same treaty, affected larger interests, and left more permanent traces upon European history. In the provinces ceded to France lay the territory of the ancient ecclesiastical princes of the empire, the Electors of Mainz, Cologne, and Trèves; but, besides these spiritual sovereigns, a variety of secular potentates, ranging from the Elector Palatine, with 600,000 subjects, to the Prince of Wiedrunkel, with a single village, owned territory upon the left bank of the Rhine; and for the dispossessed lay princes new territories had now to be formed by the destruction of other ecclesiastical States in the interior of Germany. Affairs returned to the state in which they had stood in 1798, and the comedy of Rastadt was renewed at the point where it had been broken off: the only difference was that the French statesmen who controlled the partition of ecclesiastical Germany now remained in Paris, instead of coming to the Rhine, to run the risk of being murdered by Austrian hussars. Scarcely was the Treaty of Lunéville signed when the whole company of intriguers who had touted at Rastadt posted off to the French capital with their maps and their money-bags, the keener for the work when it became known that by common consent the Free Cities of the Empire were

Settlement of Germany.

now to be thrown into the spoil, Talleyrand and his confidant Mathieu had no occasion to ask for bribes, or to manœuvre for the position of arbiters in Germany. They were overwhelmed with importunities. Solemn diplomatists of the old school toiled up four flights of stairs to the office of the needy secretary, or danced attendance at the parties of the witty Minister. They hugged Talleyrand's poodle; they vied with one another in gaining a smile from the child whom he brought up at his house.* The shrewder of them fortified their attentions with solid bargains, and made it their principal care not to be outbidden at the auction. Thus the game was kept up as long as there was a bishopric or a city in the market.

This was the real process of the German re-organisation. A pretended one was meanwhile enacted by the Diet of Ratisbon. The Diet deliberated during the whole of the summer of 1801 without arriving at a single resolution. Not even the sudden change of Russian policy that followed the death of the Emperor Paul and deprived Bonaparte of the support of the Northern Maritime League, could stimulate the German Powers to united action. The old antagonism of Austria and Prussia paralysed the Diet. Austria sought a German indemnity for the dethroned Grand Duke of Tuscany: Prussia aimed at extending its influence into Southern Germany by the annexation of Würzburg and Bam-

---

* Gagern, Mein Antheil, i., 119. He protests that he never carried the dog. The waltz was introduced about this time at Paris by Frenchmen returning from Germany, which gave occasion to the *mot* that the French had annexed even the national dance of the Germans.

berg. Thus the summer of 1801 was lost in interminable debate, until Bonaparte regained the influence over Russia which he had held before the death of Paul, and finally set himself free from all check and restraint by concluding peace with England.

No part of Bonaparte's diplomacy was more ably conceived or more likely to result in a permanent empire than that which affected the secondary States of Germany. The rivalry of Austria and Prussia, the dread of Austrian aggression felt in Bavaria, the grotesque ambition of the petty sovereigns of Baden and Würtemburg, were all understood and turned to account in the policy which from this time shaped the French protectorate beyond the Rhine. Bonaparte intended to give to Prussia such an increase of territory upon the Baltic as should counterbalance the power of Austria; and for this purpose he was willing to sacrifice Hanover or Mecklenburg: but he forbade Prussia's extension to the south. Austria, so far from gaining new territory in Bavaria, was to be deprived of its own outlying possessions in Western Germany, and excluded from all influence in this region. Bavaria, dependent upon French protection against Austria, was to be greatly strengthened. Baden and Würtemberg, enriched by the spoil of little sovereignties, of Bishoprics and Free Cities, were to look to France for further elevation and aggrandisement. Thus, while two rival Powers balanced one another upon the Baltic and the Lower Danube, the sovereigns of central and western Germany, owing everything to the Power that

German policy of Bonaparte.

had humbled Austria, would find in submission to France the best security for their own gains, and the best protection against their more powerful neighbours.

One condition alone could have frustrated a policy agreeable to so many interests, namely, the existence of a national sentiment among the Germans themselves. But the peoples of Germany cared as little about a Fatherland as their princes. To the Hessian and the Bavarian at the centre of the Empire, Germany was scarcely more than it was to the Swiss or the Dutch, who had left the Empire centuries before. The inhabitants of the Rhenish Provinces had murmured for a while at the extortionate rule of the Directory; but their severance from Germany and their incorporation with a foreign race touched no fibre of patriotic regret; and after the establishment of a better order of things under the Consulate the annexation to France appears to have become highly popular.* Among a race whose members could thus be actually conquered and annexed without doing violence to their feelings Bonaparte had no difficulty in finding willing allies. While the Diet dragged on its debates upon the settlement of the Empire, the minor States pursued their bargainings with the French Government; and on the 14th of August, 1801, Bavaria signed the first of those treaties which made the First Consul the patron of Western Germany. Two months later a secret treaty between France and Russia admitted the new Czar, Alexander, to a share in

Treaty between France and Russia for joint action in Germany, Oct. 11, 1801.

---

* Perthes, Politische Zustände, i., 311.

the reorganisation of the Empire. The Governments of Paris and St. Petersburg pledged themselves to united action for the purpose of maintaining an equilibrium between Austria and Prussia; and the Czar further stipulated for the advancement of his own relatives, the Sovereigns of Bavaria, Baden, and Würtemberg. The relationship of these petty princes to the Russian family enabled Bonaparte to present to the Czar, as a graceful concession, the very measure which most vitally advanced his own power in Germany. Alexander's intervention made resistance on the part of Austria hopeless. One after another the German Sovereigns settled with their patrons for a share in the spoil; and on the 3rd of June, 1802, a secret agreement between France and Russia embodied the whole of these arrangements, and disposed of almost all the Free Cities and the entire ecclesiastical territory of the Empire.

When everything had thus been settled by the foreigners, a Committee, to which the Diet of Ratisbon had referred the work of re-organisation, began its sessions, assisted by a French and a Russian representative. The Scheme which had been agreed upon between France and Russia was produced entire; and in spite of the anger and the threats of Austria it passed the Committee with no greater delay than was inseparable from everything connected with German affairs. The Committee presented the Scheme to the Diet: the Diet only agitated itself as to the means of passing the Scheme without violating those formalities which were the breath of its life. The

Diet of Ratisbon accepts French scheme.

proposed destruction of all the Ecclesiastical States, and of forty-five out of the fifty Free Cities, would extinguish a third part of the members of the Diet itself. If these unfortunate bodies were permitted to vote upon the measure, their votes might result in its rejection: if unsummoned, their absence would impair the validity of the resolution. By a masterpiece of conscientious pedantry it was agreed that the doomed prelates and cities should be duly called to vote in their turn, and that upon the mention of each name the answer "absent" should be returned by an officer. Thus, faithful to its formalities, the Empire voted the destruction of its ancient Constitution; and the sovereignties of the Ecclesiastics and Free Cities, which had lasted for so many centuries, vanished from Europe (March, 1803).*

End of German Ecclesiastical States and forty-five Free Cities, March, 1803.

The loss was small indeed. The internal condition of the priest-ruled districts was generally wretched; heavy ignorance, beggary, and intolerance reduced life to a gross and dismal inertia. Except in their patronage of music, the ecclesiastical princes had perhaps rendered no single service to Germany. The Free Cities, as a rule, were sunk in debt; the management of their affairs had become the perquisite of a few lawyers and privileged families. For Germany, as a nation, the destruction of these petty sovereignties was not only an advantage but an absolute necessity. The order by which they were superseded was not de-

Effect on Germany.

---

* Koch und Schoell, vi., 247. Beer, Zehn Jahre Oesterreichischer Politik, p. 35. Haüsser, ii., 398.

vised in the interest of Germany itself; yet even in the arrangements imposed by the foreigner Germany gained centres from which the institutions of modern political life entered into regions where no public authority had yet been known beyond the court of the bishop or the feudal officers of the manor.* Through the suppression of the Ecclesiastical States a Protestant majority was produced in the Diet. The change bore witness to the decline of Austrian and of Catholic energy during the past century; it scarcely indicated the future supremacy of the Protestant rival of Austria; for the real interests of Germany were but faintly imaged in the Diet, and the leadership of the race was still open to the Power which should most sincerely identify itself with the German nation. The first result of the changed character of the Diet was the confiscation of all landed property held by religious or charitable bodies, even where these had never advanced the slightest claim to political independence. The Diet declared the whole of the land held in Germany by pious foundations to be at the disposal of the Governments for purposes of religion, of education, and of financial relief. The more needy courts immediately seized so welcome an opportunity of increasing their revenues. Germany lost nothing by the dissolution of some hundreds of monasteries; the suppression of hospitals and the impoverishment of Universities was a doubtful benefit. Through the destruction of the Ecclesiastical States and the confiscation of Church lands, the support of an army of

* Perthes, Politische Zustände, ii., 402, seq.

priests was thrown upon the public revenues. The Elector of Cologne, who had been an indifferent civil ruler, became a very prosperous clergyman on £20,000 a year. All the members of the annexed or disendowed establishments, down to the acolytes and the sacristans, were credited with annuities equal in value to what they had lost. But in the confusion caused by war the means to satisfy these claims was not always forthcoming; and the ecclesiastical revolution, so beneficial on the whole to the public interest, was not effected without much severe and undeserved individual suffering.

The movement of 1803 put an end to an order of things more curious as a survival of the mixed religious and political form of the Holy Roman Empire than important in the actual state of Europe. The temporal power now lost by the Church in Germany had been held in such sluggish hands that its effect was hardly visible except in a denser prejudice and an idler life than prevailed under other Governments. The first consequence of its downfall was that a great part of Germany which had hitherto had no political organisation at all gained the benefit of a regular system of taxation, of police, of civil and of criminal justice. If harsh and despotic, the Governments which rose to power at the expense of the Church were usually not wanting in the love of order and uniformity. Officers of the State administered a fixed law where custom and privilege had hitherto been the only rule. Appointments ceased to be bought or inherited; trades and professions were thrown open; the

Governments in Germany become more absolute and more regular.

peasant was relieved of his heaviest feudal burdens. Among the newly consolidated States, Bavaria was the one where the reforming impulse of the time took the strongest form. A new dynasty, springing from the west of the Rhine, brought something of the spirit of French liberalism into a country hitherto unsurpassed in Western Europe for its ignorance and bigotry.* The Minister Montgelas, a politician of French enlightenment, entered upon the same crusade against feudal and ecclesiastical disorder which Joseph had inaugurated in Austria twenty years before. His measures for subjecting the clergy to the law, and for depriving the Church of its control over education, were almost identical with those which in 1790 had led to the revolt of Belgium; and the Bavarian landowners now unconsciously reproduced all the mediæval platitudes of the University of Louvain. Montgelas organised and levelled with a remorseless common sense. Among his victims there was a class which had escaped destruction in the recent changes. The Knights of the Empire, with their village jurisdictions, were still legally existent; but to Montgelas such a class appeared a mere absurdity, and he sent his soldiers to disperse their courts and to seize their tolls. Loud lamentation assailed the Emperor at Vienna. If the dethroned bishops had bewailed the approaching extinction of Christianity in Europe, the knights just as convincingly deplored the end of chivalry. Knightly honour, now being swept

margin notes: Bavaria. Reforms of Montgelas. Suppression of the Knights.

* Friedrich, Geschichte des Vatikanischen Konzils, i., 27, 174.

from the earth, was proved to be the true soul of German nationality, the invisible support of the Imperial throne. For a moment the intervention of the Emperor forced Montgelas to withdraw his grasp from the sacred rents and turnpikes; but the threatening storm passed over, and the example of Bavaria was gradually followed by the neighbouring Courts.

It was to the weak and unpatriotic princes who were enriched by the French that the knights fell victims. Among the knights thus despoiled by the Duke of Nassau was the Ritter vom Stein, a nobleman who had entered the Prussian service in the reign of Frederick the Great, and who had lately been placed in high office in the newly-acquired province of Münster. Stein was thoroughly familiar with the advantages of systematic government; the loss of his native parochial jurisdiction was not a serious one to a man who had become a power in Prussia; and although domestic pride had its share in Stein's resentment, the protest now published by him against the aggressions of the Duke of Nassau sounded a different note from that of his order generally. That a score of farmers should pay their dues and take off their hats to the officer of the Duke of Nassau instead of to the bailiff of the Ritter vom Stein was not a matter to excite deep feeling in Europe; but that the consolidation of Germany should be worked out in the interest of French hirelings instead of in the interests of the German people was justly treated by Stein as a subject for

Stein and the Duke of Nassau.

patriotic anger. In his letter to the Duke of Nassau,* Stein reproached his own despoiler and the whole tribe of petty princes with that treason to German interests which had won them the protection of the foreigner. He argued that the knights were a far less important obstacle to German unity than those very princes to whom the knights were sacrificed; and he invoked that distant day which should give to Germany a real national unity, over knights and princes alike, under the leadership of a single patriotic sovereign. Stein's appeal found little response among his contemporaries. Like a sober man among drunkards, he seemed to be scarcely rational. The simple conception of a nation sacrificing its internal rivalries in order to avert foreign rule was folly to the politicians who had all their lives long been outwitting one another at Vienna or Berlin, or who had just become persons of consequence in Europe through the patronage of Bonaparte. Yet, if years of intolerable suffering were necessary before any large party in Germany rose to the idea of German union, the ground had now at least been broken. In the changes that followed the Peace of Lunéville the fixity and routine of Germany received its death-blow. In all but name the Empire had ceased to exist. Change and re-constitution in one form or another had become familiar to all men's minds; and one real statesman at the least was already beginning to learn the lesson which later events were to teach to the rest of the German race.

<small>*Stein's attack on the Minor Princes.*</small>

* Pertz, Leben Stein, i., 257. Seeley's Stein, i., 125.

Four years of peace separated the Treaty of Lunéville from the next outbreak of war between France and any Continental Power. They were years of extension of French influence in every neighbouring State; in France itself, years of the consolidation of Bonaparte's power, and of the decline of everything that checked his personal rule. The legislative bodies sank into the insignificance for which they had been designed; everything that was suffered to wear the appearance of strength owed its vigour to the personal support of the First Consul. Among the institutions which date from this period, two, equally associated with the name of Napoleon, have taken a prominent place in history, the Civil Code and the Concordat. Since the middle of the eighteenth century the codification of law had been pursued with more or less success by almost every government in Europe. In France the Constituent Assembly of 1789 had ordered the statutes, by which it superseded the old variety of local customs, to be thus cast into a systematic form. A Committee of the Convention had completed the draft of a Civil Code. The Directory had in its turn appointed a Commission; but the project still remained unfulfilled when the Directory was driven from power. Bonaparte instinctively threw himself into a task so congenial to his own systematising spirit, and stimulated the efforts of the best jurists in France by his personal interest and pride in the work of legislation. A Commission of lawyers, appointed by the First Consul, presented the successive chapters of a Civil Code to the Council of State. In the discussions in the Council of State Bonaparte himself took an active, though not always a beneficial, part. The draft of each chapter, as it left the Council of State, was submitted, as a project of Law, to the Tribunate and to the Legislative Body. For a moment the free expression of opinion in the Tribunate caused Bonaparte to suspend his work in impatient jealousy. The Tribunate, however, was soon brought to silence; and in March, 1804, France received the Code which has formed from that time to the present the basis of its civil rights.

When Napoleon declared that he desired his fame to rest upon the Civil Code, he showed his appreciation of the power which names exercise over mankind. It is probable that a majority of the inhabitants of Western Europe believe that Napoleon actually invented the laws which bear his name. As a matter of fact, the substance of these laws was fixed by the successive Assemblies of the Revolution; and, in the final revision which produced the Civil Code, Napoleon appears to have originated neither more nor less than several of the members of his Council whose names have long been forgotten. He is unquestionably entitled to the honour of a great legislator, not, however, as one who, like Solon or like Mahomet, himself created a new body of law, but as one who most vigorously pursued the work of consolidating and popularising law by the help of all the skilled and scientific minds whose resources were at his command. Though faulty in parts, the Civil Code, through its conciseness,

Napoleon as a legislator.

its simplicity, and its justice, enabled Napoleon to carry a new and incomparably better social order into every country that became part of his Empire. Four other Codes, appearing at intervals from the year 1804 to the year 1810, embodied, in a corresponding form, the Law of Commerce, the Criminal Law, and the Rules of Civil and of Criminal Process.* The whole remains a monument of the legal energy of the period which began in 1789, and of the sagacity with which Napoleon associated with his own rule all the science and the reforming zeal of the jurists of his day.

Far more distinctively the work of Napoleon's own mind was the reconciliation with the Church of Rome effected by the Concordat. It was a restoration of religion similar to that restoration of political order which made the public service the engine of a single will. The bishops and priests, whose appointment the Concordat transferred from their congregations to the Government, were as much instruments of the First Consul as his prefects and his gendarmes. The spiritual wants of the public, the craving of the poor for religious consolation, were made the pretext for introducing the new theological police. But the

The Concordat.

* The first-hand account of the formation of the Code Napoleon, with the Procès-Verbal of the Council of State and the principal reports, speeches, &c., made in the Tribunate and the Legislative Bodies, is to be found in the work of Baron Locré, "La Legislation de la France," published at Paris in 1827. Locré was Secretary of the Council of State under the Consulate and the Empire, and possessed a quantity of records which had not been published before 1827. The Procès-Verbal, though perhaps not always faithful, contains the only record of Napoleon's own share in the discussions of the Council of State.

situation of the Catholic Church was in reality no worse in France at the commencement of the Consulate than its present situation in Ireland. The Republic had indeed subjected the non-juring priests to the heaviest penalties; but the exercise of Christian worship, which, even in the Reign of Terror, had only been interrupted by local and individual fanaticism, had long recovered the protection of the law, services in the open air being alone prohibited.* Since 1795 the local authorities had been compelled to admit the religious societies of their district to the use of church-buildings. Though the coup d'état of Fructidor, 1797, renewed the prosecu-

* The statement, so often repeated, that the Convention prohibited Christian worship, or "abolished Christianity," in France, is a fiction. Throughout the Reign of Terror the Convention maintained the State Church, as established by the Constituent Assembly in 1791. Though the salaries of the clergy fell into arrear, the Convention rejected a proposal to cease paying them. The non-juring priests were condemned by the Convention to transportation, and were liable to be put to death if they returned to France. But where churches were profaned, or constitutional priests molested, it was the work of local bodies, or of individual Conventionalists on mission, not of the law. The Commune of Paris shut up most, but not all, of the churches in Paris. Other local bodies did the same. After the Reign of Terror ended, the Convention adopted the proposal which it had rejected before, and abolished the State salary of the clergy (Sept. 20th, 1794). This merely placed all sects on a level. But local fanatics were still busy against religion; and the Convention accordingly had to pass a law (Feb. 23, 1795), forbidding all interference with Christian services. This law required that worship should not be held in a distinctive building (i.e., church), nor in the open air. Very soon afterwards the Convention (May 23) permitted the churches to be used for worship. The laws against non-juring priests were not now enforced, and a number of churches in Paris were actually given up to non-juring priests. The Directory was inclined to renew the persecution of this class in 1796, but the Assemblies would not permit it; and in July, 1797, the Council of Five Hundred passed a motion totally abolishing the legal penalties of non-jurors. This was immediately followed by the coup d'état of Fructidor.

tion of non-juring priests, it in no way checked the activity of the Constitutional Church, now free from all connexion with the Civil Government. While the non-juring priests, exiled as political offenders, or theatrically adoring the sacred elements in the woods, pretended that the age of the martyrs had returned to France, a Constitutional Church, ministering in 4,000 parishes, unprivileged but unharassed by the State, supplied the nation with an earnest and respectable body of clergy.* But in the eyes of the First Consul everything left to voluntary association was so much lost to the central power. In the order of nature, peasants must obey priests, priests must obey bishops, and bishops must obey the First Consul. An alliance with the Pope offered to Bonaparte the means of supplanting the popular organisation of the Constitutional Church by an imposing hierarchy, rigid in its orthodoxy and unquestioning in its devotion to himself. In return for the consecration of his own rule, Bonaparte did not shrink from inviting the Pope to an exercise of authority such as the Holy See had never even claimed in France. The whole of the existing French Bishops, both the exiled non-jurors and those of the Constitutional Church, were summoned to resign their Sees into the hands of the Pope; against all who refused to do so sentence of deposition was pronounced by the Pontiff, without a word heard in defence, or the shadow of a fault alleged. The Sees were re-organised, and filled up by

* Grégoire, Mémoires, ii., 87. Annales de la Religion, x., 441; Pressensé, L'Église et la Révolution, p. 359.

nominees of the First Consul. The position of the great body of the clergy was substantially altered in its relation to the Bishops. Episcopal power was made despotic, like all other power in France: thousands of the clergy, hitherto secure in their livings, were placed at the disposal of their bishop, and rendered liable to be transferred at the pleasure of their superior from place to place. The Constitutional Church vanished, but religion appeared to be honoured by becoming part of the State. *The Concordat destroys the Free Church.*

In its immediate action, the Napoleonic Church served the purpose for which it was intended. For some few years the clergy unflaggingly preached, prayed, and catechised to the glory of their restorer. In the greater cycle of religious change, the Concordat of Bonaparte appears in another light. How- *Results in Ultramontanism.* ever little appreciated at the time, it was the greatest, the most critical, victory which the Roman See has ever gained over the more enlightened and the more national elements in the Catholic Church. It converted the Catholicism of France from a faith already far more independent than that of Fénélon and Bossuet into the Catholicism which in our own day has outstripped the bigotry of Spain and Austria in welcoming the dogma of Papal infallibility. The lower clergy, condemned by the State to an intolerable subjection, soon found their only hope in an appeal to Rome, and instinctively worked as the emissaries of the Roman See. The Bishops, who owed their office to an unprecedented exercise of Papal power and to the destruction of religious independence in France, were not the men who could maintain a struggle with the Papacy for the ancient Gallican liberties. In the resistance to the Papacy which had been maintained by the Continental Churches in a greater or less degree during the eighteenth century, France had on the whole taken the most effective part; but, from the time when the Concordat dissolved both the ancient and the revolutionary Church system of France, the Gallican tradition of the past became as powerless among the French clergy as the philosophical liberalism of the Revolution.

In Germany the destruction of the temporal power of the Church tended equally to Ultramontanism. An archbishop of Cologne who governed half a million subjects was less likely to prostrate himself before the Papal Chair than an archbishop of Cologne who was only one among a regiment of churchmen. The spiritual Electors and Princes who lost their dominions in 1801 had understood by the interests of their order something more tangible than a body of doctrines. When not hostile to the Papacy, they had usually treated it with indifference. The conception of a Catholic society exposed to persecution at the hands of the State on account of its devotion to Rome was one which had never entered the mind of German ecclesiastics in the eighteenth century. Without the changes effected in Germany by the Treaty of Lunéville, without the Concordat of Bonaparte, Catholic orthodoxy would never have become identical with Ultramontanism. In this respect the opening years of

So do the German changes.

the present century mark a turning-point in the relation of the Church to modern life. Already, in place of the old monarchical Governments, friendly on the whole to the Catholic Church, events were preparing the way for that changed order with which the century seems destined to close;—an emancipated France, a free Italy, a secular, state-disciplined Germany, and the Church in conspiracy against them all.

CHAPTER VI.

England claims Malta—War renewed—Bonaparte occupies Hanover, and blockades the Elbe—Remonstrances of Prussia—Cadoudal's Plot—Murder of the Duke of Enghien—Napoleon Emperor—Coalition of 1805—Prussia holds aloof—State of Austria—Failure of Napoleon's attempt to gain naval superiority in the Channel—Campaign in Western Germany—Capitulation of Ulm—Trafalgar—Treaty of Potsdam between Prussia and the Allies—The French enter Vienna—Haugwitz sent to Napoleon with Prussian Ultimatum—Battle of Austerlitz—Haugwitz signs a Treaty of Alliance with Napoleon—Peace—Treaty of Presburg—End of the Holy Roman Empire—Naples given to Joseph Bonaparte—Battle of Maida—The Napoleonic Empire and Dynasty—Federation of the Rhine—State of Germany—Possibility of maintaining the Empire of 1806.

WAR was renewed between France and Great Britain in the spring of 1803. Addington's Government, in their desire for peace, had borne with Bonaparte's aggressions during all the months of negotiation at Amiens; they had met his complaints against the abuse of the English press by prosecuting his Royalist libellers; throughout the Session of 1802 they had upheld the possibility of peace against the attacks of their parliamentary opponents. The invasion of Switzerland in the autumn of 1802, following the annexation of Piedmont, forced the Ministry to alter its tone. The King's Speech at the meeting of Parliament in November declared that the changes in operation on the Continent demanded measures of security on the part of Great Britain. The naval and military forces of the country were restored to a war-footing;

England prepares for war, Nov., 1802.

the evacuation of Malta by Great Britain, which had hitherto been delayed chiefly through a misunderstanding with Russia, was no longer treated as a matter of certainty. While the English Government still wavered, a challenge was thrown down by the First Consul which forced them into decided action. The *Moniteur* published on the 13th of January, 1803, a report upon Egypt by Colonel Sebastiani, pointing in the plainest terms to the renewal of French attacks upon the East. The British Government demanded explanations, and declared that until satisfaction was given upon this point they should retain possession of Malta. Malta was in fact appropriated by Great Britain as an equivalent for the Continental territory added to France since the end of the war.*

<small>England claims Malta.</small>

It would have been better policy if, some months earlier, Bonaparte had been required to withdraw from Piedmont or from Switzerland, under pain of hostilities with England. Great Britain had as little technical right to retain Malta as Bonaparte had to annex Piedmont. The desire for peace had, however, led Addington's Government to remain inactive until Bonaparte's aggressions had become accomplished facts. It was now too late to attempt to undo them: England could only treat the settlement of Amiens as superseded, and claim compensation on its own side. Malta was the position most necessary to Great Britain, in order to prevent Bonaparte from carrying out projects in Egypt and Greece of which the Government had evidence inde-

* Papers presented to Parliament, 1802—3, p. 95.

pendent of Sebastiani's report. The value of Malta, so lately denied by Nelson, was now fully understood both in France and England. No sooner had the English Ministry avowed its intention of retaining the island than the First Consul declared himself compelled to take up arms in behalf of the faith of treaties. Ignoring his own violations of treaty-rights in Italy and Switzerland, Bonaparte declared the retention of Malta by Great Britain to be an outrage against all Europe. He assailed the British Ambassador with the utmost fury at a reception held at the Tuileries on the 13th of March; and, after a correspondence of two months, which probably marked his sense of the power and obstinacy of his enemy, the conflict was renewed which was now to continue without a break until Bonaparte was driven from his throne.

War, May 1803.

So long as England was without Continental allies its warfare was limited to the seizure of colonies and the blockade of ports: on the part of France nothing could be effected against the island Power except by actual invasion. There was, however, among the communities of Germany one which, in the arguments of a conqueror, might be treated as a dependency of England, and made to suffer for its connection with the British Crown. Hanover had hitherto by common agreement been dissociated from the wars in which its Elector engaged as King of England; even the personal presence of King George II. at the battle of Dettingen had been held no ground for violating its neutrality. Bonaparte, however, was untroubled by

Bonaparte and Hanover.

precedents in a case where he had so much to gain. Apart from its value as a possible object of exchange in the next treaty with England, Hanover would serve as a means of influencing Prussia: it was also worth so many millions in cash through the requisitions which might be imposed upon its inhabitants. The only scruple felt by Bonaparte in attacking Hanover arose from the possibility of a forcible resistance on the part of Prussia to the appearance of a French army in North Germany. Accordingly, before the invasion began, General Duroc was sent to Berlin to inform the King of the First Consul's intentions, and to soothe any irritation that might be felt at the Prussian Court by assurances of friendship and respect.

It was a moment of the most critical importance to Prussia. Prussia was the recognised guardian of Northern Germany; every consideration *Prussia and Hanover.* of interest and of honour required that its Government should forbid the proposed occupation of Hanover—if necessary, at the risk of actual war. Hanover in the hands of France meant the extinction of German independence up to the frontiers of the Prussian State. If, as it was held at Berlin, the cause of Great Britain was an unjust one, and if the connection of Hanover with the British Crown was for the future to make that province a scapegoat for the offences of England, the wisest course for Prussia would have been to deliver Hanover at once from its French and from its English enemies by occupying it with its own forces. The Foreign Minister, Count Haugwitz, appears to have recommended this step, but his counsels were overruled. King Frederick William III., who had succeeded his father in 1797, was a conscientious but a timid and spiritless being. Public affairs were in the hands of his private advisers, of whom the most influential were the so-called cabinet-secretaries, Lombard and Beyme, men credulously anxious for the goodwill of France, and perversely blind to the native force and worth which still existed in the Prussian Monarchy.* Instead of declaring the entry of the French into Hanover to be absolutely incompatible with the safety of the other North German States, King Frederick William endeavoured to avert it by diplomacy. He tendered his mediation to the British Government upon condition of the evacuation of Malta; and, when this proposal was bluntly rejected, he offered to the First Consul his personal security that Hanover should pay a sum of money in order to be spared the intended invasion.

Such a proposal marked the depth to which Prussian statesmanship had sunk; it failed to affect the First Consul in the slightest degree. While negotiations were still proceeding, a French division, commanded by General Mortier, entered Hanover (May, 1803). The

* "The King and his Ministers are in the greatest distress and embarrassment. The latter do not hesitate to avow it, and the King has for the last week shown such evident symptoms of dejection that the least observant could not but remark it. He has expressed himself most feelingly upon the unfortunate predicament in which he finds himself. He would welcome the hand that should assist him and the voice that should give him courage to extricate himself."—F. Jackson's despatch from Berlin, May 16, 1803; Records: Prussia, vol. 189.

Hanoverian army was lost through the follies of the civil Government; the Duke of Cambridge, commander of one of its divisions, less ingenious than his brother the Duke of York in finding excuses for capitulation, resigned his commission, and fled to England, along with many brave soldiers, who subsequently found in the army of Great Britain the opportunity for honourable service which was denied to them at home. Hanover passed into the possession of France, and for two years the miseries of French occupation were felt to the full. Extortion consumed the homely wealth of the country; the games and meetings of the people were prohibited; French spies violated the confidences of private life; law was administered by foreign soldiers; the press existed only for the purpose of French proselytism. It was in Hanover that the bitterness of that oppression was first felt which subsequently roused all North Germany against a foreign master, and forced upon the race the long-forgotten claims of patriotism and honour. *French enter Hanover, May, 1803. Oppression in Hanover, 1803—1805.*

Bonaparte had justly calculated upon the inaction of the Prussian Government when he gave the order to General Mortier to enter Hanover; his next step proved the growth of his confidence in Prussia's impassivity. A French force was despatched to Cuxhaven, at the mouth of the Elbe, in order to stop the commerce of Great Britain with the interior of Germany. The British Government immediately informed the Court of Berlin that it should blockade the *French blockade the Elbe.*

Elbe and the Weser against the ships of all nations unless the French soldiers withdrew from the Elbe. As the linen trade of Silesia and other branches of Prussian industry depended upon the free navigation of the Elbe, the threatened reprisals of the British Government raised very serious questions for Prussia. It was France, not England, that had first violated the neutrality of the river highway; and the King of Prussia now felt himself compelled to demand assurances from Bonaparte that the interests of Germany should suffer no further injury at his hands. A letter was written by the King to the First Consul, and entrusted to the cabinet-secretary Lombard, who carried it to Napoleon at Brussels (July, 1803). Lombard, the son of French parents who had settled at Berlin in the reign of Frederick the Great, had risen from a humble station through his skill in expression in the two languages that were native to him; and the accomplishments which would have made him a good clerk or a successful journalist made him in the eyes of Frederick William a counsellor for kings. The history of his mission to Brussels gives curious evidence both of the fascination exercised by Napoleon over common minds, and of the political helplessness which in Prussia could now be mistaken for the quality of a statesman. Lombard failed to obtain from Napoleon any guarantee or security whatever; yet he wrote back in terms of the utmost delight upon the success of his mission. Napoleon had infatuated him by the mere exercise of his personal charm. "What I cannot describe," said Lom-

Vain remonstrance of Prussia.

bard, in his report to the King relating his interview with the First Consul,* "is the tone of goodness and noble frankness with which he expressed his reverence for your Majesty's rights, and asked for that confidence from your Majesty which he so well deserves." "I only wish," he cried at the close of Napoleon's address, "that I could convey to the King, my master, every one of your words and the tone in which they are uttered; he would then, I am sure, feel a double joy at the justice with which you have always been treated at his hands." Lombard's colleagues at Berlin were perhaps not stronger men than the envoy himself, but they were at least beyond the range of Napoleon's voice and glance, and they received this rhapsody with coldness. They complained that no single concession had been made by the First Consul upon the points raised by the King. Cuxhaven continued in French hands; the British inexorably blockaded the Germans upon their own neutral waters; and the cautious statecraft of Prussia proved as valueless to Germany as the obstinate, speculating warfare of Austria.

There was, however, a Power which watched the advance of French dominion into Northern Germany with less complaisance than the Germans themselves. The Czar of Russia had gradually

<small>Alexander displeased.</small>

---

* Häusser ii., 472. There are interesting accounts of Lombard and the other leading persons of Berlin in F. Jackson's despatches of this date. The charge of gross personal immorality made against Lombard is brought against almost every German public man of the time in the writings of opponents. History and politics are, however, a bad tribunal of private character.

s

come to understand the part allotted to him by Bonaparte since the Peace of Lunéville, and was no longer inclined to serve as the instrument of French ambition. Bonaparte's occupation of Hanover changed the attitude of Alexander into one of coldness and distrust. Alexander saw and lamented the help which he himself had given to Bonaparte in Germany: events that now took place in France itself, as well as the progress of French intrigues in Turkey,* threw him into the arms of Bonaparte's enemies, and prepared the way for a new European coalition. The First Consul had determined to assume the dignity of Emperor. The renewal of war with England excited a new outburst of enthusiasm for his person; nothing was wanting to place the crown on his head but the discovery of a plot against his life. Such a plot had been long and carefully followed by the police. A Breton gentleman, Georges Cadoudal, had formed the design of attacking the First Consul in the streets of Paris in the midst of his guards. Cadoudal and his fellow-conspirators, including General Pichegru, were traced by the police from the coast of Normandy to Paris: an unsuccessful attempt was made to lure the Count of Artois, and other royal patrons of the conspiracy, from Great Britain. When all the conspirators who could be enticed to

Bonaparte about to become Emperor.

---

* Fournier, Gentz und Cobenzl, p. 79. Beer, Zehn Jahre, p. 49. The despatches of Sir J. Warren of this date from St. Petersburg (Records: Russia, vol. 175) are full of plans for meeting an expected invasion of the Morea and the possible liberation of the Greeks by Bonaparte. They give the impression that Eastern affairs were really the dominant interest with Alexander in his breach with France.

MURDER OF THE DUKE OF ENGHIEN.

(p. 275.)

France were collected within the capital, the police, who had watched every stage of the movement, began to make arrests. Moreau, the last Republican soldier of France, was charged with complicity in the plot. Pichegru and Cadoudal were thrown into prison, there to await their doom; Moreau, who probably wished for the overthrow of the Consular Government, but had no part in the design against Bonaparte's life,* was kept under arrest and loaded with official calumny. One sacrifice more remained to be made, in place of the Bourbon d'Artois, who baffled the police of the First Consul beyond the seas. In the territory of Baden, twelve miles from the French frontier, there lived a prince of the exiled house, the Duke of Enghien, a soldier under the first Coalition against France, now a harmless dependent on the bounty of England. French spies surrounded him; his excursions into the mountains gave rise to a suspicion that he was concerned in Pichegru's plot. This was enough to mark him for destruction. Bonaparte gave orders that he should be seized, brought to Paris, and executed. On the 15th of March, 1804, a troop of French soldiers crossed the Rhine and arrested the Duke in his own house at Ettenheim, They arrived with him at Paris on the 20th. He was taken to the fort of Vincennes without entering the city. On that same night a commission of six colonels sat in judgment upon the prisoner, whose grave was already dug, and pronounced sentence of death without hearing a word of

<small>Murder of the Duke of Enghien, March 20, 1804.</small>

---

* Miot de Melito, i., ch. 16.   Savary, ii., 32.

evidence. At daybreak the Duke was led out and shot.

If some barbaric instinct made the slaughter of his predecessor's kindred in Bonaparte's own eyes the omen of a successful usurpation, it was not so with Europe generally. One universal sense of horror passed over the Continent. The Court of Russia put on mourning; even the Diet of Ratisbon showed signs of human passion at the indignity done to Germany by the seizure of the Duke of Enghien on German soil. Austria kept silent, but watched the signs of coming war. France alone showed no pity. Before the Duke of Enghien had been dead a week, the Senate besought Napoleon to give to France the security of a hereditary throne. Prefects, bishops, mayors, and councils with one voice repeated the official prayer. A resolution in favour of imperial rule was brought forward in the Tribunate, and passed, after a noble and solitary protest on the part of Carnot. A decree of the Senate embodied the terms of the new Constitution; and on the 18th of May, without waiting for the sanction of a national vote, Napoleon assumed the title of Emperor of the French.

Napoleon Emperor, May 18, 1804.

In France itself the change was one more of the name than of the substance of power. Napoleon could not be vested with a more absolute authority than he already possessed; but the forms of republican equality vanished; and although the real social equality given to France by the Revolution was beyond reach of change, the nation had to put up with a bastard Court and a fictitious aristocracy of Corsican princes, Terrorist excellencies, and Jacobin dukes. The new dynasty was recognised at Vienna and Berlin: on the part of Austria it received the compliment of an imitation. Three months after the assumption of the Imperial title by Napoleon, the Emperor Francis (Emperor in Germany, but King in Hungary and Bohemia) assumed the title of Emperor of all his Austrian dominions. The true reason for this act was the virtual dissolution of the Germanic system by the Peace of Lunéville, and the probability that the old Imperial dignity, if preserved in name, would soon be transferred to some client of Napoleon or to Napoleon himself. Such an apprehension was, however, not one that could be confessed to Europe. Instead of the ruin of Germany, the grandeur of Austria was made the ostensible ground of change. In language which seemed to be borrowed from the scriptural history of Nebuchadnezzar, the Emperor Francis declared that, although no possible addition could be made to his own personal dignity, as Roman Emperor, yet the ancient glory of the Austrian House, the grandeur of the principalities and kingdoms which were united under its dominion, required that the Sovereigns of Austria should hold a title equal to that of the greatest European throne. A general war against Napoleon was already being proposed by the Court of St. Petersburg; but for the present the Corsican and the Hapsburg Cæsar exchanged their hypocritical congratulations.*

margin: Title of Emperor of Austria, Aug., 1804.

---

* A protest handed in at Vienna by Louis XVIII. against Napoleon's title was burnt in the presence of the French ambassador. The Austrian

Almost at the same time that Bonaparte ascended the throne, Pitt returned to power in Great Britain. He was summoned by the general distrust felt in Addington's Ministry, and by the belief that no statesman but himself could rally the Powers of Europe against the common enemy. Pitt was not long in framing with Russia the plan of a third Coalition. The Czar broke off diplomatic intercourse with Napoleon in September, 1804, and induced the Court of Vienna to pledge itself to resist any further extension of French power. Sweden entered into engagements with Great Britain. On the opening of Parliament at the beginning of 1805, King George III. announced that an understanding existed between Great Britain and Russia, and asked in general terms for a provision for Continental subsidies. In April, a treaty was signed at St. Petersburg by the representatives of Russia and Great Britain, far more comprehensive and more serious in its provisions than any which had yet united the Powers against France.* Russia and England bound themselves to direct their efforts to the formation of a European League capable of placing five hundred thousand men in the field. Great Britain undertook to furnish subsidies to every member of the League; no peace was to be concluded with France but by common consent; conquests

Marginal notes: Pitt again Minister, May, 1804. — Coalition of 1805.

title was assumed on August 10, but the publication was delayed a day on account of the sad memories of August 10, 1792. Fournier, p. 102. Beer, p. 60.

* Papers presented to Parliament, 28th January, 1806, and 5th May, 1815.

made by any of the belligerents were to remain unappropriated until the general peace; and at the termination of the war a Congress was to fix certain disputed points of international right, and to establish a federative European system for their maintenance and enforcement. As the immediate objects of the League, the treaty specified the expulsion of the French from Holland, Switzerland, Italy, and Northern Germany; the re-establishment of the King of Sardinia in Piedmont, with an increase of territory; and the creation of a solid barrier against any future usurpations of France. The last expression signified the union of Holland and part of Belgium under the House of Orange. In this respect, as in the provision for a common disposal of conquests and for the settlement of European affairs by a Congress, the Anglo-Russian Treaty of 1805 defined the policy actually carried out in 1814. Other territorial changes now suggested by Pitt, including the annexation of the Rhenish Provinces to the Prussian Monarchy, were not embodied in the treaty, but became from this time understood possibilities.

England and Russia had, however, some difficulty in securing allies. Although in violation of his promises to Austria, Napoleon had accepted the title of King of Italy from the Senate of the Italian Republic, and had crowned himself with the Iron Crown of Lombardy (March, 1805), the Ministers at Vienna would have preferred peace, if that had been possible; and their master reluctantly consented to a war against Napoleon when war in some form or other seemed inevitable.

The policy of Prussia was doubtful. For two years past Napoleon had made every effort to induce Prussia to enter into alliance with himself. After the invasion of Hanover he had doubled his attentions to the Court of Berlin, and had spared nothing in the way of promises and assurances of friendship to win the King over to his side. The neutrality of Prussia was of no great service to France: its support would have been of priceless value, rendering any attack upon France by Russia or Austria almost impossible, and thus enabling Napoleon to throw his whole strength into the combat with Great Britain. In the spring of 1804, the King of Prussia, uncertain of the friendship of the Czar, and still unconvinced of the vanity of Napoleon's professions, had inclined to a defensive alliance with France. The news of the murder of the Duke of Enghien, arriving almost simultaneously with a message of goodwill from St. Petersburg, led him to abandon this project of alliance, but caused no breach with Napoleon. Frederick William adhered to the temporising policy which Prussia had followed since 1795, and the Foreign Minister, Haugwitz, who had recommended bolder measures, withdrew for a time from the Court.* Baron Hardenberg, who had already acted as his deputy, stepped into his place. Hardenberg, the negotiator of the peace of Basle, had for the last ten years advocated a system of neutrality. A politician quick to grasp new social and political ideas, he was

Policy of Prussia.

* Hardenberg, ii., 50 : corrected in the articles on Hardenberg and Haugwitz in the Deutsch Allgemeine Biographie.

without that insight into the real forces at work in Europe which, in spite of errors in detail, made the political aims of Pitt, and of many far inferior men, substantially just and correct. So late as the end of the year 1804, Hardenberg not only failed to recognise the dangers to which Prussia was exposed from Napoleon's ambition, but conceived it to be still possible for Prussia to avert war between France and the Allied Powers by maintaining a good understanding with all parties alike. Hardenberg's neutrality excited the wrath of the Russian Cabinet. While Metternich, the Austrian ambassador at Berlin, cautiously felt his way, the Czar proposed in the last resort to force Prussia to take up arms. A few months more passed; and, when hostilities were on the point of breaking out, Hanover was definitely offered to Prussia by Napoleon as the price of an alliance. Hardenberg, still believing that it lay within the power of Prussia, by means of a French alliance, both to curb Napoleon and to prevent a European war, urged the King to close with the offer of the French Emperor.* But the King shrank from a decision which involved the possibility of immediate war. The offer of Hanover was rejected, and Prussia connected itself neither with Napoleon nor his enemies.

margin note: Prussia neutral.

---

* Hardenberg, v., 167. Hardenberg was meanwhile representing himself to the British and Russian envoys as the partisan of the Allies. "He declared that he saw it was become impossible for this country to remain neutral, and that he should unequivocally make known his sentiments to that effect to the King. He added that if the decision depended upon himself, Russia need entertain no apprehension as to the part he should take."—Jackson, Sept. 3, 1805; Records: Prussia, vol. 194.

Pitt, the author of the Coalition of 1805, had formed the most sanguine estimate of the armaments of his allies. Austria was said to have entered upon a new era since the peace of Lunéville, and to have turned to the best account all the disasters of its former campaigns. There had indeed been no want of fine professions from Vienna, but Pitt knew little of the real state of affairs. The Archduke Charles had been placed at the head of the military administration, and entrusted with extraordinary powers; but the whole force of routine and corruption was ranged against him. He was deceived by his subordinates; and after three years of reorganisation he resigned his post, confessing that he left the army no nearer efficiency than it was before. Charles was replaced at the War Office by General Mack. Within six months this bustling charlatan imagined himself to have effected the reorganisation of which the Archduke despaired,* while he had in fact only introduced new confusion into an army already hampered beyond any in Europe by its variety of races and languages.

State of Austria. The army.

If the military reforms of Austria were delusive, its political reforms were still more so. The Emperor had indeed consented to unite the Ministers, who had hitherto worked independently, in a Council of State; but here reform stopped. Cobenzl, who was now First Minister, understood nothing but diplomacy. Men continued in office whose presence

Political condition of Austria.

---

* Gentz, Schriften, iii., 60. Boer, 132, 141. Fournier, 104. Springer, i., 64.

was an insuperable bar to any intelligent action: even in that mechanical routine which, in the eyes of the Emperor Francis, constituted the life of the State, everything was antiquated and self-contradictory. In all that affected the mental life of the people the years that followed the peace of Lunéville were distinctly retrograde. Education was placed more than ever in the hands of the priests; the censorship of the press was given to the police; a commission was charged with the examination of all the books printed during the reign of the Emperor Joseph, and above two thousand works, which had come into being during that brief period of Austrian liberalism, were suppressed and destroyed. Trade regulations were issued which combined the extravagance of the French Reign of Terror with the ignorance of the Middle Ages. All the grain in the country was ordered to be sold before a certain date, and the Jews were prohibited from carrying on the corn-trade for a year. Such were the reforms described by Pitt in the English Parliament as having effected the regeneration of Austria. Nearer home things were judged in a truer light. Mack's paper-regiments, the helplessness and unreality of the whole system of Austrian officialism, were correctly appreciated by the men who had been most in earnest during the last war. Even Thugut now thought a contest hopeless. The Archduke Charles argued to the end for peace, and entered upon the war with the presentiment of defeat and ruin.

The plans of the Allies for the campaign of 1805

covered an immense field.* It was intended that one Austrian army should operate in Lombardy under the Archduke Charles, while a second, under General Mack, entered Bavaria, and there awaited the arrival of the Russians, who were to unite with it in invading France: British and Russian contingents were to combine with the King of Sweden in Pomerania, and with the King of Naples in Southern Italy. At the head-quarters of the Allies an impression prevailed that Napoleon was unprepared for war. It was even believed that his character had lost something of its energy under the influence of an Imperial Court. Never was there a more fatal illusion. The forces of France had never been so overwhelming; the plans of Napoleon had never been worked out with greater minuteness and certainty. From Hanover to Strasburg masses of troops had been collected upon the frontier in readiness for the order to march; and, before the campaign opened, the magnificent army of Boulogne, which had been collected for the invasion of England, was thrown into the scale against Austria.

<small>Plans of campaign, 1805.</small>

Events had occurred at sea which frustrated Napoleon's plan for an attack upon Great Britain. This attack, which in 1797 had been but lightly threatened, had, upon the renewal of war with England in 1803, become the object of Napoleon's most serious efforts. An army was concentrated at Boulogne sufficient to overwhelm the military forces of England, if once it could reach the opposite shore.

<small>Failure of Napoleon's naval designs against England.</small>

* Rüstow, Krieg von 1805, p. 55.

Napoleon's thoughts were centred on a plan for obtaining the naval superiority in the channel, if only for the few hours which it would take to transport the army from Boulogne to the English coast. It was his design to lure Nelson to the other side of the Atlantic by a feigned expedition against the West Indies, and, during the absence of the English admiral, to unite all the fleets at present lying blockaded in the French ports, as a cover for the invading armament. Admiral Villeneuve was ordered to sail to Martinique, and, after there meeting with some other ships, to re-cross the Atlantic with all possible speed, and liberate the fleets blockaded in Ferrol, Brest, and Rochefort. The junction of the fleets would give Napoleon a force of fifty sail in the British Channel, a force more than sufficient to overpower all the squadrons which Great Britain could possibly collect for the defence of its shores. Such a design exhibited all the power of combination which marked Napoleon's greatest triumphs; but it required of an indifferent marine the precision and swiftness of movement which belonged to the land-forces of France; it assumed in the seamen of Great Britain the same absence of resource which Napoleon had found among the soldiers of the Continent. In the present instance, however, Napoleon had to deal with a man as far superior to all the admirals of France as Napoleon himself was to the generals of Austria and Prussia. Villeneuve set sail for the West Indies in the spring of 1805, and succeeded in drawing Nelson after him; but, before he could re-cross the Atlantic,

<small>Nelson and Villeneuve, April—June, 1805.</small>

Nelson, incessantly pursuing the French squadron in the West-Indian seas, and at length discovering its departure homewards at Antigua (June 13), had warned the English Government of Villeneuve's movement by a message sent in the swiftest of the English brigs.* The Government, within twenty-four hours of receiving Nelson's message, sent orders to Sir Robert Calder instantly to raise the blockades of Ferrol and Rochefort, and to wait for Villeneuve off Cape Finisterre. Here Villeneuve met the English fleet (July 22). He was worsted in a partial engagement, and retired into the harbour of Ferrol. The pressing orders of Napoleon forced the French admiral, after some delay, to attempt that movement on Brest and Rochefort on which the whole plan of the invasion of England depended. But Villeneuve was no longer in a condition to meet the English force assembled against him. He put back without fighting, and retired to Cadiz. All hope of carrying out the attack upon England was lost.

It only remained for Napoleon to avenge himself upon Austria through the army which was baulked of its English prey. On the 1st of September, when the Austrians were now on the point of crossing the Inn, the camp of Boulogne was broken up. The army turned eastwards, and distributed itself over all the roads leading from the Channel to the Rhine and the Upper Danube. Far on the north-east the army of Hanover, commanded by Bernadotte, moved as its left wing, and converged upon a

March of French armies on Bavaria, Sept.

* Nelson Despatches, vi., 457.

point in Southern Germany half-way between the frontiers of France and Austria. In the fables that long disguised the true character of every action of Napoleon, the admirable order of march now given to the French armies appears as the inspiration of a moment, due to the rebound of Napoleon's genius after learning the frustration of all his naval plans. In reality, the employment of the "Army of England" against a Continental coalition had always been an alternative present to Napoleon's mind; and it was threateningly mentioned in his letters at a time when Villeneuve's failure was still unknown.

The only advantage which the Allies derived from the remoteness of the Channel army was that Austria was able to occupy Bavaria without resistance. General Mack, who was charged with this operation, crossed the Inn on the 8th of September. The Elector of Bavaria was known to be secretly hostile to the Coalition. The design of preventing his union with the French was a correct one; but in the actual situation of the allied armies it was one that could not be executed without great risk. The preparations of Russia required more time than was allowed for them; no Russian troops could reach the Inn before the end of October; and, in consequence, the entire force operating in Western Germany did not exceed seventy thousand men. Any doubts, however, as to the prudence of an advance through Bavaria were silenced by the assurance that Napoleon had to bring the bulk

Austrians invade Bavaria, Sept. 8.

of his army from the British Channel.* In ignorance of the real movements of the French, Mack pushed on to the western limit of Bavaria, and reached the river Iller, the border of Würtemberg, where he intended to stand on the defensive until the arrival of the Russians.

Here, in the first days of October, he became aware of the presence of French troops, not only in front but to the east of his own position. With some misgiving as to the situation of the enemy, Mack nevertheless refused to fall back from Ulm. Another week revealed the true state of affairs. Before the Russians were anywhere near Bavaria, the vanguard of Napoleon's Army of the Channel and the Army of Hanover had crossed North-Western Germany, and seized the roads by which Mack had advanced from Vienna. Every hour that Mack remained in Ulm brought new divisions of the French into the Bavarian towns and villages behind him. Escape was only possible by a retreat into the Tyrol, or by breaking through the French line while it was yet incompletely formed. Resolute action might still have saved the Austrian army; but the only energy that was shown was shown in opposition to the general. The Archduke Ferdinand, who was the titular commander-in-chief, cut his way through the French with part of the cavalry; Mack remained in Ulm, and the iron circle closed around him. At the last moment, after the hopelessness of the

Mack at Ulm, October.

* "The reports from General Mack are of the most satisfactory nature, and the apprehensions which were at one time entertained from the immense force which Bonaparte is bringing into Germany gradually decrease."
—Sir A. Paget's Despatch from Vienna, Sept. 18; Records: Austria, vol. 75.

situation had become clear even to himself, Mack was seized by an illusion that some great disaster had befallen the French in their rear, and that in the course of a few days Napoleon would be in full retreat. "Let no man utter the word 'Surrender'"—he proclaimed in an order of October 15th—"the enemy is in the most fearful straits; it is impossible that he can continue more than a few days in the neighbourhood. If provisions run short, we have three thousand horses to nourish us. I myself," continued the general, "will be the first to eat horseflesh." Two days later the inevitable capitulation took place; and Mack, with 25,000 men, fell into the hands of the enemy without striking a blow. A still greater number of the Austrians outside Ulm surrendered in detachments.*

<small>Capitulation of Ulm, Oct. 17.</small>

* Rüstow, p. 154. Schönhals, Krieg von, 1805, p. 33. Pagot's despatch, Oct. 25; Records: Austria, vol. 75. "The jealousy and misunderstanding among the generals had reached such a pitch that no communication took place between Ferdinand and Mack but in writing. Mack openly attributed his calamities to the ill-will and opposition of the Archduke and the rest of the generals. The Archduke accuses Mack of ignorance, of madness, of cowardice, and of treachery. The consternation which prevails here (Vienna) is at the highest pitch. The pains which are taken to keep the public in the dark naturally increase the alarm. Not a single newspaper has been delivered for several days past except the wretched *Vienna Gazette*. The Emperor is living at a miserable country-house, in order, as people say, that he may effect his escape. Every bark on the Danube has been put in requisition by the Government. The greatest apprehensions prevail on account of the Russians, of whose excesses loud complaints are made. Their arrival here is as much dreaded as that of the French. Cobenzl and Collenbach are in such a state of mind as to render them totally unfit for all business." Cobenzl was nevertheless still able to keep up his jocular style in asking the ambassador for the English subsidies:—"Vous êtes malade, je le suis aussi un peu, mais ce qui est encore plus malade que nous deux ce sont nos finances: ainsi pour l'amour de Dieu dépêchez vous de nous donner vos doux cent mille livres sterlings. Je vous embrasse de tout mon cœur."—Cobenzl to Pagot, enclosed in *id*.

T

All France read with wonder Napoleon's bulletins describing the capture of an entire army and the approaching presentation of forty Austrian standards to the Senate at Paris. No imperial rhetoric acquainted the nation with an event which, within four days of the capitulation of Ulm, inflicted a heavier blow on France than Napoleon himself had ever dealt to any adversary. On the 21st of October Nelson's crowning victory of Trafalgar, won over Villeneuve venturing out from Cadiz, annihilated the combined fleets of France and Spain. Nelson fell in the moment of his triumph; but the work which his last hours had achieved was one to which years prolonged in glory could have added nothing. He had made an end of the power of France upon the sea. Trafalgar was not only the greatest naval victory, it was the greatest and most momentous victory won either by land or by sea during the whole of the Revolutionary War. No victory, and no series of victories, of Napoleon produced the same effect upon Europe. Austria was in arms within five years of Marengo, and within four years of Austerlitz; Prussia was ready to retrieve the losses of Jena in 1813; a generation passed after Trafalgar before France again seriously threatened England at sea. The prospect of crushing the British navy, so long as England had the means to equip a navy, vanished: Napoleon henceforth set his hopes on exhausting England's resources by compelling every State on the Continent to exclude her commerce. Trafalgar forced him to impose his yoke

THE BATTLE OF TRAFALGAR.

(p. 200.)

upon all Europe, or to abandon the hope of conquering Great Britain. If national love and pride have idealised in our great sailor a character which, with its Homeric force and freshness, combined something of the violence and the self-love of the heroes of a rude age, the common estimate of Nelson's work in history is not beyond the truth. So long as France possessed a navy, Nelson sustained the spirit of England by his victories; his last triumph left England in such a position that no means remained to injure her but those which must result in the ultimate deliverance of the Continent.

The consequences of Trafalgar lay in the future; the military situation in Germany after Mack's catastrophe was such that nothing could keep the army of Napoleon out of Vienna. In the sudden awakening of Europe to its danger, one solitary gleam of hope appeared in the attitude of the Prussian Court. Napoleon had not scrupled, in his anxiety for the arrival of the Army of Hanover, to order Bernadotte, its commander, to march through the Prussian territory of Anspach, which lay on his direct route towards Ulm. It was subsequently alleged by the Allies that Bernadotte's violation of Prussian neutrality had actually saved him from arriving too late to prevent Mack's escape; but, apart from all imaginary grounds of reproach, the insult offered to Prussia by Napoleon was sufficient to incline even Frederick William to decided action. Some weeks earlier the approach of Russian forces to his frontier had led Frederick William to arm; the French had now more than carried out

Violation of Prussian territory.

what the Russians had only suggested. When the outrage was made known to the King of Prussia, that cold and reserved monarch displayed an emotion which those who surrounded him had seldom witnessed.* The Czar was forthwith offered a free passage for his armies through Silesia; and, before the news of Mack's capitulation reached the Russian frontier, Alexander himself was on the way to Berlin. The result of the deliberations of the two monarchs was the Treaty of Potsdam, signed on November 3rd. By this treaty Prussia undertook to demand from Napoleon an indemnity for the King of Piedmont, and the evacuation of Germany, Switzerland, and Holland: failing Napoleon's acceptance of Prussia's mediation upon these terms, Prussia engaged to take the field with 180,000 men.

Treaty of Potsdam, Nov. 3.

Napoleon was now close upon Vienna. A few days after the capitulation of Ulm thirty thousand Russians, commanded by General Kutusoff, had reached Bavaria; but Mack's disaster rendered it impossible to defend the line of the Inn, and the last detachments of the Allies disappeared as soon as Napoleon's vanguard approached the river. The French pushed forth in overpowering strength upon the capital. Kutusoff and the weakened Austrian army could neither defend Vienna nor meet the invader in the field. It was

French enter Vienna, Nov 13.

---

* Hardenberg, ii., 268. Jackson, Oct. 7. Records: Prussia, vol. 195. "The intelligence was received yesterday at Potsdam, while M. de Hardenberg was with the King of Prussia. His Prussian Majesty was very violently affected by it, and in the first moment of anger ordered M. de Hardenberg to return to Berlin and immediately to dismiss the French ambassador. After a little reflection, however, he said that that measure should be postponed."

resolved to abandon the city, and to unite the retreating forces on the northern side of the Danube with a second Russian army now entering Moravia. On the 7th of November the Court quitted Vienna. Six days later the French entered the capital, and by an audacious stratagem of Murat's gained possession of the bridge connecting the city with the north bank of the Danube, at the moment when the Austrian gunners were about to blow it into the air.* The capture of this bridge deprived the allied army of the last object protecting it from Napoleon's pursuit. Vienna remained in the possession of the French. All the resources of a great capital were now added to the means of the conqueror; and Napoleon prepared to follow his retreating adversary beyond the Danube, and to annihilate him before he could reach his supports.

The retreat of the Russian army into Moravia was conducted with great skill by General Kutusoff, who retorted upon Murat the stratagem practised at the bridge of Vienna, and by means of a pretended armistice effected his junction with the newly-arrived Russian corps between Olmütz and Brünn. Napoleon's anger at the escape of his prey was shown in the bitterness of his attacks upon Murat. The junction of the allied armies in Moravia had in fact most seriously altered the prospects of the war. For the first time since the opening of the campaign, the Allies had concentrated a force superior in numbers to anything that Napoleon could bring against

The Allies and Napoleon in Moravia, Nov.

---

* Rapp, Mémoires, p. 58. Beer, p. 188.

it. It was impossible for Napoleon, while compelled to protect himself on the Italian side, to lead more than 70,000 men into Moravia. The Allies had now 80,000 in camp, with the prospect of receiving heavy reinforcements. The war, which lately seemed to be at its close, might now, in the hands of a skilful general, be but beginning. Although the lines of Napoleon's communication with France were well guarded, his position in the heart of Europe exposed him to many perils; the Archduke Charles had defeated Massena at Caldiero on the Adige, and was hastening northwards; above all, the army of Prussia was preparing to enter the field. Every mile that Napoleon advanced into Moravia increased the strain upon his resources; every day that postponed the decision of the campaign brought new strength to his enemies. Merely to keep the French in their camp until a Prussian force was ready to assail their communications seemed enough to ensure the Allies victory; and such was the counsel of Kutusoff, who made war in the temper of the wariest diplomatist. But the scarcity of provisions was telling upon the discipline of the army, and the Czar was eager for battle.* The Emperor Francis gave way to the ardour of his allies. Weyrother, the Austrian chief of the staff, drew up the

* "The scarcity of provisions had been very great indeed. Much discouragement had arisen in consequence, and a considerable degree of insubordination, which, though less easy to produce in a Russian army than in any other, is, when it does make its appearance, most prejudicial, was beginning to manifest itself in various ways. The bread waggons were pillaged on their way to the camp, and it became very difficult to repress the excesses of the troops."—Report of General Ramsay, Dec. 10; Records: Austria, vol. 78.

most scientific plans for a great victory that had ever been seen even at the Austrian head-quarters; and towards the end of November it was agreed by the two Emperors that the allied army should march right round Napoleon's position near Brünn, and fight a battle with the object of cutting off his retreat upon Vienna.

It was in the days immediately preceding the intended battle, and after Napoleon had divined the plans of his enemy, that Count Haugwitz, bearing the demands of the Cabinet of Berlin, reached the French camp at Brünn.* Napoleon had already heard something of the Treaty of Potsdam, and was aware that Haugwitz had started from Berlin. He had no intention of making any of those concessions which Prussia required; at the same time it was of vital importance to him to avoid the issue of a declaration of war by Prussia, which would nerve both Austria and Russia to the last extremities. He therefore resolved to prevent Haugwitz by every possible method from delivering his ultimatum, until a decisive victory over the allied armies should have entirely changed the political situation. The Prussian envoy himself played into Napoleon's hands. Haugwitz had obtained a disgraceful permission from his sovereign to submit to all Napoleon's wishes, if, before his arrival, Austria should be separately treating for peace; and he had an excuse for delay in the fact that the military preparations of Prussia were not capable of being com-

Haugwitz comes with Prussian demands to Napoleon, Nov. 28.

---

* Hardenberg, ii., 345. Haugwitz had just become joint Foreign Minister with Hardenberg.

pleted before the middle of December. He passed twelve days on the journey from Berlin, and presented himself before Napoleon on the 28th of November. The Emperor, after a long conversation, requested that he would proceed to Vienna and transact business with Talleyrand. He was weak enough to permit himself to be removed to a distance with his ultimatum to Napoleon undelivered. When next the Prussian Government heard of their envoy, he was sauntering in Talleyrand's drawing-rooms at Vienna, with the cordon of the French Legion of Honour on his breast, exchanging civilities with officials who politely declined to enter upon any question of business.

<small>Haugwitz goes away to Vienna.</small>

Haugwitz once removed to Vienna, and the Allies thus deprived of the certainty that Prussia would take the field, Napoleon trusted that a single great defeat would suffice to break up the Coalition. The movements of the Allies were exactly those which he expected and desired. He chose his own positions between Brünn and Austerlitz in the full confidence of victory; and on the morning of the 2nd of December, when the mists disappeared before a bright wintry sun, he saw with the utmost delight that the Russian columns were moving round him in a vast arc, in execution of the turning-movement of which he had forewarned his own army on the day before. Napoleon waited until the foremost columns were stretched far in advance of their supports; then, throwing Soult's division upon the gap left in the centre of the allied line, he cut the army into halves, and crushed its severed divisions

<small>Austerlitz, Dec. 2.</small>

at every point along the whole line of attack. The Allies, although they outnumbered Napoleon, believed themselves to be overpowered by an army double their own size. The incoherence of the allied movements was as marked as the unity and effectiveness of those of the French. It was alleged in the army that Kutusoff, the commander-in-chief, had fallen asleep while the Austrian Weyrother was expounding his plans for the battle; a truer explanation of the palpable errors in the allied generalship was that the Russian commander had been forced by the Czar to carry out a plan of which he disapproved. The destruction in the ranks of the Allies was enormous, for the Russians fought with the same obstinacy as at the Trebbia and at Novi. Austria had lost a second army in addition to its capital; and the one condition which could have steeled its Government against all thoughts of peace—the certainty of an immediate Prussian attack upon Napoleon— *Armistice, Dec. 4.* had vanished with the silent disappearance of the Prussian envoy. Two days after the battle, the Emperor Francis met his conqueror in the open field, and accepted an armistice, which involved the withdrawal of the Russian army from his dominions.

Yet even now the Czar sent appeals to Berlin for help, and the negotiation begun by Austria would possibly have been broken off if help had been given. But the Cabinet of Frederick William had itself determined to evade its engagements; and as soon as the news of Austerlitz reached Vienna, Haugwitz had gone over heart and soul to the conqueror. While negotiations for peace were carried on between France and Austria, a parallel negotiation was carried on with the envoy of Prussia; and even before the Emperor Francis gave way to the conqueror's demands, Haugwitz signed a treaty with Napoleon at Schönbrunn, by which Prussia, instead of attacking Napoleon, entered into an alliance with him, and received from him in return the dominion of Hanover (December 15, 1805).* Had Prussia been the defeated power at Austerlitz, the Treaty of Schönbrunn could not have more completely reversed the policy to which King Frederick William had pledged himself six weeks before. While Haugwitz was making his pact with Napoleon, Hardenberg had been arranging with an English envoy for the combination of English and Russian forces in Northern Germany.† There were some among the

<small>Haugwitz signs Treaty with Napoleon, Dec. 15.</small>

* Haugwitz' justification of himself, with Hardenberg's comments upon it, is to be seen in Hardenberg, v., 220. But see also, for Hardenberg's own bad faith, *id.*, i., 551.

† Lord Harrowby's despatch from Berlin, Dec. 7; Records: Prussia, vol. 196. The news of Austerlitz reached Berlin on the night of Dec. 7, Next day Lord Harrowby called on Hardenberg. "He told me that in a council of war held since the arrival of the first accounts of the disaster, it had been decided to order a part of the Prussian army to march into Bohemia. These events, he said, need not interrupt our negotiations." Then, on the 12th came the news of the armistice: Harrowby saw Hardenberg that evening. "I was struck with something like irritation in his manner, with a sort of reference to the orders of the King, and with an expression which dropped from him that circumstances might possibly arise in which Prussia could look only to her own defence and security. I attributed this in a great degree to the agitation of the moment, and I should have pushed the question to a point if the entrance of Count Metternich and M. d'Alopeus had not interrupted me. . . Baron Hardenberg assured us that the military movements of the Prussian army were proceeding without a moment's loss of time." On the 25th Haugwitz arrived with his treaty. Hardenberg then feigned illness. "Baron Har-

King's advisers who declared that the treaty must be repudiated, and the envoy disgraced. But the catastrophe of Austerlitz, and the knowledge that the Government of Vienna was entering upon a separate negotiation, had damped the courage of the men in power. The conduct of Haugwitz was first excused, then supported, then admired. The Duke of Brunswick disgraced himself by representing to the French Ambassador in Berlin that the whole course of Prussian policy since the beginning of the campaign had been an elaborate piece of dissimulation in the interest of France.* The leaders of the patriotic party in the army found themselves without influence or following; the mass of the nation looked on with the same stupid unconcern with which it had viewed every event of the last twenty years. The King finally decided that the treaty by which Haugwitz had thrown the obligations of his country to the winds should be ratified, with certain modifications, including one that should nominally reserve to King George III. a voice in the disposal of Hanover.

Ten days after the departure of the Prussian envoy from Vienna, peace was concluded between France and Austria by the Treaty of Presburg† (December 27). At the outbreak of the war Napoleon had declared to his army that he would not again spare Austria, as he had spared her at Campo

<small>Treaty of Presburg, Dec. 27.</small>

---

denberg was too ill to see me, or, as far as I could learn, any other person; and it has been impossible for me to discover what intelligence is brought by Count Haugwitz."

* Lefebvre, Histoire des Cabinets, ii., 217.

† Martens, viii., 388; viii., 479. Beer, p., 232.

Formio and at Lunéville; and he kept his word. The Peace of Presburg left the Austrian State in a condition very different from that in which it had emerged from the two previous wars. The Treaty of Campo Formio had only deprived Austria of Belgium in order to replace it by Venice; the Settlement of Lunéville had only substituted French for Austrian influence in Western Germany: the Treaty that followed the battle of Austerlitz wrested from the House of Hapsburg two of its most important provinces, and cut it off at once from Italy, from Switzerland, and from the Rhine. Venetia was ceded to Napoleon's kingdom of Italy; the Tyrol was ceded to Bavaria; the outlying districts belonging to Austria in Western Germany were ceded to Baden and to Würtemberg. Austria lost 28,000 square miles of territory and 3,000,000 inhabitants. The Emperor recognised the sovereignty and independence of Bavaria, Baden, and Würtemberg, and renounced all rights over those countries as head of the Germanic Body. The Electors of Bavaria and Würtemberg, along with a large increase of territory, received the title of King. The constitution of the Empire ceased to exist even in name. It only remained for its chief, the successor of the Roman Cæsars, to abandon his title at Napoleon's bidding; and on the 6th of August, 1806, an Act, published by Francis II. at Vienna, made an end of the outworn and dishonoured fiction of a Holy Roman Empire.

End of the Holy Roman Empire, Aug. 6, 1806.

Though Russia had not made peace with Napoleon, the European Coalition was at an end. Now, as in 1801, the defeat of the Austrian armies left the Neapolitan Monarchy to settle its account with the conqueror. Naples had struck no blow; but it was only through the delays of the Allies that the Neapolitan army had not united with an English and a Russian force in an attack upon Lombardy. What had been pardoned in 1801 was now avenged upon the Bourbon despot of Naples and his Austrian Queen, who from the first had shown such bitter enmity to France. Assuming the character of a judge over the sovereigns of Europe, Napoleon pronounced from Vienna that the House of Naples had ceased to reign (Dec. 27, 1805). The sentence was immediately carried into execution. Ferdinand fled, as he had fled in 1798, to place himself under the protection of the navy of Great Britain. The vacant throne was given by Napoleon to his own brother, Joseph Bonaparte. Ferdinand, with the help of the English fleet, maintained himself in Sicily. A thread of sea two miles broad was sufficient barrier against the Power which had subdued half the Continent; and no attempt was made either by Napoleon or his brother to gain a footing beyond the Straits of Messina. In Southern Italy the same fanatical movements took place among the peasantry as in the previous period of French occupation. When the armies of Austria and Russia were crushed, and the continent lay at the mercy of France, Great Britain imagined that it could effect something against Napoleon in a corner of Italy, with the help of some ferocious villagers. A British force, landing near Maida, on the Calabrian coast, in the sum-

Naples given to Joseph Bonaparte.

mer of 1806, had the satisfaction of defeating the French at the point of the bayonet, of exciting a horde of priests and brigands to fruitless barbarities, and of abandoning them to their well-merited chastisement

Battle of Maida, July 6, 1806.

The elevation of Napoleon's brother Joseph to the throne of Naples was the first of a series of appointments now made by Napoleon in the character of Emperor of the West.

The Empire. Napoleonic dynasty and titles.

He began to style himself the new Charlemagne; his thoughts and his language were filled with pictures of universal sovereignty; his authority, as a military despot who had crushed his neighbours, became strangely confused in his own mind with that half-sacred right of the Cæsars from which the Middle Ages derived all subordinate forms of power. He began to treat the government of the different countries of Western Europe as a function to be exercised by delegation from himself. Even the territorial grants which under the Feudal System accompanied military or civil office were now revived; and the commander of a French army-corps or the chief of the French Foreign Office became the titular lord of some obscure Italian principality.* Napoleon's own family were to reign in many lands, as the Bourbons and the Hapsburgs had reigned before them, but in strict dependence on their head. Joseph Bonaparte had not long been installed at Naples when his brother Louis was compelled to accept the Crown of Holland. Jerome, for whom no kingdom was at present vacant, was forced

* Correspondance de Napoleon, xii., 253.

to renounce his American wife, in order that he might marry the daughter of the King of Würtemberg. Eugène Beauharnais, Napoleon's step-son, held the office of Viceroy of Italy; Murat, who had married Napoleon's sister, had the German Duchy of Berg. Bernadotte, Talleyrand, and Berthier found themselves suzerains of districts whose names were almost unknown to them. Out of the revenues of Northern Italy a yearly sum was reserved as an endowment for the generals whom the Emperor chose to raise to princely honours.

More statesmanlike, more practical than Napoleon's dynastic policy, was his organisation of Western Germany under its native princes as a dependency of France. The object at which all French politicians had aimed since the outbreak of the Revolutionary War, the exclusion of both Austria and Prussia from influence in Western Germany, was now completely attained. The triumph of French statesmanship, the consummation of two centuries of German discord, was seen in the Act of Federation subscribed by the Western German Sovereigns in the summer of 1806. By this Act the Kings of Bavaria and Würtemberg, the Elector of Baden, and thirteen minor princes, united themselves, in the League known as the Rhenish Confederacy, under the protection of the French Emperor, and undertook to furnish contingents, amounting to 63,000 men, in all wars in which the French Empire should engage. Their connection with the ancient Germanic Body was completely severed; the very town in which the Diet of the Empire had held its meetings was

Federation of the Rhine.

annexed by one of the members of the Confederacy. The Confederacy itself, with a population of 8,000,000, became for all purposes of war and foreign policy a part of France. Its armies were organised by French officers; its frontiers were fortified by French engineers; its treaties were made for it at Paris. In the domestic changes which took place within these States the work of consolidation begun in 1801 was carried forward with increased vigour. Scores of tiny principalities which had escaped dissolution in the earlier movement were now absorbed by their stronger neighbours. Governments became more energetic, more orderly, more ambitious. The princes who made themselves the vassals of Napoleon assumed a more despotic power over their own subjects. Old constitutional forms which had imposed some check on the will of the sovereign, like the Estates of Würtemberg, were contemptuously suppressed; the careless, ineffective routine of the last age gave place to a system of rigorous precision throughout the public services. Military service was enforced in countries hitherto free from it. The burdens of the people became greater, but they were more fairly distributed. The taxes were more equally levied; justice was made more regular and more simple. A career both in the army and the offices of Government was opened to a people to whom the very conception of public life had hitherto been unknown.

No national unity in Germany. The establishment of German unity in our own day after a victorious struggle with France renders it difficult to imagine the voluntary submission of a great part of the race to a

French sovereign, or to excuse a policy which, like that of 1806, appears the opposite of everything honourable and patriotic. But what seems strange now was not strange then. No expression more truly describes the conditions of that period than one of the great German poet who was himself so little of a patriot. "Germany," said Goethe, "is not a nation." Germany had indeed the unity of race; but all that truly constitutes a nation, the sense of common interest, a common history, pride, and desire, Germany did not possess at all. Bavaria, the strongest of the western States, attached itself to France from a well-grounded fear of Austrian aggression. To be conquered by Austria was just as much conquest for Bavaria as to be conquered by any other Power; it was no step to German unity, but a step in the aggrandisement of the House of Hapsburg. The interests of the Austrian House were not the interests of Germany any more than they were the interests of Croatia, or of Venice, or of Hungary. Nor, on the other hand, had Prussia yet shown a form of political life sufficiently attractive to lead the Southern States to desire to unite with it. Frederick's genius had indeed made him the hero of Germany, but his military system was harsh and tyrannical. In the actual condition of Austria and Prussia, it is doubtful whether the population of the minor States would have been happier united to these Powers than under their own Governments. Conquest in any case was impossible, and there was nothing to stimulate to voluntary union. It followed that the smaller States were destined to remain without a nationality, until the violence of some foreign Power rendered weakness an intolerable evil, and forced upon the better minds of Germany the thought of a common Fatherland. The necessity of German unity is no self-evident political truth. Holland and Switzerland in past centuries detached themselves from the Empire, and became independent States, with the highest advantage to themselves. Identity of blood is no more conclusive reason for political union between Holstein and the Tyrol than between Great Britain and the United States of America. The conditions which determine both the true area and the true quality of German unity are in fact something more complex than an ethnological law or an outburst of patriotic indignation against the French. Where local circumstances rendered it possible for a German district, after detaching itself from the race, to maintain a real national life and defend itself from foreign conquest, there it was perhaps better that the connection with Germany should be severed: where, as in the great majority of minor States, independence resulted only in military helplessness and internal stagnation, there it was better that independence should give place to German unity. But the conditions of any tolerable unity were not present so long as Austria was the leading Power. Less was imperilled in the future of the German people by the submission of the western States to France than would have been lost by their permanent incorporation under Austria.

With the establishment of the Rhenish Confederacy

and the conquest of Naples, Napoleon's empire reached, but did not overpass, the limits within which the sovereignty of France might probably have been long maintained. It has been usual to draw the line between the sound statesmanship and the hazardous enterprises of Napoleon at the Peace of Lunéville: a juster appreciation of the condition of Western Europe would perhaps include within the range of a practical, though mischievous, ideal the whole of the political changes which immediately followed the war of 1805, and which extended Napoleon's dominion to the Inn and to the Straits of Messina. Italy and Germany were not then what they have since become. The districts that lay between the Rhine and the Inn were not more hostile to the foreigner than those Rhenish Provinces which so readily accepted their union with France. The more enterprising minds in Italy found that the Napoleonic rule, with all its faults, was superior to anything that Italy had known in recent times. If we may judge from the feeling with which Napoleon was regarded in Germany down to the middle of the year 1806, and in Italy down to a much later date, the Empire then founded might have been permanently upheld, if Napoleon had abstained from attacking other States. No comparison can be made between the attractive power exercised by the social equality of France, its military glory, and its good administration, and the slow and feeble process of assimilation which went on within the dominions of Austria; yet Austria succeeded in uniting a greater variety of races than France sought to unite

The Empire of 1806 might have been permanent.

in 1806. The limits of a possible France were indeed fixed, and fixed more firmly than by any geographical line, in the history and national character of two other peoples. France could not permanently overpower Prussia, and it could not permanently overpower Spain. But within a boundary-line drawn roughly from the mouth of the Elbe to the head of the Adriatic, that union of national sentiment and material force which checks the formation of empires did not exist. The true turning-point in Napoleon's career was the moment when he passed beyond the policy which had planned the Federation of the Rhine, and roused by his oppression the one State which was still capable of giving a national life to Germany.

Limits of a possible Napoleonic Empire.

CHAPTER VII.

Death of Pitt—Ministry of Fox and Grenville—Napoleon forces Prussia into war with England, and then offers Hanover to England—Prussia resolves on war with Napoleon—State of Prussia—Decline of the Army—Southern Germany with Napoleon—Austria neutral—England and Russia about to help Prussia, but not immediately—Campaign of 1806—Battles of Jena and Auerstädt—Ruin of the Prussian Army—Capitulation of Fortresses—Demands of Napoleon—The War continues—Berlin Decree—Exclusion of English goods from the Continent—Russia enters the war—Campaign in Poland and East Prussia—Eylau—Treaty of Bartenstein—Friedland—Interview at Tilsit—Alliance of Napoleon and Alexander—Secret Articles—English expedition to Denmark—The French enter Portugal—Prussia after the Peace of Tilsit—Stein's Edict of Emancipation—The Prussian Peasant—Reform of the Prussian Army, and creation of Municipalities—Stein's other projects of reform, which are not carried out.

SIX weeks after the tidings of Austerlitz reached Great Britain, the statesman who had been the soul of every European coalition against France was carried to the grave.* Pitt passed away at

<small>Death of Pitt, Jan. 23, 1806.</small>

<small>* The story of Pitt's "Austerlitz look" preceding his death is so impressive and so well known that I cannot resist giving the real facts about the reception of the news of Austerlitz in England. There were four Englishmen who were expected to witness the battle, Sir A. Paget, ambassador at Vienna, Lord L. Gower, ambassador with the Czar, Lord Harrington and General Ramsay, military envoys. Of these, Lord Harrington had left England too late to reach the armies; Sir A. Paget sat writing despatches at Olmutz without hearing the firing, and on going out after the post left, was astonished to fall in with the retreating army; Gower was too far in the rear; and General Ramsay unfortunately went off on that very day to get some new passes. In consequence no Englishman witnessed the awful destruction that took place; and Paget's despatch, the first that reached England, quite misrepresented the battle, treating the defeat as not a decisive one. Pitt actually thought at first that the effect of the battle was favourable to his policy, and likely to encourage</small>

a moment of the deepest gloom. His victories at sea appeared to have effected nothing; his combinations on land had ended in disaster and ruin. If during Pitt's lifetime a just sense of the greatness and patriotism of all his aims condoned the innumerable faults of his military administration, that personal ascendancy which might have disarmed criticism even after the disaster of Austerlitz belonged to no other member of his Ministry. His colleagues felt their position to be hopeless. Though the King attempted to set one of Pitt's subordinates in the vacant place, the prospects of Europe were too dark, the situation of the country too serious, to allow a Ministry to be formed upon the ordinary principles of party-organisation or in accordance with the personal preferences of the monarch. The nation called for the union of the ablest men of all parties in the work of government; and, in spite of the life-long hatred of King George to Mr. Fox, a Ministry entered upon office framed by Fox and Grenville conjointly; Fox taking the post of Foreign Secretary, with a leading influence in the Cabinet, and yielding

Coalition Ministry of Fox and Grenville.

Prussia in its determination to fight. So late as December 20th the following instructions were sent to Harrowby at Berlin : " Even supposing the advantage of the day to have been decidedly with Bonaparte, it must have been obtained with a loss which cannot have left his force in a condition to contend with the army of Prussia and at the same time to make head against the Allies. If on the other hand it should appear that the advantage has been with the Allies, there is every reason to hope that Prussia will come forward with vigour to decide the contest." Records: Prussia, vol. 196. It was the surrender of Ulm which really gave Pitt the shock attributed to Austerlitz. The despatch then written—evidently from Pitt's dictation—exhorting the Emperor to do his duty, is the most impassioned and soul-stirring thing in the whole political correspondence of the time.

to Grenville the title of Premier. Addington received a place in the Ministry, and carried with him the support of a section of the Tory party, which was willing to countenance a policy of peace.

Fox had from the first given his whole sympathy to the French Revolution, as the cause of freedom. He had ascribed the calamities of Europe to the intervention of foreign Powers in favour of the Bourbon monarchy: he had palliated the aggressions of the French Republic as the consequences of unjust and unprovoked attack: even the extinction of liberty in France itself had not wholly destroyed his faith in the honour and the generosity of the soldier of the Revolution. In the brief interval of peace which in 1802 opened the Continent to English travellers, Fox had been the guest of the First Consul. His personal feeling towards the French Government had in it nothing of that proud and suspicious hatred which made negotiation so difficult while Pitt continued in power.

Napoleon hopes to intimidate Fox through Prussia.

It was believed at Paris, and with good reason, that the first object of Fox on entering upon office would be the restoration of peace. Napoleon adopted his own plan in view of the change likely to arise in the spirit of the British Cabinet. It was his habit, wherever he saw signs of concession, to apply more violent means of intimidation. In the present instance he determined to work upon the pacific leanings of Fox by adding Prussia to the forces arrayed against Great Britain. Prussia, isolated and discredited since the battle of Austerlitz, might first be driven into hostilities with England, and then be made to furnish the very satisfaction demanded by England as the primary condition of peace.

At the moment when Napoleon heard of Pitt's death, he was expecting the arrival of Count Haugwitz at Paris for the purpose of obtaining some modification in the treaty which he had signed on behalf of Prussia after the battle of Austerlitz. The principal feature in that treaty had been the grant of Hanover to Prussia by the French Emperor in return for its alliance. This was the point which above all others excited King Frederick William's fears and scruples. He desired to retain Hanover, but he also desired to derive his title rather from its English owner than from its French invader. It was the object of Haugwitz' visit to Paris to obtain an alteration in the terms of the treaty which should make the Prussian occupation of Hanover appear to be merely provisional, and reserve to the King of England at least a nominal voice in its ultimate transfer. In full confidence that Napoleon would agree to such a change, the King of Prussia had concealed the fact of its cession to himself by Napoleon, and published an untruthful proclamation, stating that, in the interests of the Hanoverian people themselves, a treaty had been signed and ratified by the French and Prussian Governments, in virtue of which Hanover was placed under the protection of the King of Prussia until peace should be concluded between Great Britain and France. The British Government received assurances of Prussia's respect for the rights of King George III.: the bitter truth that the treaty between France and

Prussia contained no single word reserving the rights of the Elector, and that the very idea of qualifying the absolute cession of Hanover was an afterthought, lay hidden in the conscience of the Prussian Cabinet. Never had a Government more completely placed itself at the mercy of a pitiless enemy. Count Haugwitz, on reaching Paris, was received by Napoleon with a storm of invective against the supposed partisans of England at the Prussian Court. Napoleon declared that the ill faith of Prussia had made an end even of that miserable pact which had been extorted after Austerlitz, and insisted that King Frederick William should openly defy Great Britain by closing the ports of Northern Germany to British vessels, and by declaring himself endowed by Napoleon with Hanover in virtue of Napoleon's own right of conquest. Haugwitz signed a second and more humiliating treaty embodying these conditions; and the Prussian Government, now brought into the depths of contempt, but unready for immediate war, executed the orders of its master.* A proclamation, stating that Prussia had

Napoleon forces Prussia into war with England, March, 1806.

---

* Hardenberg, ii., 463. Hardenberg, who, in spite of his weak and ambiguous conduct up to the end of 1805, felt bitterly the disgraceful position in which Prussia had placed itself, now withdrew from office. "I received this morning a message from Baron Hardenberg requesting me to call on him. He said that he could no longer remain in office consistently with his honour, and that he waited only for the return of Count Haugwitz to give up to him the management of his department. 'You know,' he said, 'my principles, and the efforts that I have made in favour of the good cause; judge then of the pain that I must experience when I am condemned to be accessory to this measure. You know, probably, that I was an advocate for the acquisition of Hanover, but I wished it upon terms honourable to both parties. I thought it a necessary bulwark to cover the Prussian dominions, and I thought that the House of Hanover might have

received the absolute dominion of Hanover from its conqueror Napoleon, gave the lie to the earlier announcements of King Frederick William. A decree was published excluding the ships of England from the ports of Prussia and from those of Hanover itself (March 28, 1806). It was promptly answered by the seizure of four hundred Prussian vessels in British harbours, and by the total extinction of Prussian maritime commerce by British privateers.*

been indemnified elsewhere. But now,' he added, 'j'abhorre les moyens infames par lesquels nous faisons cette acquisition. Nous pourrions rester les amis de Bonaparte sans être ses esclaves.'. He apologised for this language, and said I must not consider it as coming from a Prussian Minister, but from a man who unbosomed himself to his friend. . . . I have only omitted the distressing picture of M. de Hardenberg's agitation during this conversation. He bewailed the fate of Prussia, and complained of the hardships he had undergone for the last three months, and of the want of firmness and resolution in His Prussian Majesty. He several times expressed the hope that His Majesty's Government and that of Russia would make some allowances for the situation of this country. They had the means, he said, to do it an infinity of mischief. The British navy might destroy the Prussian commerce, and a Russian army might conquer some of her eastern provinces; but Bonaparte would be the only gainer, as thereby Prussia would be thrown completely into his arms."—F. Jackson's despatch from Berlin, March 27, 1806; Records: Prussia, vol. 197.

* On the British envoy demanding his passports, Haugwitz entered into a long defence of his conduct, alleging grounds of necessity. Mr. Jackson said that there could be no accommodation with England till the note excluding British vessels was reversed. " M. de Haugwitz immediately rejoined, 'I was much surprised when I found that that note had been delivered to you.' 'How,' I said, 'can *you* be surprised who was the author of the measures that gave rise to it?' The only answer I received was, 'Ah! ne dites pas cela.' He observed that it would be worth considering whether our refusal to acquiesce in the present state of things might not bring about one still more disastrous. I smiled, and asked if I was to understand that a Prussian army would take a part in the threatened invasion of England. He replied that he did not now mean to insinuate any such thing, but that it might be impossible to answer for events."—*Id.*, April 25.

Scarcely was Prussia committed to this ruinous conflict with Great Britain, when Napoleon opened negotiations for peace with Mr. Fox's Government. The first condition required by Great Britain was the restitution of Hanover to King George III. It was unhesitatingly granted by Napoleon.* Thus was Prussia to be mocked of its prey, after it had been robbed of all its honour. For the present, however, no rumour of this part of the negotiation reached Berlin. The negotiation itself, which dragged on through several months, turned chiefly upon the future ownership of Sicily. Napoleon had in the first instance agreed that Sicily should be left in the hands of Ferdinand of Naples, who had never been expelled from it by the French. Finding, however, that the Russian envoy d'Oubril, who had been sent to Paris with indefinite instructions by the Emperor Alexander, was willing to separate the cause of Russia from that of England, and to sign a separate peace, Napoleon retracted his promise relating to Sicily, and demanded that this island should be ceded to his brother Joseph. D'Oubril signed Preliminaries on behalf of Russia on the 20th of July, and left the English negotiator to obtain what terms he could. Fox had been willing to recognise the order of things established by Napoleon on the Italian mainland; he would even have ceded Sicily, if Russia had urged this in a joint negotiation; but he was too good a statesman to be cheated out of Sicily by a mere trick. He recalled the English envoy from Paris, and

Napoleon negotiates with Fox Offers Hanover to England.

* Papers presented to Parliament, 1806, p. 63.

waited for the judgment of the Czar upon the conduct of his own representative. The Czar disavowed d'Oubril's negotiations, and repudiated the treaty which he brought back to St. Petersburg. Napoleon had thus completely overreached himself, and, instead of severing Great Britain and Russia by separate agreements, had only irritated and displeased them both. The negotiations went no farther; their importance lay only in the effect which they produced upon Prussia, when Napoleon's offer of Hanover to Great Britain became known at Berlin.

From the time when Haugwitz' second treaty placed his master at Napoleon's feet, Prussia had been subjected to an unbroken series of insults and wrongs. Murat, as Duke of Berg, had seized upon territory allotted to Prussia in the distribution of the ecclesiastical lands; the establishment of a North German Confederacy under Prussian leadership was suggested by Napoleon himself, only to be summarily forbidden as soon as Prussia attempted to carry the proposal into execution. There was scarcely a courtier in Berlin who did not feel that the yoke of the French had become past endurance; even Haugwitz himself now considered war as a question of time. The patriotic party in the capital and the younger officers of the army bitterly denounced the dishonoured Government, and urged the King to strike for the credit of his country.* In the midst of this deepening agitation, a

Prussia learns of Napoleon's offer of Hanover to England, Aug. 7.

---

* "An order has been issued to the officers of the garrison of Berlin to abstain, under severe penalties, from speaking of the state of public affairs. This order was given in consequence of the very general and loud expressions of dissatisfaction which issued from all classes of people, but parti-

despatch arrived from Lucchesini, the Prussian Ambassador at Paris (August 7), relating the offer of Hanover made by Napoleon to the British Government. For nearly three months Lucchesini had caught no glimpse of the negotiations between Great Britain and France; suddenly, on entering into conversation with the English envoy at a dinner-party, he learnt the blow which Napoleon had intended to deal to Prussia. Lucchesini instantly communicated with the Court of Berlin; but his despatch was opened by Talleyrand's agents before it left Paris, and the French Government was thus placed on its guard against the sudden explosion of Prussian wrath. Lucchesini's despatch had indeed all the importance that Talleyrand attributed to it. It brought that spasmodic access of resolution to the irresolute King which Bernadotte's violation of his territory had brought in the year before. The whole Prussian army was ordered to prepare for war; Brunswick was summoned to form plans of a campaign; and appeals for help were sent to Vienna, to St. Petersburg, and even to the hostile Court of London.

<small>Prussia determines on war.</small>

<small>cularly from the military, at the recent conduct of the Government; for it has been in contemplation to publish an edict prohibiting the public at large from discussing questions of state policy. The experience of a very few days must convince the authors of this measure of the reverse of their expectation, the satires and sarcasms upon their conduct having become more universal than before."—Jackson's Despatch, March 22, *id.* "On Thursday night the windows of Count Haugwitz's house were completely demolished by some unknown person. As carbine bullets were chiefly made use of for the purpose, it is suspected to have been done by some of the garrison. The same thing had happened some nights before, but the Count took no notice of it. Now a party of the police patrol the street." *Id.*, April 27.</small>

The condition of Prussia at this critical moment was one which filled with the deepest alarm those few patriotic statesmen who were not blinded by national vanity or by slavery to routine. The foreign policy of Prussia in 1805, miserable as it was, had been but a single manifestation of the helplessness, the moral deadness that ran through every part of its official and public life. Early in the year 1806 a paper was drawn up by Stein,* exposing, in language seldom used by a statesman, the character of the men by whom Frederick William was surrounded, and declaring that nothing but a speedy change of system could save the Prussian State from utter downfall and ruin. Two measures of immediate necessity were specified by Stein, the establishment of a responsible council of Ministers, and the removal of Haugwitz and all his friends from power. In the existing system of government the Ministers were not the monarch's confidential advisers. The Ministers performed their work in isolation from one another; the Cabinet, or confidential council of the King, was composed of persons holding no public function, and free from all public responsibility. No guarantee existed that the policy of the country would be the same for two days together. The Ministers were often unaware of the turn that affairs had taken in the Cabinet; and the history of Haugwitz' mission to Austerlitz showed that an individual might commit the State to engagements the very opposite of those which he was sent to contract. The

margin notes: Condition of Prussia. Ministers not in the King's Cabinet.

---

* Pertz, i., 331. Seeley, i., 271.

first necessity for Prussia was a responsible governing council : with such a council, formed from the heads of the actual Administration, the reform of the army and of the other branches of the public service, which was absolutely hopeless under the present system, might be attended with some chance of success.

The army of Prussia, at an epoch when the conscription and the genius of Napoleon had revolutionised the art of war, was nothing but the army of Frederick the Great grown twenty years older.* It was obvious to all the world that its commissariat and marching-regulations belonged to a time when weeks were allowed for movements now reckoned by days; but there were circumstances less conspicuous from the outside which had paralysed the very spirit of soldiership, and prepared the way for a military collapse in which defeats in the field were the least dishonourable event. Old age had rendered the majority of the higher officers totally unfit for military service. In that barrack-like routine of officialism which passed in Prussia for the wisdom of government, the upper ranks of the army formed a species of administrative corps in time of peace, and received for their civil employment double the pay that they could earn in actual war. Aged men, with the rank of majors, colonels, and generals, mouldered in the offices of country towns, and murmured at the very mention of a war, which would deprive them of half their salaries. Except in the case of certain princes, who were placed in high rank while

State of the Prussian Army.

Higher officers.

* Hopfner, Der Krieg von 1806, i., 48.

young, and of a few vigorous patriarchs like Blücher, all the energy and military spirit of the army was to be found in men who had not passed the grade of captain. The higher officers were, on an average, nearly double the age of French officers of corresponding rank.* Of the twenty-four lieutenant-generals, eighteen were over sixty; the younger ones, with a single exception, were princes. Five out of the seven commanders of infantry were over seventy; even the sixteen cavalry generals included only two who had not reached sixty-five. These were the men who, when the armies of Prussia were beaten in the field, surrendered its fortresses with as little concern as if they had been receiving the French on a visit of ceremony. Their vanity was as lamentable as their faint-heartedness. "The army of his Majesty," said General Rüchel on parade, "possesses several generals equal to Bonaparte." Faults of another character belonged to the generation which had grown up since Frederick. The arrogance and licentiousness of the younger officers was such that their ruin on the field of Jena caused positive joy to a great part of the middle classes of Prussia. But, however hateful their manners, and however rash their self-confidence, the vices of these younger men had no direct connection with the disasters of 1806. The gallants who sharpened their swords on the window-sill of the French Ambassador received a bitter lesson from the plebeian troopers of

---

* A list of all Prussian officers in 1806 of and above the rank of major is given in Henckel von Donnersmarck, Erinnerungen, with their years of service. The average of a colonel's service is 42 years; of a major's, 35.

Murat; but they showed courage in disaster, and subsequently gave to their country many officers of ability and honour.

What was bad in the higher grades of the army was not retrieved by any excellence on the part of the private soldier. The Prussian army was recruited in part from foreigners, but chiefly from Prussian serfs, who were compelled to serve. Men remained with their regiments till old age; the rough character of the soldiers and the frequency of crimes and desertions occasioned the use of brutal punishments, which made the military service an object of horror to the better part of the middle and lower classes. The soldiers themselves, who could be flogged and drilled into high military perfection by a great general like Frederick, felt a surly indifference to their present taskmasters, and were ready to desert in masses to their homes as soon as a defeat broke up the regimental muster and roll-call. A proposal made in the previous year to introduce that system of general service which has since made Prussia so great a military power was rejected by a committee of generals, on the ground that it "would convert the most formidable army of Europe into a militia." But whether Prussia entered the war with a militia or a regular army, under the men who held command in 1806 it could have met with but one fate. Neither soldiery nor fortresses could have saved a kingdom whose generals knew only how to capitulate.

Common soldiers.

All southern Germany was still in Napoleon's hands.

v

As the probability of a war with Prussia became greater and greater, Napoleon had tightened his grasp upon the Confederate States. Publications originating among the patriotic circles of Austria were beginning to appeal to the German people to unite against a foreign oppressor. An anonymous pamphlet, entitled "Germany in its Deep Humiliation," was sold by various booksellers in Bavaria, among others by Palm, a citizen of Nuremberg. There is no evidence that Palm was even acquainted with the contents of the pamphlet; but as in the case of the Duke of Enghien, two years before, Napoleon had required a victim to terrify the House of Bourbon, so now he required a victim to terrify those who among the German people might be inclined to listen to the call of patriotism. Palm was not too obscure for the new Charlemagne. The innocent and unoffending man, innocent even of the honourable crime of attempting to save his country, was dragged before a tribunal of French soldiers, and executed within twenty-four hours, in pursuance of the imperative orders of Napoleon (August 26). The murder was an unnecessary one, for the Bavarians and the Würtembergers were in fact content with the yoke they bore; its only effect was to arouse among a patient and home-loving class the doubt whether the German citizen and his family might not after all have some interest in the preservation of national independence.

Southern Germany. Execution of Palm, Aug. 26.

When, several years later, the oppressions of Napoleon had given to a great part of the German race at least the transient nobleness of a real patriotism, the story of Palm's death was one of those that kindled the bitterest sense of wrong: at the time, it exercised no influence upon the course of political events. Southern Germany remained passive, and supplied Napoleon with a reserve of soldiers: Prussia had to look elsewhere for allies. Its prospects of receiving support were good, if the war should prove a protracted one, but not otherwise. Austria, crippled by the disasters of 1805, could only hope to renew the struggle if victory should declare against Napoleon. In other quarters help might be promised, but it could not be given at the time and at the place where it was needed. The Czar proffered the whole forces of his Empire; King George III. forgave the despoilers of his patrimony when he found that they really intended to fight the French; but the troops of Alexander lay far in the East, and the action of England in any Continental war was certain to be dilatory and ineffective. Prussia was exposed to the first shock of the war alone. In the existing situation of the French armies, a blow unusually swift and crushing might well be expected by all who understood Napoleon's warfare.

Austria neutral. England and Russia can give Prussia no prompt help.

A hundred and seventy thousand French soldiers, with contingents from the Rhenish Confederate States, lay between the Main and the Inn. The last weeks of peace, in which the Prussian Government imagined themselves to be deceiving the enemy while they pushed forward their own preparations, were employed by Napoleon in quietly

Situation of the French and Prussian armies, Sept., 1806.

concentrating this vast force upon the Main (September, 1806). Napoleon himself appeared to be absorbed in friendly negotiations with General Knobelsdorff, the new Prussian Ambassador at Paris. In order to lull Napoleon's suspicions, Haugwitz had recalled Lucchesini from Paris, and intentionally deceived his successor as to the real designs of the Prussian Cabinet. Knobelsdorff confidentially informed the Emperor that Prussia was not serious in its preparations for war. Napoleon, caring very little whether Prussia intended to fight or not, continued at Paris in the appearance of the greatest calm, while his lieutenants in Southern Germany executed those unobserved movements which were to collect the entire army upon the Upper Main. In the meantime the advisers of King Frederick William supposed themselves to have made everything ready for a vigorous offensive. Divisions of the Prussian army, numbering nearly 130,000 men, were concentrated in the neighbourhood of Jena, on the Saale. The bolder spirits in the military council pressed for an immediate advance through the Thuringian Forest, and for an attack upon what were supposed to be the scattered detachments of the French in Bavaria. Military pride and all the traditions of the Great Frederick impelled Prussia to take the offensive rather than to wait for the enemy upon the strong line of the Elbe. Political motives pointed in the same direction, for the support of Saxony was doubtful if once the French were permitted to approach Dresden.

French on the Main.

Prussians on the Saale.

On the 23rd of September King Frederick William

arrived at the head-quarters of the army, which were now at Naumburg, on the Saale. But his presence brought no controlling mind to the direction of affairs. Councils of war held on the two succeeding days only revealed the discord and the irresolution of the military leaders of Prussia. Brunswick, the commander-in-chief, sketched the boldest plans, and shrank from the responsibility of executing them. Hohenlohe, who commanded the left wing, lost no opportunity of opposing his superior; the suggestions of officers of real ability, like Scharnhorst, chief of the staff, fell unnoticed among the wrangling of pedants and partisans. Brunswick, himself a man of great intelligence though of little resolution, saw the true quality of the men who surrounded him. "Rüchel," he cried, "is a tin trumpet, Möllendorf a dotard, Kalkreuth a cunning trickster. The generals of division are a set ofstupid journeymen. Are these the people with whom one can make war on Napoleon? No. The best service that I could render to the King would be to persuade him to keep the peace."* It was ultimately decided, after two days of argument, that the army should advance through the Thuringian Forest, while feints on the right and left deceived the French as to its real direction. The diplomatists, however, who were mad enough to think that an ultimatum which they had just despatched to Paris would bring Napoleon on to his knees, insisted that the opening of hostilities should be deferred till the 8th of

Confusion of the Prussians.

---

* Müffling, Aus Meinem Leben, p. 15. Hopfner, i., 157. Correspondance de Napoleon, xiii., 150.

October, when the term of grace which they had given to Napoleon would expire.

A few days after this decision had been formed, intelligence arrived at head-quarters that Napoleon himself was upon the Rhine. Before the ultimatum reached the hands of General Knobelsdorff in Paris, Napoleon had quitted the capital, and the astonished Ambassador could only send the ultimatum in pursuit of him after he had gone to place himself at the head of 200,000 men. The news that Napoleon was actually in Mainz confounded the diplomatists in the Prussian camp, and produced an order for an immediate advance. This was the wisest as well as the boldest determination that had yet been formed; and an instant assault upon the French divisions on the Main might perhaps even now have given the Prussian army the superiority in the first encounter. But some fatal excuse was always at hand to justify Brunswick in receding from his resolutions. A positive assurance was brought into camp by Lucchesini that Napoleon had laid his plans for remaining on the defensive on the south of the Thuringian Forest. If this were true, there might yet be time to improve the plan of the campaign; and on the 4th of October, when every hour was of priceless value, the forward march was arrested, and a new series of deliberations began at the head-quarters at Erfurt. In the council held on the 4th of October, a total change in the plan of operations was urged by Hohenlohe's staff. They contended, and rightly, that it was the design of Napoleon to pass the Prussian army on the

Prussians at Erfurt, Oct. 4.

east by the valley of the Saale, and to cut it off from the roads to the Elbe. The delay in Brunswick's movements had in fact brought the French within striking distance of the Prussian communications. Hohenlohe urged the King to draw back the army from Erfurt to the Saale, or even to the east of it, in order to cover the roads to Leipzig and the Elbe. His theory of Napoleon's movements, which was the correct one, was adopted by the council, and the advance into the Thuringian Forest was abandoned; but instead of immediately marching eastwards with the whole army, the generals wasted two more days in hesitations and half-measures. At length it was agreed that Hohenlohe should take post at Jena, and that the mass of the army should fall back to Weimar, with the object of striking a blow at some undetermined point on the line of Napoleon's advance.

Napoleon, who had just received the Prussian ultimatum with unbounded ridicule and contempt, was now moving along the roads that lead from Bamberg and Baireuth to the Upper Saale. On the 10th of October, as the division of Lannes was approaching Saalfeld, it was attacked by Prince Louis Ferdinand at the head of Hohenlohe's advanced guard. The attack was made against Hohenlohe's orders. It resulted in the total rout of the Prussian force. Though the numbers engaged were small, the loss of magazines and artillery, and the death of Prince Louis Ferdinand, the hero of the war-party, gave to this first repulse the moral effect of a great military disaster. Hohenlohe's troops at Jena were seized with panic; numbers of men

Encounter at Saalfeld, Oct. 10.

threw away their arms and dispersed; the drivers of artillery-waggons and provision-carts cut the traces and rode off with their horses. Brunswick, however, and the main body of the army, were now at Weimar, close at hand; and if Brunswick had decided to fight a great battle at Jena, the Prussians might have brought nearly 90,000 men into action. But the plans of the irresolute commander were again changed. It was resolved to fall back upon Magdeburg and the Elbe. Brunswick himself moved northwards to Naumburg; Hohenlohe was ordered to hold the French in check at Jena until this movement was completed. Napoleon reached Jena. He had no intelligence of Brunswick's retreat, and imagined the mass of the Prussian army to be gathered round Hohenlohe, on the plateau before him. He sent Davoust, with a corps 27,000 strong, to outflank the enemy by a march in the direction of Naumburg, and himself prepared to make the attack in front with 90,000 men, a force more than double Hohenlohe's real army. The attack was made on the 14th of October.

Napoleon defeats Hohenlohe at Jena, Oct. 14.

Hohenlohe's army was dashed to pieces by Napoleon, and fled in wild disorder. Davoust's weak corps, which had not expected to meet with any important forces until it fell upon Hohenlohe's flank, found itself in the presence of Brunswick's main army, when it arrived at Auerstädt, a few miles to the north. Fortune had given to the Prussian commander an extraordinary chance of retrieving what strategy had lost. A battle conducted with common military skill would not only have destroyed Davoust, but have secured, at least for the larger portion of the Prussian forces, a safe retreat to Leipzig or the Elbe. The French general, availing himself of steep and broken ground, defeated numbers nearly double his own through the confusion of his adversary, who sent up detachment after detachment instead of throwing himself upon Davoust with his entire strength. The fighting was as furious on the Prussian side as its conduct was unskilful. King Frederick William, who led the earlier cavalry charges, had two horses killed under him. Brunswick was mortally wounded. Many of the other generals were killed or disabled. There remained, however, a sufficient number of unbroken regiments to preserve some order in the retreat until the army came into contact with the remnant of Hohenlohe's forces, flying for their lives before the cavalry of Murat. Then all hope was lost. The fugitive mass struck panic and confusion into the retreating columns; and with the exception of a few regiments which gathered round well-known leaders, the soldiers threw away their arms and spread over the country in headlong rout. There was no line of retreat, and no rallying-point. The disaster of a single day made an end of the Prussian army as a force capable of meeting the enemy in the field. A great part of the troops was captured by the pursuing enemy during the next few days. The regiments which preserved their coherence were too weak to make any attempt to check Napoleon's advance, and could only hope to save themselves by escaping to the fortresses on the Oder.

Davoust defeats Brunswick at Auerstadt, Oct. 14.

Ruin of the Prussian Army.

Two days before the battle of Jena, an English envoy, Lord Morpeth, had arrived at the head-quarters of the King of Prussia, claiming the restoration of Hanover, and bearing an offer of the friendship and support of Great Britain. At the moment when the Prussian monarchy was on the point of being hurled to the ground, its Government might have been thought likely to welcome any security that it should not be abandoned in its utmost need. Haugwitz, however, was at head-quarters, dictating lying bulletins, and perplexing the generals with ridiculous arguments of policy until the French actually opened fire. When the English envoy made known his arrival, he found that no one would transact business with him. Haugwitz had determined to evade all negotiations until the battle had been fought. He was unwilling to part with Hanover, and he hoped that a victory over Napoleon would enable him to meet Lord Morpeth with a bolder countenance on the following day. When that day arrived, Ministers and diplomatists were flying headlong over the country. The King made his escape to Weimar, and wrote to Napoleon, begging for an armistice; but the armistice was refused, and the pursuit of the broken army was followed up without a moment's pause. The capital offered no safe halting-place; and Frederick William only rested when he had arrived at Graudenz, upon the Vistula. Hohenlohe's poor remnant of an army passed the Elbe at Magdeburg, and took the road for Stettin, at the mouth of the Oder, leaving Berlin to its fate. The retreat was badly conducted; alternate halts and strained marches discouraged the best of the soldiers. As the men passed their native villages they abandoned the famishing and broken-spirited columns; and at the end of a fortnight's disasters Prince Hohenlohe surrendered to his pursuers at Prenzlau with his main body, now numbering only 10,000 men (Oct. 28).

Blücher, who had showed the utmost energy and fortitude after the catastrophe of Jena, was moving in the rear of Hohenlohe with a considerable force which his courage had gathered around him. On learning of Hohenlohe's capitulation, he instantly reversed his line of march, and made for the Hanoverian fortress of Hameln, in order to continue the war in the rear of the French. Overwhelming forces, however, cut off his retreat to the Elbe; he was hemmed in on the east and on the west; and nothing remained for him but to throw himself into the neutral town of Lübeck, and fight until food and ammunition failed him. *Blucher at Lubeck.* The French were at his heels. The magistrates of Lübeck prayed that their city might not be made into a battle-field, but in vain; Blücher refused to move into the open country. The town was stormed by the French, and put to the sack. Blücher was driven out, desperately fighting, and pent in between the Danish frontier and the sea. Here, surrounded by overpowering numbers, without food, without ammunition, he capitulated on the 7th of November, after his courage and resolution had done everything that could ennoble both general and soldiers in the midst of overwhelming calamity.

The honour of entering the Prussian capital was given by Napoleon to Davoust, whose victory at Auerstädt had in fact far surpassed his own. Davoust entered Berlin without resistance on the 25th of October; Napoleon himself went to Potsdam, and carried off the sword and the scarf that lay upon the grave of Frederick the Great. Two days after Davoust, the Emperor made his own triumphal entry into the capital. He assumed the part of the protector of the people against the aristocracy, ordering the formation of a municipal body and of a civic guard for the city of Berlin. The military aristocracy he treated with the bitterest hatred and contempt. "I will make that noblesse," he cried, "so poor that they shall beg their bread." The disaster of Jena had indeed fearfully punished the insolence with which the officers of the army had treated the rest of the nation. The Guards were marched past the windows of the citizens of Berlin, a miserable troop of captives; soldiers of rank who remained in the city had to attend upon the French Emperor to receive his orders. But calamity was only beginning. The overthrow of Jena had been caused by faults of generalship, and cast no stain upon the courage of the officers; the surrender of the Prussian fortresses, which began on the day when the French entered Berlin, attached the utmost personal disgrace to their commanders. Even after the destruction of the army in the field, Prussia's situation would not have been hopeless if the commanders of fortresses had acted on the ordinary rules of military duty. Magdeburg and the strongholds upon the Oder were sufficiently armed and provisioned to detain the entire French army, and to give time to the King to collect upon the Vistula a force as numerous as that which he had lost. But whatever is weakest in human nature—old age, fear, and credulity—seemed to have been placed at the head of Prussia's defences. The very object for which fortresses exist was forgotten; and the fact that one army had been beaten in the field was made a reason for permitting the enemy to forestall the organisation of another. Spandau surrendered on the 25th of October, Stettin on the 29th. These were places of no great strength; but the next fortress to capitulate, Küstrin on the Oder, was in full order for a long siege. It was surrendered by the older officers, amidst the curses of the subalterns and the common soldiers: the artillerymen had to be dragged from their guns by force. Magdeburg, with a garrison of 24,000 men and enormous supplies, fell before a French force not numerous enough to beleaguer it (Nov. 8).

Neither Napoleon himself nor any one else in Europe could have foreseen such conduct on the part of the Prussian commanders. The unexpected series of capitulations made him demand totally different terms of peace from those which he had offered after the battle of Jena. A week after the victory, Napoleon had demanded, as the price of peace, the cession of Prussia's territory west of the Elbe, with the exception of the town of Magdeburg, and the withdrawal of Prussia from the affairs of Germany. These

Napoleon's demands.

terms were communicated to King Frederick William; he accepted them, and sent Lucchesini to Berlin to negotiate for peace upon this basis. Lucchesini had scarcely reached the capital when the tidings arrived of Hohenlohe's capitulation, followed by the surrender of Stettin and Küstrin. The Prussian envoy now sought in vain to procure Napoleon's ratification of the terms which he had himself proposed. No word of peace could be obtained: an armistice was all that the Emperor would grant, and the terms on which the armistice was offered rose with each new disaster to the Prussian arms. On the fall of Magdeburg becoming known, Napoleon demanded that the troops of Prussia should retire behind the Vistula, and surrender every fortress that they still retained, with the single exception of Königsberg. Much as Prussia had lost, it would have cost Napoleon a second campaign to make himself master of what he now asked; but to such a depth had the Prussian Government sunk, that Lucchesini actually signed a convention at Charlottenburg (November 16), surrendering to Napoleon, in return for an armistice, the entire list of uncaptured fortresses, including Dantzig and Thorn on the Lower Vistula, Breslau, with the rest of the untouched defences of Silesia, Warsaw and Praga in Prussian Poland, and Colberg upon the Pomeranian coast.*

Frederick William continues the war. The treaty, however, required the King's ratification. Frederick William, timorous as he was, hesitated to confirm an agreement which ousted him from his dominions as completely

* Hopfner, ii., 392. Hardenberg. iii., 230.

as if the last soldier of Prussia had gone into captivity. The patriotic party, headed by Stein, pleaded for the honour of the country against the miserable Cabinet which now sought to complete its work of ruin. Assurances of support arrived from St. Petersburg. The King determined to reject the treaty, and to continue the war to the last extremity. Haugwitz hereupon tendered his resignation, and terminated a political career disastrous beyond any recorded in modern times. For a moment, it seemed as if the real interests of the country were at length to be recognised in the appointment of Stein to one of the three principal offices of State. But the King still remained blind to the necessity of unity in the government, and angrily dismissed Stein when he refused to hold the Ministry if representatives of the old Cabinet and of the peace-party were to have places beside him. The King's act was ill calculated to serve the interests of Prussia, either at home or abroad. Stein was the one Minister on whom the patriotic party of Prussia and the Governments of Europe could rely with perfect confidence.* His dismissal at this crisis proved

---

* "Count Stein, the only man of real talents in the administration, has resigned or was dismissed. He is a considerable man, of great energy, character, and superiority of mind, who possessed the public esteem in a high degree, and, I have no doubt, deserved it. ... During the negotiation for an armistice, the expenses of Bonaparte's table and household at Berlin were defrayed by the King of Prussia. Since that period one of the Ministers called upon Stein, who was the chief of the finances, to pay 300,000 crowns on the same account. Stein refused with strong expressions of indignation. The King spoke to him: he remonstrated with His Majesty in the most forcible terms, descanted on the wretched humiliation of such mean conduct, and said that he never could pay money on such an account unless he had the order in writing from His Majesty. This order was

the incurable poverty of Frederick William's mental nature; it also proved that, so long as any hope remained of saving the Prussian State by the help of the Czar of Russia, the patriotic party had little chance of creating a responsible government at home.

<small>Napoleon at Berlin.</small> Throughout the month of November French armies overran Northern Germany: Napoleon himself remained at Berlin, and laid the foundations of a political system corresponding to that which he had imposed upon Southern Germany after the victory of Austerlitz. The Houses of Brunswick and Hesse-Cassel were deposed, in order to create a new client-kingdom of Westphalia; Saxony, with Weimar and four other duchies, entered the Confederation of the Rhine. A measure more widely affecting the Continent of Europe dated from the last days of the Emperor's residence at the Prussian capital. On the 21st of November, 1806, a decree was published at Berlin prohibiting the inhabitants of the entire European territory allied with France from carrying on any commerce with Great Britain, or admitting any merchandise that had been produced in Great Britain or in its colonies.* The line of coast thus closed to the shipping and the produce of the British Empire included everything from the Vistula to the southern point of Dalmatia, with the exception of Denmark and Portugal and the Austrian port of Trieste. All property

<small>The Berlin decree against English commerce, Nov. 21, 1806.</small>

given a few days after the conversation."—Hutchinson's Despatch, Jan. 1, 1807; Records: Prussia, vol. 200.

* Corr. Nap. xiii., 555.

belonging to English subjects, all merchandise of British origin, whoever might be the owner, was ordered to be confiscated: no vessel that had even touched at a British port was permitted to enter a Continental harbour. It was the fixed purpose of Napoleon to exhaust Great Britain, since he could not destroy its navies, or, according to his own expression, to conquer England upon the Continent. All that was most harsh and unjust in the operation of the Berlin Decree fell, however, more upon Napoleon's own subjects than upon Great Britain. The exclusion of British ships from the harbours of the allies of France was no more than the exercise of a common right in war; even the seizure of the property of Englishmen, though a violation of international law, bore at least an analogy to the seizure of French property at sea; but the confiscation of the merchandise of German and Dutch traders, after it had lain for weeks in their own warehouses, solely because it had been produced in the British Empire, was an act of flagrant and odious oppression. The first result of the Berlin Decree was to fill the trading towns of North Germany with French revenue-officers and inquisitors. Peaceable tradesmen began to understand the import of the battle of Jena when French gendarmes threw their stock into the common furnace, or dragged them to prison for possessing a hogshead of Jamaica sugar or a bale of Leeds cloth. The merchants who possessed a large quantity of English or colonial wares were the heaviest sufferers by Napoleon's commercial policy: the public found the markets supplied by American and Danish traders, until, at a later period, the British Government adopted reprisals, and prevented the ships of neutrals from entering any port from which English vessels were excluded. Then every cottage felt the stress of the war. But if the full consequences of the Berlin Decree were delayed until the retaliation of Great Britain reached the dimensions of Napoleon's own tyranny, the Decree itself marked on the part of Napoleon the assumption of a power in conflict with the needs and habits of European life. Like most of the schemes of Napoleon subsequent to the victories of 1806, it transgressed the limits of practical statesmanship, and displayed an ambition no longer raised above mere tyranny by its harmony with forms of progress and with the better tendencies of the age.

Immediately after signing the Berlin Decree, Napoleon quitted the Prussian capital (Nov. 25).

Napoleon and the Poles.

The first act of the war had now closed. The Prussian State was overthrown; its territory as far as the Vistula lay at the mercy of the invader; its king was a fugitive at Königsberg, at the eastern extremity of his dominions. The second act of the war began with the rejection of the armistice which had been signed by Lucchesini, and with the entry of Russia into the field against Napoleon. The scene of hostilities was henceforward in Prussian Poland and in the Baltic Province lying between the lower Vistula and the Russian frontier. Napoleon entered Poland, as he had entered Italy ten years before, with the pretence of restoring liberty to an enslaved people. Kosciusko's name was fraudulently attached to a proclamation summoning the Polish nation to arms; and although Kosciusko himself declined to place any trust in the betrayer of Venice, thousands of his countrymen flocked to Napoleon's standard, or anticipated his arrival by capturing and expelling the Prussian detachments scattered through their country. Promises of the restoration of Polish independence were given by Napoleon in abundance; but the cause of Poland was the last to attract the sympathy of a man who considered the sacrifice of the weak to the strong to be the first principle of all good policy. To have attempted the restoration of Polish independence would have been to make permanent enemies of Russia and Prussia for the sake of an ally weaker than either of them. The project was not at this time seriously entertained by Napoleon. He had no motive to face a work of such enormous difficulty as the creation of a solid political order among the most unpractical race in Europe. He was glad to enrol the Polish nobles among his soldiers; he knew the value of their enthusiasm, and took pains to excite it; but, when the battle was over, it was with Russia, not Poland, that France had to settle; and no better fate remained, even for the Prussian provinces of Poland, than in part to be formed into a client-state, in part to be surrendered as a means of accommodation with the Czar.

The armies of Russia were at some distance from the Vistula when, in November, 1806, Napoleon entered Polish territory. Their movements were slow, their numbers insufficient. At the moment when all the forces of the Empire were required for the struggle against Napoleon, troops were being sent into Moldavia against the Sultan. Nor were the Russian commanders anxious to save what still remained of the Prussian kingdom. The disasters of Prussia, like those of Austria at the beginning of the campaign of 1805, excited less sympathy than contempt; and the inclination of the Czar's generals was rather to carry on the war upon the frontier of their own country than to commit themselves to a distant campaign with a despised ally. Lestocq, who commanded the remnant of the Prussian army upon the Vistula, was therefore directed to abandon his position at Thorn and to move eastwards. The French crossed the Vistula higher up the river; and by the middle of December the armies of France and Russia lay opposite to one another in the neighbourhood of Pultusk, upon the Ukra and the Narew. The first encounter, though not of a decisive character, resulted in the retreat of the Russians. Heavy rains and fathomless mud checked the pursuit. War seemed almost impossible in such a country and such a climate; and Napoleon ordered his troops to take up their winter quarters along the Vistula, believing that nothing more could be attempted on either side before the spring.

Campaign in Poland against Russia, Dec., 1806.

But the command of the Russian forces was now transferred from the aged and half-mad Kamenski,* who

---

* "It is still doubtful who commands, and whether Kamensky has or has not given up the command. I wrote to him on the first moment of my arrival, but have received no answer from him. On the 23rd, the day of the first attack, he took off his coat and waistcoat, put all his stars and ribbons over his shirt, and ran about the streets of Pultusk encouraging the soldiers, over whom he is said to have great influence."—Lord Hutchinson's Despatch, Jan. 1, 1807; Records: Prussia, vol. 200.

had opened the campaign, to a general better qualified to cope with Napoleon. Bennigsen, the new commander-in-chief, was an active and daring soldier. Though a German by birth, his soldiership was of that dogged and resolute order which suits the character of Russian troops; and, in the mid-winter of 1806, Napoleon found beyond the Vistula such an enemy as he had never encountered in Western Europe. Bennigsen conceived the design of surprising the extreme left of the French line, where Ney's division lay stretched towards the Baltic, far to the north-east of Napoleon's main body. *Napoleon and Bennigsen in East Prussia.* Forest and marsh concealed the movement of the Russian troops, and both Ney and Bernadotte narrowly escaped destruction. Napoleon now broke up his winter quarters, and marched in great force against Bennigsen in the district between Königsberg and the mouth of the Vistula. Bennigsen manœuvred and retired until his troops clamoured for battle. He then took up a position at Eylau, and waited for the attack of the French. The battle of Eylau, fought in the midst of snow- *Eylau. Feb. 8, 1807.* storms on the 8th of February, 1807, was unlike anything that Napoleon had ever yet seen. His columns threw themselves in vain upon the Russian infantry. Augereau's corps was totally destroyed in the beginning of the battle. The Russians pressed upon the ground where Napoleon himself stood; and although the superiority of the Emperor's tactics at length turned the scale, and the French began a forward movement, their advance was stopped by the arrival of Lestocq and a body of 13,000 Prussians. At the close of the engagement 30,000 men lay wounded or dead in the snow; the positions of the armies remained what they had been in the morning. Bennigsen's lieutenants urged him to renew the combat on the next day; but the confusion of the Russian army was such that the French, in spite of their losses and discouragement, would probably have gained the victory in a second battle; * and the Russian commander determined to fall back towards Königsberg, content with having disabled the enemy and given Napoleon such a check as he had never received before. Napoleon, who had announced his intention of entering Königsberg in triumph, fell back upon the river Passarge, and awaited the arrival of reinforcements.

The warfare of the next few months was confined to the reduction of the Prussian fortresses which had not yet fallen into the hands of the French.

Sieges of Dantzig and Colberg, March, 1807.

Dantzig surrendered after a long and difficult siege; the little town of Colberg upon the Pomeranian coast prolonged a defence as honourable to its inhabitants as to the military leaders. Two soldiers of singularly different character, each destined to play a conspicuous part in coming years, first distinguished themselves in the defence of Colberg. Gneisenau, a scientific soldier of the highest order, the future guide of Blücher's victorious campaigns, commanded the garrison; Schill, a cavalry officer of adventurous daring, gathered round him a troop of hardy riders, and harassed the French with an audacity as perplexing to his military superiors as

* Hutchinson's letter, in Adair, Mission to Vienna, p. 373.

to the enemy. The citizens, led by their burgomaster, threw themselves into the work of defence with a vigour in striking contrast to the general apathy of the Prussian people; and up to the end of the war Colberg remained uncaptured. Obscure as Colberg was, its defence might have given a new turn to the war if the Government of Great Britain had listened to the entreaties of the Emperor Alexander, and despatched a force to the Baltic to threaten the communications of Napoleon. The task was not a difficult one for a Power which could find troops, as England now did, to send to Constantinople, to Alexandria, and to Buenos Ayres; but military judgment was more than ever wanting to the British Cabinet. Fox had died at the beginning of the war; his successors in Grenville's Ministry, though they possessed a sound theory of foreign policy,* were not fortunate in its application, nor were they prompt enough in giving financial help to their allies. Suddenly, however, King George quarrelled with his Ministers upon the ancient question of Catholic Disabilities, and drove them from office (March 24). The country sided with the King. A Ministry came into power, composed of the old supporters of Pitt, men, with the exception of Canning and Castlereagh, of narrow views and poor capacity, headed by the Duke of Portland, who, in 1793, had given his name to the section of the Whig party which

Inaction of England

Fall of Grenville's Ministry, March 24, 1807.

---

* For the Whig foreign policy, see Adair, p. 11—13. Its principle was to relinquish the attempt to raise coalitions of half-hearted Governments against France by means of British subsidies, but to give help to States which of their own free will entered into war with Napoleon.

joined Pitt. The foreign policy of the new Cabinet, which concealed its total lack of all other statesmanship, returned to the lines laid down by Pitt in 1805. Negotiations were opened with Russia for the despatch of an English army to the Baltic; arms and money were promised to the Prussian King. For a moment it seemed as if the Powers of Europe had never been united in so cordial a league. The Czar embraced the King of Prussia in the midst of his soldiers, and declared with tears that the two should stand or fall together. The Treaty of Bartenstein, signed in April, 1807, pledged the Courts of St. Petersburg, Stockholm, and Berlin to a joint prosecution of the war, and the common conclusion of peace.

Treaty of Bartenstein between Russia, Prussia, England, and Sweden, April, 1807.

Great Britain joined the pact, and prepared to fulfil its part in the conflict upon the Baltic. But the task was a difficult one, for Grenville's Ministry had dispersed the fleet of transports; and, although Canning determined upon the Baltic expedition in April, two months passed before the fleet was ready to sail.

In the meantime army upon army was moving to the support of Napoleon, from France, from Spain, from Holland, and from Southern Germany. The fortresses of the Elbe and the Oder, which ought to have been his barrier, had become his base of operations; and so enormous were the forces at his command, that, after manning every stronghold in Central Europe, he was able at the beginning of June to bring 140,000 men into the field beyond the Vistula. The Russians had also received reinforcements, but Ben-

Summer campaign in East Prussia 1807.

nigsen's army was still weaker than that of the enemy. It was Bennigsen, nevertheless, who began the attack; and now, as in the winter campaign, he attempted to surprise and crush the northern corps of Ney. The same general movement of the French army followed as in January. The Russian commander, outnumbered by the French, retired to his fortified camp at Heilsberg. After sustaining a bloody repulse in an attack upon this position, Napoleon drew Bennigsen from his lair by marching straight upon Königsberg. Bennigsen supposed himself to be in time to deal with an isolated corps; he found himself face to face with the whole forces of the enemy at Friedland, accepted battle, and was unable to save his army from a severe and decisive defeat (June 14). The victory of Friedland brought the French into Königsberg. Bennigsen retired behind the Niemen; and on the 19th of June an armistice closed the operations of the hostile forces upon the frontiers of Russia.*

Battle of Friedland, June 14.

The situation of Bennigsen's army was by no means desperate. His men had not been surrounded; they had lost scarcely any prisoners; they felt no fear of the French. But the general exaggerated the seriousness of his defeat. Like most of his officers, he was weary of the war, and felt no sympathy with the motives which led the Emperor to fight for the common cause of

---

* The battle of Friedland is described in Lord Hutchinson's despatch (Records: Prussia, vol. 200—in which volume are also Colonel Sonntag's reports, containing curious details about the Russians, and some personal matter about Napoleon in a letter from an inhabitant of Eylau; also Gneisenau's appeal to Mr. Canning from Colberg).

Europe. The politicians who surrounded Alexander urged him to withdraw Russia from a conflict in which she had nothing to gain. The Emperor wavered. The tardiness of Great Britain, the continued neutrality of Austria, cast a doubt upon the wisdom of his own disinterestedness; and he determined to meet Napoleon, and ascertain the terms on which Russia might be reconciled to the master of half the Continent.

On the 25th of June the two sovereigns met one another on the raft of Tilsit, in the midstream of the river Niemen. The conversation, which is alleged to have been opened by Alexander with an expression of hatred towards England, was heard by no one but the speakers. But whatever the eagerness or the reluctance of the Russian monarch to sever himself from Great Britain, the purpose of Napoleon was effected. Alexander surrendered himself to the addresses of a conqueror who seemed to ask for nothing and to offer everything. The negotiations were prolonged; the relations of the two monarchs became more and more intimate; and the issue of the struggle for life or death was that Russia accepted the whole scheme of Napoleonic conquest, and took its place by the side of the despoiler in return for its share of the prey. It was in vain that the King of Prussia had rejected Napoleon's offers after the battle of Eylau, in fidelity to his engagements towards his ally. Promises, treaties, and pity were alike cast to the winds. The unfortunate Frederick William received no more embraces; the friend with whom he was to stand or fall

Interview of Napoleon and Alexander at Tilsit, June 25.

bargained away the larger half of his dominions to Napoleon, and even rectified the Russian frontier at his expense. Prussia's continued existence in any shape whatever was described as a concession made by Napoleon to Alexander. By the public articles of the Treaties of Tilsit, signed by France, Russia, and Prussia in the first week of July, the King of Prussia ceded to Napoleon the whole of his dominions west of the Elbe, and the entire territory which Prussia had gained in the three partitions of Poland, with the exception of a district upon the Lower Vistula connecting Pomerania with Eastern Prussia. Out of the ceded territory on the west of the Elbe a Kingdom of Westphalia was created for Napoleon's brother Jerome; the Polish provinces of Prussia, with the exception of a strip made over to Alexander, were formed into the Grand-Duchy of Warsaw, and presented to Napoleon's vassal, the King of Saxony. Russia recognised the Napoleonic client-states in Italy, Holland, and Germany. The Czar undertook to offer his mediation in the conflict between France and Great Britain; a secret article provided that, in the event of Great Britain and France being at war on the ensuing 1st of December, Prussia should declare war against Great Britain.

Treaties of Tilsit, July, 1807.

Such were the stipulations contained in the formal Treaties of Peace between the three Powers. These, however, contained but a small part of the terms agreed upon between the masters of the east and of the west. A secret Treaty of Alliance, distinct from the Treaty of Peace, was also signed by

Secret Treaty of Alliance.

Napoleon and Alexander. In the conversations which won over the Czar to the cause of France, Napoleon had offered to Alexander the spoils of Sweden and the Ottoman Empire. Finland and the Danubian provinces were not too high a price for the support of a Power whose arms could paralyse Austria and Prussia. In return for the promise of this extension of his Empire, Alexander undertook, in the event of Great Britain refusing terms of peace dictated by himself, to unite his arms to those of Napoleon, and to force the neutral maritime Powers, Denmark and Portugal, to take part in the struggle against England. The annexation of Moldavia and Wallachia to the Russian Empire was provided for under the form of a French mediation. In the event of the Porte declining this mediation, Napoleon undertook to assist Russia to liberate all the European territory subject to the yoke of the Sultan, with the exception of Roumelia and Constantinople. A partition of the liberated territory between France and Russia, as well as the establishment of the Napoleonic house in Spain, probably formed the subject rather of a verbal understanding than of any written agreement.*

<small>Conspiracy of the two Emperors.</small> Such was this vast and threatening scheme, conceived by the man whose whole career had been one consistent struggle for personal domination, accepted by the man who among the rulers of the Continent had hitherto shown the greatest power of acting for a European end, and of interesting himself in a cause not directly his own. In the imagination of

* Bignon, vi., 342.

Napoleon, the national forces of the western continent had now ceased to exist. Austria excepted, there was no State upon the mainland whose army and navy were not prospectively in the hands of himself and his new ally. The commerce of Great Britain, already excluded from the greater part of Europe, was now to be shut out from all the rest; the armies which had hitherto fought under British subsidies for the independence of Europe, the navies which had preserved their existence by neutrality or by friendship with England, were soon to be thrown without distinction against that last foe. If even at this moment an English statesman who had learnt the secret agreement of Tilsit might have looked without fear to the future of his country, it was not from any imperfection in the structure of Continental tyranny. The fleets of Denmark and Portugal might be of little real avail against English seamen; the homes of the English people might still be as secure from foreign invasion as when Nelson guarded the seas; but it was not from any vestige of political honour surviving in the Emperor Alexander. Where Alexander's action was of decisive importance, in his mediation between France and Prussia, he threw himself without scruple on to the side of oppression. It lay within his power to gain terms of peace for Prussia as lenient as those which Austria had gained at Campo Formio and at Lunéville: he sacrificed Prussia, as he allied himself against the last upholders of national independence in Europe, in order that he might himself receive Finland and the Danubian Provinces.

Two days before the signature of the Treaty of Tilsit the British troops which had once been so anxiously expected by the Czar landed in the island of Rügen. The struggle in which they were intended to take their part was over. Sweden alone remained in arms; and even the Quixotic pugnacity of King Gustavus was unable to save Stralsund from a speedy capitulation. But the troops of Great Britain were not destined to return without striking a blow. The negotiations between Napoleon and Alexander had scarcely begun, when secret intelligence of their purport was sent to the British Government.* It became known in London that the fleet of Denmark was to be seized by Napoleon, and forced to fight against Great Britain. Canning and his colleagues acted with the promptitude that seldom failed the British Government when it could effect its object by the fleet alone. They determined to anticipate Napoleon's violation of Danish neutrality, and to seize upon the navy which would otherwise be seized by France and Russia.

English expedition against Denmark, July, 1807.

On the 28th of July a fleet with 20,000 men on board set sail from the British coast. The troops landed

* Papers presented to Parliament 1808, p. 106. The intelligence reached Canning on the 21st of July. Canning's despatch to Brook Taylor, July 22; Records: Denmark, vol. 196. It has never been known who sent the information, but it must have been some one very near the Czar, for it purported to give the very words used by Napoleon in his interview with Alexander on the raft. It is clear, from Canning's despatch of July 22, that this conversation and nothing else had up till then been reported. The informant was probably one of the authors of the English alliance of 1805.

in Denmark in the middle of August, and united with the corps which had already been despatched to Rügen. The Danish Government was summoned to place its navy in the hands of Great Britain, in order that it might remain as a deposit in some British port until the conclusion of peace. While demanding this sacrifice of Danish neutrality, England undertook to protect the Danish nation and colonies from the hostility of Napoleon, and to place at the disposal of its Government every means of naval and military defence. Failing the surrender of the fleet, the English declared that they would bombard Copenhagen. The reply given to this summons was such as might be expected from a courageous nation exasperated against Great Britain by its harsh treatment of neutral ships of commerce, and inclined to submit to the despot of the Continent rather than to the tyrants of the seas. Negotiations proved fruitless, and on the 2nd of September the English opened fire on Copenhagen. For three days and nights the city underwent a bombardment of cruel efficiency. Eighteen hundred houses were levelled, the town was set on fire in several places, and a large number of the inhabitants lost their lives. At length the commander found himself compelled to capitulate. The fleet was handed over to Great Britain, with all the stores in the arsenal of Copenhagen. It was brought to England, no longer under the terms of a friendly neutrality, but as a prize of war.

Bombardment of Copenhagen, Sept. 2.

The captors themselves were ashamed of their spoil. England received an armament which had been taken from a people who were not our enemies, and by an attack which was not war, with more misgiving than applause. In Europe the seemingly unprovoked assault upon a weak neutral State excited the utmost indignation. The British Ministry, who were prevented from making public the evidence which they had received of the intention of the two Emperors, were believed to have invented the story of the Secret Treaty. The Danish Government denied that Napoleon had demanded their co-operation; Napoleon and Alexander themselves assumed the air of indignant astonishment. But the facts alleged by Canning and his colleagues were correct. The conspiracy of the two Emperors was no fiction. The only question still remaining open—and this is indeed an essential one—relates to the engagements entered into by the Danish Government itself. Napoleon in his correspondence of this date alludes to certain promises made to him by the Court of Denmark, but he also complains that these promises had not been fulfilled; and the context of the letter renders it almost certain that, whatever may have been demanded by Napoleon, nothing more was promised by Denmark than that its ports should be closed to English vessels.* Had the British Cabinet possessed evidence of the determination

---

* Napoleon to Talleyrand, July 31, 1807. He instructs Talleyrand to enter into certain negotiations with the Danish Minister, which would be meaningless if the Crown Prince had already promised to hand over the fleet. The original English documents, in Records: Denmark, vols. 196, 197, really show that Canning never considered that he had any proof of the intentions of Denmark, and that he justified his action only by the inability of Denmark to resist Napoleon's demands.

of the Danish Government to transfer its fleet to Napoleon without resistance, the attack upon Denmark, considered as virtually an act of war, would not have been unjust. But beyond an alleged expression of Napoleon at Tilsit, no such evidence was even stated to have reached London; and the undoubted conspiracy of the Emperors against Danish neutrality was no sufficient ground for an action on the part of Great Britain which went so far beyond the mere frustration of their designs. The surrender of the Danish fleet demanded by England would have been an unqualified act of war on the part of Denmark against Napoleon; it was no mere guarantee for a continued neutrality. Nor had the British Government the last excuse of an urgent and overwhelming necessity. Nineteen Danish men-of-war would not have turned the scale against England. The memory of Trafalgar might well have given a British Ministry courage to meet its enemies by the ordinary methods of war. Had the forces of Denmark been far larger than they actually were, the peril of Great Britain was not so extreme as to excuse the wrong done to mankind by an example encouraging all future belligerents to anticipate one another in forcing each neutral state to take part with themselves.

The fleet which Napoleon had meant to turn against this country now lay safe within Portsmouth harbour. Denmark, in bitter resentment, declared war against Great Britain, and rendered some service to the Continental League by the attacks of its privateers upon British merchant-vessels in the Baltic. The second neutral power whose fate had been decided by the two Emperors at Tilsit received the summons of Napoleon a few days before the attack on Copenhagen. The Regent of Portugal himself informed the British Government that he had been required by Napoleon to close his ports to British vessels, to declare war on England, and to confiscate all British property within his dominions. Placed between a Power which could strip him of his dominions on land, and one which could despoil him of everything he possessed beyond the sea, the Regent determined to maintain his ancient friendship with Great Britain, and to submit to Napoleon only in so far as the English Government would excuse him, as acting under coercion. Although a nominal state of war arose between Portugal and England, the Regent really acted in the interest of England, and followed the advice of the British Cabinet up to the end.

<small>Napoleon's demands upon Portugal.</small>

The end was soon to come. The demands of Napoleon, arbitrary and oppressive as they were, by no means expressed his full intentions towards Portugal. He had determined to seize upon this country, and to employ it as a means for extending his own dominion over the whole of the Spanish Peninsula. An army-corps, under the command of Junot, had been already placed in the Pyrenees. On the 12th of October Napoleon received the answer of the Regent of Portugal, consenting to declare war upon England, and only rejecting the dishonourable order to confiscate all English property. This single act of resistance was sufficient for Napoleon's purpose. He immediately recalled his ambassador from Lisbon, and gave orders to Junot to cross the frontier, and march upon Portugal. The King of Spain, who was to be Napoleon's next victim, was for the moment employed as his accomplice. A treaty was concluded at Fontainebleau between Napoleon and King Charles IV. for the partition of Portugal (Oct. 27).* In return for the cession of the kingdom of Etruria, which was still nominally governed by a member of the Spanish house, the King of Spain was promised half the Portuguese colonies, along with the title of Emperor of the Indies; the northern provinces of Portugal were reserved for the infant King of Etruria, its southern provinces for Godoy, minister of Charles IV.; the central districts were to remain in the hands of France, and to be employed as a means of regaining the Spanish colonies from England upon the conclusion of a general peace.

<small>Treaty of Fontainebleau between France and Spain for the partition of Portugal, Oct. 27.</small>

Not one of these provisions was intended to be carried into effect. The conquest of Portugal was but a part of the conquest of the whole peninsula. But neither the Spanish Court nor the Spanish people suspected Napoleon's design. Junot advanced without resistance through the intervening Spanish territory, and pushed forward upon Lisbon with the utmost haste. The speed at which Napoleon's orders forced him to march reduced his army to utter prostration, and the least resistance would have resulted in its ruin. But the Court of Lisbon had determined to quit a country which they could not hope to defend

<small>Junot invades Portugal, Nov., 1807.</small>

* Cevallos, p. 78.

against the master of the Continent. Already in the seventeenth and eighteenth centuries the House of Braganza had been familiar with the project of transferring the seat of their Government to Brazil; and now, with the approval of Great Britain, the Regent resolved to maintain the independence of his family by flight across the Atlantic. As Junot's troops approached the capital, the servants of the palace hastily stowed the royal property on ship-board. On the 29th of November, when the French were now close at hand, the squadron which bore the House of Braganza to its colonial home dropped down the Tagus, saluted by the cannon of the English fleet that lay in the same river. Junot entered the capital a few hours later, and placed himself at the head of the Government without encountering any opposition. The occupation of Portugal was described by Napoleon as a reprisal for the bombardment of Copenhagen. It excited but little attention in Europe; and even at the Spanish Court the only feeling was one of satisfaction at the approaching aggrandisement of the Bourbon monarchy. The full significance of Napoleon's intervention in the affairs of the Peninsula was not discovered until some months were passed.

Portugal and Denmark had felt the consequences of the peace made at Tilsit. Less, however, depended upon the fate of the Danish fleet and the Portuguese Royal Family than upon the fate of Prussia, the most cruelly wronged of all the victims sacrificed by Alexander's ambition. The unfortunate Prussian State, reduced to half its former extent, devastated and impoverished by war, and burdened with the support of a French army, found in the crisis of its ruin the beginning of a worthier national life. Napoleon, in his own vindictive jealousy, unwittingly brought to the head of the Prussian Government the ablest and most patriotic statesman of the Continent. Since the spring of 1807 Baron Hardenberg had again been the leading Minister of Prussia, and it was to his counsel that the King's honourable rejection of a separate peace after the battle of Eylau was due. Napoleon could not permit this Minister, whom he had already branded as a partisan of Great Britain, to remain in power: he insisted upon Hardenberg's dismissal, and recommended the King of Prussia to summon Stein, who was as yet known to Napoleon only as a skilful financier, likely to succeed in raising the money which the French intended to extort. *Stein Minister, Oct. 5, 1807.*

Stein entered upon office on the 5th of October, 1807, with almost dictatorial power. The need of the most radical changes in the public services, as well as in the social order of the Prussian State, had been brought home to all enlightened men by the disasters of the war; and a commission, which included among its members the historian Niebuhr, had already sketched large measures of reform before Hardenberg quitted office. Stein's appointment brought to the head of the State a man immeasurably superior to Hardenberg in the energy necessary for the execution of great changes, and gave to those who were the most sincerely engaged in civil or military reform a leader unrivalled in patriotic zeal, in boldness, and in purity of character. The first great legislative measure of Stein was the abolition of serfage, and of all the legal distinctions which fixed within the limits of their caste the noble, the citizen, and the peasant. In setting his name to the edict* which, on the 9th of October, 1807, made an end of the mediæval framework of Prussian society, Stein was indeed but consummating a change which the progress of neighbouring States must have forced upon Prussia, whoever held its government. The Decree was framed upon the report of Hardenberg's Commission, and was published by Stein within six days after his own entry upon office. Great as were the changes involved in this edict of emancipation, it contained no more than was necessary to bring Prussia up to the level of the least advanced of the western Continental States. In Austria pure serfage had been abolished by Maria Theresa thirty years before; it vanished, along with most of the legal distinctions of class, wherever the victories of France carried a new political order; even the misused peasantry of Poland had been freed from their degrading yoke within the borders of the newly-founded Duchy of Warsaw. If Prussia was not to renounce its partnership in European progress and range itself with its barbarous eastern neighbour, that order which fettered the peasant to the soil, and limited every Prussian to the hereditary occupations of his class could no longer be maintained. It is not as an achievement of individual genius, but as

Marginal note: Edict of Emancipation, Oct. 9, 1807.

---

* Pertz, ii., 23. Seeley, i., 430.

the most vivid expression of the differences between the old and the new Europe, that the first measure of Stein deserves a closer examination.

The Edict of October 9, 1807, extinguished all personal servitude; it permitted the noble, the citizen, and the peasant to follow any calling; it abolished the rule which prevented land held by a member of one class from passing into the hands of another class; it empowered families to free their estates from entail. Taken together, these enactments substitute the free disposition of labour and property for the outworn doctrine which Prussia had inherited from the feudal ages, that what a man is born that he shall live and die. The extinction of serfage, though not the most prominent provision of the Edict, was the one whose effects were the soonest felt. *The Prussian peasant before and after the Edict of Oct 9.* In the greater part of Prussia the marks of serfage, as distinct from payments and services amounting to a kind of rent, were the obligation of the peasant to remain on his holding, and the right of the lord to take the peasant's children as unpaid servants into his house. A general relation of obedience and command existed, as between an hereditary subject and master, although the lord could neither exact an arbitrary amount of labour nor inflict the cruel punishments which had been common in Poland and Hungary. What the villein was in England in the thirteenth century, that the serf was in Prussia in the year 1806; and the change which in England gradually elevated the villein into the free copyholder was that change which, so many centuries later, the Prussian legislator effected by one great measure. Stein made the Prussian peasant what the English copyholder had become at the accession of Henry VII., and what the French peasant had been before 1789, a free person, but one bound to render fixed dues and service to the lord of the manor in virtue of the occupation of his land. These feudal dues and services, which the French peasant, accustomed for centuries before the Revolution to consider himself as the full proprietor of the land, treated as a mere grievance and abuse, Stein considered to be the best form in which the joint interest of the lord and the peasant could be maintained. It was reserved for Hardenberg, four years later, to free the peasant from all obligations towards his lord, and to place him in unshackled proprietorship of two-thirds of his former holding, the lord receiving the remaining one-third in compensation for the loss of feudal dues. Neither Stein nor Hardenberg interfered with the right of the lord to act as judge and police-magistrate within the limits of his manor; and the hereditary legal jurisdiction, which was abolished in Scotland in 1747, and in France in 1789, continued unchanged in Prussia down to the year 1848.

The history of Agrarian Reform upon the Continent shows how vast was the interval of time by which some of the greatest social changes in England had anticipated the corresponding changes in almost all other nations. But if the Prussian peasant at the beginning of this century remained in the servile condition which had passed out of mind in Great Britain before the Reformation, the early prosperity of

Relative position of the peasant in Prussia and England.

the peasant in England was dearly purchased by a subsequent decline which has made his present lot far inferior to that of the children or grandchildren of the Prussian serf. However heavy the load of the Prussian serf, his holding was at least protected by law from absorption into the domain of his lord. Before sufficient capital had been amassed in Prussia to render landed property an object of competition, the forced military service of Frederick had made it a rule of State that the farmsteads of the peasant class must remain undiminished in number, at whatever violence to the laws of the market or the desires of great landlords. No process was permitted to take place corresponding to that by which, in England, after the villein had become the free copyholder, the lord, with or without technical legal right, terminated the copyhold tenure of his retainer, and made the land as much his own exclusive property as the chairs and tables in his house. In Prussia, if the law kept the peasant on the land, it also kept the land for the peasant. Economic conditions, in the absence of such control in England, worked against the class of small holders. Their early enfranchisement in fact contributed to their extinction. It would perhaps have been better for the English labouring class to remain bound by a semi-servile tie to their land, than to gain a free holding which the law, siding with the landlord, treated as terminable at the expiration of particular lives, and which the increasing capital of the rich made its favourite prey. It is little profit to the landless, resourceless English labourer to know that his ancestor was a yeoman when the Prussian was a serf. Long as the bondage of the peasant on the mainland endured, prosperity came at last. The conditions which once distinguished agricultural England from the Continent are now reversed. Nowhere on the Continent is there a labouring class so stripped and despoiled of all interest in the soil, so sedulously excluded from all possibilities of proprietorship, as in England. In England alone the absence of internal revolution and foreign pressure has preserved a class whom a life spent in toil leaves as bare and dependent as when it began, and to whom the only boon which their country can offer is the education which may lead them to quit it.

Besides the commission which had drafted the Edict of Emancipation, Stein found a military commission engaged on a plan for the reorganisation of the Prussian army. The existing system forced the peasant to serve in the ranks for twenty years, and drew the officers from the nobility, leaving the inhabitants of towns without either the duty or the right to enter the army at all. Since the battle of Jena, no one doubted that the principle of universal liability to military service must be introduced into Prussia; on the other hand, the very disasters of the State rendered it impossible to maintain an army on anything approaching to its former scale. With half its territory torn from it, and the remainder devastated by war, Prussia could barely afford to keep 40,000 soldiers in arms. Such were the conditions laid before the men who were charged with the construction of a new

Prussian military system. Their conclusions, imperfect in themselves, and but partially carried out in the succeeding years, have nevertheless been the basis of the latest military organisation of Prussia and of Europe generally. The problem was solved by the adoption of a short period of service and the rapid drafting of the trained conscript into a reserve-force. *Short service.* Scharnhorst, President of the Military Commission, to whom more than to any one man Prussia owed its military revival, proposed to maintain an Active Army of 40,000 men; a Reserve, into which soldiers should pass after short service in the active army; a Landwehr, to be employed only for the internal defence of the country; and a Landsturm, or general arming of the population, for a species of guerilla warfare. Scharnhorst's project was warmly supported by Stein, who held a seat and a vote on the Military Commission; and the system of short service, with a Reserve, was immediately brought into action, though on a very limited scale. The remainder of the scheme had to wait for the assistance of events. The principle of universal military obligation was first proclaimed in the war of 1813, when also the Landwehr was first enrolled.

The reorganisation of the Prussian military system and the emancipation of the peasant, though promoted by Stein's accession to power, did not originate in Stein himself; the distinctive work of Stein was a great scheme of political reform. *Stein's plans of political reform.* Had Stein remained longer in power, he would have given to Prussia at least the beginnings of constitutional government. Events drove him from office when but a small part of his project was carried into effect; but the project itself was great and comprehensive. He designed to give Prussia a Parliament, and to establish a system of self-government in its towns and country districts. Stein had visited England in his youth. The history and the literature of England interested him beyond those of any other country; and he had learnt from England that the partnership of the nation in the work of government, so far from weakening authority, animates it with a force which no despotic system can long preserve. Almost every important state-paper written by Stein denounces the apathy of the civil population of Prussia, and attributes it to their exclusion from all exercise of public duties. He declared that the nation must be raised from its torpor by the establishment of representative government and the creation of free local institutions in town and country. Stein was no friend of democracy. Like every other Prussian statesman he took for granted the exercise of a vigorous monarchical power at the centre of the State; but around the permanent executive he desired to gather the Council of the Nation, checking at least the caprices of Cabinet-rule, and making the opinion of the people felt by the monarch. Stein's Parliament would have been a far weaker body than the English House of Commons, but it was at least not intended to be a mockery, like those legislative bodies which Napoleon and his clients erected as the disguise

Design for a Parliament, for Municipalities, and District Boards.

of despotism. The transaction of local business in the towns and country districts, which had hitherto belonged to officials of the Crown, Stein desired to transfer in part to bodies elected by the inhabitants themselves. The functions allotted to the new municipal bodies illustrated the modest and cautious nature of Stein's attempt in the direction of self-government, including no more than the care of the poor, the superintendence of schools, and the maintenance of streets and public buildings. Finance remained partly, police wholly, in the hands of the central Government. Equally limited were the powers which Stein proposed to entrust to the district councils elected by the rural population. In comparison with the self-government of England or America, the self-government which Stein would have introduced into Prussia was of the most elementary character; yet his policy stood out in striking contrast to that which in every client-state of Napoleon was now crushing out the last elements of local independence under a rigid official centralisation.

Stein was indeed unable to transform Prussia as he desired. Of the legislative, the municipal, and the district reforms which he had sketched, the municipal reform was the only one which he had time to carry out before being driven from power; and for forty years the municipal institutions created by Stein were the only fragment of liberty which Prussia enjoyed. A vehement opposition to reform was excited among the landowners, and supported by a powerful party at the Court. Stein was

Municipal reform alone carried out.

detested by the nobles whose peasants he had emancipated, and by the Berlin aristocracy, which for the last ten years had maintained the policy of friendship with France, and now declared the only safety of the Prussian State to lie in unconditional submission to Napoleon. The fire of patriotism, of energy, of self-sacrifice, which burned in Stein made him no representative of the Prussian governing classes of his time. It was not long before the landowners, who deemed him a Jacobin, and the friends of the French, who called him a madman, had the satisfaction of seeing the Minister sent into banishment by order of Napoleon himself (Dec., 1808). Stein left the greater part of his work uncompleted, but he had not laboured in vain. The years of his ministry in 1807 and 1808 were the years that gathered together everything that was worthiest in Prussia in the dawn of a national revival, and prepared the way for that great movement in which, after an interval of the deepest gloom, Stein was himself to light the nation to its victory.

CHAPTER VIII.

Spain in 1806—Napoleon uses the quarrel between Ferdinand and Godoy—He affects to be Ferdinand's protector—Dupont's army enters Spain—Murat in Spain—Charles abdicates—Ferdinand King—Savary brings Ferdinand to Bayonne—Napoleon makes both Charles and Ferdinand resign—Spirit of the Spanish Nation—Contrast with Germany—Rising of all Spain—The Notables at Bayonne—Campaign of 1808—Capitulation of Baylen—Wellesley lands in Portugal—Vimieiro—Convention of Cintra—Effect of the Spanish Rising on Europe—War Party in Prussia—Napoleon and Alexander at Erfurt—Stein resigns, and is proscribed—Napoleon in Spain—Spanish Misgovernment—Campaign on the Ebro—Campaign of Sir John Moore—Corunna—Napoléon leaves Spain—Siege of Saragossa—Successes of the French.

SPAIN, which had played so insignificant a part throughout the Revolutionary War, was now about to become the theatre of events that opened a new world of hope to Europe. Its king, the Bourbon Charles IV., was more weak and more pitiful than any sovereign of the age. Power belonged to the Queen and to her paramour Godoy, who for the last fourteen years had so conducted the affairs of the country that every change in its policy had brought with it new disaster. In the war of the First Coalition Spain had joined the Allies, and French armies had crossed the Pyrenees. In 1796 Spain entered the service of France, and lost the battle of St. Vincent. At the Peace of Amiens, Napoleon surrendered its colony Trinidad to England; on the renewal of the war he again forced it into hostilities with Great Britain, and brought upon it

Spanish affairs, 1793–1806.

the disaster of Trafalgar. This unbroken humiliation of the Spanish arms, combined with intolerable oppression and impoverishment at home, raised so bitter an outcry against Godoy's government, that foreign observers, who underrated the loyalty of the Spanish people, believed the country to be on the verge of revolution. At the Court itself the Crown Prince Ferdinand, under the influence of his Neapolitan wife, headed a party in opposition to Godoy and the supporters of French dominion.

Spain in 1806. Godoy, insecure at home, threw himself the more unreservedly into the arms of Napoleon, who bestowed upon him a contemptuous patronage, and flattered him with the promise of an independent principality in Portugal. Izquierdo, Godoy's agent at Paris, received proposals from Napoleon which were concealed from the Spanish Ambassador; and during the first months of 1806 Napoleon possessed no more devoted servant than the man who virtually held the government of Spain.

The opening of negotiations between Napoleon and Fox's Ministry in May, 1806, first shook this relation of confidence and obedience. Peace between France and England involved the abandonment on the part of Napoleon of any attack upon Portugal; and Napoleon now began to meet Godoy's inquiries after his Portuguese principality with an ominous silence. The next intelligence received was that the Spanish Balearic Islands had been offered by Napoleon to Great Britain, with the view of providing an indemnity for Ferdinand of Naples, if he should give up Sicily to Joseph Bonaparte (July, 1806). This contemptuous appropriation of Spanish territory, without even the pretence of consulting the Spanish Government, excited scarcely less anger at Madrid than the corresponding proposal with regard to Hanover excited at Berlin. The Court began to meditate a change of policy, and watched the events which were leading Prussia to arm for the war of 1806. A few weeks more passed, and news arrived that Buenos Ayres, the capital of Spanish South America, had fallen into the hands of the English. This disaster produced the deepest impression, for the loss of Buenos Ayres was believed, and with good reason, to be but the prelude to the loss of the entire American empire of Spain. Continuance of the war with England was certain ruin; alliance with the enemies of Napoleon was at least not hopeless, now that Prussia was on the point of throwing its army into the scale against France. An agent was despatched by the Spanish Government to London (Sept., 1806); and, upon the commencement of hostilities by Prussia, a proclamation was issued by Godoy, which, without naming any actual enemy, summoned the Spanish people to prepare for a war on behalf of their country.

Spain intends to join Prussia in 1806.

Scarcely had the manifesto been read by the Spaniards when the Prussian army was annihilated at Jena. The dream of resistance to Napoleon vanished away; the only anxiety of the Spanish Government was to escape from the consequences of its untimely daring. Godoy hastened to explain that his martial proclamation had been directed not against the Emperor of the French, but against the

Y

Emperor of Morocco. Napoleon professed himself satisfied with this palpable absurdity: it appeared as if the events of the last few months had left no trace on his mind. Immediately after the Peace of Tilsit he resumed his negotiations with Godoy upon the old friendly footing, and brought them to a conclusion in the Treaty of Fontainebleau (Oct., 1807), which provided for the invasion of Portugal by a French and a Spanish army, and for its division into principalities, one of which was to be conferred upon Godoy himself. The occupation of Portugal was duly effected, and Godoy looked forward to the speedy retirement of the French from the province which was to be his portion of the spoil.

Treaty of Fontainebleau, Oct., 1807.

Napoleon, however, had other ends in view. Spain, not Portugal, was the true prize. Napoleon had gradually formed the determination of taking Spain into his own hands, and the dissensions of the Court itself enabled him to appear upon the scene as the judge to whom all parties appealed. The Crown Prince Ferdinand had long been at open enmity with Godoy and his own mother. So long as Ferdinand's Neapolitan wife was alive, her influence made the Crown Prince the centre of the party hostile to France; but after her death in 1806, at a time when Godoy himself inclined to join Napoleon's enemies, Ferdinand took up a new position, and allied himself with the French Ambassador, at whose instigation he wrote to Napoleon, soliciting the hand of a princess of the Napoleonic House.* Godoy, though unaware of

Napoleon uses the enmity of Ferdinand against Godoy.

* Cevallos, p. 13. Baumgarten, Geschichte Spaniens, i., 131.

the letter, discovered that Ferdinand was engaged in some intrigue. King Charles was made to believe that his son had entered into a conspiracy to dethrone him. The Prince was placed under arrest, and on the 30th of October, 1807, a royal proclamation appeared at Madrid, announcing that Ferdinand had been detected in a conspiracy against his parents, and that he was about to be brought to justice along with his accomplices. King Charles at the same time wrote a letter to Napoleon, of whose connection with Ferdinand he had not the slightest suspicion, stating that he intended to exclude the Crown Prince from the succession to the throne of Spain. No sooner had Napoleon received the communication from the simple King than he saw himself in possession of the pretext for intervention which he had so long desired. The most pressing orders were given for the concentration of troops on the Spanish frontier; Napoleon appeared to be on the point of entering Spain as the defender of the hereditary rights of Ferdinand. *Napoleon about to intervene as protector of Ferdinand.* The opportunity, however, proved less favourable than Napoleon had expected. The Crown Prince, overcome by his fears, begged forgiveness of his father, and disclosed the negotiations which had taken place between himself and the French Ambassador. Godoy, dismayed at finding Napoleon's hand in what he had supposed to be a mere palace-intrigue, abandoned all thought of proceeding further against the Crown Prince; and a manifesto announced that Ferdinand was restored to the favour of his father. Napoleon now countermanded the order which he had given for the despatch of the Rhenish troops to the Pyrenees, and contented himself with directing General Dupont, the commander of an army-corps nominally destined for Portugal, to cross the Spanish frontier and advance as far as Vittoria.

Dupont enters Spain, Dec. 1807.

Dupont's troops entered Spain in the last days of the year 1807, and were received with acclamations. It was universally believed that Napoleon had espoused the cause of Ferdinand, and intended to deliver the Spanish nation from the detested rule of Godoy. Since the open attack made upon Ferdinand in the publication of the pretended conspiracy, the Crown Prince, who was personally as contemptible as any of his enemies, had become the idol of the people. For years past the hatred of the nation towards Godoy and the Queen had been constantly deepening, and the very reforms which Godoy effected in the hope of attaching to himself the more enlightened classes only served to complete his unpopularity with the fanatical mass of the nation. The French, who gradually entered the Peninsula to the number of 80,000, and who described themselves as the protectors of Ferdinand and of the true Catholic faith, were able to spread themselves over the northern provinces without exciting suspicion. It was only when their commanders, by a series of tricks worthy of American savages, obtained possession of the frontier citadels and fortresses, that the wiser part of the nation began to entertain some doubt as to the real purpose of their ally. At the Court

French welcomed in Spain as Ferdinand's protectors.

itself and among the enemies of Ferdinand the advance of the French roused the utmost alarm. King Charles wrote to Napoleon in the tone of ancient friendship; but the answer he received was threatening and mysterious. The utterances which the Emperor let fall in the presence of persons likely to report them at Madrid were even more alarming, and were intended to terrify the Court into the resolution to take flight from Madrid. The capital once abandoned by the King, Napoleon judged that he might safely take everything into his own hands on the pretence of restoring to Spain the government which it had lost.

On the 20th of February, 1808, Murat was ordered to quit Paris in order to assume the command in Spain. Not a word was said by Napoleon to him before his departure. His instructions first reached him at Bayonne; they were of a military nature, and gave no indication of the ultimate political object of his mission. Murat entered Spain on the 1st of March, knowing no more than that he was ordered to reassure all parties and to commit himself to none, but with full confidence that he himself was intended by Napoleon to be the successor of the Bourbon dynasty. It was now that the Spanish Court, expecting the appearance of the French army in Madrid, resolved upon that flight which Napoleon considered so necessary to his own success. The project was not kept a secret. It passed from Godoy to the Ministers of State, and from them to the friends of Ferdinand. The populace of Madrid was inflamed by the report that Godoy was about to carry the

Murat sent to Spain, Feb. 1808.

King to a distance, in order to prolong the misgovernment which the French had determined to overthrow. A tumultuous crowd marched from the capital to Aranjuez, the residence of the Court. On the evening of the 17th of March, the palace of Godoy was stormed by the mob. Godoy himself was seized, and carried to the barracks amid the blows and curses of the populace. The terrified King, who already saw before him the fate of his cousin, Louis XVI., first published a decree depriving Godoy of all his dignities, and then abdicated in favour of his son. On the 19th of March Ferdinand was proclaimed King.

Charles IV. abdicates, March 17, 1808.

Such was the unexpected intelligence that met Murat as he approached Madrid. The dissensions of the Court, which were to supply his ground of intervention, had been terminated by the Spaniards themselves: in the place of a despised dotard and a menaced favourite, Spain had gained a youthful sovereign around whom all classes of the nation rallied with the utmost enthusiasm. Murat's position became a very difficult one; but he supplied what was wanting in his instructions by the craft of a man bent upon creating a vacancy in his own favour. He sent his aide-de-camp, Monthieu, to visit the dethroned sovereign, and obtained a protest from King Charles IV., declaring his abdication to have been extorted from him by force, and consequently to be null and void. This document Murat kept secret; but he carefully abstained from doing anything which might involve a recognition of Ferdinand's title. On the 23rd of March the French

French enter Madrid, March 23.

MURAT ENTERING MADRID.

(p. 374.)

troops entered Madrid. Nothing had as yet become
known to the public that indicated an altered policy on
the part of the French; and the soldiers of Murat, as
the supposed friends of Ferdinand, met with as friendly
a reception in Madrid as in the other towns of Spain.
On the following day Ferdinand himself made his solemn
entry into the capital, amid wild demonstrations of an
almost barbaric loyalty.

In the tumult of popular joy it was noticed that
Murat's troops continued their exercises without the
least regard to the pageant that so deeply stirred the
hearts of the Spaniards. Suspicions were aroused; the
enthusiasm of the people for the French soldiers began
to change into irritation and ill-will. The end of the
long drama of deceit was in fact now close at hand.
On the 4th of April General Savary arrived at Madrid
with instructions independent of those given to Murat.
He was charged to entice the new Spanish
sovereign from his capital, and to bring him, *Savary brings Ferdinand to Bayonne, April, 1808.*
either as a dupe or as a prisoner, on to
French soil. The task was not a difficult one. Savary
pretended that Napoleon had actually entered Spain,
and that he only required an assurance of Ferdinand's
continued friendship before recognising him as the legitimate successor of Charles IV. Ferdinand, he added,
could show no greater mark of cordiality to his patron
than by advancing to meet him on the road. Snared by
these hopes, Ferdinand set out from Madrid, in company
with Savary and some of his own foolish confidants.
On reaching Burgos the party found no signs of the

Emperor. They continued their journey to Vittoria. Here Ferdinand's suspicions were aroused, and he declined to proceed farther. Savary hastened to Bayonne to report the delay to Napoleon. He returned with a letter which overcame Ferdinand's scruples and induced him to cross the Pyrenees, in spite of the prayers or statesmen and the loyal violence of the simple inhabitants of the district. At Bayonne Ferdinand was visited by Napoleon, but not a word was spoken on the object of his journey. In the afternoon the Emperor received Ferdinand and his suite at a neighbouring château, but preserved the same ominous silence. When the other guests departed, the Canon Escoiquiz, a member of Ferdinand's retinue, was detained, and learned from Napoleon's own lips the fate in store for the Bourbon Monarchy. Savary returned to Bayonne with Ferdinand, and informed the prince that he must renounce the crown of Spain.*

For some days Ferdinand held out against Napoleon's demands with a stubbornness not often shown by him in the course of his mean and hypocritical career. He was assailed not only by Napoleon but by those whose fall had been his own rise; for Godoy was sent to Bayonne by Murat, and the old King and Queen hurried after their son in order to witness his humiliation. Ferdinand's parents attacked him with an indecency that astonished even Napoleon himself; but the Prince maintained his refusal until news arrived from Madrid which terrified him into submission. The

* Escoiquiz, Exposé, p. 57, 107.

irritation of the capital had culminated in an armed conflict between the populace and the French troops. On an attempt being made by Murat to remove the remaining members of the royal family from the palace, the capital had broken into open insurrection, and wherever French soldiers were found alone or in small bodies they were massacred. (May 2.) Some hundreds of the French perished; but the victory of Murat was speedy, and his vengeance ruthless. The insurgents were driven into the great central square of the city, and cut down by repeated charges of cavalry. When all resistance was over, numbers of the citizens were shot in cold blood. Such was the intelligence which reached Bayonne in the midst of Napoleon's struggle with Ferdinand. There was no further need of argument. Ferdinand was informed that if he withheld his resignation for twenty-four hours longer he would be treated as a rebel. He yielded; and for a couple of country houses and two life-annuities the crown of Spain and the Indies was renounced in favour of Napoleon by father and son. *Attack on the French in Madrid, May 2.* *Charles and Ferdinand surrender their rights to Napoleon.*

The crown had indeed been won without a battle. That there remained a Spanish nation ready to fight to the death for its independence was not a circumstance which Napoleon had taken into account. His experience had as yet taught him of no force, but that of Governments and armies. In the larger States, or groups of States, which had hitherto been the spoil of France, the sense of nationality scarcely *National spirit of the Spaniards.*

existed. Italy had felt it no disgrace to pass under the rule of Napoleon. The Germans on both sides of the Rhine knew of a fatherland only as an arena of the keenest jealousies. In Prussia and in Austria the bond of citizenship was far less the love of country than the habit of obedience to government. England and Russia, where patriotism existed in the sense in which it existed in Spain, had as yet been untouched by French armies. Judging from the action of the Germans and the Italians, Napoleon might well suppose that in settling with the Spanish Government he had also settled with the Spanish people, or, at the worst, that his troops might have to fight some fanatical peasants, like those who resisted the expulsion of the Bourbons from Naples. But the Spanish nation was no mosaic of political curiosities like the Holy Roman Empire, and no divided and oblivious family like the population of Italy. Spain, as a single nation united under its King, had once played the foremost part in Europe: when its grandeur departed, its pride had remained behind: the Spaniard, in all his torpor and impoverishment, retained the impulse of honour, the spirited self-respect, which periods of national greatness leave behind them among a race capable of cherishing their memory. Nor had those influences of a common European culture, which directly opposed themselves to patriotism in Germany, affected the home-bred energy of Spain. The temper of mind which could find satisfaction in the revival of a form of Greek art when Napoleon's cavalry were scouring Germany, or which could inquire whether mankind would not profit by the removal of the barriers between nations, was unknown among the Spanish people. Their feeling towards a foreign invader was less distant from that of African savages than from that of the civilised and literary nations which had fallen so easy a prey to the French. Government, if it had degenerated into everything that was contemptible, had at least failed to reduce the people to the passive helplessness which resulted from the perfection of uniformity in Prussia. Provincial institutions, though corrupted, were not extinguished; provincial attachments and prejudices existed in unbounded strength. Like the passion of the Spaniard for his native district, his passion for Spain was of a blind and furious character. Enlightened conviction, though not altogether absent, had small place in the Spanish war of defence. Religious fanaticism, hatred of the foreigner, delight in physical barbarity, played their full part by the side of nobler elements in the struggle for national independence.

The captivity of Ferdinand, and the conflict of Murat's troops with the inhabitants of Madrid, had become known in the Spanish cities before the middle of May. On the 20th of the same month the *Gaceta* announced the abdication of the Bourbon family. Nothing more was wanting to throw Spain into tumult. The same irresistible impulse seized provinces and cities separated by the whole breadth of the Peninsula. Without communication, and without the guidance of any central authority, the Spanish people in every part of the kingdom armed themselves

Rising of Spain, May, 1808.

against the usurper. Carthagena rose on the 22nd. Valencia forced its magistrates to proclaim King Ferdinand on the 23rd. Two days later the mountain-district of Asturias, with a population of half a million, formally declared war on Napoleon, and despatched envoys to Great Britain to ask for assistance. On the 26th, Santander and Seville, on opposite sides of the Peninsula, joined the national movement. Corunna, Badajoz, and Granada declared themselves on the Feast of St. Ferdinand, the 30th of May. Thus within a week the entire country was in arms, except in those districts where the presence of French troops rendered revolt impossible. The action of the insurgents was everywhere the same. They seized upon the arms and munitions of war collected in the magazines, and forced the magistrates or commanders of towns to place themselves at their head. Where the latter resisted, or were suspected of treachery to the national cause, they were in many cases put to death. Committees of Government were formed in the principal cities, and as many armies came into being as there were independent centres of the insurrection.

Napoleon was in the meantime collecting a body of prelates and grandees at Bayonne, under the pretence of consulting the representatives of the Spanish nation. Half the members of the intended Assembly received a personal summons from the Emperor; the other half were ordered to be chosen by popular election. When the order, however, was issued from Bayonne, the country was already in

Napoleon's Assembly at Bayonne, June, 1808.

full revolt. Elections were held only in the districts occupied by the French, and not more than twenty representatives so elected proceeded to Bayonne. The remainder of the Assembly, which numbered in all ninety-one persons, was composed of courtiers who had accompanied the Royal Family across the Pyrenees, and of any Spaniards of distinction upon whom the French could lay their hands. Joseph Bonaparte was brought from Naples to receive the crown of Spain.* On the 15th of June the Assembly of the Notables was opened. Its discussions followed the order prescribed by Napoleon on all similar occasions. Articles disguising a central absolute power with some pretence of national representation were laid before the Assembly, and adopted without criticism. Except in the privileges accorded to the Church, little indicated that the Constitution of Bayonne was intended for the Spanish rather than for any other nation. Its political forms were as valuable or as valueless as those which Napoleon had given to his other client States; its principles of social order were those which even now despotism could not dissever from French supremacy—the abolition of feudal services, equality of taxation, admission of all ranks to public employment. Titles of nobility were preserved, the privileges of nobility abolished One genuine act of homage was rendered to the national character. The Catholic religion was declared to be the only one permitted in Spain.

_{Joseph Bonaparte made King}

While Napoleon was thus emancipating the peasants

* Miot de Melito, ii., ch. 7.

from the nobles, and reconciling his supremacy with the claims of the Church, peasants and townspeople were flocking to arms at the call of the priests, who so little appreciated the orthodoxy of their patron as to identify him in their manifestos with Calvin, with the Antichrist, and with Apollyon.* The Emperor underrated the military efficiency of the national revolt, and contented himself with sending his lieutenants to repress it, while he himself, expecting a speedy report of victory, remained in Bayonne.

Attempts of Napoleon to suppress the Spanish rising.

Divisions of the French army moved in all directions against the insurgents. Dupont was ordered to march upon Seville from the capital, Moncey upon Valencia; Marshal Bessières took command of a force intended to disperse the main army of the Spaniards, which threatened the roads from the Pyrenees to Madrid. The first encounters were all favourable to the practised French troops; yet the objects which Napoleon set before his generals were not achieved. Moncey failed to reduce Valencia; Dupont found himself outnumbered on passing the Sierra Morena, and had to retace his steps and halt at Andujar, where the road to Madrid leaves the valley of the Guadalquivir. Without sustaining any severe loss, the French divisions were disheartened by exhausting and resultless marches; the Spaniards gained new confidence on each successive day which passed without inflicting upon them a defeat. At length, however, the commanders of the northern army were forced by Marshal Bessières to fight a pitched battle at

* Baumgarten, i., 242.

Rio Seco, on the west of Valladolid (July 13th). Bessières won a complete victory, and gained the lavish praises of his master for a battle which, according to Napoleon's own conception, ended the Spanish war by securing the roads from the Pyrenees to Madrid.

Never had Napoleon so gravely mistaken the true character of a campaign. The vitality of the Spanish insurrection lay not in the support of the capital, which had never passed out of the hands of the French, but in the very independence of the several provincial movements. Unlike Vienna and Berlin, Madrid might be held by the French without the loss being felt by their adversary; Cadiz, Corunna, Lisbon, were equally serviceable bases for the insurrection. The victory of Marshal Bessières in the north preserved the communication between France and Madrid, and it did nothing more. It failed to restore the balance of military force in the south of Spain, or to affect the operations of the Spanish troops which were now closing round Dupont upon the Guadalquivir. On the 15th of July Dupont was attacked at Andujar by greatly superior forces. His lieutenant, Vedel, knowing the Spaniards to be engaged in a turning movement, made a long march northwards in order to guard the line of retreat. In his absence the position of Baylen, immediately in Dupont's rear, was seized by the Spanish general Reding. Dupont discovered himself to be surrounded. He divided his army into two columns, and moved on the night of the 18th from Andujar towards Baylen, in the hope of overpowering Reding's division.

Dupont in Andalusia.

At daybreak on the 19th the positions of Reding were attacked by the French. The struggle continued until mid-day, though the French soldiers sank exhausted with thirst and with the burning heat. At length the sound of cannon was heard in the rear. Castanos, the Spanish general commanding at Andujar, had discovered Dupont's retreat, and pressed behind him with troops fresh and unwearied by conflict. Further resistance was hopeless. Dupont had to negotiate for a surrender. He consented to deliver up Vedel's division as well as his own, although Vedel's troops were in possession of the road to Madrid, the Spanish commander promising, on this condition, that the captives should not be retained as prisoners of war in Spain, but be permitted to return by sea to their native country. The entire army of Andalusia, numbering 23,000 men, thus passed into the hands of an enemy whom Napoleon had not believed to possess a military existence. Dupont's anxiety to save something for France only aggravated the extent of the calamity; for the Junta of Seville declined to ratify the terms of the capitulation, and the prisoners, with the exception of the superior officers, were sent to the galleys at Cadiz. The victorious Spaniards pushed forwards upon Madrid. King Joseph, who had entered the city only a week before, had to fly from his capital. The whole of the French troops in Spain were compelled to retire to a defensive position upon the Ebro.

Capitulation of Baylen, July 19.

The disaster of Baylen did not come alone. Napoleon's attack upon Portugal had brought him within the striking-range of Great Britain. On the 1st of August an English army, commanded by Sir Arthur Wellesley, landed on the Portuguese coast at the mouth of the Mondego. Junot, the first invader of the Peninsula, was still at Lisbon; his forces in occupation of Portugal numbered nearly 30,000 men, but they were widely dispersed, and he was unable to bring more than 13,000 men into the field against the 16,000 with whom Wellesley moved upon Lisbon. Junot advanced to meet the invader. A battle was fought at Vimieiro, thirty miles north of Lisbon, on the 21st of August. The victory was gained by the British; and had the first advantage been followed up, Junot's army would scarcely have escaped capture. But the command had passed out of Wellesley's hands. His superior officer, Sir Harry Burrard, took up the direction of the army immediately the battle ended, and Wellesley had to acquiesce in a suspension of operations at a moment when the enemy seemed to be within his grasp. Junot made the best use of his reprieve. He entered into negotiations for the evacuation of Portugal, and obtained the most favourable terms in the Convention of Cintra, signed on the 30th of August. The French army was permitted to return to France with its arms and baggage. Wellesley, who had strongly condemned the inaction of his superior officers after the battle of the 21st, agreed with them that, after the enemy had once been permitted to escape, the evacuation of Portugal was the best result which the English could obtain.* Junot's troops were accordingly conveyed to French ports at the expense of the British Government, to the great displeasure of the public, who expected to see the marshal and his army brought prisoners into Portsmouth. The English were as ill-humoured with their victory as the French with their defeat. When on the point of sending Junot to a court-martial for his capitulation, Napoleon learnt that the British Government had ordered its own generals to be brought to trial for permitting the enemy to escape them.

If the Convention of Cintra gained little glory for England, the tidings of the successful uprising of the Spanish people against Napoleon, and of Dupont's capitulation at Baylen, created the deepest impression in every country of Europe that still entertained the thought of resistance to France. The first great disaster had befallen Napoleon's arms. It had been inflicted by a nation without a government, without a policy, without a plan beyond that of the liberation of its fatherland from the foreigner. What Coalition after Coalition had failed to effect, the patriotism and energy of a single people deserted by its rulers seemed about to accomplish. The victory of the regular troops at Baylen was but a part of that great national movement in which every isolated outbreak had had its share in dividing and paralysing the Emperor's force. The capacity of untrained popular levies to resist practised troops might be exaggerated in the first outburst of wonder and admiration caused by the Spanish rising;

Effect of Spanish rising on Europe.

* Wellington Despatches, iii., 135.

but the difference made in the nature of the struggle by the spirit of popular resentment and determination was one upon which mistake was impossible. A sudden light broke in upon the politicians of Austria and Prussia, and explained the powerlessness of those Coalitions in which the wars had always been the affair of the Cabinets, and never the affair of the people. What the Spanish nation had effected for itself against Napoleon was not impossible for the German nation, if once a national movement like that of Spain sprang up among the German race. "I do not see," wrote Blücher some time afterwards, "why we should not think ourselves as good as the Spaniards." The best men in the Austrian and Prussian Governments began to look forward to the kindling of popular spirit as the surest means for combating the tyranny of Napoleon. *War-party in Austria and Prussia.* Military preparations were pushed forward in Austria with unprecedented energy and on a scale rivalling that of France itself. In Prussia the party of Stein determined upon a renewal of the war, and decided to risk the extinction of the Prussian State rather than submit to the extortions by which Napoleon was completing the ruin of their country. *Napoleon and Prussia.* It was among the patriots of Northern Germany that the course of the Spanish struggle excited the deepest emotion, and gave rise to the most resolute purpose of striking for European liberty.

Since the nominal restoration of peace between France and Prussia by the cession of half the Prussian kingdom, not a month had passed without the infliction of some gross injustice upon the conquered nation. The evacuation of the country had in the first instance been made conditional upon the payment of certain requisitions in arrear. While the amount of this sum was being settled, all Prussia, except Königsberg, remained in the hands of the French, and 157,000 French soldiers lived at free quarters upon the unfortunate inhabitants. At the end of the year 1807 King Frederick William was informed that, besides paying to Napoleon 60,000,000 francs in money, and ceding domain lands of the same value, he must continue to support 40,000 French troops in five garrison-towns upon the Oder. Such was the dismay caused by this announcement, that Setin quitted Königsberg, now the seat of government, and passed three months at the head-quarters of the French at Berlin, endeavouring to frame some settlement less disastrous to his country. Count Daru, Napoleon's administrator in Prussia, treated the Minister with respect, and accepted his proposal for the evacuation of Prussian territory on payment of a fixed sum to the French. But the agreement required Napoleon's ratification, and for this Stein waited in vain.*

Month after month dragged on, and Napoleon made no reply. At length the victories of the Spanish insurrection in the summer of 1808 forced the Emperor to draw in his troops from beyond the Elbe. He placed a bold front upon his necessities, and demanded from the Prussian Government, as the price of evacuation, a still larger sum than that which had been named in the

* Häusser, iii., 133. Seeley, i., 480.

previous winter: he insisted that the Prussian army should be limited to 40,000 men, and the formation of the Landwehr abandoned; and he required the support of a Prussian corps of 16,000 men, in the event of hostilities breaking out between France and Austria. Not even on these conditions was Prussia offered the complete evacuation of her territory. Napoleon still insisted on holding the three principal fortresses on the Oder with a garrison of 10,000 men. Such was the treaty proposed to the Prussian Court (September, 1808) at a time when every soldierly spirit thrilled with the tidings from Spain, and every statesman was convinced by the events of the last few months that Napoleon's treaties were but stages in a progression of wrongs. Stein and Scharnhorst urged the King to arm the nation for a struggle as desperate as that of Spain, and to delay only until Napoleon himself was busied in the warfare of the Peninsula. Continued submission was ruin; revolt was at least not hopeless. However forlorn the condition of Prussia, its alliances were of the most formidable character. Austria was arming without disguise; Great Britain had intervened in the warfare of the Peninsula with an efficiency hitherto unknown in its military operations; Spain, on the estimate of Napoleon himself, required an army of 200,000 men. Since the beginning of the Spanish insurrection Stein had occupied himself with the organisation of a general outbreak throughout Northern Germany. Rightly or wrongly, he believed the train to be now laid, and encouraged the King of Prussia to count upon the support of a popular insurrection against the French in all the territories which they had taken from Prussia, from Hanover, and from Hesse.

In one point alone Stein was completely misinformed. He believed that Alexander, in spite of the Treaty of Tilsit, would not be unwilling to see the storm burst upon Napoleon, and that in the event of another general war the forces of Russia would more probably be employed against France than in its favour. The illusion was a fatal one. Alexander was still the accomplice of Napoleon. For the sake of the Danubian Principalities, Alexander was willing to hold central Europe in check while Napoleon crushed the Spaniards, and to stifle every bolder impulse in the simple King of Prussia. Napoleon himself dreaded the general explosion of Europe before Spain was conquered, and drew closer to his Russian ally. Difficulties that had been placed in the way of the Russian annexation of Roumania vanished. The Czar and the Emperor determined to display to all Europe the intimacy of their union by a festal meeting at Erfurt in the midst of their victims and their dependents. The whole tribe of vassal German sovereigns was summoned to the meeting-place; representatives attended from the Courts of Vienna and Berlin. On the 7th of October Napoleon and Alexander made their entry into Erfurt. Pageants and festivities required the attendance of the crowned and titled rabble for several days; but the only serious business was the settlement of a treaty confirming the alliance of France and Russia, and the notification of the Czar to the envoy of the King of Prussia that his master must accept the terms demanded by Napoleon, and relinquish the idea of a struggle with France.* Count Goltz, the Prussian envoy, unwillingly signed the treaty which gave Prussia but a partial evacuation at so dear a cost, and wrote to the King that no course now remained for him but to abandon himself to unreserved dependence upon France, and to permit Stein and the patriotic party to retire from the direction of the State. Unless the King could summon up courage to declare war in defiance of Alexander, there was in fact no alternative left open to him. Napoleon had discovered Stein's plans for raising an insurrection in Germany several weeks before, and had given vent to the most furious outburst of wrath against Stein in the presence of the Prussian Ambassador at Erfurt. If the great struggle on which Stein's whole heart and soul were set was to be relinquished, if Spain was to be crushed before Prussia moved an arm, and Austria was to be left to fight its inevitable battle alone, then the presence of Stein at the head of the Prussian State was only a snare to Europe, a peril to Prussia, and a misery to himself. Stein asked for and received his dismissal. (Nov. 24, 1808.)

Stein resigns, Nov. 24. Proscribed by Napoleon.

Stein's retirement averted the wrath of Napoleon from the King of Prussia; but the whole malignity of

---

* For the striking part played at Erfurt by Talleyrand in opposition to Napoleon see Metternich's paper of December 4, in Beer, p. 516. It seems that Napoleon wished to involve the Czar in active measures against Austria, but was thwarted by Talleyrand.

that Corsican nature broke out against the high-spirited patriot as soon as fresh victories had released Napoleon from the ill-endured necessity of self-control. On the 16th of December, when Madrid had again passed into the possession of the French, an imperial order appeared, which gave the measure of Napoleon's hatred of the fallen Minister. Stein was denounced as the enemy of the Empire; his property was confiscated; he was ordered to be seized by the troops of the Emperor or his allies wherever they could lay their hands upon him. As in the days of Roman tyranny, the west of Europe could now afford no asylum to the enemies of the Emperor. Russia and Austria remained the only refuge of the exile. Stein escaped into Bohemia; and, as the crowning humiliation of the Prussian State, its police were forced to pursue as a criminal the statesman whose fortitude had still made it possible in the darkest days for Prussian patriots not to despair of their country.

Central Europe secured by the negotiations with Alexander at Erfurt, Napoleon was now able to place himself at the head of the French forces in Spain without fear of any immediate attack from the side of Germany. Since the victory of Baylen the Spaniards had made little progress either towards good government or towards a good military administration. The provincial Juntas had consented to subordinate themselves to a central committee chosen from among their own members; but this new supreme authority, which held its meetings at Aranjuez, proved one of the worst governments that

Napoleon goes to Spain, Nov., 1808.

even Spain itself had ever endured. It numbered thirty persons, twenty-eight of whom were priests, nobles, or officials.* Its qualities were those engrained in Spanish official life. In legislation it attempted absolutely nothing but the restoration of the Inquisition and the protection of Church lands; its administration was confined to a foolish interference with the better generals, and the acquisition of enormous supplies of war from Great Britain, which were either stolen by contractors or allowed to fall into the hands of the French. While the members of the Junta discussed the titles of honour which were to attach to them collectively and individually, and voted themselves salaries equal to those of Napoleon's generals, the armies fell into a state of destitution which scarcely any but Spanish troops would have been capable of enduring. The energy of the humbler classes alone prolonged the military existence of the insurrection; the Government organised nothing, comprehended nothing. Its part in the national movement was confined to a system of begging and boasting, which demoralised the Spaniards, and bewildered the agents and generals of England who first attempted the difficult task of assisting the Spaniards to help themselves. When the approach of army after army, the levies of Germany, Poland, Holland, and Italy, in addition to Napoleon's own veteran troops of Austerlitz and Jena, gave to the rest of the world some idea of the enormous force which Napoleon was about to throw on

marginal note: Misgovernment of the Spanish Junta.

* Baumgarten, i., 311.

to Spain, the Spanish Government could form no better design than to repeat the movement of Baylen against Napoleon himself on the banks of the Ebro.

The Emperor for the first time crossed the Pyrenees in the beginning of November, 1808. The victory of the Spaniards in the summer had forced the invaders to retire into the district between the Ebro and the Pyrenees, and the Ebro now formed the dividing-line between the hostile armies. It was the intention of Napoleon to roll back the extremes of the Spanish line to the east and the west, and, breaking through its centre, to move straight upon Burgos and Madrid. The Spaniards, for their part, were not content to act upon the defensive. When Napoleon arrived at Vittoria on the 5th of November, the left wing of the Spanish army under General Blake had already received orders to move eastwards from the upper waters of the Ebro, and to cut the French off from their communication with the Pyrenees. The movement was exactly that which Napoleon desired; for in executing it, Blake had only to march far enough eastwards to find himself completely surrounded by French divisions. A premature movement of the French generals themselves alone saved Blake from total destruction. He was attacked and defeated at Espinosa, on the upper Ebro, before he had advanced far enough to lose his line of retreat (Nov. 10); and, after suffering great losses, he succeeded in leading off a remnant of his army into the mountains of Asturias. In the centre, Soult drove the enemy before him, and captured

Burgos. Of the army which was to have cleared Spain of the French, nothing now remained but a corps on the right at Tudela, commanded by Palafox. The destruction of this body was committed by the Emperor to Lannes and Ney. Ney was ordered to take a long march southwards in order to cut off the retreat of the Spaniards; he found it impossible, however, to execute his march within the time prescribed; and Palafox, beaten by Lannes at Tudela, made good his retreat into Saragossa. A series of accidents had thus saved the divisions of the Spanish army from actual capture, but there no longer existed a force capable of meeting the enemy in the field. Napoleon moved forward from Burgos upon Madrid. The rest of his march was a triumph. The batteries defending the mountain-pass of Somo Sierra were captured by a charge of Polish cavalry; and the capital itself surrendered, after a short artillery fire, on the 4th of December, four weeks after the opening of the campaign.

Napoleon enters Madrid, Dec. 4.

An English army was slowly and painfully making its way towards the Ebro at the time when Napoleon broke in pieces the Spanish line of defence. On the 14th of October Sir John Moore had assumed the command of 20,000 British troops at Lisbon. He was instructed to march to the neighbourhood of Burgos, and to co-operate with the Spanish generals upon the Ebro. According to the habit of the English, no allowance was made for the movements of the enemy while their own were under consideration; and the mountain-country which Moore had to traverse placed

Campaign of Sir John Moore.

additional obstacles in the way of an expedition at least a month too late in its starting. Moore believed it to be impossible to carry his artillery over the direct road from Lisbon to Salamanca, and sent it round by way of Madrid, while he himself advanced through Ciudad Rodrigo, reaching Salamanca on the 13th of November. Here, while still waiting for his artillery, rumours reached him of the destruction of Blake's army at Espinosa, and of the fall of Burgos. Later came the report of Palafox's overthrow at Tudela. Yet even now Moore could get no trustworthy information from the Spanish authorities. He remained for some time in suspense, and finally determined to retreat into Portugal. Orders were sent to Sir David Baird, who was approaching with reinforcements from Corunna, to turn back towards the northern coast. Scarcely had Moore formed this decision, when despatches arrived from Frere, the British agent at Madrid, stating that the Spaniards were about to defend the capital to the last extremity, and that Moore would be responsible for the ruin of Spain and the disgrace of England if he failed to advance to its relief. To the great joy of his soldiers, Moore gave orders for a forward march. The army advanced upon Valladolid, with the view of attacking the French upon their line of communication, while the siege of the capital engaged them in front. Baird was again ordered southwards. It was not until the 14th of December, ten days after Madrid had passed into the hands of the French, that Moore received intelligence of its fall. Neither the Spanish Government nor the British agent who had caused Moore to advance took the trouble to inform him of the surrender of the capital; he learnt it from an intercepted French despatch. From the same despatch Moore learnt that to the north of him, at Saldanha, on the river Carrion, there lay a comparatively small French force under the command of Soult. The information was enough for Moore, heart-sick at the mockery to which his army had been subjected, and burning for decisive action. He turned northwards, and marched against Soult, in the hope of surprising him before the news of his danger could reach Napoleon in the capital.

On the 19th of December a report reached Madrid that Moore had suspended his retreat on Portugal. Napoleon instantly divined the actual movement of the English, and hurried from Madrid against Moore at the head of 40,000 men. Moore had met Baird on the 20th at Mayorga; on the 23rd the united British divisions reached Sahagun, scarcely a day's march from Soult at Saldanha. Here the English commander learnt that Napoleon himself was on his track. Escape was a question of hours. Napoleon had pushed across the Guadarama mountains in forced marches through snow and storm. Had his vanguard been able to seize the bridge over the river Esla at Benavente before the English crossed it, Moore would have been cut off from all possibility of escape. The English reached the river first and blew up the bridge. This rescued them from immediate danger. The defence of the river gave Moore's army a start which rendered the superiority of

Napoleon marches against Moore, Dec. 19.

Retreat of the English.

Napoleon's numbers of little effect. For a while Napoleon followed Moore towards the northern coast. On the 1st of January, 1809, he wrote an order which showed that he looked upon Moore's escape as now inevitable, and on the next day he quitted the army, leaving to his marshals the honour of toiling after Moore to the coast, and of seizing some thousands of frozen or drunken British stragglers. Moore himself pushed on towards Corunna with a rapidity which was dearly paid for by the demoralisation of his army. The sufferings and the excesses of the troops were frightful; only the rearguard, which had to face the enemy, preserved soldierly order. At length Moore found it necessary to halt and take up position, in order to restore the discipline of his army. He turned upon Soult at Lugo, and offered battle for two successive days; but the French general declined an engagement; and Moore, satisfied with having recruited his troops, continued his march upon Corunna. Soult still followed. On January 11th the English army reached the sea; but the ships which were to convey them back to England were nowhere to be seen. A battle was inevitable, and Moore drew up his troops, 14,000 in number, on a range of low hills outside the town, to await the attack of the French. On the 16th, when the fleet had now come into harbour, Soult gave battle. The French were defeated at every point of their attack. Moore fell at the moment of his victory, conscious that the army which he had so bravely led had nothing more to fear. The embarkation

Corunna, Jan. 16, 1809.

DEATH OF MOORE AT CORUNNA.

(p. 808.)

was effected that night; on the next day the fleet put out to sea.

Napoleon quitted Spain on the 19th of January, 1809, leaving his brother Joseph again in possession of the capital, and an army of 300,000 men under the best generals of France engaged with the remnants of a defeated force which had never reached half that number. *(Napoleon leaves Spain, Jan. 19, 1809.)* No brilliant victories remained to be won; no enemy remained in the field important enough to require the presence of Napoleon. Difficulties of transit and the hostility of the people might render the subjugation of Spain a slower process than the subjugation of Prussia or Italy; but, to all appearance, the ultimate success of the Emperor's plans was certain, and the worst that lay before his lieutenants was a series of wearisome and obscure exertions against an inconsiderable foe. Yet, before the Emperor had been many weeks in Paris, a report reached him from Marshal Lannes which told of some strange form of military capacity among the people whose armies were so contemptible in the field. The city of Saragossa, after successfully resisting its besiegers in the summer of 1808, had been a second time invested after the defeats of the Spanish armies upon the Ebro.* *(Siege of Saragossa, Dec. 1808.)* The besiegers themselves were suffering from extreme scarcity when, on the 22nd of January, 1809, Lannes took up the command. Lannes immediately called up all the troops within reach, and pressed the battering operations with the utmost vigour.

* Napier, ii., 17.

On the 29th, the walls of Saragossa were stormed in four different places.

According to all ordinary precedents of war, the French were now in possession of the city. But the besiegers found that their real work was only beginning. The streets were trenched and barricaded; every dwelling was converted into a fortress; for twenty days the French were forced to besiege house by house. In the centre of the town the popular leaders erected a gallows, and there they hanged every one who flinched from meeting the enemy. Disease was added to the horrors of warfare. In the cellars, where the women and children crowded in filth and darkness, a malignant pestilence broke out, which, at the beginning of February, raised the deaths to five hundred a day. The dead bodies were unburied; in that poisoned atmosphere the slightest wound produced mortification and death. At length the powers of the defenders sank. A fourth part of the town had been won by the French; of the townspeople and peasants who were within the walls at the beginning of the siege, it is said that thirty thousand had perished; the remainder could only prolong their defence to fall in a few days more before disease or the enemy. Even now there were members of the Junta who wished to fight as long as a man remained, but they were outnumbered. On the 20th of February what was left of Saragossa capitulated. Its resistance gave to the bravest of Napoleon's soldiers an impression of horror and dismay new even to men who had passed through seventeen years of revolutionary warfare, but it failed to retard Napoleon's armies in the conquest of Spain. No attempt was made to relieve the heroic or ferocious city. Everywhere the tide of French conquest appeared to be steadily making its advance. Soult invaded Portugal; in combination with him, two armies moved from Madrid upon the southern and the south-western provinces of Spain. Oporto fell on the 28th of March; in the same week the Spanish forces covering the south were decisively beaten at Ciudad Real and at Medellin upon the line of the Guadiana. The hopes of Europe fell. Spain itself could expect no second Saragossa. It appeared as if the complete subjugation of the Peninsula could now only be delayed by the mistakes of the French generals themselves, and by the untimely removal of that controlling will which had hitherto made every movement a step forward in conquest.

Defeats of the Spaniards, March, 1809.

CHAPTER IX.

Austria preparing for war—The war to be one on behalf of the German Nation—Patriotic movement in Prussia—Expected Insurrection in North Germany—Plans of Campaign—Austrian Manifesto to the Germans—Rising of the Tyrolese—Defeats of the Archduke Charles in Bavaria—French in Vienna—Attempts of Dörnberg and Schill—Battle of Aspern—Second Passage of the Danube—Battle of Wagram—Armistice of Znaim—Austria waiting for events—Wellesley in Spain—He gains the Battle of Talavera, but retreats—Expedition against Antwerp fails—Austria makes Peace—Treaty of Vienna—Real Effects of the War of 1809—Austria after 1809—Metternich—Marriage of Napoleon with Marie Louise—Severance of Napoleon and Alexander—Napoleon annexes the Papal States, Holland, La Valais, and the North German Coast—The Napoleonic Empire: Its benefits and wrongs—The Czar withdraws from Napoleon's Commercial System—War with Russia imminent—Wellington in Portugal: Lines of Torres Vedras; Massena's Campaign of 1810, and retreat—Soult in Andalusia—Wellington's Campaign of 1811—Capture of Ciudad Rodrigo and Badajoz—Salamanca.

NAPOLEON, quitting Spain in the third week of January, 1809, travelled to Paris with the utmost haste. He believed Austria to be on the point of declaring war; and on the very day of his arrival at the capital he called out the contingents of the Rhenish Federation. In the course of the next few weeks, however, he formed the opinion that Austria would either decline hostilities altogether, or at least find it impossible to declare war before the middle of May. For once the efforts of Austria outstripped the calculations of her enemy. Count Stadion, the earnest and enlightened statesman who had held power in Austria since the Peace of Presburg, had

Austria preparing for war, 1808-9.

steadily prepared for a renewal of the struggle with France. He was convinced that Napoleon would soon enter upon new enterprises of conquest, and still farther extend his empire at the expense of Austria, unless attacked before Spain had fallen under his dominion. Metternich, now Austrian Ambassador at Paris, reported that Napoleon was intending to divide Turkey as soon as he had conquered Spain; and, although he advised delay, he agreed with the Cabinet at Vienna that Austria must sooner or later strike in self-defence.* Stadion, more sanguine, was only prevented from declaring war in 1808 by the counsels of the Archduke Charles and of other generals who were engaged in bringing the immense mass of new levies into military formation. Charles himself attached little value to the patriotic enthusiasm which, since the outbreak of the Spanish insurrection, had sprung up in the German provinces of Austria. He saw the approach of war with more apprehension than pleasure; but, however faint his own hopes, he laboured earnestly in creating for Austria a force far superior to anything that she had possessed before, and infused into the mass of the army that confident and patriotic spirit which he saw in others rather than felt in himself. By the beginning of March, 1809, Austria had 260,000 men ready to take the field.

The war now breaking out was to be a war for the German nation, as the struggle of the Spaniards had been a struggle for Spain. The animated appeals of the Emperor's generals

<small>The war of 1809 to be a war for Germany.</small>

* Metternich, ii., 147.

formed a singular contrast to the silence with which the Austrian Cabinet had hitherto entered into its wars. The Hapsburg sovereign now stood before the world less as the inheritor of an ancient empire and the representative of the Balance of Power than as the disinterested champion of the German race. On the part of the Emperor himself the language of devotion for Germany was scarcely more than ironical. Francis belonged to an age and to a system in which the idea of nationality had no existence; and, like other sovereigns, he regarded his possessions as a sort of superior property which ought to be defended by obedient domestic dogs against marauding foreign wolves. The same personal view of public affairs had hitherto satisfied the Austrians. It had been enough for them to be addressed as the dutiful children of a wise and affectionate father. The Emperor spoke the familiar Viennese dialect; he was as homely in his notions and his prejudices as any beerseller in his dominions; his subjects might see him at almost any hour of the day or night; and out of the somewhat tough material of his character popular imagination had no difficulty in framing an idol of parental geniality and wisdom. Fifteen years of failure and mismanagement had, however, impaired the beauty of the domestic fiction; and although old-fashioned Austrians, like Haydn, the composer of the Austrian Hymn, were ready to go down to the grave invoking a blessing on their gracious master, the Emperor himself and his confidants were shrewd enough to see that the newly-excited sense of

German patriotism would put them in possession of a force which they could hardly evoke by the old methods.

One element of reality lay in the professions which were not for the most part meant very seriously. There was probably now no statesman in Austria who any longer felt a jealousy of the power of Prussia. With Count Stadion and his few real supporters the restoration of Germany was a genuine and deeply-cherished desire; with the majority of Austrian politicians the interests of Austria herself seemed at least for the present to require the liberation of North Germany. Thus the impassioned appeals of the Archduke Charles to all men of German race to rise against their foreign oppressor, and against their native princes who betrayed the interests of the Fatherland, gained the sanction of a Court hitherto very little inclined to form an alliance with popular agitation. If the chaotic disorder of the Austrian Government had been better understood in Europe, less importance would have been attached to this sudden change in its tone. No one in the higher ranks at Vienna was bound by the action of his colleagues. The Emperor, though industrious, had not the capacity to enforce any coherent system of government. His brothers caballed against one another, and against the persons who figured as responsible ministers. State-papers were brought by soldiers to the Emperor for his signature without the knowledge of his advisers. The very manifestos which seemed to herald a new era for Germany owed most of their vigour to

Austrian parties.

the literary men who were entrusted with their composition.*

The answer likely to be rendered by Germany to the appeal of Austria was uncertain. In the Rhenish Federation there were undoubted signs of discontent with French rule among the common people; but the official classes were universally on the side of Napoleon, who had given them their posts and their salaries; while the troops, and especially the officers, who remembered the time when they had been mocked by the Austrians as "harlequins" and "nose-bags," were won by the kindness of the great conqueror, who organised them under the hands of his own generals, and gave them the companionship of his own victorious legions. Little could be expected from districts where to the mass of the population the old régime of German independence had meant nothing more than attendance at the manor-court of a knight, or the occasional spectacle of a ducal wedding, or a deferred interest in the droning jobbery of some hereditary town-councillor. In Northern Germany there was far more prospect of a national insurrection. There the spirit of Stein and of those who had worked with him was making itself felt, in spite of the fall of the Minister. Scharnhorst's reforms had made the Prussian army a school of patriotism, and the work of statesmen and soldiers was promoted by men who spoke to the feelings and the intelligence of the nation. Literature lost its indifference to nationality and to home. The

Governing classes in South Germany on the side of Napoleon.

Patriotic movement in Prussia.

* Gentz, Tagebücher, i., 60.

philosopher Fichte, the poet Arndt, the theologian
Schleiermacher pressed the claims of Germany and of the
manlier virtues upon a middle class singularly open to
literary influences, singularly wanting in the experience
and the impulses of active public life.* In the Kingdom of Westphalia preparations for an insurrection
against the French were made by officers who had
served in the Prussian and the Hessian armies. In
Prussia itself, by the side of many nobler agencies, the
newly-founded Masonic society of the Tugendbund, or
League of Virtue, made the cause of the Fatherland
popular among thousands to whom it was an agreeable
novelty to belong to any society at all. No spontaneous,
irresistible uprising, like that which Europe had seen in
the Spanish Peninsula, was to be expected among the
unimpulsive population of the North German plains;
but the military circles of Prussia were generally in
favour of war, and an insurrection of the population
west of the Elbe was not improbable in the event of
Napoleon's army being defeated by Austria in the field.
King Frederick William, too timid to resolve upon war
himself, too timid even to look with satisfaction upon
the bold attitude of Austria, had every reason for
striking, if once the balance should incline against Napoleon: even against his own inclination it was possible
that the ardour of his soldiers might force him into war.

So strong were the hopes of a general rising in
Northern Germany, that the Austrian Government to
some extent based its plans for the campaign on this

* Steffens, vi., 153. Mémoires du Roi Jérome, iii., 340.

event. In the ordinary course of hostilities between France and Austria the line of operations in Germany is the valley of the Danube; but in preparing for the war of 1809 the Austrian Government massed its forces in the north-west of Bohemia, with the object of throwing them directly upon Central Germany. The French troops which were now evacuating Prussia were still on their way westwards at the time when Austria was ready to open the campaign. Davoust, with about 60,000 men, was in Northern Bavaria, separated by a great distance from the nearest French divisions in Baden and on the Rhine. By a sudden incursion of the main army of Austria across the Bohemian mountains, followed by an uprising in Northern Germany, Davoust and his scattered detachments could hardly escape destruction. Such was the original plan of the campaign, and it was probably a wise one in the present exceptional superiority of the Austrian preparations over those of France. For the first time since the creation of the Consulate it appeared as if the opening advantages of the war must inevitably be upon the side of the enemies of France. Napoleon had underrated both the energy and the resources of his adversary. By the middle of March, when the Austrians were ready to descend upon Davoust from Bohemia, Napoleon's first troops had hardly crossed the Rhine. Fortunately for the French commander, the Austrian Government, at the moment of delivering its well-planned blow, was seized with fear at its own boldness. Recollections of Hohenlinden and Ulm filled anxious minds with the thought that the valley of the Danube was insufficiently defended; and on the 20th of March, when the army was on the point of breaking into Northern Bavaria, orders were given to divert the line of march to the south, and to enter the Rhenish Confederacy by the roads of the Danube and the Inn. Thus the fruit of so much energy, and of the enemy's rare neglectfulness, was sacrificed at the last moment. It was not until the 9th of April that the Austrian movement southward was completed, and that the army lay upon the line of the Inn, ready to attack Napoleon in the territory of his principal German ally.

The proclamations now published by the Emperor and the Archduke bore striking testimony to the influence of the Spanish insurrection in exciting the sense of national right, and awakening the Governments of Europe to the force which this placed in their hands. For the first time in history a manifesto was addressed "to the German nation." The contrast drawn in the Archduke's address to his army between the Spanish patriots dying in the defence of their country, and the German vassal-contingents dragged by Napoleon into Spain to deprive a gallant nation of its freedom, was one of the most just and the most telling that tyranny has ever given to the leaders of a righteous cause.* The Emperor's address "to the German nation" breathed the same spirit. It was not difficult for the politicians of the Rhenish Federation to ridicule the sudden enthusiasm for liberty

Austrian manifesto to the Germans.

---

* Beer, p. 370. Häusser, iii., 278.

and nationality shown by a Government which up to the present time had dreaded nothing so much as the excitement of popular movements; but, however unconcernedly the Emperor and the old school of Austrian statesmen might adopt patriotic phrases which they had no intention to remember when the struggle was over, such language was a reality in the effect which it produced upon the thousands who, both in Austria and other parts of Germany, now for the first time heard the summons to unite in defence of a common Fatherland.

The leading divisions of the Archduke's army crossed the Inn on the 9th of April. Besides the forces intended for the invasion of Bavaria, which numbered 170,000 men, the Austrian Government had formed two smaller armies, with which the Princes Ferdinand and John were to take up the offensive in the Grand Duchy of Warsaw and in Northern Italy. On every side Austria was first in the field; but even before its regular forces could encounter the enemy, a popular outbreak of the kind that the Government had invoked wrested from the French the whole of an important province. While the army crossed the Inn, the Tyrolese people rose, and overpowered the French and Bavarian detachments stationed in their country. The Tyrol had been taken from Austria at the Peace of Presburg, and attached to Napoleon's vassal kingdom of Bavaria. In geographical position and in relationship of blood the Tyrolese were as closely connected with the Bavarians as with the Austrians; and the annexation would pro-

Austrians invade Bavaria, April 9, 1809.

Rising of the Tyrol, April, 1809.

bably have caused no lasting discontent if the Bavarian Government had condescended to take some account of the character of its new subjects. Under the rule of Austria the Tyrolese had enjoyed many privileges. They were exempt from military service, except in their own militia; they paid few taxes; they possessed forms of self-government which were at least popular enough to be regretted after they had been lost. The people adored their bishops and clergy. Nowhere could the Church exhibit a more winning example of unbroken accord between a simple people and a Catholic Crown. Protestantism and the unholy activities of reason had never brought trouble into the land. The people believed exactly what the priests told them, and delighted in the innumerable holidays provided by the Church. They had so little cupidity that no bribe could induce a Tyrolese peasant to inform the French of any movement; they had so little intelligence that, when their own courage and stout-heartedness had won their first battle, they persuaded one another that they had been led by a Saint on a white horse. Grievances of a substantial character were not wanting under the new Bavarian rule; but it was less the increased taxation and the enforcement of military service that exasperated the people than the attacks made by the Government upon the property and rights of the Church. Montgelas, the reforming Bavarian minister, treated the Tyrolese bishops with as little ceremony as the Swabian knights. The State laid claim to all advowsons; and upon the refusal of the bishops

Its causes religious.

to give up their patronage, the bishops themselves were banished and their revenues sequestrated. A passion for uniformity and common sense prompted the Government to revive the Emperor Joseph's edicts against pilgrimages and Church holidays. It became a police-offence to shut up a shop on a saint's day, or to wear a gay dress at a festival. Bavarian soldiers closed the churches at the end of a prescribed number of masses. At a sale of Church property, ordered by the Government, some of the sacred vessels were permitted to fall into the hands of the Jews.

These were the wrongs that fired the simple Tyrolese. They could have borne the visits of the tax-gatherer and the lists of conscription; they could not bear that their priests should be overruled, or that their observances should be limited to those sufficient for ordinary Catholics. Yet, with all its aspect of unreason, the question in the Tyrol was also part of that larger question whether Napoleon's pleasure should be the rule of European life, or nations should have some voice in the disposal of their own affairs. The Tyrolese were not more superstitious, and they were certainly much less cruel, than the Spaniards. They fought for ecclesiastical absurdities; but their cause was also the cause of national right, and the admiration which their courage excited in Europe was well deserved.

Tyrolese expel Bavarians and French, April, 1809. Early in the year 1809 the Archduke John had met the leaders of the Tyrolese peasantry, and planned the first movements of a national insurrection. As soon as the Austrian army crossed the Inn, the peasants thronged to their appointed meeting-places. Scattered detachments of the Bavarians were surrounded, and on the 12th of April the main body of the Tyrolese, numbering about 15,000 men, advanced upon Innsbruck. The town was invested; the Bavarian garrison, consisting of 3,000 regular troops, found itself forced to surrender after a severe engagement. On the next morning a French column, on the march from Italy to the Danube, approached Innsbruck, totally unaware of the events of the preceding day. The Tyrolese closed behind it as it advanced. It was not until the column was close to the town that its commander, General Brisson, discovered that Innsbruck had fallen into an enemy's hands. Retreat was impossible; ammunition was wanting for a battle; and Brisson had no choice but to surrender to the peasants, who had already proved more than a match for the Bavarian regular troops. The Tyrolese had done their work without the help of a single Austrian regiment. In five days the weak fabric of Bavarian rule had been thrown to the ground. The French only maintained themselves in the lower valley of the Adige; and before the end of April their last positions at Trent and Roveredo were evacuated, and no foreign soldier remained on Tyrolese soil.

The operations of the Austrian commanders upon the Inn formed a melancholy contrast to the activity of the mountaineers. In spite of the delay of three weeks in opening the campaign, Davoust had still not effected his junction

Campaign of Archduke Charles in Bavaria.

with the French troops in Southern Bavaria, and a rapid movement of the Austrians might even now have overwhelmed his isolated divisions at Ratisbon. Napoleon himself had remained in Paris till the last moment, instructing Berthier, the chief of the staff, to concentrate the vanguard at Ratisbon, if by the 15th of April the enemy had not crossed the Inn, but to draw back to the line of the Lech if the enemy crossed the Inn before that day.* The Archduke entered Bavaria on the 9th; but, instead of retiring to the Lech, Berthier allowed the army to be scattered over an area sixty miles broad, from Ratisbon to points above Augsburg. Davoust lay at Ratisbon, a certain prey if the Archduke pushed forwards with vigour and thrust his army between the northern and the southern positions of the French. But nothing could change the sluggishness of the Austrian march. The Archduke was six days in moving from the Inn to the Isar; and before the order was given for an advance upon Ratisbon, Napoleon himself had arrived at Donauwörth, and taken the command out of the hands of his feeble lieutenant.

It needed all the Emperor's energy to snatch victory from the enemy's grasp. Davoust was bidden to fall back from Ratisbon to Neustadt; the most pressing orders were sent to Massena, who commanded the right at Augsburg, to push forward to the north-east in the direction of his colleague, before the Austrians could throw the mass

Napoleon restores superiority of French. April 18, 19.

---

* Correspondance de Napoleon, xviii., 459, 472. Gentz, Tagebücher, i., 120. Pelet, Mémoires sur la Guerre de 1809, i., 223.

of their forces upon Davoust's weak corps. Both generals understood the urgency of the command. Davoust set out from Ratisbon on the morning of the 19th. He was attacked by the Archduke, but so feebly and irresolutely that, with all their superiority in numbers, the Austrians failed to overpower the enemy at any one point. Massena, immediately after receiving his orders, hurried from Augsburg north-eastwards, while Napoleon himself advanced into the mid-space between the two generals, and brought the right and left wings of the French army into communication with one another. In two days after the Emperor's arrival all the advantages of the Austrians were gone: the French, so lately exposed to destruction, formed a concentrated mass in the presence of a scattered enemy. The issue of the campaign was decided by the movements of these two days. Napoleon was again at the head of 150,000 men; the Archduke, already baulked in his first attack upon Davoust, was seized with unworthy terror when he found that Napoleon himself was before him, and resigned himself to anticipations of ruin.

A series of manœuvres and engagements in the finest style of Napoleonic warfare filled the next three days with French victories and Austrian disasters. On April the 20th the long line of the Archduke's army was cut in halves by an attack at Abensberg. The left was driven across the Isar at Landshut; the right, commanded by the Archduke himself, was overpowered at Eggmühl on the 22nd, and forced northwards. The unbroken mass of the French

Austrian defeats at Landshut and Eggmühl, April 22.

army now thrust itself between the two defeated wings of the enemy. The only road remaining open to the Archduke was that through Ratisbon to the north of the Danube. In five days, although no engagement of the first order had taken place between the French and Austrian armies, Charles had lost 60,000 men; the mass of his army was retreating into Bohemia, and the road to Vienna lay scarcely less open than after Mack's capitulation at Ulm four years before. A desperate battle fought against the advancing French at Edelsberg by the weak divisions that had remained on the south of the Danube, proved that the disasters of the campaign were due to the faults of the general, not to the men whom he commanded. But whatever hopes of ultimate success might still be based on the gallant temper of the army, it was impossible to prevent the fall of the capital. The French, leaving the Archduke on the north of the Danube, pressed forwards along the direct route from the Inn to Vienna. The capital was bombarded and occupied. On the 13th of May Napoleon again took up his quarters in the palace of the Austrian monarchs where he had signed the Peace of 1806. The divisions which had fallen back before him along the southern road crossed the Danube at Vienna, and joined the Archduke on the bank of the river opposite the capital.

<small>French enter Vienna, May 13.</small>

The disasters of the Bavarian campaign involved the sacrifice of all that had resulted from Austrian victories elsewhere, and of all that might have been won by a general insurrection in Northern Germany. In Poland

and in Italy the war had opened favourably for Austria. Warsaw had been seized; Eugène Beauharnais, the Viceroy of Italy, had been defeated by the Archduke John at Sacile, in Venetia; but it was impossible to pursue these advantages when the capital itself was on the point of falling into the hands of the enemy. The invading armies halted, and ere long the Archduke John commenced his retreat into the mountains. In Northern Germany no popular uprising could be expected when once Austria had been defeated. The only movements that took place were undertaken by soldiers, and undertaken before the disasters in Bavaria became known. The leaders in this military conspiracy were Dörnberg, an officer in the service of King Jerome of Westphalia, and Schill, the Prussian cavalry leader who had so brilliantly distinguished himself in the defence of Colberg. Dörnberg had taken service under Jerome with the design of raising Jerome's own army against him. It had been agreed by the conspirators that at the same moment Dörnberg should raise the Hessian standard in Westphalia, and Schill, marching from Berlin with any part of the Prussian army that would follow him, should proclaim war against the French in defiance of the Prussian Government. Dörnberg had made sure of the support of his own regiment; but at the last moment the plot was discovered, and he was transferred to the command of a body of men upon whom he could not rely. He placed himself at the head of a band of peasants, and raised the standard of insurrection. King

Attempts of Dörnberg and Schill in Northern Germany. April, 1809.

Jerome's troops met the solicitations of their countrymen with a volley of bullets. Dörnberg fled for his life; and the revolt ended on the day after it had begun (April 23). Schill, unconscious of Dörnberg's ruin, and deceived by reports of Austrian victories upon the Danube, led out his regiment from Berlin as if for a day's manœuvring, and then summoned his men to follow him in raising a national insurrection against Napoleon. The soldiers answered Schill's eloquent words with shouts of applause; the march was continued westwards, and Schill crossed the Elbe, intending to fall upon the communications of Napoleon's army, already, as he believed, staggering under the blows delivered by the Archduke in the valley of the Danube.

On reaching Halle, Schill learnt of the overthrow of the Archduke and of Dörnberg's ruin in Westphalia. All hope of success in the enterprise on which he had quitted Berlin was dashed to the ground. The possibility of raising a popular insurrection vanished. Schill, however, had gone too far to recede; and even now it was not too late to join the armies of Napoleon's enemies. Schill might move into Bohemia, or to some point on the northern coast where he would be within reach of English vessels. But in any case quick and steady decision was necessary; and this Schill could not attain. Though brave even to recklessness, and gifted with qualities which made him the idol of the public, Schill lacked the disinterestedness and self-mastery which calm the judgment in time of trial. The sudden ruin of his hopes left him without a plan. He wasted day after day in purposeless marches, while the enemy collected a force to overwhelm him. His influence over his men became impaired; the denunciations of the Prussian Government prevented other soldiers from joining him. At length Schill determined to recross the Elbe, and to throw himself into the coast town of Stralsund, in Swedish Pomerania. He marched through Mecklenburg, and suddenly appeared before Stralsund at the moment when the French cannoneers in garrison were firing a salvo in honour of Napoleon's entry into Vienna. A hand-to-hand fight gave Schill possession of the town, with all its stores. For a moment it seemed as if Stralsund might become a second Saragossa; but the French were at hand before it was possible to create works of defence. Schill had but eighteen hundred men, half of whom were cavalry; he understood nothing of military science, and would listen to no counsels. A week after his entry into Stralsund the town was stormed by a force four times more numerous than its defenders. Capitulation was no word for the man who had dared to make a private war upon Napoleon; Schill could only set the example of an heroic death.* The officers who were not so fortunate as to fall with their leader were shot in cold blood, after trial by a French court-martial. Six hundred common soldiers who surrendered were sent to the galleys of Toulon to sicken among French thieves and murderers. The cruelty of the conqueror, the

Schill at Stralsund. May 25.

---

* "Je n'ai jamais vu d'affaire aussi sanglante et aussi meurtrière." Report of the French General, Mémoires de Jérome, iv. 109.

heroism of the conquered, gave to Schill's ill-planned venture the importance of a great act of patriotic martyrdom. Another example had been given of self-sacrifice in the just cause. Schill's faults were forgotten; his memory deepened the passion with which all the braver spirits of Germany now looked for the day of reckoning with their oppressor.*

Napoleon had finished the first act of the war of 1809 by the occupation of Vienna; but no peace was possible until the Austrian army, which lay upon the opposite bank of the river, had been attacked and beaten. Four miles below Vienna the Danube is divided into two streams by the island of Lobau: the southern stream is the main channel of the river, the northern is only a hundred and fifty yards broad. It was here that Napoleon determined to make the passage. The broad arm of the Danube, sheltered by the island from the enemy's fire, was easily bridged by boats; the passage from the island to the northern bank, though liable to be disputed by the Austrians, was facilitated by the narrowing of the stream. On the 18th of May, Napoleon, supposing himself to have made good the connection between the island and the southern bank, began to bridge the northern arm of the river. His movements were observed by the enemy, but no opposition was offered. On the 20th a body of 40,000 French crossed to the northern bank, and occupied the villages of Aspern and Essling. This was the movement for which the Archduke

<small>Napoleon crosses the Danube, May 20.</small>

<small>* See Arndt's Poem on Schill. Gedichte, i. 328 (ed. 1837).</small>

Charles, who had now 80,000 men under arms, had been waiting. Early on the 21st a mass of heavily-laden barges was let loose by the Austrians above the island. The waters of the Danube were swollen by the melting of the snows, and at midday the bridges of the French over the broad arm of the river were swept away. A little later, dense Austrian columns were seen advancing upon the villages of Aspern and Essling, where the French, cut off from their supports, had to meet an overpowering enemy in front, with an impassable river in their rear. The attack began at four in the afternoon; when night fell the French had been driven out of Aspern, though they still held the Austrians at bay in their other position at Essling. During the night the long bridges were repaired; forty thousand additional troops moved across the island to the northern bank of the Danube; and the engagement was renewed, now between equal numbers, on the following morning. Five times the village of Aspern was lost and won. In the midst of the struggle the long bridges were again carried away. Unable to break the enemy, unable to bring up any new forces from Vienna, Napoleon ordered a retreat. The army was slowly withdrawn into the island of Lobau. There for the next two days it lay without food and without ammunition, severed from Vienna, and exposed to certain destruction if the Archduke could have thrown his army across the narrow arm of the river and renewed the engagement. But the Austrians were in no condition to follow up their victory.

Battle of Aspern, May 21, 22.

Their losses were enormous; their stores were exhausted. The moments in which a single stroke might have overthrown the whole fabric of Napoleon's power were spent in forced inaction. By the third day after the battle of Aspern the communications between the island and the mainland were restored, and Napoleon's energy had brought the army out of immediate danger.

Nevertheless, although the worst was averted, and the French now lay secure in their island fortress, the defeat of Aspern changed the position of Napoleon in the eyes of all Europe. The belief in his invincibility was destroyed; he had suffered a defeat in person, at the head of his finest troops, from an enemy little superior in strength to himself. The disasters of the Austrians in the opening of the campaign were forgotten; everywhere the hopes of resistance woke into new life. Prussian statesmen urged their King to promise his support if Austria should gain one more victory. Other enemies were ready to fall upon Napoleon without waiting for this condition. England collected an immense armament destined for an attack upon some point of the northern coast. Germany, lately mute and nerveless, gave threatening signs. The Duke of Brunswick, driven from his inheritance after his father's death at Jena, invaded the dominions of Napoleon's vassal, the King of Saxony, and expelled him from his capital. Popular insurrections broke out in Würtemberg and in Westphalia, and proved the rising force of national

Effect on Europe.

Brunswick invades Saxony.

feeling even in districts where the cause of Germany lately seemed so hopelessly lost.

But Napoleon concerned himself little with these remoter enemies. Every energy of his mind was bent to the one great issue on which victory depended, the passage of the Danube. His chances of success were still good, if the French troops watching the enemy between Vienna and the Adriatic could be brought up in time for the final struggle. The Archduke Charles was in no hurry for a battle, believing that every hour increased the probability of an attack upon Napoleon by England or Prussia, or insurgent Germany. Never was the difference between Napoleon and his ablest adversaries more strikingly displayed than in the work which was accomplished by him during this same interval. He had determined that in the next battle his army should march across the Danube as safely and as rapidly as it could march along the streets of Vienna. Two solid bridges were built on piles across the broad arm of the river; no less than six bridges of rafts were made ready to be thrown across the narrow arm when the moment arrived for the attack. By the end of June all the outlying divisions of the French army had gathered to the great rallying-point; a hundred and eighty thousand men were in the island, or ready to enter it; every movement, every position to be occupied by each member of this vast mass in its passage and advance, was fixed down to the minutest details. Napoleon had decided to cross from the eastern, not from the northern side of the island,

Napoleon's preparations for the second passage of the Danube. June.

and thus to pass outside the fortifications which the Archduke had erected on the former battle-field. Towards midnight on the 4th of July, in the midst of a violent storm, the six bridges were successively swung across the river. The artillery opened fire. One army corps after another, each drawn up opposite to its own bridge, marched to the northern shore, and by sunrise nearly the whole of Napoleon's force deployed on the left bank of the Danube. The river had been converted into a great highway; the fortifications which had been erected by the Archduke were turned by the eastward direction of the passage. All that remained for the Austrian commander was to fight a pitched battle on ground that was now at least thoroughly familiar to him. Charles had taken up a good position on the hills that look over the village of Wagram. Here, with 130,000 men, he awaited the attack of the French. The first attack was made in the afternoon after the crossing of the river. It failed; and the French army lay stretched during the night between the river and the hills, while the Archduke prepared to descend upon their left on the morrow, and to force himself between the enemy and the bridges behind them.

French cross the Danube. July 4.

Early on the morning of the 6th the two largest armies that had ever been brought face to face in Europe began their onslaught. Spectators from the steeples of Vienna saw the fire of the French little by little receding on their left, and dense masses of the Austrians pressing on

Battle of Wagram July 5, 6.

towards the bridges, on whose safety the existence of the French army depended. But ere long the forward movement stopped. Napoleon had thrown an overpowering force against the Austrian centre, and the Archduke found himself compelled to recall his victorious divisions and defend his own threatened line. Gradually the superior numbers of the French forced the enemy back. The Archduke John, who had been ordered up from Presburg, failed to appear on the field; and at two o'clock Charles ordered a retreat. The order of the Austrians was unbroken; they had captured more prisoners than they had lost; their retreat was covered by so powerful an artillery that the French could make no pursuit. The victory was no doubt Napoleon's, but it was a victory that had nothing in common with Jena and Austerlitz. Nothing was lost by the Austrians at Wagram but their positions and the reputation of their general. The army was still in fighting-order, with the fortresses of Bohemia behind it. Whether Austria would continue the war depended on the action of the other European Powers. If Great Britain successfully landed an armament in Northern Germany or dealt any overwhelming blow in Spain, if Prussia declared war on Napoleon, Austria might fight on. If the other Powers failed, Austria must make peace. The armistice of Znaim, concluded on the 12th of July, was recognised on all sides as a mere device to gain time. There was a pause in the great struggle in the central Continent. Its renewal or its termination depended upon the issue of events at a distance.

<small>Armistice of Znaim. July 12.</small>

For the moment the eyes of all Europe were fixed upon the British army in Spain. Sir Arthur Wellesley, who took command at Lisbon in the spring, had driven Soult out of Oporto, and was advancing by the valley of the Tagus upon the Spanish capital. Some appearance of additional strength was given to him by the support of a Spanish army under the command of General Cuesta. Wellesley's march had, however, been delayed by the neglect and bad faith of the Spanish Government, and time had been given to Soult to collect a large force in the neighbourhood of Salamanca, ready either to fall upon Wellesley from the north, or to unite with another French army which lay at Talavera, if its commander, Victor, had the wisdom to postpone an engagement. The English general knew nothing of Soult's presence on his flank: he continued his march towards Madrid along the valley of the Tagus, and finally drew up for battle at Talavera, when Victor, after retreating before Cuesta to some distance, hunted back his Spanish pursuer to the point from which he had started.* The first attack was made by Victor upon the English positions at evening on the 27th of July. Next morning the assault was renewed, and the battle became general. Wellesley gained a complete victory, but the English themselves suffered heavily, and the army remained in its position. Within the next few days Soult was discovered to be descending from the mountains between Salamanca and the Tagus. A force

* Wellington Despatches, iv. 533. Sup. Desp. vi. 319. Napier, ii. 357.

superior to Wellesley's own threatened to close upon him from the rear, and to hem him in between two fires. The sacrifices of Talavera proved to have been made in vain. Wellesley had no choice but to abandon his advance upon the Spanish capital, and to fall back upon Portugal by the roads south of the Tagus. In spite of the defeat of Victor, the French were the winners of the campaign. Madrid was still secure; the fabric of French rule in the Spanish Peninsula was still unshaken. The tidings of Wellesley's retreat reached Napoleon and the Austrian negotiators, damping the hopes of Austria, and easing Napoleon's fears. Austria's continuance of the war now depended upon the success or failure of the long-expected descent of an English army upon the northern coast of Europe. *Wellesley retreats to Portugal.*

Three months before the Austrian Government declared war upon Napoleon, it had acquainted Great Britain with its own plans, and urged the Cabinet to dispatch an English force to Northern Germany. Such a force, landing at the time of the battle of Aspern, would certainly have aroused both Prussia and the country between the Elbe and the Maine. But the difference between a movement executed in time and one executed weeks and months too late was still unknown at the English War Office. The Ministry did not even begin their preparations till the middle of June, and then they determined, in pursuance of a plan made some years earlier, to attack the French fleet and docks at Antwerp, and to ignore that patriotic movement in Northern Germany from which they had so much to hope.

English Expedition against Antwerp. July, 1809.

On the 28th of July, two months after the battle of Aspern and three weeks after the battle of Wagram, a fleet of thirty-seven ships of the line, with innumerable transports and gunboats, set sail from Dover for the Schelde. Forty thousand troops were on board; the commander of the expedition was the Earl of Chatham, a court-favourite in whom Nature avenged herself upon Great Britain for what she had given to this country in his father and his younger brother. The troops were landed on the island of Walcheren. Instead of pushing forward to Antwerp with all possible haste, and surprising it before any preparations could be made for its defence, Lord Chatham placed half his army on the banks of various canals, and with the other half proceeded to invest Flushing. On the 16th of August this unfortunate town surrendered, after a bombardment that had reduced it to a mass of ruins. During the next ten days the English commander advanced about as many miles, and then discovered that for all prospect of taking Antwerp he might as well have remained in England. Whilst Chatham was groping about in Walcheren, the fortifications of Antwerp were restored, the fleet carried up the river, and a mass of troops collected sufficient to defend the town against a regular siege. Defeat stared the English in the face. At the end of August the general recommended the Government to recall the expedition, only leaving a

Total failure.

force of 15,000 soldiers to occupy the marshes of Walcheren. Chatham's recommendations were accepted; and on a spot so notoriously pestiferous that Napoleon had refused to permit a single French soldier to serve there on garrison duty,* an English army-corps, which might at least have earned the same honour as Schill and Brunswick in Northern Germany, was left to perish of fever and ague. When two thousand soldiers were in their graves, the rest were recalled to England.

Great Britain had failed to weaken or to alarm Napoleon; the King of Prussia made no movement on behalf of the losing cause; and the Austrian Government unwillingly found itself compelled to accept conditions of peace. *Austria makes peace.* It was not so much a deficiency in its forces as the universal distrust of its generals that made it impossible for Austria to continue the war. The soldiers had fought as bravely as the French, but in vain. "If we had a million soldiers," it was said, "we must make peace; for we have no one to command them." Count Stadion, who was for carrying on the war to the bitter end, despaired of throwing his own energetic courage into the men who surrounded the Emperor, and withdrew from public affairs. For week after week the Emperor fluctuated between the acceptance of Napoleon's hard conditions and the renewal of a struggle which was likely to involve his own dethronement as well the total conquest of the Austrian State. At length Napoleon's demands

* Correspondance de Napoleon: Décision, Mai 28, 1806. Parliamentary Papers 1810, p. 123, 697.

were presented in the form of an ultimatum. In his distress the Emperor's thoughts turned towards the Minister who, eight years before, had been so strong, so resolute, when all around him wavered. Thugut, now seventy-six years old, was living in retirement. The Emperor sent one of his generals to ask his opinion on peace or war. "I thought to find him," reported the general, "broken in mind and body; but the fire of his spirit is in its full force." Thugut's reply did honour to his foresight: "Make peace at any price. The existence of the Austrian monarchy is at stake: the dissolution of the French Empire is not far off." On the 14th of October the Emperor Francis accepted his conqueror's terms, and signed conditions of peace.*

The Treaty of Vienna, the last which Napoleon signed as a conqueror, took from the Austrian Empire 50,000 square miles of territory and more than 4,000,000 inhabitants. Salzburg, with part of Upper Austria, was ceded to Bavaria; Western Galicia, the territory gained by Austria in the final partition of Poland, was transferred to the Grand-Duchy of Warsaw; part of Carinthia, with the whole of the country lying between the Adriatic and the Save as far as the frontier of Bosnia, was annexed to Napoleon's own Empire, under the title of the Illyrian Provinces. Austria was cut off from the sea, and the dominion of Napoleon extended without a break to the borders of Turkey. Bavaria and Saxony, the outposts of French sovereignty in Central Europe, were enriched

Peace of Vienna, Oct. 14, 1809.

* Beer, p. 445. Gentz, Tagebücher i. 82, 118.

at the expense of the Power which had called Germany to arms; Austria, which at the beginning of the Revolutionary War had owned territory upon the Rhine and exercised a predominating influence over all Italy, seemed now to be finally excluded both from Germany and the Mediterranean. Yet, however striking the change of frontier which gave to Napoleon continuous dominion from the Straits of Calais to the border of Bosnia, the victories of France in 1809 brought in their train none of those great moral changes which had hitherto made each French conquest a stage in European progress. The campaign of 1796 had aroused the hope of national independence in Italy; the settlements of 1801 and 1806 had put an end to Feudalism in Western Germany; the victories of 1809 originated nothing but a change of frontier such as the next war might obliterate and undo. All that was permanent in the effects of the year 1809 was due, not to any new creations of Napoleon, but to the spirit of resistance which France had at length excited in Europe. The revolt of the Tyrol, the exploits of Brunswick and Schill, gave a stimulus to German patriotism which survived the defeat of Austria. Austria itself, though overpowered, had inflicted a deadly injury upon Napoleon, by withdrawing him from Spain at the moment when he might have completed its conquest, and by enabling Wellesley to gain a footing in the Peninsula. Napoleon appeared to have gathered a richer spoil from the victories of 1809 than from any of his previous wars; in reality he had never surrounded himself with

Real effects of the war of 1809.

so many dangers. Russia was alienated by the annexation of West Galicia to the Polish Grand Duchy of Warsaw; Northern Germany had profited by the examples of courage and patriotism shown so largely in 1809 on behalf of the Fatherland; Spain, supported by Wellesley's army, was still far from submission. The old indifference which had smoothed the way for the earlier French conquests was no longer the characteristic of Europe. The estrangement of Russia, the growth of national spirit in Germany and in Spain, involved a danger to Napoleon's power which far outweighed the visible results of his victory.

Austria itself could only acquiesce in defeat: nor perhaps would the permanent interests of Europe have been promoted by its success. The championship of Germany which it assumed at the beginning of the war would no doubt have resulted in the temporary establishment of some form of German union under Austrian leadership, if the event of the war had been different; but the sovereign of Hungary and Croatia could never be the true head of the German people; and the conduct of the Austrian Government after the peace of 1809 gave little reason to regret its failure to revive a Teutonic Empire. No portion of the Emperor's subjects had fought for him with such determined loyalty as the Tyrolese. After having been the first to throw off the yoke of the stranger, they had again and again freed their country when Napoleon's generals supposed all resistance overcome; and in return for their efforts the Emperor had solemnly assured them

Austria and the Tyrol.

that he would never accept a peace which did not restore them to his Empire. If fair dealing was due anywhere it was due from the Court of Austria to the Tyrolese Yet the only reward of the simple courage of these mountaineers was that the war-party at head-quarters recklessly employed them as a means of prolonging hostilities after the armistice of Znaim, and that up to the moment when peace was signed they were left in the belief that the Emperor meant to keep his promise. Austria, however, could not ruin herself to please the Tyrolese. Circumstances were changed; and the phrases of patriotism which had excited so much rejoicing at the beginning of the war were now fallen out of fashion at Vienna. Nothing more was heard about the rights of nations and the deliverance of Germany. Austria had made a great venture and failed; and the Government rather resumed than abandoned its normal attitude in turning its back upon the professions of 1809.

Henceforward the policy of Austria was one of calculation, untinged by national sympathies. France had been a cruel enemy; yet if there was a prospect of winning something for Austria by a French alliance, considerations of sentiment could not be allowed to stand in the way. A statesman who, like Count Stadion, had identified the interests of Austria with the liberation of Germany, was no fitting helmsman for the State in the shifting course that now lay before it. A diplomatist was called to power who had hitherto by Napoleon's own desire represented the Austrian State at Paris. Count

Austrian policy after 1809.

Metternich.

Metternich, the new Chief Minister, was the son of a Rhenish nobleman who had held high office under the Austrian crown. His youth had been passed at Coblentz, and his character and tastes were those which in the eighteenth century had marked the court-circles of the little Rhenish Principalities, French in their outer life, unconscious of the instinct of nationality, polished and seductive in that personal management which passed for the highest type of statesmanship. Metternich had been ambassador at Dresden and at Berlin before he went to Paris. Napoleon had requested that he might be transferred to the Court of the Tuileries, on account of the marked personal courtesy shown by Metternich to the French ambassador at Berlin during the war between France and Austria in 1805. Metternich carried with him all the friendliness of personal intercourse which Napoleon expected in him, but he also carried with him a calm and penetrating self-possession, and the conviction that Napoleon would give Europe no rest until his power was greatly diminished. He served Austria well at Paris, and in the negotiations for peace which followed the battle of Wagram he took a leading part. After the disasters of 1809, when war was impossible and isolation ruin, no statesman could so well serve Austria as one who had never confessed himself the enemy of any Power; and, with the full approval of Napoleon, the late Ambassador at Paris was placed at the head of the Austrian State.

Metternich's first undertaking gave singular evidence

of the flexibility of system which was henceforward to guard Austria's interests. Before the grass had grown over the graves at Wagram, the Emperor Francis was persuaded to give his daughter in marriage to Napoleon. For some time past Napoleon had determined on divorcing Josephine and allying himself to one of the reigning houses of the Continent. His first advances were made at St. Petersburg; but the Czar hesitated to form a connection which his subjects would view as a dishonour; and the opportunity was seized by the less fastidious Austrians as soon as the fancies of the imperial suitor turned towards Vienna. The Emperor Francis, who had been bullied by Napoleon upon the field of Austerlitz, ridiculed and insulted in every proclamation issued during the late campaign, gave up his daughter for what was called the good of his people, and reconciled himself to a son-in-law who had taken so many provinces for his dowry. Peace had not been proclaimed four months when the treaty was signed which united the House of Bonaparte to the family of Marie Antoinette. The Archduke Charles represented Napoleon in the espousals; the Archbishop of Vienna anointed the bride with the same sacred oil with which he had consecrated the banners of 1809; the servile press which narrated the wedding festivities found no space to mention that the Emperor's bravest subject, the Tyrolese leader Hofer, was executed by Napoleon as a brigand in the interval between the contract and the celebration of the marriage. Old Austrian families, members of the only aristocracy

Marriage of Napoleon with Marie Louise, 1810.

upon the Continent that still possessed political weight and a political tradition, lamented the Emperor's consent to a union which their prejudices called a mis-alliance, and their consciences an adultery; but the object of Metternich was attained. The friendship between France and Russia, which had inflicted so much evil on the Continent since the Peace of Tilsit, was dissolved; the sword of Napoleon was turned away from Austria for at least some years; the restoration of the lost provinces of the Hapsburg seemed not impossible, now that Napoleon and Alexander were left face to face in Europe, and the alliance of Austria had become so important to the power which had hitherto enriched itself at Austria's expense.

Severance of Napoleon and Alexander.

Napoleon crowned his new bride, and felt himself at length the equal of the Hapsburgs and the Bourbons. Except in Spain, his arms were no longer resisted upon the Continent, and the period immediately succeeding the Peace of Vienna was that which brought the Napoleonic Empire to its widest bounds. Already, in the pride of the first victories of 1809, Napoleon had completed his aggressions upon the Papal sovereignty by declaring the Ecclesiastical States to be united to the French Empire (May 17, 1809). The Pope retorted upon his despoiler with a Bull of Excommunication; but the spiritual terrors were among the least formidable of those then active in Europe, and the sanctity of the Pontiff did not prevent Napoleon's soldiers from arresting him in the Quirinal, and carrying him as a prisoner to Savona. Here

Napoleon annexes Papal States, May, 1809.

Pius VII. was detained for the next three years. The Roman States received the laws and the civil organisation of France.* Bishops and clergy who refused the oath of fidelity to Napoleon were imprisoned or exiled; the monasteries and convents were dissolved; the cardinals and great officers, along with the archives and the whole apparatus of ecclesiastical rule, were carried to Paris. In relation to the future of European Catholicism, the breach between Napoleon and Pius VII. was a more important event than was understood at the time: its immediate and visible result was that there was one sovereign the fewer in Europe, and one more province opened to the French conscription.

The next of Napoleon's vassals who lost his throne was the King of Holland. Like Joseph in Spain, and like Murat in Naples, Louis Bonaparte had made an honest effort to govern for the benefit of his subjects. He had endeavoured to lighten the burdens which Napoleon laid upon the Dutch nation, already deprived of its colonies, its commerce, and its independence; and every plea which Louis had made for his subjects had been treated by Napoleon as a breach of duty towards himself. The offence of the unfortunate King of Holland became unpardonable when he neglected to enforce the orders of Napoleon against the admission of English goods. Louis was summoned to Paris, and compelled to sign a treaty, ceding part of his dominions and placing his customhouses in the hands of French officers. He returned to

Napoleon annexes Holland, July, 1810.

---

* Correspondance de Napoleon, xix., 15, 265.

Holland, but affairs grew worse and worse. French troops overran the country; Napoleon's letters were each more menacing than the last; and at length Louis fled from his dominions (July 1, 1810), and delivered himself from a royalty which had proved the most intolerable kind of servitude. A week later Holland was incorporated with the French Empire.

Two more annexations followed before the end of the year. The Republic of the Valais was declared to have neglected the duty imposed upon it of repairing the road over the Simplon, and forfeited its independence. The North-German coast-district, comprising the Hanse towns, Oldenburg, and part of the Kingdom of Westphalia, was annexed to the French Empire, with the alleged object of more effectually shutting out British goods from the ports of the Elbe and the Weser. Hamburg, however, and most of the territory now incorporated with France, had been occupied by French troops ever since the war of 1806, and the legal change in its position scarcely made its subjection more complete. Had the history of this annexation been written by men of the peasant-class, it would probably have been described in terms of unmixed thankfulness and praise. In the Decree introducing the French principle of the free tenure of land, thirty-six distinct forms of feudal service are enumerated, as abolished without compensation.*

Napoleon's dominion had now reached its widest bounds. The frontier of the Empire began at Lübeck

Marginal note: Annexation of Le Valais, and of the North German coast.

* Corresp. de Napoleon, xxiii., 62. Décret, 9 Déc., 1811.

on the Baltic, touched the Rhine at Wesel, and followed the river and the Jura mountains to the foot of the Lake of Geneva; then, crossing the Alps above the source of the Rhone, it ran with the rivers Sesia and Po to a point nearly opposite Mantua, mounted to the watershed of the Apennines, and descended to the Mediterranean at Terracina. The late Ecclesiastical States were formed into the two Departments of the Tiber and of Trasimene; Tuscany, also divided into French Departments, and represented in the French Legislative Body, gave the title of Archduchess and the ceremonial of a Court to Napoleon's sister Eliza; the Kingdom of Italy, formed by Lombardy, Venice, and the country east of the Apennines as far south as Ascoli, belonged to Napoleon himself, but was not constitutionally united with the French Empire. On the east of the Adriatic the Illyrian Provinces extended Napoleon's rule to the borders of Bosnia and Montenegro. Outside the frontier of this great Empire an order of feudatories ruled in Italy, in Germany, and in Poland. Murat, King of Naples, and the client-princes of the Confederation of the Rhine, holding all Germany up to the frontiers of Prussia and Austria, as well as the Grand-Duchy of Warsaw, were nominally sovereigns within their own dominions; but they held their dignities at Napoleon's pleasure, and the population and revenues of their States were at his service.

Extent of Napoleon's Empire and Dependencies, 1810.

The close of the year 1810 saw the last changes effected which Europe was destined to receive at the hands of Napoleon. The fabric of his sovereignty was raised upon the ruins of all that was obsolete and forceless upon the western Continent; the benefits as well as the wrongs of his supremacy were now seen in their widest operation. All Italy, the northern districts of Germany which were incorporated with the Empire, and a great part of the Confederate Territory of the Rhine, received in the Code Napoleon a law which, to an extent hitherto unknown in Europe, brought social justice into the daily affairs of life. The privileges of the noble, the feudal burdens of the peasant, the monopolies of the guilds, passed away, in most instances for ever. The comfort and improvement of mankind were vindicated as the true aim of property by the abolition of the devices which convert the soil into an instrument of family pride, and by the enforcement of a fair division of inheritances among the children of the possessor. Legal process, both civil and criminal, was brought within the comprehension of ordinary citizens, and submitted to the test of publicity. These were among the fruits of an earlier enlightenment which Napoleon's supremacy bestowed upon a great part of Europe. The price which was paid for them was the suppression of every vestige of liberty, the conscription, and the Continental blockade. On the whole, the yoke was patiently borne. The Italians and the Germans of the Rhenish Confederacy cared little what Government they obeyed; their recruits who were sent to be killed by the Austrians or the Spaniards felt it no especial hardship to fight Napoleon's battles. More galling was the pressure of

Napoleon's commercial system and of the agencies by which he attempted to enforce it. In the *Commercial blockade.* hope of ruining the trade of Great Britain, Napoleon spared no severity against the owners of anything that had touched British hands, and deprived the Continent of its entire supply of colonial produce, with the exception of such as was imported at enormous charges by traders licensed by himself. The possession of English goods became a capital offence. In the great trading towns a system of permanent terrorism was put in force against the merchants. Soldiers ransacked their houses; their letters were opened; spies dogged their steps. It was in Hamburg, where Davoust exercised a sort of independent sovereignty, that the violence and injustice of the Napoleonic commercial system was seen in its most repulsive form; in the greater part of the Empire it was felt more in the general decline of trade and in a multitude of annoying privations than in acts of obtrusive cruelty.* The French were themselves compelled to extract sugar from beetroot, and to substitute chicory for coffee; the Germans, less favoured by nature, and less rapid in adaptation, thirsted and sulked. Even in such torpid communities as Saxony political discontent was at length engendered by bodily discomfort. Men who were proof against all the patriotic exaltation of Stein and Fichte felt that there must be something wrong in a system which sent up the price of coffee to five shillings a pound, and reduced the tobacconist to exclusive dependence upon the market-gardener.

* Mémoires de Jérome, v., 185.

It was not, however, by its effects upon Napoleon's German vassals that the Continental system contributed to the fall of its author. Whatever the discontent of these communities, they obeyed Napoleon as long as he was victorious, and abandoned him only when his cause was lost. Its real political importance lay in the hostility which it excited between France and Russia.

The Czar withdraws from Napoleon's commercial system, Dec., 1810.
The Czar, who had attached himself to Napoleon's commercial system at the Peace of Tilsit, withdrew from it in the year succeeding the Peace of Vienna. The trade of the Russian Empire had been ruined by the closure of its ports to British vessels and British goods. Napoleon had broken his promise to Russia by adding West Galicia to the Polish Duchy of Warsaw; and the Czar refused to sacrifice the wealth of his subjects any longer in the interest of an insincere ally. At the end of the year 1810 an order was published at St. Petersburg, opening the harbours of Russia to all ships bearing a neutral flag, and imposing a duty upon many of the products of France. This edict was scarcely less than a direct challenge to the French Emperor. Napoleon exaggerated the effect of his Continental prohibitions upon English traffic. He imagined that the command of the European coast-line, and nothing short of this, would enable him to exhaust his enemy; and he was prepared to risk a war with Russia rather than permit it to frustrate his long-cherished hopes. Already in the Austrian marriage Napoleon had marked the severance of his interest from those of Alexander. An

attempted compromise upon the affairs of Poland produced only new alienation and distrust, an open affront was offered to Alexander in the annexation of the Duchy of Oldenburg, whose sovereign was a member of his own family. The last event was immediately followed by the publication of the new Russian tariff. In the spring of 1811 Napoleon had determined upon war. With Spain still unsubdued, he had no motive to hurry on hostilities; Alexander on his part was still less ready for action; and the forms of diplomatic intercourse were in consequence maintained for some time longer at Paris and St. Petersburg. But the true nature of the situation was shown by the immense levies that were ordered both in France and Russia; and the rest of the year was spent in preparations for the campaign which was destined to decide the fate of Europe.

France and Russia preparing for war, 1811.

We have seen that during the period of more than two years that elapsed between the Peace of Vienna and the outbreak of war with Russia, Napoleon had no enemy in arms upon the Continent except in the Spanish Peninsula. Had the Emperor himself taken up the command in Spain, he would probably within a few months have crushed both the Spanish armies and their English ally. A fatal error in judgment made him willing to look on from a distance whilst his generals engaged with this last foe. The disputes with the Pope and the King of Holland might well have been adjourned for another year; but Napoleon felt no suspicions that the conquest

Affairs in Spain and Portugal, 1809—1812.

of the Spanish Peninsula was too difficult a task for his marshals; nor perhaps would it have been so if Wellington had been like any of the generals whom Napoleon had himself encountered. The French forces in the Peninsula numbered over 300,000 men: in spite of the victory of Talavera, the English had been forced to retreat into Portugal. But the warfare of Wellington was a different thing from that even of the best Austrian or Russian commanders. From the time of the retreat from Talavera he had foreseen that Portugal would be invaded by an army far outnumbering his own; and he planned a scheme of defence as original, as strongly marked with true military insight, as Napoleon's own most daring schemes of attack. Behind Lisbon a rugged mountainous tract stretches from the Tagus to the sea: here, while the English army wintered in the neighbourhood of Almeida, Wellington employed thousands of Portuguese labourers in turning the promontory into one vast fortress. No rumour of the operation was allowed to reach the enemy. A double series of fortifications, known as the Lines of Torres Vedras, followed the mountain-bastion on the north of Lisbon, and left no single point open between the Tagus and the sea. This was the barrier to which Wellington meant in the last resort to draw his assailants, whilst the country was swept of everything that might sustain an invading army, and the irregular troops of Portugal closed in upon its rear.*

Lines of Torres Vedras, 1809–1810.

In June, 1810, Marshal Massena, who had won the

* Wellington Supplementary Despatches, vi., 41. Napier, iii., 250.

highest distinction at Aspern and Wagram, arrived in Spain, and took up the command of the army destined for the conquest of Portugal. Ciudad Rodrigo was invested: Wellington, too weak to effect its relief, too wise to jeopardise his army for the sake of Spanish praise, lay motionless while this great fortress fell into the hands of the invader. In September, the French, 70,000 strong, entered Portugal. Wellington retreated down the valley of the Mondego, devastating the country. At length he halted at Busaco and gave battle (September 27). The French were defeated; the victory gave the Portuguese full confidence in the English leader, but other roads were open to the invader, and Wellington continued his retreat. Massena followed, and heard for the first time of the fortifications of Torres Vedras when he was within five days' march of them. On nearing the mountain-barrier, Massena searched in vain for an unprotected point. Fifty thousand English and Portuguese regular troops, besides a multitude of Portuguese militia, were collected behind the lines; with the present number of the French an assault was hopeless. Massena waited for reinforcements. It was with the utmost difficulty that he could keep his army from starving; at length, when the country was utterly exhausted, he commenced his retreat (Nov. 14). Wellington descended from the heights, but his marching force was still too weak to risk a pitched battle. Massena halted and took post at Santarem, on the Tagus. Here, and in the neighbouring valley of the Zezere, he maintained himself during the winter. But

Massena's campaign against Wellington, 1810.

in March, 1811, reinforcements arrived from England: Wellington moved forward against his enemy, and the retreat of the French began in real earnest. Massena made his way northwards, hard pressed by the English, and devastating the country with merciless severity in order to retard pursuit. Fire and ruin marked the track of the retreating army; but such were the sufferings of the French themselves, both during the invasion and the retreat, that when Massena re-entered Spain, after a campaign in which only one pitched battle had been fought, his loss exceeded 30,000 men.

Retreat of Massena, 1810-11.

Other French armies, in spite of a most destructive guerilla warfare, were in the meantime completing the conquest of the south and the east of Spain. Soult captured Seville, and began to lay siege to Cadiz. Here, at the end of 1810, an order reached him from Napoleon to move to the support of Massena. Leaving Victor in command at Cadiz, Soult marched northwards, routed the Spaniards, and conquered the fortress of Badajoz, commanding the southern road into Portugal. Massena, however, was already in retreat, and Soult's own advance was cut short by intelligence that Graham, the English general in Cadiz, had broken out upon the besiegers and inflicted a heavy defeat. Soult returned to Cadiz and resumed the blockade. Wellington, thus freed from danger of attack from the south, and believing Massena to be thoroughly disabled, considered that the time had come for a forward movement into Spain. It was necessary for him to capture the

Soult conquers Spain as far as Cadiz.

fortresses of Almeida and Ciudad Rodrigo on the northern road, and to secure his own communications with Portugal by wresting back Badajoz from the French. He left a small force to besiege Almeida, and moved to Elvas to make arrangements with Beresford for the siege of Badajoz. But before the English commander had deemed it possible, the energy of Massena had restored his troops to efficiency, and the two armies of Massena and Soult were now ready to assail the English on the north and the south. Massena marched against the corps investing Almeida. Wellington hastened back to meet him, and fought a battle at Fuentes d'Onoro. The French were defeated; Almeida passed into the hands of the English. In the south, Soult advanced to the relief of Badajoz. He was overthrown by Beresford in the bloody engagement of Albuera (May 16th); but his junction with the army of the north, which was now transferred from Massena to Marmont, forced the English to raise the siege; and Wellington, after audaciously offering battle to the combined French armies, retired within the Portuguese frontier, and marched northwards with the design of laying siege to Ciudad Rodrigo. Again outnumbered by the French, he was compelled to retire to cantonments on the Coa.

Wellington's campaign of 1811.

Throughout the autumn months, which were spent in forced inaction, Wellington held patiently to his belief that the French would be unable to keep their armies long united, on account of the scarcity of food. His calculations were correct, and at the close of the year 1811 the English were again superior in the field. Wellington moved against Ciudad Rodrigo, and took it by storm on the 19th of January, 1812. The road into Spain was opened; it only remained to secure Portugal itself by the capture of Badajoz. Wellington crossed the Tagus on the 8th of March, and completed the investment of Badajoz ten days later. It was necessary to gain possession of the city, at whatever cost, before Soult could advance to its relief. On the night of the 6th of April Wellington gave orders for the assault. The fury of the attack, the ferocity of the English soldiers in the moment of their victory, have made the storm of Badajoz conspicuous amongst the most terrible events of war. But the purpose of Wellington was effected; the base of the English army in Portugal was secured from all possibility of attack; and at the moment when Napoleon was summoning his veteran regiments from beyond the Pyrenees for the invasion of Russia, the English commander, master of the frontier fortresses of Spain, was preparing to overwhelm the weakened armies in the Peninsula, and to drive the French from Madrid.

Capture of Ciudad Rodrigo, Jan. 19, 1812.

Capture of Badajoz, April 6.

It was in the summer of 1812, when Napoleon was now upon the point of opening the Russian campaign, that Wellington advanced against Marmont's positions in the north of Spain and the French lines of communication with the capital. Marmont fell back and allowed Wellington to pass Salamanca; but on reaching the Douro he turned upon his

Wellington invades Spain, June, 1812.

adversary, and by a succession of swift and skilful marches brought the English into some danger of losing their communications with Portugal. Wellington himself now retreated as far as Salamanca, and there gave battle (July 22). A decisive victory freed the English army from its peril, and annihilated all the advantages gained by Marmont's strategy and speed. The French were so heavily defeated that they had to fall back on Burgos. Wellington marched upon Madrid. At his approach King Joseph fled from the capital, and ordered Soult to evacuate Andalusia, and to meet him at Valencia, on the eastern coast. Wellington entered Madrid amidst the wild rejoicing of the Spaniards, and then turned northwards to complete the destruction of the army which he had beaten at Salamanca. But the hour of his final success was not yet come. His advance upon Madrid, though wise as a political measure, had given the French northern army time to rally. He was checked by the obstinate defence of Burgos; and finding the French strengthened by the very abandonment of territory which his victory had forced upon them, he retired to Portugal, giving to King Joseph a few months' more precarious enjoyment of his vassal-sovereignty before his final and irrevocable overthrow. *Salamanca, July 22.* *Wellington retires to Portugal.*

In Spain itself the struggle of the nation for its independence had produced a political revolution as little foreseen by the Spaniards as by Napoleon himself when the conflict began. When, in 1808, the people had taken up arms for its *The war excites a constitutional movement in Spain.*

native dynasty, the voices of those who demanded a reform in the abuses of the Bourbon government had scarcely been heard amid the tumult of loyal enthusiasm for Ferdinand. There existed, however, a group of liberally-minded men in Spain; and as soon as the invasion of the French and the subsequent successes of the Spaniards had overthrown both the old repressive system of the Bourbons and that which Napoleon attempted to put in its place, the opinions of these men, hitherto scarcely known outside the circle of their own acquaintances, suddenly became a power in the country through the liberation of the press. Jovellanos, an upright and large-minded statesman, who had suffered a long imprisonment in the last reign in consequence of his labours in the cause of progress, now represented in the Central Junta the party of constitutional reform. The Junta itself acted with but little insight or sincerity. A majority of its members neither desired nor understood the great changes in government which Jovellanos advocated; yet the Junta itself was an irregular and revolutionary body, and was forced to appeal to the nation in order to hold its ground against the old legal Councils of the monarchy, which possessed not only a better formal right, but all the habits of authority. The victories of Napoleon at the end of 1808, and the threatening attitude both of the old official bodies and of the new provincial governments which had sprung up in every part of the kingdom, extorted from the Junta in the spring of 1809 a declaration in favour of the assembling of the Cortes, or National Parliament, in the following year. Once made, the declaration could not be nullified or withdrawn. It was in vain that the Junta, alarmed at the progress of popular opinions, restored the censorship of the press, and attempted to suppress the liberal journals. The current of political agitation swept steadily on; and before the end of the year 1809 the conflict of parties, which Spain was henceforward to experience in common with the other Mediterranean States, had fairly begun.*

The Spanish Liberals of 1809 made the same attack upon despotic power, and upheld the same theories of popular right, as the leaders of the French nation twenty years before. Against them was ranged the whole force of Spanish officialism, soon to be supported by the overwhelming power of the clergy. In the outset, however, the Liberals carefully avoided infringing on the prerogatives of the Church. Thus accommodating its policy to the Catholic spirit of the nation, the party of reform gathered strength throughout the year 1809, as disaster after disaster excited the wrath of the people against both the past and the present holders of power. It was determined by the Junta that the Cortes should assemble on the 1st of March, 1810. According to the ancient usage of Spain, each of the Three Estates, the Clergy, the Nobles, and the Commons, would have been represented in the Cortes by a separate assembly. The opponents of reform pressed for the maintenance of this mediæval order, the Liberals declared for a single Chamber; the Junta, guided by Jovellanos, adopted a middle course, and decided that the higher clergy and nobles should be jointly represented by one Chamber, the

Spanish Liberals in 1809 and 1810.

* Baumgarten, Geschichte Spaniens, i. 405.

D D 2

Commons by a second. Writs of election had already been issued, when the Junta, driven to Cadiz by the advance of the French armies, and assailed alike by Liberals, by reactionists, and by city mobs, ended its ineffective career, and resigned its powers into the hands of a Regency composed of five persons (Jan. 30, 1810). Had the Regency immediately taken steps to assemble the Cortes, Spain would probably have been content with the moderate reforms which two Chambers, formed according to the plans of Jovellanos, would have been likely to sanction. The Regency, however, preferred to keep power in its own hands, and ignored the promise which the Junta had given to the nation. Its policy of obstruction, which was continued for months after the time when the Cortes ought to have assembled, threw the Liberal party into the hands of men of extremes, and prepared the way for revolution instead of reform. It was only when the report reached Spain that Ferdinand was about to marry the daughter of King Joseph, and to accept the succession to the Spanish crown from the usurper himself, that the Regency consented to convoke the Cortes. But it was now no longer possible to create an Upper House to serve as a check upon the popular Assembly. A single Chamber was elected, and elected in great part within the walls of Cadiz itself; for the representatives of districts where the presence of French soldiery rendered election impossible were chosen by refugees from those districts within Cadiz, amid the tumults of political passion which stir a great city in time of war and revolution.

On the 24th of September, 1810, the Cortes opened.

Its first act was to declare the sovereignty of the people, its next act to declare the freedom of the Press. In every debate a spirit of bitter hatred towards the old system of government and of deep distrust towards Ferdinand himself revealed itself in the speeches of the Liberal deputies, although no one in the Assembly dared to avow the least want of loyalty towards the exiled House. *Constitution made by the Cortes, 1812.* The Liberals knew how passionate was the love of the Spanish people for their Prince; but they resolved that, if Ferdinand returned to his throne, he should return without the power to revive the old abuses of Bourbon rule. In this spirit the Assembly proceeded to frame a Constitution for Spain. The Crown was treated as the antagonist and corrupter of the people; its administrative powers were jealously reduced; it was confronted by an Assembly to be elected every two years, and the members of this Assembly were prohibited both from holding office under the Crown, and from presenting themselves for re-election at the end of their two years' service. To a Representative Body thus excluded from all possibility of gaining any practical acquaintance with public affairs was entrusted not only the right of making laws, but the control of every branch of government. The executive was reduced to a mere cypher.

Such was the Constitution which, under the fire of the French artillery now encompassing Cadiz, the Cortes of Spain proclaimed in the spring of the year 1812. Its principles had excited the most vehement opposition within the Assembly itself; by the nation, or at least that part of it which was in communication with Cadiz, it appeared to be received with enthusiasm.

The Clergy against the Constitution. The Liberals, who had triumphed over their opponents in the debates in the Assembly, believed that their own victory was the victory of the Spanish people over the forces of despotism. But before the first rejoicings were over, ominous signs appeared of the strength of the opposite party, and of the incapacity of the Liberals themselves to form any effective Government. The fanaticism of the clergy was excited by a law partly ratifying the suppression of monasteries begun by Joseph Bonaparte; the enactments of the Cortes regarding the censorship of religious writings threw the Church into open revolt. In declaring the freedom of the Press, the Cortes had expressly guarded themselves against extending this freedom to religious discussion; the clergy now demanded the restoration of the powers of the Inquisition, which had been in abeyance since the beginning of the war. The Cortes were willing to grant to the Bishops the right of condemning any writing as heretical, and they were willing to enforce by means of the ordinary tribunals the law which declared the Catholic religion to be the only one permitted in Spain; but they declined to restore the jurisdiction of the Holy Office (Feb., 1813). Without this engine for the suppression of all mental independence the priesthood of Spain conceived its cause to be lost. The anathema of the Church went out against the new order. Uniting with the partisans of absolutism, whom Wellington, provoked by the extravagances of the

Liberals, now took under his protection, the clergy excited an ignorant people against its own emancipators, and awaited the time when the return of Ferdinand, and a combination of all the interests hostile to reform, should overthrow the Constitution which the Liberals fondly imagined to have given freedom to Spain.

CHAPTER X.

War approaching between France and Russia—Policy of Prussia—Hardenberg's Ministry—Prussia forced into Alliance with Napoleon—Austrian Alliance—Napoleon's Preparations—He enters Russia—Alexander and Bernadotte—Plan of the Russians to fight a battle at Drissa frustrated—They retreat on Witepsk—Sufferings of the French—French enter Smolensko—Battle of Borodino—Evacuation of Moscow—Moscow fired—The Retreat from Moscow—The French at Smolensko—Advance of Russian Armies from North and South—Battle of Krasnoi—Passage of the Beresina—The French reach the Niemen—York's Convention with the Russians—The Czar and Stein—Russian Army enters Prussia—Stein raises East Prussia—Treaty of Kalisch—Prussia declares War—Enthusiasm of the Nation—Idea of German Unity—The Landwehr.

WAR between France and Russia was known to be imminent as early as the spring of 1811. The approach of the conflict was watched with the deepest anxiety by the two States of central Europe which still retained some degree of independence. The Governments of Berlin and Vienna had been drawn together by misfortune.

Austria and Prussia in 1811.

The same ultimate deliverance formed the secret hope of both; but their danger was too great to permit them to combine in open resistance to Napoleon's will. In spite of a tacit understanding between the two powers, each was compelled for the present to accept the conditions necessary to secure its own existence. The situation of Prussia in especial was one of the utmost danger. Its territory lay directly between the French Empire and Russia; its fortresses were in the hands of Napoleon; its resources were certain to be seized by one or other of the hostile armies. Neutrality was impossible, however much desired by Prussia itself; and the only question to be decided by the Government was whether Prussia should enter the war as the ally of France or of Russia. Had the party of Stein been in power, Prussia would have taken arms against Napoleon at every risk. Stein, however, was in exile; his friends, though strong in the army, were not masters of the Government; the foreign policy of the country was directed by a statesman who trusted more to time and prudent management than to desperate resolves. Hardenberg had been recalled to office in 1810, *Hardenberg's Ministry.* and permitted to resume the great measures of civil reform which had been broken off two years before. The machinery of Government was reconstructed upon principles that had been laid down by Stein; agrarian reform was carried still farther by the abolition of peasant's service, and the partition of peasant's land between the occupant and his lord; an experiment, though a very ill-managed one, was made in the forms of constitutional Government by the convocation of three successive assemblies of the Notables. On the part of the privileged orders Hardenberg encountered the most bitter opposition; his own love of absolute power prevented him from winning popular confidence by any real approach towards a Representative System. Nor was the foreign policy of the Minister of a character to excite enthusiasm. A true patriot at heart, he seemed at times to be destitute of patriotism, when he was in fact only destitute of the power to reveal his real motives.

Convinced that Prussia could not remain neutral in the coming war, and believing some relief from its present burdens to be absolutely necessary, Hardenberg determined in the first instance to offer Prussia's support to Napoleon, demanding in return for it a reduction of the payments still due to France, and the removal of the limits imposed upon the Prussian army.* The offer of the Prussian alliance reached Napoleon in the spring of 1811 : he maintained an obstinate silence. While the Prussian envoy at Paris vainly waited for an audience, masses of troops advanced from the Rhine towards the Prussian frontier, and the French garrisons on the Oder were raised far beyond their stipulated strength. In July the envoy returned from Paris, announcing that Napoleon declined even to enter upon a discussion of the terms proposed by Hardenberg. King Frederick William now wrote to the Czar, proposing an alliance between Prussia and Russia. It was not long before the report of Hardenberg's military preparations reached Paris. Napoleon announced that if they were not immediately suspended he should order Davoust to march on Berlin; and he presented a counter-proposition for a Prussian alliance, which was in fact one of unqualified submission. The Government had to decide between accepting a treaty which placed Prussia among Napoleon's vassals, or certain war. Hardenberg, expecting favourable news from St. Petersburg, pronounced in favour of war; but the Czar, though anxious for the support of Prussia, had determined on a

Marginal note: Hardenberg's foreign policy, 1811.

* Hardenberg (Ranke), iv. 268. Häusser, iii. 535. Seeley, ii. 447.

defensive plan of operations, and declared that he could send no troops beyond the Russian frontier.

Prussia was thus left to face Napoleon alone. Hardenberg shrank from the responsibility of proclaiming a war for life or death, and a treaty was signed which added the people of Frederick the Great to that inglorious crowd which fought at Napoleon's orders against whatever remained of independence and nationality in Europe.* (Feb. 24th, 1812.) Prussia undertook to supply Napoleon with 20,000 men for the impending campaign, and to raise no levies and to give no orders to its troops without Napoleon's consent. Such was the bitter termination of all those patriotic hopes and efforts which had carried Prussia through its darkest days. Hardenberg himself might make a merit of bending before the storm, and of preserving for Prussia the means of striking when the time should come; but the simpler instincts of the patriotic party felt his submission to be the very surrender of national existence. Stein in his exile denounced the Minister with unsparing bitterness. Scharnhorst resigned his post; many of the best officers in the Prussian army quitted the service of King Frederick William in order to join the Russians in the last struggle for European liberty.

Prussia accepts alliance with Napoleon, Feb., 1812.

The alliance which Napoleon pressed upon Austria was not of the same humiliating character as that which

---

* Martens, Nouveau Recueil i. 417. A copy, or the original, of this Treaty was captured by the Russians with other of Napoleon's papers during the retreat from Moscow, and a draft of it sent to London, which remains in the Records.

Prussia was forced to accept. Both Metternich and
the Emperor Francis would have preferred
to remain neutral, for the country was
suffering from a fearful State-bankruptcy,
and the Government had been compelled to reduce its
paper money, in which all debts and salaries were
payable, to a fifth of its nominal value. Napoleon,
however, insisted on Austria's co-operation. The
family-relations of the two Emperors pointed to a close
alliance, and the reward which Napoleon held out to
Austria, the restoration of the Illyrian provinces, was
one of the utmost value. Nor was the Austrian contingent to be treated, like the Prussian, as a mere French
army-corps. Its operations were to be separate from
those of the French, and its command was to be held
by an Austrian general, subordinate only to Napoleon
himself. On these terms Metternich was not unwilling
to enter the campaign. He satisfied his scruples by
inventing a strange diplomatic form in which Austria
was still described as a neutral, although she took part
in the war,* and felt as little compunction in uniting
with France as in explaining to the Courts of St.
Petersburg and Berlin that the union was a hypocritical
one. The Sovereign who was about to be attacked by
Napoleon, and the Sovereigns who sent their troops
to Napoleon's support, perfectly well understood one
another's position. The Prussian corps, watched and
outnumbered by the French, might have to fight the
Russians because they could not help it; the Austrians,

Alliance of Austria with Napoleon.

* Metternich, i., 122.

directed by their own commander, would do no serious harm to the Russians so long as the Russians did no harm to them. Should the Czar succeed in giving a good account of his adversary, he would have no difficulty in coming to a settlement with his adversary's forced allies.

The Treaties which gave to Napoleon the hollow support of Austria and Prussia were signed early in the year 1812. During the next three months all Northern Germany was covered with enormous masses of troops and waggon-trains, on their way from the Rhine to the Vistula. No expedition had ever been organised on anything approaching to the scale of the invasion of Russia. In all the wars of the French since 1793 the enemy's country had furnished their armies with supplies, and the generals had trusted to their own exertions for everything but guns and ammunition. Such a method could not, however, be followed in an invasion of Russia. The country beyond the Niemen was no well-stocked garden, like Lombardy or Bavaria. Provisions for a mass of 450,000 men, with all the means of transport for carrying them far into Russia, had to be collected at Dantzig and the fortresses of the Vistula. No mercy was shown to the unfortunate countries whose position now made them Napoleon's harvest-field and storehouse. Prussia was forced to supplement its military assistance with colossal grants of supplies. The whole of Napoleon's troops upon the march through Germany lived at the expense of the towns and villages

Preparations of Napoleon for invasion of Russia.

through which they passed; in Westphalia such was the ruin caused by military requisitions that King Jerome wrote to Napoleon, warning him to fear the despair of men who had nothing more to lose.*

At length the vast stores were collected, and the invading army reached the Vistula. Napoleon himself quitted Paris on the 9th of May, and received the homage of the Austrian and Prussian Sovereigns at Dresden. The eastward movement of the army continued. The Polish and East Prussian districts which had been the scene of the combats of 1807 were again traversed by French columns. On the 23rd of June the order was given to cross the Niemen and enter Russian territory. Out of 600,000 troops whom Napoleon had organised for this campaign, 450,000 were actually upon the frontier. Of these, 380,000 formed the central army, under Napoleon's own command, at Kowno, on the Niemen, to the north, at Tilsit, there was formed a corps of 32,000, which included the contingent furnished by Prussia; the Austrians, under Schwarzenburg, with a small French division, lay to the south, on the borders of Galicia. Against the main army of Napoleon, the real invading force, the Russians could only bring up 150,000 men. These were formed into the First and Second Armies of the West. The First, or Northern Army, with which the Czar himself was present, numbered about 100,000, under the command of Barclay de Tolly; the Second Army, half that strength, was led by Prince Bagration.

<small>Napoleon crosses Russian frontier, June, 1812.</small>

* Mémoires de Jérome, v. 247.

In Southern Poland and on the Lower Niemen the French auxiliary corps were faced by weak divisions. In all, the Russians had only 220,000 men to oppose to more than double that number of the enemy. The principal reinforcements which they had to expect were from the armies hitherto engaged with the Turks upon the Danube. Alexander found it necessary to make peace with the Porte at the cost of a part of the spoils of Tilsit. The Danubian provinces, with the exception of Bessarabia, were restored to the Sultan, in order that Russia might withdraw its forces from the south. Bernadotte, Crown Prince of Sweden, <small>Alexander and Bernadotte.</small> who was threatened with the loss of his own dominions in the event of Napoleon's victory, concluded an alliance with the Czar. In return for the co-operation of a Swedish army, Alexander undertook, with an indifference to national right worthy of Napoleon himself, to wrest Norway from Denmark, and to annex it to the Swedish crown.

The head-quarters of the Russian army were at Wilna when Napoleon crossed the Niemen. It was unknown whether the French intended to advance upon Moscow or upon St. Petersburg; nor had any systematic plan of the campaign been adopted by the Czar. The idea of falling back before the enemy was indeed familiar in Russia since the war between Peter the Great and Charles XII. of Sweden, and there was no want of good counsel in favour of a defensive warfare;* but neither the Czar

---

* Bogdanowitsch, i. 72; Chambray, i. 186. Sir R. Wilson, Invasion of Russia, p. 15.

nor any one of his generals understood the simple theory of a retreat in which no battles at all should be fought. The most that was understood by a defensive system was the occupation of an entrenched position for battle, and a retreat to a second line of entrenchments before the engagement was repeated. The actual course of the campaign was no result of a profound design; it resulted from the disagreement of the generals' plans, and the frustration of them all. It was intended in the first instance to fight a battle at Drissa, on the river Dwina. In this position, which was supposed to cover the roads both to Moscow and St. Petersburg, a great entrenched camp had been formed, and here the Russian army was to make its first stand against Napoleon. Accordingly, as soon as the French crossed the Niemen, both Barclay and Bagration were ordered by the Czar to fall back upon Drissa. But the movements of the French army were too rapid for the Russian commanders to effect their junction. Bagration, who lay at some distance to the south, was cut off from his colleague, and forced to retreat along the eastern road towards Witepsk. Barclay reached Drissa in safety, but he knew himself to be unable to hold it alone against 300,000 men. He evacuated the lines without waiting for the approach of the French, and fell back in the direction taken by the second army. The first movement of defence had thus failed, and the Czar now quitted the camp, leaving to Barclay the command of the whole Russian forces.

Russians intend to fight at Drissa.

Russian armies severed, and retreat on Witepsk.

Napoleon entered Wilna, the capital of Russian Poland, on the 28th of June. The last Russian detachments had only left it a few hours before; but the French were in no condition for immediate pursuit. Before the army reached the Niemen the unparalleled difficulties of the campaign had become only too clear. *Collapse of the French transport.* The vast waggon-trains broke down on the highways. The stores were abundant, but the animals which had to transport them died of exhaustion. No human genius, no perfection of foresight and care, could have achieved the enormous task which Napoleon had undertaken. In spite of a year's preparations the French suffered from hunger and thirst from the moment that they set foot on Russian soil. Thirty thousand stragglers had left the army before it reached Wilna; twenty-five thousand sick were in the hospitals; the transports were at an unknown distance in the rear. At the end of six days' march from the Niemen, Napoleon found himself compelled to halt for nearly three weeks. The army did not leave Wilna till the 16th of July, when Barclay had already evacuated the camp at Drissa. When at length a march became possible, Napoleon moved upon the Upper Dwina, hoping to intercept Barclay upon the road to Witepsk; but difficulties of transport again brought him to a halt, and the Russian commander reached Witepsk before his adversary. Here Barclay drew up for battle, supposing Bagration's army to be but a short distance to the south. In the course of the night intelligence arrived that Bagration's army was nowhere near the rallying-point, but had been driven back towards Smolensko. Barclay immediately gave up the thought of fighting a battle, and took the road to Smolensko himself, leaving his watch-fires burning. His movement was unperceived by the French, the retreat was made in good order; and the two severed Russian armies at length effected their junction at a point three hundred miles distant from the frontier.

Barclay and Bagration unite at Smolensko, Aug. 3.

Napoleon, disappointed of battle, entered Witepsk on the evening after the Russians had abandoned it (July 28). Barclay's escape was, for the French, a disaster of the first magnitude, since it extinguished all hope of crushing the larger of the two Russian armies by overwhelming numbers in one great and decisive engagement. The march of the French during the last twelve days showed at what cost every further step must be made. Since quitting Wilna the 50,000 sick and stragglers had risen to 100,000. Fever and disease struck down whole regiments. The provisioning of the army was beyond all human power. Of the 200,000 men who still remained, it might almost be calculated in how many weeks the last would perish. So fearful was the prospect that Napoleon himself thought of abandoning any further advance until the next year, and of permitting the army to enter into winter-quarters upon the Dwina. But the conviction that all Russian resistance would end with the capture of Moscow hurried him on. The army left Witepsk on the 13th of August, and followed the Russians to Smolensko. Here the entire Russian army clamoured for battle. Barclay stood

The French waste away.

alone in perceiving the necessity for retreat. The generals caballed against him; the soldiers were on the point of mutiny; the Czar himself wrote to express his impatience for an attack upon the French. Barclay nevertheless persisted in his resolution to abandon Smolensko. He so far yielded to the army as to permit the rearguard to engage in a bloody struggle with the French when they assaulted the town; but the evacuation was completed under cover of night; and when the French made their entrance into Smolensko on the next morning they found it deserted and in ruins. The surrender of Smolensko was the last sacrifice that Barclay could extort from Russian pride. He no longer opposed the universal cry for battle, and the retreat was continued only with the intention of halting at the first strong position. Barclay himself was surveying a battle-ground when he heard that the command had been taken out of his hands. The Czar had been forced by national indignation at the loss of Smolensko to remove this able soldier, who was a Livonian by birth, and to transfer the command to Kutusoff, a thorough Russian, whom a life-time spent in victories over the Turk had made, in spite of his defeat at Austerlitz, the idol of the nation.

French enter Smolensko, Aug. 18.

Barclay superseded by Kutusoff.

When Kutusoff reached the camp, the prolonged miseries of the French advance had already reduced the invaders to the number of the army opposed to them. As far as Smolensko the French had at least not suffered from the hostility of the population, who were Poles, not Russians; but on

The French advance from Smolensko.

reaching Smolensko they entered a country where every peasant was a fanatical enemy. The villages were burnt down by their inhabitants, the corn destroyed, and the cattle driven into the woods. Every day's march onward from Smolensko cost the French three thousand men. On reaching the river Moskwa in the first week of September, a hundred and seventy-five thousand out of Napoleon's three hundred and eighty thousand soldiers were in the hospitals, or missing, or dead. About sixty thousand guarded the line of march. The Russians, on the other hand, had received reinforcements which covered their losses at Smolensko; and although detachments had been sent to support the army of Riga, Kutusoff was still able to place over one hundred thousand men in the field.

On the 5th of September the Russian army drew up for battle at Borodino, on the Moskwa, seventy miles west of the capital. At early morning on the 7th the French advanced to the attack. The battle was, in proportion to its numbers, the most sanguinary of modern times. Forty thousand French, thirty thousand Russians were struck down. At the close of the day the French were in possession of the enemy's ground, but the Russians, unbroken in their order, had only retreated to a second line of defence. Both sides claimed the victory; neither had won it. It was no catastrophe such as Napoleon required for the decision of the war, it was no triumph sufficient to save Russia from the necessity of abandoning its capital. Kutusoff had sustained too heavy a loss to face the French beneath the

Battle of Borodino, Sept. 7.

walls of Moscow. Peace was no nearer for the 70,000 men who had been killed or wounded in the fight. The French steadily advanced; the Russians retreated to Moscow, and evacuated the capital when their generals decided that they could not encounter the French assault. The Holy City was left undefended before the invader. But the departure of the army was the smallest part of the evacuation. The inhabitants, partly of their own free will, partly under the compulsion of the Governor, abandoned the city in a mass. No gloomy or excited crowd, as at Vienna and Berlin, thronged the streets to witness the entrance of the great conqueror, when on the 14th of September Napoleon took possession of Moscow. His troops marched through silent and deserted streets. In the solitude of the Kremlin Napoleon received the homage of a few foreigners, who alone could be collected by his servants to tender to him the submission of the city.

Evacuation of Moscow. French enter Moscow, Sept. 14.

But the worst was yet to come. On the night after Napoleon's entry, fires broke out in different parts of Moscow. They were ascribed at first to accident; but when on the next day the French saw the flames gaining ground in every direction, and found that all the means for extinguishing fire had been removed from the city, they understood the doom to which Moscow had been devoted by its own defenders. Count Rostopchin, the governor, had determined on the destruction of Moscow without the knowledge of the Czar. The doors of the prisons were thrown open. Rostopchin gave the signal by setting fire to his own palace, and let

Moscow fired.

loose his bands of incendiaries over the city. For five days the flames rose and fell; and when, on the evening of the 20th, the last fires ceased, three-fourths of Moscow lay in ruins.

Such was the prize for which Napoleon had sacrificed 200,000 men, and engulfed the weak remnant of his army six hundred miles deep in an enemy's country. Throughout all the terrors of the advance Napoleon had held fast to the belief that Alexander's resistance would end with the fall of his capital. The events that accompanied the entry of the French into Moscow shook his confidence; yet even now Napoleon could not believe that the Czar remained firm against all thoughts of peace. His experience in all earlier wars had given him confidence in the power of one conspicuous disaster to unhinge the resolution of kings. His trust in the deepening impression made by the fall of Moscow was fostered by negotiations begun by Kutusoff for the very purpose of delaying the French retreat. For five weeks Napoleon remained at Moscow as if spellbound, unable to convince himself of his powerlessness to break Alexander's determination, unable to face a retreat which would display to all Europe the failure of his arms and the termination of his career of victory. At length the approach of winter forced him to action. It was impossible to provision the army at Moscow during the winter months, even if there had been nothing to fear from the enemy. Even the mocking overtures of Kutusoff had ceased. The frightful reality could no longer be concealed. On the 19th of October the order for retreat was given.

Napoleon at Moscow, Sept 14—Oct 19.

It was not the destruction of Moscow, but the departure of its inhabitants, that had brought the conqueror to ruin. Above two thousand houses were still standing; but whether the buildings remained or perished made little difference; the whole value of the capital to Napoleon was lost when the inhabitants, whom he could have forced to procure supplies for his army, disappeared. Vienna and Berlin had been of such incalculable service to Napoleon because the whole native administration placed itself under his orders, and every rich and important citizen became a hostage for the activity of the rest. When the French gained Moscow, they gained nothing beyond the supplies which were at that moment in the city. All was lost to Napoleon when the class who in other capitals had been his instruments fled at his approach. The conflagration of Moscow acted upon all Europe as a signal of inextinguishable national hatred; as a military operation, it neither accelerated the retreat of Napoleon nor added to the miseries which his army had to undergo.

The French forces which quitted Moscow in October numbered about 100,000 men. Reinforcements had come in during the occupation of the city, and the health of the soldiers had been in some degree restored by a month's rest. *Napoleon leaves Moscow, Oct. 19.* Everything now depended upon gaining a line of retreat where food could be found. Though but a fourth part of the army which entered Russia in the summer, the army which left Moscow was still large enough to protect itself against the enemy, if allowed to retreat through a fresh country; if forced back upon the devastated line of its advance it was impossible for it to escape destruction. Napoleon therefore determined to make for Kaluga, on the south of Moscow, and to endeavour to gain a road to Smolensko far distant from that by which he had come. The army moved from Moscow in a southern direction. But its route had been foreseen by Kutusoff. At the end of four days' march it was met by a Russian corps at Jaroslavitz. A bloody struggle left the French in possession of the road: they continued their advance; but it was only to find that Kutusoff, with his full strength, had occupied a line of heights farther south, and barred the way to Kaluga. The effort of an assault was beyond the powers of the French. Napoleon surveyed the enemy's position, and recognised the fatal necessity of abandoning the march southwards and returning to the wasted road by which he had advanced. The meaning of the backward movement was quickly understood by the army. From the moment of quitting Jaroslavitz, disorder and despair increased with every march. Thirty thousand men were lost upon the road before a pursuer appeared in sight. When, on the 2nd of November, the army reached Wiazma, it numbered no more than 65,000 men.

Forced to retreat by the same road.

Kutusoff was unadventurous in pursuit. The necessity of moving his army along a parallel road south of the French, in order to avoid starvation, diminished the opportunities for attack; but the general himself disliked risking his forces, and preferred to see the enemy's destruction effected by the elements. At Wiazma, where, on the

Kutusoff follows by parallel road.

3rd of November, the French were for the first time attacked in force, Kutusoff's own delay alone saved them from total ruin. In spite of heavy loss the French kept possession of the road, and secured their retreat to Smolensko, where stores of food had been accumulated, and where other and less exhausted French troops were at hand.

Up to the 6th of November the weather had been sunny and dry. On the 6th the long-delayed terrors of Russian winter broke upon the pursuers and the pursued. *Frost, Nov. 6.* Snow darkened the air, and hid the last traces of vegetation from the starving cavalry trains. The temperature sank at times to forty degrees of frost. Death came, sometimes in the unfelt release from misery, sometimes in horrible forms of mutilation and disease. Both armies were exposed to the same sufferings; but the Russians had at least such succour as their countrymen could give: where the French sank, they died. The order of war disappeared under conditions which made life itself the accident of a meal or of a place by the camp-fire. Though most of the French soldiery continued to carry their arms, the Guard alone kept its separate formation; the other regiments marched in confused masses. *French reach Smolensko, Nov. 9.* From the 9th to the 13th of November these starving bands arrived one after another at Smolensko, expecting that here their sufferings would end. But the organisation for distributing the stores accumulated in Smolensko no longer existed. The perishing crowds were left to find shelter where they could; sacks of corn were thrown to them for food.

It was impossible for Napoleon to give his wearied soldiers rest, for new Russian armies were advancing from the north and the south to cut off their retreat. From the Danube and from the Baltic Sea troops were pressing forward to their meeting-point upon the rear of the invader. Witgenstein, moving southwards at the head of the army of the Dwina, had overpowered the French corps stationed upon that river, and made himself master of Witepsk. The army of Bucharest, which had been toiling northwards ever since the beginning of August, had advanced to within a few days' march of its meeting-point with the army of the Dwina upon the line of Napoleon's communications. Before Napoleon reached Smolensko he sent orders to Victor, who was at Smolensko with some reserves, to march against Witgenstein and drive him back upon the Dwina. Victor set out on his mission. During the short halt of Napoleon in Smolensko, Kutusoff pushed forward to the west of the French, and took post at Krasnoi, thirty miles farther along the road by which Napoleon had to pass. The retreat of the French seemed to be actually cut off. Had the Russian general dared to face Napoleon and his Guards, he might have held the French in check until the arrival of the two auxiliary armies from the north and south enabled him to capture Napoleon and his entire force. Kutusoff, however, preferred a partial and certain victory to a struggle with Napoleon for life or death. He permitted Napoleon and the Guard to pass by unattacked, and then fell upon the hinder divisions of the French army. (Nov. 17.) These unfortunate troops were successively cut to pieces. Twenty-six thousand were made prisoners. Ney, with a part of the rear-guard, only escaped by crossing the Dnieper on the ice. Of the army that had quitted Moscow there now remained but 10,000 combatants and 20,000 followers. Kutusoff himself was brought to such a state of exhaustion that he could carry the pursuit no further, and entered into quarters upon the Dnieper.

It was a few days after the battle at Krasnoi that the divisions of Victor, coming from the direction of the Dwina, suddenly encountered the remnant of Napoleon's army. *Victor joins Napoleon.* Though aware that Napoleon was in retreat, they knew nothing of the calamities that had befallen him, and were struck with amazement when, in the middle of a forest, they met with what seemed more like a miserable troop of captives than an army upon the march. Victor's soldiers of a mere auxiliary corps found themselves more than double the effective strength of the whole army of Moscow. Their arrival again placed Napoleon at the head of 30,000 disciplined troops, and gave the French a gleam of victory in the last and seemingly most hopeless struggle in the campaign. Admiral Tchitchagoff, in command of the army marching from the Danube, had at length reached the line of Napoleon's retreat, and established himself at Borisov, where the road through Poland crosses the river Beresina. The bridge was destroyed by the Russians, and Tchitchagoff opened communication with Witgenstein's army, which lay only a few miles to the north. It appeared as if the retreat of the French was now finally intercepted, and the surrender of Napoleon inevitable. Yet even in this hopeless situation the military skill and daring of the French worked with something of its ancient power. The army reached the Beresina; Napoleon succeeded in withdrawing the enemy from the real point of passage; bridges were thrown across the river, and after desperate fighting a great part of the army made good its footing upon the western bank (Nov. 28). But the losses even among the effective troops were enormous. The fate of the miserable crowd that followed them, torn by the cannon-fire of the Russians, and precipitated into the river by the breaking of one of the bridges, has made the passage of the Beresina a synonym for the utmost degree of human woe.

Passage of the Beresina, Nov. 28th.

This was the last engagement fought by the army. The Guards still preserved their order: Marshal Ney still found soldiers capable of turning upon the pursuer with his own steady and unflagging courage; but the bulk of the army struggled forward in confused crowds, harassed by the Cossacks, and laying down their arms by thousands before the enemy. The frost, which had broken up on the 19th, returned on the 30th of November with even greater severity. Twenty thousand fresh troops which joined the army between the Beresina and Wilna scarcely arrested the process of dissolution. On the 3rd of December Napoleon quitted the army. Wilna itself was abandoned with all its stores; and when at length the fugitives reached the Niemen, they numbered little more than twenty thousand. *French reach the Niemen, Dec. 13.* Here, six months earlier, three hundred and eighty thousand men had crossed with Napoleon. A hundred thousand more had joined the army in the course of its retreat. Of all this host, not the twentieth part reached the Prussian frontier. A hundred and seventy thousand remained prisoners in the hands of the Russians; a greater number had perished. Of the twenty thousand men who now beheld the Niemen, probably not seven thousand had crossed with Napoleon. In the presence of a catastrophe so overwhelming and so un-paralleled the Russian generals might well be content with their own share in the work of destruction. Yet the event proved that Kutusoff had done ill in sparing the extremest effort to capture or annihilate his foe. Not only was Napoleon's own escape the pledge of continued war, but the remnant that escaped with him possessed a military value out of all proportion to its insignificant numbers. The best of the army were the last to succumb. Out of those few thousands who endured to the end, a very large proportion were veteran officers, who immediately took their place at the head of Napoleon's newly-raised armies, and gave to them a military efficiency soon to be bitterly proved by Europe on many a German battle-field.

Four hundred thousand men were lost to a conqueror who could still stake the lives of half a million more. The material power of Napoleon, though largely, was not fatally diminished by the Russian campaign; it was through its moral effect, first proved in the action of Prussia, that the retreat from Moscow created a new order of things in Europe. The Prussian contingent, commanded by General von York, lay in front of Riga, where it formed part of the French subsidiary army-corps led by Marshal Macdonald. Early in November the Russian governor of Riga addressed himself to York, assuring him that Napoleon was ruined, and soliciting York himself to take up arms against Macdonald.* York had no evidence, beyond the word of the Russian commander, of the extent of Napoleon's losses; and even if the facts were as stated, it was by no means clear that the Czar might not be inclined to take vengeance on Prussia on account of its alliance with Napoleon. York returned a guarded answer to the Russian, and sent an officer to Wilna to ascertain the real state of the French army. On the 8th of December the officer returned, and described what he had himself seen. Soon afterwards the Russian commandant produced a letter from the Czar, declaring his intention to deal with Prussia as a friend, not as an enemy. On these points all doubt was removed; York's decision was thrown upon himself. York was a rigid soldier of the old Prussian type, dominated by the idea of military duty. The act to which the Russian commander invited him, and which the younger officers were ready to hail as the liberation of Prussia, might be branded by his sovereign as desertion and treason. Whatever scruples

York and the Prussian contingent at Riga.

* Droysen, Leben des Grafen York. I., 394.

and perplexity might be felt in such a situation by a loyal and obedient soldier were felt by York. He nevertheless chose the course which seemed to be for his country's good; and having chosen it, he accepted all the consequences which it involved. On the 30th of December a convention was signed at Tauroggen, which, under the guise of a truce, practically withdrew the Prussian army from Napoleon, and gave the Russians possession of Königsberg. The momentous character of the act was recognised by Napoleon as soon as the news reached Paris. York's force was the strongest military body upon the Russian frontier; united with Macdonald, it would have forced the Russian pursuit to stop at the Niemen; abandoning Napoleon, it brought his enemies on to the Vistula, and threatened incalculable danger by its example to all the rest of Germany. For the moment, however, Napoleon could count upon the spiritless obedience of King Frederick William. In the midst of the French regiments that garrisoned Berlin, the King wrote orders pronouncing York's convention null and void, and ordering York himself to be tried by court-martial. The news reached the loyal soldier: he received it with grief, but maintained his resolution to act for his country's good. "With bleeding heart," he wrote, "I burst the bond of obedience, and carry on the war upon my own responsibility. The army desires war with France; the nation desires it; the King himself desires it, but his will is not free. The army must make his will free."

York's convention with the Russians, Dec. 30.

York's act was nothing less than the turning-point in Prussian history. Another Prussian, at this great crisis of Europe, played as great, though not so conspicuous, a part. Before the outbreak of the Russian war, the Czar had requested the exile Stein to come to St. Petersburg to aid him with his counsels during the struggle with Napoleon. Stein gladly accepted the call; and throughout the campaign he encouraged the Czar in the resolute resistance which the Russian nation itself required of its Government. So long as French soldiers remained on Russian soil, there was indeed little need for a foreigner to stimulate the Czar's energies; but when the pursuit had gloriously ended on the Niemen, the case became very different. Kutusoff and the generals were disinclined to carry the war into Germany. The Russian army had itself lost three-fourths of its numbers; Russian honour was satisfied; the liberation of Western Europe might be left to Western Europe itself. Among the politicians who surrounded Alexander, there were a considerable number, including the first minister Romanzoff, who still believed in the good policy of a French alliance. These were the influences with which Stein had to contend, when the question arose whether Russia should rest satisfied with its own victories, or summon all Europe to unite in overthrowing Napoleon's tyranny. No record remains of the stages by which Alexander's mind rose to the clear and firm conception of a single European interest against Napoleon; indications exist that it was Stein's personal influence which most largely affected his decision. Even

The Czar and Stein.

in the darkest moments of the war, when the forces of Russia seemed wholly incapable of checking Napoleon's advance, Stein had never abandoned his scheme for raising the German nation against Napoleon. The confidence with which he had assured Alexander of ultimate victory over the invader had been thoroughly justified; the triumph which he had predicted had come with a rapidity and completeness even surpassing his hopes. For a moment Alexander identified himself with the statesman who, in the midst of Germany's humiliation, had been so resolute, so far-sighted, so aspiring.* The minister of the peace-party was dismissed: Alexander ordered his troops to advance into Prussia, and charged Stein himself to assume the government of the Prussian districts occupied by Russian armies. Stein's mission was to arm the Landwehr, and to gather all the resources of the country for war against France; his powers were to continue until some definite arrangement should be made between the King of Prussia and the Czar. *(Alexander enters Prussia, Jan., 1813.)*

Armed with this commission from a foreign sovereign, Stein appeared at Königsberg on the 22nd of January, 1813, and published an order requiring the governor of the province of East Prussia to convoke an assembly for the purpose of arming the people. Stein would have desired York to appear as President of the Assembly; but York, like most of the Prussian officials, was alarmed and indignant at Stein's assumption of power in Prussia as the *(Stein's commission from Alexander.)*

* Pertz, iii. 211, seq. Seeley, iii. 21.

representative of the Russian Czar, and hesitated to connect himself with so revolutionary a measure as the arming of the people. It was only upon condition that Stein himself should not appear in the Assembly that York consented to recognise its powers. The Assembly met. York entered the house, and spoke a few soul-stirring words. His undisguised declaration of war with France was received with enthusiastic cheers. A plan for the formation of a Landwehr, based on Scharnhorst's plans of 1808, was laid before the Assembly, and accepted.

<small>Province of East Prussia arms, Jan., 1813.</small> Forty thousand men were called to arms in a province which included nothing west of the Vistula. The nation itself had begun the war, and left its Government no choice but to follow. Stein's task was fulfilled, and he retired to the quarters of Alexander, unwilling to mar by the appearance of foreign intervention the work to which the Prussian nation had now committed itself beyond power of recall. It was the fortune of the Prussian State, while its King dissembled before the French in Berlin, to possess a soldier brave enough to emancipate its army, and a citizen bold enough to usurp the government of its provinces. Frederick William forgave York his intrepidity; Stein's action was never forgiven by the timid and jealous sovereign whose subjects he had summoned to arm themselves for their country's deliverance.

The Government of Berlin, which since the beginning of the Revolutionary War had neither been able to fight, nor to deceive, nor to be honest, was at length forced by circumstances into a certain effectiveness in all three forms of action. In the interval between the first tidings of Napoleon's disasters and the announcement of York's convention with the Russians, Hardenberg had been assuring Napoleon of his devotion, and collecting troops which he carefully prevented from joining him.* The desire of the King was to gain concessions without taking part in the war either against Napoleon or on his side. When, however, the balance turned more decidedly against Napoleon, he grew bolder; and the news of York's defection, though it seriously embarrassed the Cabinet for the moment, practically decided it in favour of war with France. The messenger who was sent to remove York from his command received private instructions to fall into the hands of the Russians, and to inform the Czar that, if his troops advanced as far as the Oder, King Frederick William would be ready to conclude an alliance. Every post that arrived from East Prussia strengthened the warlike resolutions of the Government. At length the King ventured on the decisive step of quitting Berlin and placing himself at Breslau (Jan. 25). At Berlin he was in the power of the French; at Breslau he was within easy reach of Alexander. The significance of the journey could not be mistaken: it was immediately followed by open preparation for war with France. On February 3rd there appeared an edict inviting volunteers to enrol themselves: a week later all exemptions from military service were abolished, and the entire male population of Prussia between the ages of seventeen

margin: Policy of Hardenberg.

* Oncken, Oesterreich und Preussen, i. 28.

and twenty-four was declared liable to serve. General Knesebeck was sent to the headquarters of the Czar, which were now between Warsaw and Kalisch, to conclude a treaty of alliance. Knesebeck demanded securities for the restoration to Prussia of all the Polish territory which it had possessed before 1806; the Czar, unwilling either to grant this condition or to lose the Prussian alliance, kept Knesebeck at his quarters, and sent Stein with a Russian plenipotentiary to Breslau to conclude the treaty with Hardenberg himself. Stein and Hardenberg met at Breslau on the 26th February. Hardenberg accepted the Czar's terms, and the treaty, known as the Treaty of Kalisch,* was signed on the following day. By this treaty, without guaranteeing the restoration of Prussian Poland, Russia undertook not to lay down its arms until the Prussian State as a whole was restored to the area and strength which it had possessed before 1806. For this purpose annexations were promised in Northern Germany. With regard to Poland, Russia promised no more than to permit Prussia to retain what it had received in 1772, together with a strip of territory to connect this district with Silesia. The meaning of the agreement was that Prussia should abandon to Russia the greater part of its late Polish provinces, and receive an equivalent German territory in its stead. The Treaty of Kalisch virtually surrendered to the Czar all that Prussia had gained in the partitions of Poland made in 1793 and in 1795. The

Treaty of Kalisch, Feb. 27.

* Martens, N. R., III. 234. British and Foreign State Papers (Hertslet), i. 49.

sacrifice was deemed a most severe one by every Prussian politician, and was accepted only as a less evil than the loss of Russia's friendship, and a renewed submission to Napoleon. No single statesman, not even Stein himself, appears to have understood that in exchanging its Polish conquests for German annexations, in turning to the German west instead of to the alien Slavonic east, Prussia was in fact taking the very step which made it the possible head of a future united Germany.

War was still not declared upon Napoleon by King Frederick William, but throughout the month of February the light cavalry of the Russians pushed forward unhindered through Prussian territory towards the Oder, and crowds of volunteers, marching through Berlin on their way to the camps in Silesia, gave the French clear signs of the storm that was about to burst upon them.* The remnant of Napoleon's army, now commanded by Eugène Beauharnais, had fallen back step by step to the Oder. Here, resting on the fortresses, it might probably have checked the Russian advance: but the heart of Eugène failed; the line of the Oder was abandoned, and the retreat continued to Berlin and the Elbe. The Cossacks followed. On the 20th of February they actually entered Berlin and fought with the French in the streets. The French garrison was far superior in force; but the appearance of the Cossacks caused such a ferment that, although the alliance between France and Prussia was still in nominal existence, the French

French retreat to the Elbe.

* For Breslau in February, see Steffens, 7. 69.

troops expected to be cut to pieces by the people. For some days they continued to bivouac in the streets, and as soon as it became known that a regular Russian force had reached the Oder, Eugène determined to evacuate Berlin. On the 4th of March the last French soldier quitted the Prussian capital. The Cossacks rode through the town as the French left it, and fought with their rear-guard. Some days later Witgenstein appeared with Russian infantry. On March 17th York made his triumphal entry at the head of his corps, himself cold and rigid in the midst of tumultuous outbursts of patriotic joy.

It was on this same day that King Frederick William issued his proclamation to the Prussian people, declaring that war had begun with France, and summoning the nation to enter upon the struggle as one that must end either in victory or in total destruction. The proclamation was such as became a monarch conscious that his own faint-heartedness had been the principal cause of Prussia's humiliation. It was simple and unboastful, admitting that the King had made every effort to preserve the French alliance, and ascribing the necessity for war to the intolerable wrongs inflicted by Napoleon in spite of Prussia's fulfilment of its treaty-obligations. The appeal to the great memories of Prussia's earlier sovereigns, and to the example of Russia, Spain, and all countries which in present or in earlier times had fought for their independence against a stronger foe, was worthy of the truthful and modest tone in which the King spoke of the misfortunes of Prussia under his own rule.

King of Prussia declares war, March 17.

But no exhortations were necessary to fire the spirit of the Prussian people. Seven years of suffering and humiliation had done their work. The old apathy of all classes had vanished under the pressure of a bitter sense of wrong. If among the Court party of Berlin and the Conservative landowners there existed a secret dread of the awakening of popular forces, the suspicion could not be now avowed. A movement as penetrating and as universal as that which France had experienced in 1792 swept through the Prussian State. It had required the experience of years of wretchedness, the intrusion of the French soldier upon the peace of the family, the sight of the homestead swept bare of its stock to supply the invaders of Russia, the memory of Schill's companions shot in cold blood for the cause of the Fatherland, before the Prussian nation caught that flame which had spontaneously burst out in France, in Spain, and in Russia at the first shock of foreign aggression. But the passion of the Prussian people, if it had taken long to kindle, was deep, steadfast, and rational. It was undisgraced by the frenzies of 1792, or by the religious fanaticism of the Spanish war of liberation; where religion entered into the struggle, it heightened the spirit of self-sacrifice rather than that of hatred to the enemy. Nor was it a thing of small moment to the future of Europe that in every leading mind the cause of Prussia was identified with the cause of the whole German race. The actual condition of Germany warranted no such conclusion, for Saxony, Bavaria, and the whole of the Rhenish Federation still followed Napoleon: but the spirit and the ideas which became a living force when at length the contest with Napoleon broke out were those of men like Stein, who in the depths of Germany's humiliation had created the bright and noble image of a common Fatherland. It was no more given to Stein to see his hopes fulfilled than it was given to Mirabeau to establish constitutional liberty in France, or to the Italian patriots of 1797 to create a united Italy. A group of States where kings like Frederick William and Francis, ministers like Hardenberg and Metternich, governed millions of people totally destitute of political instincts and training, was not to be suddenly transformed into a free nation by the genius of an individual or the patriotism of a single epoch. But if the work of German union was one which, even in the barren form of military empire, required the efforts of two more generations, the ideals of 1813 were no transient and ineffective fancy. Time was on the side of those who called the Prussian monarchy the true centre round which Germany could gather. If in the sequel Prussia was slow to recognise its own opportunities, the fault was less with patriots who hoped too much than with kings and ministers who dared too little.

For the moment, the measures of the Prussian Government were worthy of the spirit shown by the nation. Scharnhorst's military system had given Prussia 100,000 trained soldiers ready to join the existing army of 45,000. The scheme for the formation of a Landwehr, though not yet carried into effect,

Formation of the Landwehr.

needed only to receive the sanction of the King. On the same day that Frederick William issued his proclamation to the people, he decreed the formation of the Landwehr and the Landsturm. The latter force, which was intended in case of necessity to imitate the peasant warfare of Spain and La Vendée, had no occasion to act: the Landwehr, though its arming was delayed by the poverty and exhaustion of the country, gradually became a most formidable reserve, and sent its battalions to fight by the side of the regulars in some of the greatest engagements in the war. It was the want of arms and money, not of willing soldiers, that prevented Prussia from instantly attacking Napoleon with 200,000 men. The conscription was scarcely needed from the immense number of volunteers who joined the ranks. Though the completion of the Prussian armaments required some months more, Prussia did not need to stand upon the defensive. An army of 50,000 men was ready to cross the Elbe immediately on the arrival of the Russians, and to open the next campaign in the territory of Napoleon's allies of the Rhenish Federation.

CHAPTER XI.

The War of Liberation—Blücher crosses the Elbe—Battle of Lützen—The Allies retreat to Silesia—Battle of Bautzen—Armistice—Napoleon intends to intimidate Austria—Mistaken as to the forces of Austria—Metternich's Policy—Treaty of Reichenbach—Austria offers its Mediation—Congress of Prague—Austria enters the War—Armies and Plans of Napoleon and the Allies—Campaign of August—Battles of Dresden, Grosbeeren, the Katzbach, and Kulm—Effect of these Actions—Battle of Dennewitz—German Policy of Austria favourable to the Princes of the Rhenish Confederacy—Frustrated hopes of German Unity—Battle of Leipzig—The Allies reach the Rhine—Offers of Peace at Frankfort—Plan of Invasion of France—Backwardness of Austria—The Allies enter France—Campaign of 1814—Congress of Châtillon—Napoleon moves to the rear of the Allies—The Allies advance on Paris—Capitulation of Paris—Entry of the Allies—Dethronement of Napoleon—Restoration of the Bourbons—The Charta—Treaty of Paris—Territorial effects of the War, 1792-1814—Every Power except France had gained—France relatively weaker in Europe—Summary of the permanent effects of this period on Europe.

THE first three months of the year 1813 were spent by Napoleon in vigorous preparation for a campaign in Northern Germany. Immediately after receiving the news of York's convention with the Russians he had ordered a levy of 350,000 men. It was in vain that Frederick William and Hardenberg affected to disavow the general as a traitor; Napoleon divined the national character of York's act, and laid his account for a war against the combined forces of Prussia and Russia. In spite of the catastrophe of the last campaign, Napoleon was still stronger than his enemies. Italy and the Rhenish Federation had never wavered in their allegiance;

Napoleon in 1813.

Austria, though a cold ally, had at least shown no signs of hostility. The resources of an empire of forty million inhabitants were still at Napoleon's command. It was in the youth and inexperience of the new soldiers, and in the scarcity of good officers,* that the losses of the previous year showed their most visible effect. Lads of seventeen, commanded in great part by officers who had never been through a campaign, took the place of the soldiers who had fought at Friedland and Wagram. They were as brave as their predecessors, but they failed in bodily strength and endurance. Against them came the remnant of the men who had pursued Napoleon from Moscow, and a Prussian army which was but the vanguard of an armed nation. Nevertheless, Napoleon had no cause to expect defeat, provided that Austria remained on his side. Though the Prussian nation entered upon the conflict in the most determined spirit, a war on the Elbe against Russia and Prussia combined was a less desperate venture than a war with Russia alone beyond the Niemen.

When King Frederick William published his declaration of war (March 17), the army of Eugène had already fallen back as far west as Magdeburg, leaving garrisons in most of the fortresses between the Elbe and the Russian frontier. Napoleon was massing troops on the Main, and preparing for an advance in force, when the Prussians, commanded by Blücher, and some weak divisions of the Russian army, pushed forward to the Elbe. On the 18th of March the

Blücher crosses the Elbe, March, 1813.

---

* For the difference between the old and the new officers, see Correspondance de Napoléon, 27 Avril, 1813.

Cossacks appeared in the suburbs of Dresden, on the right bank of the river. Davoust, who was in command of the French garrison, blew up two arches of the bridge, and retired to Magdeburg: Blücher soon afterwards entered Dresden, and called upon the Saxon nation to rise against Napoleon. But he spoke to deaf ears. The common people were indifferent; the officials waited to see which side would conquer. Blücher could scarcely obtain provisions for his army; he passed on westwards, and came into the neighbourhood of Leipzig. Here he found himself forced to halt, and to wait for his allies. Though a detachment of the Russian army under Witgenstein had already crossed the Elbe, the main army, with Kutusoff, was still lingering at Kalisch on the Polish frontier, where it had arrived six weeks before. As yet the Prussians had only 50,000 men ready for action; until the Russians came up, it was unsafe to advance far beyond the Elbe. Blücher counted every moment lost that kept him from battle: the Russian commander-in-chief, sated with glory and sinking beneath the infirmities of a veteran, could scarcely be induced to sign an order of march. At length Kutusoff's illness placed the command in younger hands. His strength failed him during the march from Poland; he was left dying in Silesia; and on the 24th of April the Czar and the King of Prussia led forward his veteran troops into Dresden.

Napoleon was now known to be approaching with considerable force by the roads of the Saale. A pitched battle west of the Elbe was necessary before the Allies could hope to win over any of the States of the Rhenish

Confederacy; the flat country beyond Leipzig offered the best possible field for cavalry, in which the Allies were strong and Napoleon extremely deficient. It was accordingly determined to unite all the divisions of the army with Blücher on the west of Leipzig, and to attack the French as soon as they descended from the hilly country of the Saale, and began their march across the Saxon plain. The Allies took post at Lützen: the French advanced, and at midday on the 2nd of May the battle of Lützen began. Till evening, victory inclined to the Allies. The Prussian soldiery fought with the utmost spirit; for the first time in Napoleon's campaigns, the French infantry proved weaker than an enemy when fighting against them in equal numbers. But the generalship of Napoleon turned the scale. Seventy thousand of the French were thrown upon fifty thousand of the Allies; the battle was fought in village streets and gardens, where cavalry were useless; and at the close of the day, though the losses on each side were equal, the Allies were forced from the positions which they had gained. Such a result was equivalent to a lost battle. Napoleon's junction with the army of Eugène at Magdeburg was now inevitable, unless a second engagement was fought and won. No course remained to the Allies but to stake everything upon a renewed attack, or to retire behind the Elbe and meet the reinforcements assembling in Silesia. King Frederick William declared for a second battle*; he was over-ruled, and the retreat commenced.

<small>Battle of Lutzen, May 2.</small>

---

* Henckel von Donnersmarck, p. 187. The battles of Lützen, Bautzen, and Leipzig are described in the despatches of Lord Cathcart, who wit-

Napoleon entered Dresden on May 14th. No attempt was made by the Allies to hold the line of the Elbe; all the sanguine hopes with which Blücher and his comrades had advanced to attack Napoleon within the borders of the Rhenish Confederacy were dashed to the ground. The Fatherland remained divided against itself. Saxony and the rest of the vassal States were secured to France by the victory of Lützen; the liberation of Germany was only to be wrought by prolonged and obstinate warfare, and by the wholesale sacrifice of Prussian life.

Napoleon enters Dresden, May 14.

It was with deep disappointment, but not with any wavering of purpose, that the allied generals fell back before Napoleon towards the Silesian fortresses. The Prussian troops which had hitherto taken part in the war were not the third part of those which the Government was arming; new Russian divisions were on the march from Poland. As the Allies moved eastwards from the Elbe, both their own forces and those of Napoleon gathered strength. The retreat stopped at Bautzen, on the river Spree; and here, on the 19th of May, 90,000 of the Allies and the same number of the French drew up in order of battle. The Allies held a long, broken chain of hills behind the river, and the ground lying between these hills and the village of Bautzen. On the 20th the French began the attack, and won the passage of the river. In spite of the approach of Ney with 40,000

Battle of Bautzen, May 21.

nessed them in company with the Czar and King Frederick William. Records: Russia, 207, 209.

more troops, the Czar and the King of Prussia determined to continue the battle on the following day. The struggle of the 21st was of the same obstinate and indecisive character as that at Lützen. Twenty-five thousand French had been killed or wounded before the day was over, but the bad generalship of the Allies had again given Napoleon the victory. The Prussian and Russian commanders were all at variance; Alexander, who had to decide in their contentions, possessed no real military faculty. It was not for want of brave fighting and steadfastness before the enemy that Bautzen was lost. The Allies retreated in perfect order, and without the loss of a single gun. Napoleon followed, forcing his wearied regiments to ceaseless exertion, in the hope of ruining by pursuit an enemy whom he could not overthrow in battle. In a few more days the discord of the allied generals and the sufferings of the troops would probably have made them unable to resist Napoleon's army, weakened as it was. But the conqueror himself halted in the moment of victory. On the 4th of June an armistice of seven weeks arrested the pursuit, and brought the first act of the War of Liberation to a close.

<small>Armistice, June 4.</small>

Napoleon's motive for granting this interval to his enemies, the most fatal step in his whole career, has been vaguely sought among the general reasons for military delay; as a matter of fact, Napoleon was thinking neither of the condition of his own army nor of that of the Allies when he broke off

<small>Napoleon and Austria.</small>

hostilities, but of the probable action of the Court of Vienna.* " I shall grant a truce," he wrote to the Viceroy of Italy (June 2, 1813), "on account of the armaments of Austria, and in order to gain time to bring up the Italian army to Laibach to threaten Vienna." Austria had indeed resolved to regain, either by war or negotiation, the provinces which it had lost in 1809. It was now preparing to offer its mediation, but it was also preparing to join the Allies in case Napoleon rejected its demands. Metternich was anxious to attain his object, if possible, without war. The Austrian State was bankrupt; its army had greatly deteriorated since 1809; Metternich himself dreaded both the ambition of Russia and what he considered the revolutionary schemes of the German patriots. It was his object not to drive Napoleon from his throne, but to establish a European system in which neither France nor Russia should be absolutely dominant. Soon after the retreat from Moscow the Cabinet of Vienna had informed Napoleon, though in the most friendly terms, that Austria could not longer remain in the position of a dependent ally.† Metternich stated, and not insincerely, that by certain concessions Napoleon might still count on Austria's friendship; but at the same time he negotiated with the

* The account given in the following pages of Napoleon's motives and action during the armistice is based upon the following letters printed in the twenty-fifth volume of the Correspondence:—To Eugène, June 2, July 1, July 17, Aug. 4; to Maret, July 8; to Daru, July 17; to Berthier, July 23; to Davoust, July 24, Aug. 5; to Ney, Aug. 4, Aug. 12. The statement of Napoleon's error as to the strength of the Austrian force is confirmed by Metternich, i. 150.

† Oncken, i. 80.

allied Powers, and encouraged them to believe that Austria would, under certain circumstances, strike on their behalf. The course of the campaign of May was singularly favourable to Metternich's policy. Napoleon had not won a decided victory; the Allies, on the other hand, were so far from success that Austria could set almost any price it pleased upon its alliance. By the beginning of June it had become a settled matter in the Austrian Cabinet that Napoleon must be made to resign the Illyrian Provinces conquered in 1809 and the districts of North Germany annexed in 1810; but it was still the hope of the Government to obtain this result by peaceful means. Napoleon saw that Austria was about to change its attitude, but he had by no means penetrated the real intentions of Metternich. He credited the Viennese Government with a stronger sentiment of hostility towards himself than it actually possessed; at the same time he failed to appreciate the fixed and settled character of its purpose. He believed that the action of Austria would depend simply upon the means which he possessed to intimidate it; that, if the army of Italy were absent, Austria would attack him; that, on the other hand, if he could gain time to bring the army of Italy into Carniola, Austria would keep the peace. It was with this belief, and solely for the purpose of bringing up a force to menace Austria, that Napoleon stayed his hand against the Prussian and Russian armies after the battle of Bautzen, and gave time for the gathering of the immense forces which were destined to effect his destruction.

Immediately after the conclusion of the armistice of June 4th, Metternich invited Napoleon to accept Austria's mediation for a general peace. The settlement which Metternich contemplated was a very different one from that on which Stein and the Prussian patriots had set their hopes. Austria was willing to leave to Napoleon the whole of Italy and Holland, the frontier of the Rhine, and the Protectorate of Western Germany: all that was required by Metternich, as arbiter of Europe, was the restoration of the provinces taken from Austria after the war of 1809, the reinstatement of Prussia in Western Poland, and the abandonment by France of the North-German district annexed in 1810. But to Napoleon the greater or less extent of the concessions asked by Austria was a matter of no moment. He was determined to make no concessions at all, and he entered into negotiations only for the purpose of disguising from Austria the real object with which he had granted the armistice. While Napoleon affected to be weighing the proposals of Austria, he was in fact calculating the number of marches which would place the Italian army on the Austrian frontier; this once effected, he expected to hear nothing more of Metternich's demands.

Metternich offers Austria's mediation.

It was a game of deceit; but there was no one who was so thoroughly deceived as Napoleon himself. By some extraordinary miscalculation on the part of his secret agents he was led to believe that the whole force of Austria, both in the north and the south, amounted to only 100,000

Napoleon deceived as to the forces of Austria.

men,* and it was on this estimate that he had formed his plans of intimidation. In reality Austria had double that number of men ready to take the field. By degrees Napoleon saw reason to suspect himself in error. On the 11th of July he wrote to his Foreign Minister, Maret, bitterly reproaching him with the failure of the secret service to gain any trustworthy information. It was not too late to accept Metternich's terms. Yet even now, when the design of intimidating Austria had proved an utter delusion, and Napoleon was convinced that Austria would fight, and fight with very powerful forces, his pride and his invincible belief in his own superiority prevented him from drawing back. He made an attempt to enter upon a separate negotiation with Russia, and, when this failed, he resolved to face the conflict with the whole of Europe.

There was no longer any uncertainty among Napoleon's enemies. On the 27th of June, Austria had signed a treaty at Reichenbach, pledging itself to join the allied Powers in the event of Napoleon rejecting the conditions to be proposed by Austria as mediator; and the conditions so to be proposed were fixed by the same treaty. *Treaty of Reichenbach, June 27.* They were the following :—The suppression of the Duchy of Warsaw; the restoration to Austria of the Illyrian Provinces; and the surrender by Napoleon of the North-German district annexed to his Empire in 1810. Terms more hostile to France than these Austria declined to embody in its mediation. The Elbe might still sever

* Napoleon to Eugène, 1st July, 1813.

Prussia from its German provinces lost in 1807; Napoleon might still retain, as chief of the Rhenish Confederacy, his sovereignty over the greater part of the German race.

From the moment when these conditions were fixed, there was nothing which the Prussian generals so much dreaded as that Napoleon might accept them, and so rob the Allies of the chance of crushing him by means of Austria's support. But their fears were groundless. The counsels of Napoleon were exactly those which his worst enemies would have desired him to adopt. War, and nothing but war, was his fixed resolve. He affected to entertain Austria's propositions, and sent his envoy Caulaincourt to a Congress which Austria summoned at Prague; but it was only for the purpose of gaining a few more weeks of preparation. The Congress met; the armistice was prolonged to the 10th of August. Caulaincourt, however, was given no power to close with Austria's demands. He was ignorant that he had only been sent to Prague in order to gain time. He saw the storm gathering: unable to believe that Napoleon intended to fight all Europe rather than make the concessions demanded of him, he imagined that his master still felt some doubt whether Austria and the other Powers meant to adhere to their word. As the day drew nigh which closed the armistice and the period given for a reply to Austria's ultimatum, Caulaincourt implored Napoleon not to deceive himself with hopes that Austria would draw back. Napoleon had no such hope; he knew well that

Congress of Prague, July 15 —Aug. 10.

Austria would declare war, and he accepted the issue. Caulaincourt heard nothing more. At midnight on the 10th of August the Congress declared itself dissolved. Before the dawn of the next morning the army in Silesia saw the blaze of the beacon-fires which told that negotiation was at an end, and that Austria was entering the war on the side of the Allies.*

<small>Austria enters the war, Aug. 10.</small>

Seven days' notice was necessary before the commencement of actual hostilities. Napoleon, himself stationed at Dresden, held all the lower course of the Elbe; and his generals had long had orders to be ready to march on the morning of the 18th. Forces had come up from all parts of the Empire, raising the French army at the front to 300,000 men; but, for the first time in Napoleon's career, his enemies had won from a pause in war results even surpassing his own. The strength of the Prussian and Russian armies was now enormously different from what it had been at Lützen and Bautzen. The Prussian Landwehr, then a weaponless and ill-clad militia drilling in the villages, was now fully armed, and in great part at the front. New Russian divisions had reached Silesia. Austria took the field with a force as numerous as that which had checked Napoleon in 1809. At the close of the armistice, 350,000 men actually faced the French positions upon the Elbe; 300,000 more were on the march, or watching the German fortresses and the frontier of Italy. The allied troops operating against Napoleon were divided into three armies. In the north,

<small>Armies of Napoleon and the Allies.</small>

---

* Metternich, i. 163.

between Wittenberg and Berlin, Bernadotte commanded 60,000 Russians and Prussians, in addition to his own Swedish contingent. Blücher was placed at the head of 100,000 Russians and Prussians in Silesia. The Austrians remained undivided, and formed, together with some Russian and Prussian divisions, the great army of Bohemia, 200,000 strong, under the command of Schwarzenberg. The plan of the campaign had been agreed upon by the Allies soon after the Treaty of Reichenbach had been made with Austria. It was a sound, though not a daring one. The three armies, now forming an arc from Wittenberg to the north of Bohemia, were to converge upon the line of Napoleon's communications behind Dresden; if separately attacked, their generals were to avoid all hazardous engagements, and to manœuvre so as to weary the enemy and preserve their own general relations, as far as possible, unchanged. Blücher, as the most exposed, was expected to content himself the longest with the defensive; the great army of Bohemia, after securing the mountain-passes between Bohemia and Saxony, might safely turn Napoleon's position at Dresden, and so draw the two weaker armies towards it for one vast and combined engagement in the plain of Leipzig.

Plan of the Allies.

In outline, the plan of the Allies was that which Napoleon expected them to adopt. His own design was to anticipate it by an offensive of extraordinary suddenness and effect. Hostilities could not begin before the morning of the 18th of August;

Napoleon's plan of attack.

by the 21st or the 22nd, Napoleon calculated that he should have captured Berlin. Oudinot, who was at Wittenberg with 80,000 men, had received orders to advance upon the Prussian capital at the moment that the armistice expired, and to force it, if necessary by bombardment, into immediate surrender. The effect of this blow, as Napoleon supposed, would be to disperse the entire reserve-force of the Prussian monarchy, and paralyse the action of its army in the field. While Oudinot marched on Berlin, Blücher was to be attacked in Silesia, and prevented from rendering any assistance either on the north or on the south. The mass of Napoleon's forces, centred at Dresden, and keeping watch upon the movements of the army of Bohemia, would either fight a great battle, or, if the Allies made a false movement, march straight upon Prague, the centre of Austria's supplies, and reach it before the enemy. All the daring imagination of Napoleon's earlier campaigns displayed itself in such a project, which, if successful, would have terminated the war within ten days; but this imagination was no longer, as in those earlier campaigns, identical with insight into real possibilities. The success of Napoleon's plan involved the surprise or total defeat of Bernadotte before Berlin, the disablement of Blücher, and a victory, or a strategical success equivalent to a victory, over the vast army of the south. It demanded of a soldiery, inferior to the enemy in numerical strength, the personal superiority which had belonged to the men of Jena and Austerlitz, when in fact the French regiments of conscripts had ceased to be a match for equal numbers of the enemy. But no experience could alter Napoleon's fixed belief in the fatuity of all warfare except his own. After the havoc of Borodino, after the even struggles of Lützen and Bautzen, he still reasoned as if he had before him the armies of Brunswick and Mack. His plan assumed the certainty of success in each of its parts; for the failure of a single operation hazarded all the rest, by requiring the transfer of reinforcements from armies already too weak for the tasks assigned to them. Nevertheless, the utmost that Napoleon would acknowledge was that the execution of his design needed energy. He still underrated the force which Austria had brought into the field against him. Though ignorant of the real position and strength of the army in Bohemia, and compelled to wait for the enemy's movements before striking on this side, he already in imagination saw the war decided by the fall of the Prussian capital.

On the 18th of August the forward movement began. Oudinot advanced from Wittenberg towards Berlin; Napoleon himself hurried into Silesia, intending to deal Blücher one heavy blow, and instantly to return and place himself before Schwarzenberg. On the 21st, and following days, the Prussian general was attacked and driven eastwards. Napoleon committed the pursuit to Macdonald, and hastened back to Dresden, already threatened by the advance of the Austrians from Bohemia. Schwarzenberg and the allied sovereigns, as soon as they heard that Napoleon had gone to seek Blücher in Silesia, had in fact abandoned their cautious plans, and determined to make

Triple movement, Aug. 18 —26.

an assault upon Dresden with the Bohemian army alone. But it was in vain that they tried to surprise Napoleon. He was back at Dresden on the 25th, and ready for the attack. Never were Napoleon's hopes higher than on this day. His success in Silesia had filled him with confidence. He imagined Oudinot to be already in Berlin; and the advance of Schwarzenberg against Dresden gave him the very opportunity which he desired for crushing the Bohemian army in one great battle, before it could draw support either from Blücher or from Bernadotte. Another Austerlitz seemed to be at hand. Napoleon wrote to Paris that he should be in Prague before the enemy; and, while he completed his defences in front of Dresden, he ordered Vandamme, with 40,000 men, to cross the Elbe at Königstein, and force his way south-westwards on to the roads into Bohemia, in the rear of the Great Army, in order to destroy its magazines and menace its line of retreat on Prague. On August 26th Schwarzenberg's host assailed the positions of Napoleon on the slopes and gardens outside Dresden. Austrians, Russians, and Prussians all took part in the attack. Moreau, the victor of Hohenlinden, stood by the side of the Emperor Alexander, whom he had come to help against his own countrymen. He lived only to witness one of the last and greatest victories of France. The attack was everywhere repelled: the Austrian divisions were not only beaten, but disgraced and overthrown. At the end of two days' fighting the Allies were in full retreat, leaving 20,000 prisoners in the hands of Napoleon. It was a moment

Battle of Dresden, Aug. 26, 27.

when the hearts of the bravest sank, and when hope itself might well vanish, as the rumour passed through the Prussian regiments that Metternich was again in friendly communication with Napoleon. But in the midst of Napoleon's triumph intelligence arrived which robbed it of all its worth. Oudinot, instead of conquering Berlin, had been defeated by the Prussians of Bernadotte's army at Grossbeeren (Aug. 23), and driven back upon the Elbe. Blücher had turned upon Macdonald in Silesia, and completely overthrown his army on the river Katzbach, at the very moment when the Allies were making their assault upon Dresden. It was vain to think of a march upon Prague, or of the annihilation of the Austrians, when on the north and the east Napoleon's troops were meeting with nothing but disaster. The divisions which had been intended to support Vandamme's movement from Königstein upon the rear of the Great Army were retained in the neighbourhood of Dresden, in order to be within reach of the points where their aid might be needed. Vandamme, ignorant of his isolation, was left with scarcely 40,000 men to encounter the Great Army in its retreat. He threw himself upon a Russian corps at Kulm, in the Bohemian mountains, on the morning of the 29th. The Russians, at first few in number, held their ground during the day; in the night, and after the battle had recommenced on the morrow, vast masses of the allied troops poured in. The French fought desperately, but were overwhelmed. Vandamme himself was made prisoner, with

Battles of Grossbeeren, Aug. 23, and the Katzbach, Aug. 26.

Battle of Kulm, Aug. 29, 30.

10,000 of his men. The whole of the stores and most of the cannon of his army remained in the enemy's hands.

The victory at Kulm secured the Bohemian army from pursuit, and almost extinguished the effects of its defeat at Dresden. Thanks to the successes of Blücher and of Bernadotte's Prussian generals, which prevented Napoleon from throwing all his forces on to the rear of the Great Army, Schwarzenberg's rash attack had proved of no worse significance than an unsuccessful raid. The Austrians were again in the situation assigned to them in the original plan of the campaign, and capable of resuming their advance into the interior of Saxony: Blücher and the northern commanders had not only escaped separate destruction, but won great victories over the French: Napoleon, weakened by the loss of 100,000 men, remained exactly where he had been at the beginning of the campaign. Had the triple movement by which he meant to overwhelm his adversaries been capable of execution, it would now have been fully executed. The balance, however, had turned against Napoleon; and the twelve days from the 18th to the 29th of August, though marked by no catastrophe like Leipzig or Waterloo, were in fact the decisive period in the struggle of Europe against Napoleon. The attack by which he intended to prevent the junction of the three armies had been made, and had failed. Nothing now remained for him but to repeat the same movements with a discouraged force against an emboldened enemy, or to quit the line of the Elbe, and prepare for one

Effect of the twelve days, Aug. 18—30.

vast and decisive encounter with all three armies combined. Napoleon drove from his mind the thought of failure; he ordered Ney to take command of Oudinot's army, and to lead it again, in increased strength, upon Berlin; he himself hastened to Macdonald's beaten troops in Silesia, and rallied them for a new assault upon Blücher. All was in vain. Ney, advancing on Berlin, was met by the Prussian general Bülow at Dennewitz, and totally routed (Sept. 6): Blücher, finding that Napoleon himself was before him, skilfully avoided battle, and forced his adversary to waste in fruitless marches the brief interval which he had snatched from his watch on Schwarzenberg. Each conflict with the enemy, each vain and exhausting march, told that the superiority had passed from the French to their foes, and that Napoleon's retreat was now only a matter of time. "These creatures have learnt something," said Napoleon in the bitterness of his heart, as he saw the columns of Blücher manœuvring out of his grasp. Ney's report of his own overthrow at Dennewitz sounded like an omen of the ruin of Waterloo. "I have been totally defeated," he wrote, "and do not yet know whether my army has re-assembled. The spirit of the generals and officers is shattered. To command in such conditions is but half to command. I had rather be a common grenadier."

Battle of Dennewitz, Sept. 6.

The accession of Austria had turned the scale in favour of the Allies; it rested only with the allied generals themselves to terminate the warfare round Dresden, and to lead their

German policy of Stein and of Austria.

armies into the heart of Saxony. For a while the course of the war flagged, and military interests gave place to political. It was in the interval between the first great battles and the final advance on Leipzig that the future of Germany was fixed by the three allied Powers. In the excitement of the last twelve months little thought had been given, except by Stein and his friends, to the political form to be set in the place of the Napoleonic Federation of the Rhine. Stein, in the midst of the Russian campaign, had hoped for a universal rising of the German people against Napoleon, and had proposed the dethronement of all the German princes who supported his cause. His policy had received the general approval of Alexander, and, on the entrance of the Russian army into Germany, a manifesto had been issued appealing to the whole German nation, and warning the vassals of Napoleon that they could only save themselves by submission.* A committee had been appointed by the allied sovereigns, under the presidency of Stein himself, to administer the revenues of all Confederate territory that should be occupied by the allied armies. Whether the reigning Houses should be actually expelled might remain in uncertainty; but it was the fixed hope of Stein and his friends that those princes who were permitted to retain their thrones would be permitted to retain them only as officers in a great German Empire, without sovereign rights either over their own

* Häusser, iv. 59. One of the originals is contained in Lord Cathcart's despatch from Kalisch, March 28th, 1813. Records: Russia, Vol. 206.

subjects or in relation to foreign States. The Kings of Bavaria and Würtemberg had gained their titles and much of their despotic power at home from Napoleon; their independence of the Head of Germany had made them nothing more than the instruments of a foreign conqueror. Under whatever form the central authority might be revived, Stein desired that it should be the true and only sovereign Power in Germany, a Power to which every German might appeal against the oppression of a minor Government, and in which the whole nation should find its representative before the rest of Europe. In the face of such a central authority, whether an elected Parliament or an Imperial Council, the minor princes could at best retain but a fragment of their powers; and such was the theory accepted at the allied head-quarters down to the time when Austria proffered its mediation and support. Then everything changed. The views of the Austrian Government upon the future system of Germany were in direct opposition to those of Stein's party.

Metternich. Metternich dreaded the thought of popular agitation, and looked upon Stein, with his idea of a National Parliament, and his plans for dethroning the Rhenish princes, as little better than the Jacobins of 1792. The offer of a restored imperial dignity in Germany was declined by the Emperor of Austria at the instance of his Minister. With characteristic sense of present difficulties, and blindness to the great forces which really contained their solution, Metternich argued that the minor princes would only be driven into the arms of the foreigner by the establishment of any supreme German Power. They would probably desert Napoleon if the Allies guaranteed to them everything that they at present possessed; they would be freed from all future temptation to attach themselves to France if Austria contented itself with a diplomatic influence and with the ties of a well-constructed system of treaties. In spite of the influence of Stein with the Emperor Alexander, Metternich's views prevailed. Austria had so deliberately kept itself in balance during the first part of the year 1813, that the Allies were now willing to concede everything, both in this matter and in others, in return for its support. Nothing more was heard of the dethronement of the Confederate princes, or even of the limitation of their powers. It was agreed by the Treaty of Teplitz, signed by Prussia, Russia, and Austria on September 9th, that every State of the Rhenish Confederacy should be placed in a position of absolute independence. Negotiations were opened with the King of Bavaria, whose army had steadily fought on the side of Napoleon in every campaign since 1806. Instead of being outlawed as a criminal, he was welcomed as an ally. The Treaty of Ried, signed on the 3rd of October, guaranteed to the King of Bavaria, in return for his desertion of Napoleon, full sovereign rights, and the whole of the territory which he had received from Napoleon, except the Tyrol and the Austrian district on the Inn. What had been accorded to the King of Bavaria could not be refused to the rest of Napoleon's vassals who were willing to make their peace with the Allies in time. Germany was thus left at the mercy of a score of petty Cabinets. It was seen by the patriotic party in Prussia at what price the alliance of Austria had been purchased. Austria had indeed made it possible to conquer Napoleon, but it had also made an end of all prospect of the union of the German nation.

Till the last days of September the position of the hostile armies round Dresden remained little changed. *Allies cross the Elbe, Oct. 3.* Napoleon unweariedly repeated his attacks, now on one side, now on another, but without result. The Allies on their part seemed rooted to the soil. Bernadotte, balanced between the desire to obtain Norway from the Allies and a foolish hope of being called to the throne of France, was bent on doing the French as little harm as possible; Schwarzenberg, himself an indifferent general, was distracted by the councillors of all the three monarchs; Blücher alone pressed for decided and rapid action. At length the Prussian commander gained permission to march northwards, and unite his army with Bernadotte's in a forward movement across the Elbe. The long-expected Russian reserves, led by Bennigsen, reached the Bohemian mountains; and at the beginning of October the operation began which was to collect the whole of the allied forces in the plain of Leipzig. Blücher forced the passage of the Elbe at Wartenburg. It was not until Napoleon learnt that the army of Silesia had actually crossed the river that he finally quitted Dresden. Then, hastening northwards, he threw himself upon the

Prussian general; but Blücher again avoided battle, as he had done in Silesia; and on the 7th of October his army united with Bernadotte's, which had crossed the Elbe two days before.

The enemy was closing in upon Napoleon. Obstinately as he had held on to the line of the Elbe, he could hold on no longer. In the frustration of all his hopes there flashed across his mind the wild project of a march eastwards to the Oder, and the gathering of all the besieged garrisons for a campaign in which the enemy should stand between himself and France; but the dream lasted only long enough to gain a record. Napoleon ventured no more than to send a corps back to the Elbe to threaten Berlin, in the hope of tempting Blücher and Bernadotte to abandon the advance which they had now begun in co-operation with the great army of Schwarzenberg. From the 10th to the 14th of October, Napoleon lingered at Düben, between Dresden and Leipzig, restlessly expecting to hear of Blücher's or Bernadotte's retreat. The only definite information that he could gain was that Schwarzenberg was pressing on towards the west. At length he fell back to Leipzig, believing that Blücher, but not Bernadotte, was advancing to meet Schwarzenberg and take part in a great engagement. As he entered Leipzig on October 14th the cannon of Schwarzenberg was heard on the south. Napoleon drew up for battle. The number of his troops in position around the city was 170,000: about 15,000 others lay within call. He placed Marmont and Ney on the north of Leipzig at the

Battle of Leipzig, Oct. 16—19.

village of Möckern, to meet the expected onslaught of Blücher; and himself, with the great mass of his army, took post on the south, facing Schwarzenberg. On the morning of the 16th, Schwarzenberg began the attack. His numbers did not exceed 150,000, for the greater part of the Russian army was a march in the rear. The battle was an even one. The Austrians failed to gain ground: with one more army-corps Napoleon saw that he could overpower the enemy. He was still without intelligence of Blücher's actual appearance in the north; and in the rash hope that Blücher's coming might be delayed, he sent orders to Ney and Marmont to leave their positions and hurry to the south to throw themselves upon Schwarzenberg. Ney obeyed. Marmont, when the order reached him, was actually receiving Blücher's first fire. He determined to remain and defend the village of Möckern, though left without support. York, commanding the van-guard of Blücher's army, assailed him with the utmost fury. A third part of the troops engaged on each side were killed or wounded before the day closed; but in the end the victory of the Prussians was complete. It was the only triumph won by the Allies on this first day of the battle, but it turned the scale against Napoleon. Marmont's corps was destroyed; Ney, divided between Napoleon and Marmont, had rendered no effective help to either. Schwarzenberg, saved from a great disaster, needed only to wait for Bernadotte and the Russian reserves, and to renew the battle with an additional force of 100,000 men.

In the course of the night Napoleon sent proposals for peace. It was in the vain hope of receiving some friendly answer from his father-in-law, the Austrian Emperor, that he delayed making his retreat during the next day, while it might still have been unmolested. No answer was returned to his letter. In the evening of the 17th, Bennigsen's army reached the field of battle. Next morning began that vast and decisive encounter known in the language of Germany as "the battle of the nations," the greatest battle in all authentic history, the culmination of all the military effort of the Napoleonic age. Not less than 300,000 men fought on the side of the Allies; Napoleon's own forces numbered 170,000. The battle raged all round Leipzig, except on the west, where no attempt was made to interpose between Napoleon and the line of his retreat. As in the first engagement, the decisive successes were those of Blücher, now tardily aided by Bernadotte, on the north; Schwarzenberg's divisions, on the south side of the town, fought steadily, but without gaining much ground. But there was no longer any doubt as to the issue of the struggle. If Napoleon could not break the Allies in the first engagement, he had no chance against them now when they had been joined by 100,000 more men. The storm of attack grew wilder and wilder: there were no new forces to call up for the defence. Before the day was half over Napoleon drew in his outer line, and began to make dispositions for a retreat from Leipzig. At evening long trains of wounded from the hospitals passed through

Battle of the 18th.

the western gates of the city along the road towards the Rhine. In the darkness of night the whole army was withdrawn from its positions, and dense masses poured into the town, until every street was blocked with confused and impenetrable crowds of cavalry and infantry. The leading divisions moved out of the gates before sunrise. As the throng lessened, some degree of order was restored, and the troops which Napoleon intended to cover the retreat took their places under the walls of Leipzig. The Allies advanced to the storm on the morning of the 19th. The French were driven into the town; the victorious enemy pressed on towards the rear of the retreating columns. In the midst of the struggle an explosion was heard above the roar of the battle. The bridge over the Elster, the only outlet from Leipzig to the west, had been blown up by the mistake of a French soldier before the rear-guard began to cross. The mass of fugitives, driven from the streets of the town, found before them an impassable river. Some swam to the opposite bank or perished in attempting to do so; the rest, to the number of 15,000, laid down their arms. This was the end of the battle. Napoleon had lost in the three days 40,000 killed and wounded, 260 guns, and 30,000 prisoners. The killed and wounded of the Allies reached the enormous sum of 54,000.

Storm of Leipzig, 19th. French retreat.

The campaign was at an end. Napoleon led off a large army, but one that was in no condition to turn upon its pursuers. At each stage in the retreat thousands of fever-stricken wretches were left to terrify even the pursuing army with the dread of their infection. It was only when the French found the road to Frankfort blocked at Hanau by a Bavarian force that they rallied to the order of battle. The Bavarians were cut to pieces; the road was opened; and, a fortnight after the Battle of Leipzig, Napoleon, with the remnant of his great army, re-crossed the Rhine. Behind him the fabric of his Empire fell to the ground. Jerome fled from Westphalia;* the princes of the Rhenish Confederacy came one after another to make their peace with the Allies; Bülow, with the army which had conquered Ney at Dennewitz, marched through the north of Germany to the deliverance of Holland. Three days after Napoleon had crossed the Rhine the Czar reached Frankfort; and here, on the 7th of November, a military council was held, in which Blücher and Gneisenau, against almost all the other generals, advocated an immediate invasion of France. The soldiers, however, had time to re-consider their opinions, for, on the 9th, it was decided by the representatives of the Powers to send an offer of peace to Napoleon, and the operations of the war were suspended by common consent. The condition on which peace was offered to Napoleon was the surrender of the conquests of France beyond the Alps and the Rhine. The Allies were still willing to permit the Emperor to retain Belgium, Savoy, and the Rhenish Provinces; they declined, however, to enter into any negotiation until Napoleon had accepted this basis of

*Mémoires de Jérome, vi., 223.

peace; and they demanded a distinct reply before the end of the month of November.

Napoleon, who had now arrived in Paris, and saw around him all the signs of power, returned indefinite answers. The month ended without the reply which the Allies required; and on the 1st of December the offer of peace was declared to be withdrawn. It was still undecided whether the war should take the form of an actual invasion of France. The memory of Brunswick's campaign of 1792, and of the disasters of the first coalition in 1793, even now exercised a powerful influence over men's minds. Austria was unwilling to drive Napoleon to extremities, or to give to Russia and Prussia the increased influence which they would gain in Europe from the total overthrow of Napoleon's power. It was ultimately determined that the allied armies should enter France, but that the Austrians, instead of crossing the north-eastern frontier, should make a détour by Switzerland, and gain the plateau of Langres in Champagne, from which the rivers Seine, Marne, and Aube, with the roads following their valleys, descend in the direction of the capital. The plateau of Langres was said to be of such strategical importance that its occupation by an invader would immediately force Napoleon to make peace. As a matter of fact, the plateau was of no strategical importance whatever; but the Austrians desired to occupy it, partly with the view of guarding against any attack from the direction of Italy and Lyons, partly from their want of the heavy artillery necessary for

Offer of peace withdrawn, Dec. 1.

Plan of invasion of France.

besieging the fortresses farther north,* and from a just appreciation of the dangers of a campaign conducted in a hostile country intersected by several rivers. Anything was welcomed by Metternich that seemed likely to avert, or even to postpone, a struggle with Napoleon for life or death. Blücher correctly judged the march through Switzerland to be mere procrastination. He was himself permitted to take the straight road into France, though his movements were retarded in order to keep pace with the cautious steps of Schwarzenberg. On the last day of the year 1813 the Prussian general crossed the Rhine near Coblentz; on the 18th of January, 1814, the Austrian army, having advanced from Switzerland by Belfort and Vesoul, reached its halting-place on the plateau of Langres. Here the march stopped; and here it was expected that terms of peace would be proposed by Napoleon.

Allies enter France, Jan., 1814.

It was not on the eastern side alone that the invader was now entering France. Wellington had passed the Pyrenees. His last victorious march into the north of

---

* "Your lordship has only to recollect the four days' continued fighting at Leipzig, followed by fourteen days' forced marches in the worst weather, in order to understand the reasons that made some repose absolutely necessary. The total loss of the Austrians alone, since the 10th of August, at the time of our arrival at Frankfort, was 80,000 men. We were entirely unprovided with heavy artillery, the nearest battery train not having advanced further than the frontiers of Bohemia." It was thought for a moment that the gates of Strasburg and Huningen might be opened by bribery, and the Austrian Government authorised the expenditure of a million florins for this purpose; in that case the march into Switzerland would have been abandoned. The bribing plan, however, broke down.—Lord Aberdeen's despatches, Nov. 24, Dec. 25, 1813. Records: Austria, 107.

Spain began on the day when the Prussian and Russian armies were defeated by Napoleon at Bautzen (May 21, 1813). During the armistice of Dresden, a week before Austria signed the treaty which fixed the conditions of its armed mediation, he had gained an overwhelming triumph at Vittoria over King Joseph and the French army, as it retreated with all the spoils gathered in five years' occupation of Spain (June 21). A series of bloody engagements had given the English the passes of the Pyrenees in those same days of August and September that saw the allied armies close around Napoleon at Dresden: and when, after the catastrophe of Leipzig, the wreck of Napoleon's host was retreating beyond the Rhine, Soult, the defender of the Pyrenees, was driven by the British general from his entrenchments on the Nivelle, and forced back under the walls of Bayonne.

<small>Wellington entering France from the south.</small>

Twenty years had passed since, in the tempestuous morn of the Revolution, Hoche swept the armies of the first coalition across the Alsatian frontier. Since then, French soldiers had visited every capital, and watered every soil with their blood; but no foreign soldier had set foot on French soil. Now the cruel goads of Napoleon's military glory had spent the nation's strength, and the force no longer existed which could bar the way to its gathered enemies. The armies placed upon the eastern frontier had to fall back before an enemy five times more numerous than themselves. Napoleon had not expected that the Allies would enter France before the spring.

<small>French armies unable to hold the frontier.</small>

With three months given him for organisation, he could have made the frontier-armies strong enough to maintain their actual positions: the winter advance of the Allies compelled him to abandon the border districts of France, and to concentrate his defence in Champagne, between the Marne, the Seine, and the Aube. This district was one which offered extraordinary advantages to a great general acting against an irresolute and ill-commanded enemy. By holding the bridges over the three rivers, and drawing his own supplies along the central road from Paris to Arcis-sur-Aube, Napoleon could securely throw the bulk of his forces from one side to the other against the flank of the Allies, while his own movements were covered by the rivers, which could not be passed except at the bridges. A capable commander at the head of the Allies would have employed the same river-strategy against Napoleon himself, after conquering one or two points of passage by main force; but Napoleon had nothing of the kind to fear from Schwarzenberg; and if the Austrian headquarters continued to control the movements of the allied armies, it was even now doubtful whether the campaign would close at Paris or on the Rhine.

Napoleon's plan of defence.

For some days after the arrival of the monarchs and diplomatists at Langres (Jan. 22), Metternich and the more timorous among the generals opposed any further advance into France, and argued that the army had already gained all it needed by the occupation of the border provinces. It was only upon the threat of the Czar to continue the war by him-

Campaign of 1814.

self that the Austrians consented to move forward upon Paris. After several days had been lost in discussion, the advance from Langres was begun. Orders were given to Blücher, who had pushed back the French divisions commanded by Marmont and Mortier, and who was now near St. Dizier on the Marne, to meet the Great Army at Brienne. This was the situation of the Allies when, on the 25th of January, Napoleon left Paris, and placed himself at Châlons on the Marne, at the head of his left wing, having his right at Troyes and at Arcis, guarding the bridges over the Seine and the Aube. Napoleon knew that Blücher was moving towards the Austrians; he hoped to hold the Prussian general in check at St. Dizier, and to throw himself upon the heads of Schwarzenberg's columns as they moved towards the Aube. Blücher, however, had already passed St. Dizier when Napoleon reached it. Napoleon pursued, and overtook the Prussians at Brienne. After an indecisive battle, Blücher fell back towards Schwarzenberg. The allied armies effected their junction, and Blücher, now supported by the Austrians, turned and marched down the right bank of the Aube to meet Napoleon. Napoleon, though far outnumbered, accepted battle. He was attacked at La Rothière, close above Brienne, and defeated with heavy loss (Feb. 1). A vigorous pursuit would probably have ended the war; but the Austrians held back. Schwarzenberg believed peace to be already gained, and condemned all further action as useless waste of life. In spite of the protests of the Emperor Alexander, he allowed Napoleon to retire unmolested. Schwarzenberg's inaction was no mere error in military judgment. There was a direct conflict between the Czar and the Austrian Cabinet as to the end to be obtained by the war. Alexander already insisted on the dethronement of Napoleon; the Austrian Government would have been content to leave Napoleon in power if he would accept a peace giving France no worse a frontier than it had possessed in 1791. Castlereagh, who had come from England, and Hardenberg were as yet inclined to support Metternich's policy, although the whole Prussian army, the public opinion of Great Britain, and the counsels of Stein and all the bolder Prussian statesmen, were on the side of the Czar.*

Already the influence of the peace-party was so far in the ascendant that negotiations had been opened with Napoleon. Representatives of all the Powers assembled at Châtillon, in Burgundy; and there, towards the end of January, Caulaincourt appeared on behalf of France. The first sitting took place on the 5th of February; on the following day Caulaincourt received full powers from Napoleon to conclude peace. The Allies laid down as the condition of peace the limitation of France to the frontiers of 1791. Had Caulaincourt dared to conclude peace instantly on these terms, Napoleon would have retained

Congress of Châtillon, Feb. 5-9.

---

* Castlereagh's despatch from Langres, Jan. 29, 1814. Records: Continent, Vol. II.: "As far as I have hitherto felt myself called on to give an opinion, I have stated that the British Government did not decline treating with Buonaparte." "The Czar said he observed my view of the question was different from what he believed prevailed in England" (*id.* Feb. 16). See Southey's fine Ode on he Negotiations of 1814.

his throne; but he was aware that Napoleon had only granted him full powers in consequence of the disastrous battle of La Rothière, and he feared to be disavowed by his master as soon as the army had escaped from danger. Instead of simply accepting the Allies' offer, he raised questions as to the future of Italy and Germany. The moment was lost; on the 9th of February the Czar recalled his envoy from Châtillon, and the sittings of the Congress were broken off.

Schwarzenberg was now slowly and unwillingly moving forwards along the Seine towards Troyes. Blücher was permitted to return to the Marne, and to advance upon Paris by an independent line of march. He crossed the country between the Aube and the Marne, and joined some divisions which he had left behind him on the latter river. But his dispositions were outrageously careless: his troops were scattered over a space of sixty miles from Châlons westward, as if he had no enemy to guard against except the weak divisions commanded by Mortier and Marmont, which had uniformly fallen back before his advance. Suddenly Napoleon himself appeared at the centre of the long Prussian line at Champaubert. He had hastened northwards in pursuit of Blücher with 30,000 men, as soon as Schwarzenberg entered Troyes; and on February 10th a weak Russian corps that lay in the centre of Blücher's column was overwhelmed before it was known the Emperor had left the Seine. Then, turning leftwards, Napoleon overthrew the Prussian van-guard at Montmirail, and two days later attacked and defeated Blücher

Defeats of Blücher on the Marne, Feb. 10—14.

himself, who was bringing up the remainder of his troops in total ignorance of the enemy with whom he had to deal. In four days Blücher's army, which numbered 70,000 men, had thrice been defeated in detail by a force of 30,000. Blücher was compelled to fall back upon Châlons; Napoleon instantly returned to the support of Oudinot's division, which he had left in front of Schwarzenberg. In order to relieve Blücher, the Austrians had pushed forward on the Seine beyond Montereau. Within three days after the battle with Blücher, Napoleon was back upon the Seine, and attacking the heads of the Austrian column. On the 18th of February he gained so decisive a victory at Montereau that Schwarzenberg abandoned the advance, and fell back upon Troyes, sending word to Blücher to come *Montereau, Feb. 18.* southwards again and help him to fight a great battle. Blücher moved off with admirable energy, and came into the neighbourhood of Troyes within a week after his defeats upon the Marne. But the design of fighting a great battle was given up. The disinclination of the Austrians to vigorous action was too strong to be overcome; and it was finally determined that Schwarzenberg should fall back almost to the plateau of Langres, leaving Blücher to unite with the *Austrians fall back towards Langres.* troops of Bülow which had conquered Holland, and to operate on the enemy's flank and rear.

The effect of Napoleon's sudden victories on the Marne was instantly seen in the councils of the allied sovereigns. Alexander, who had withdrawn his envoy from Châtillon, could no longer hold out against negotiations with Napoleon. He restored the powers of his envoy, and the Congress re-assembled. But Napoleon already saw himself in imagination driving the invaders beyond the Rhine, and sent orders to Caulaincourt to insist upon the terms proposed at Frankfort, which left to France both the Rhenish Provinces and Belgium. At the same time he attempted to open a private negotiation with his father-in-law the Emperor of Austria, and to detach him from the cause of the Allies. The attempt failed; the demands now made by Caulaincourt overcame even the peaceful inclinations of the Austrian Minister; and on the 1st of March the Allies signed a new treaty at Chaumont, pledging themselves to conclude no peace with Napoleon that did not restore the frontier of 1791, and to maintain a defensive alliance against France for a period of twenty years.* Caulaincourt continued for another fortnight at Châtillon, instructed by Napoleon to prolong the negotiations, but forbidden to accept the only conditions which the Allies were willing to grant.

Congress of Châtillon resumed, Feb. 17 —March 15.

Blücher was now on his way northwards to join the so-called army of Bernadotte upon the Aisne. Since the Battle of Leipzig, Bernadotte himself had taken no part in the movements of the army nominally under his command. The Netherlands had been conquered by Bülow and the Russian general Winzingerode, and these officers were now pushing southwards in order to take part with Blücher in a movement against Paris. Napoleon calculated that the

Napoleon follows Blücher to the north. Battle of Laon, Mar. 10.

* British and Foreign State Papers, 1. 121.

fortress of Soissons would bar the way to the northern army, and enable him to attack and crush Blücher before he could effect a junction with his colleagues. He set out in pursuit of the Prussians, still hoping for a second series of victories like those he had won upon the Marne. But the cowardice of the commander of Soissons ruined his chances of success. The fortress surrendered to the Russians at the first summons. Blücher met the advanced guard of the northern army upon the Aisne on the 4th of March, and continued his march towards Laon for the purpose of uniting with its divisions which lay in the rear. The French followed, but the only advantage gained by Napoleon was a victory over a detached Russian corps at Craonne. Marmont was defeated with heavy loss by a sally of Blücher from his strong position on the hill of Laon (March 10); and the Emperor himself, unable to restore the fortune of the battle, fell back upon Soissons, and thence marched southward to throw himself again upon the line of the southern army.

Schwarzenberg had once more begun to move forward on the news of Blücher's victory at Laon. His troops were so widely dispersed that Napoleon might even now have cut the line in halves had he known Schwarzenberg's real position. But he made a détour in order to meet Oudinot's corps, and gave the Austrians time to concentrate at Arcis-sur-Aube. *Napoleon marches to the rear of the Allies, March 23.*
Here, on the 20th of March, Napoleon found himself in face of an army of 100,000 men. His own army was less than a third of that number; yet with unalterable contempt for the enemy he risked another battle. No

decided issue was reached in the first day's fighting, and Napoleon remained in position, expecting that Schwarzenberg would retreat during the night. But on the morrow the Austrians were still fronting him. Schwarzenberg had at length learnt his own real superiority, and resolved to assist the enemy no longer by a wretched system of retreat. A single act of firmness on the part of the Austrian commander showed Napoleon that the war of battles was at an end. He abandoned all hope of resisting the invaders in front: it only remained for him to throw himself on to their rear, and, in company with the frontier-garrisons and the army of Lyons, to attack their communications with Germany. The plan was no unreasonable one, if Paris could either have sustained a siege or have fallen into the enemy's hands without terminating the war. But the Allies rightly judged that Napoleon's power would be extinct from the moment that Paris submitted. They received the intelligence of the Emperor's march to the east, and declined to follow him. The armies of Schwarzenberg and Blücher approached one another, and moved together on Paris. It was at Vitry, on March 27th, that Napoleon first discovered that the troops which had appeared to be following his eastward movement were but a detachment of cavalry, and that the allied armies were in full march upon the capital. He instantly called up every division within reach, and pushed forward by forced marches for the Seine, hoping to fall upon Schwarzenberg's rear before the allied van-guard could reach Paris. But at each hour of the march it became more evident that the enemy was far in advance. For two days Napoleon urged his men forward; at length, unable to bear the intolerable suspense, he quitted the army on the morning of the 30th, and drove forward at the utmost speed along the road through Fontainebleau to the capital. As day sank, he met reports of a battle already begun. When he reached the village of Fromenteau, fifteen miles from Paris, at ten o'clock at night, he heard that Paris had actually surrendered. *The Allies advance on Paris.*

The Allies had pressed forward without taking any notice of Napoleon's movements, and at early morning on the 30th they had opened the attack on the north-eastern heights of Paris. Marmont, with the fragments of a beaten army and some weak divisions of the National Guard, had but 35,000 men to oppose to three times that number of the enemy. The Government had taken no steps to arm the people, or to prolong resistance after the outside line of defence was lost, although the erection of barricades would have held the Allies in check until Napoleon arrived with his army. While Marmont fought in the outer suburbs, masses of the people were drawn up on Montmartre, expecting the Emperor's appearance, and the spectacle of a great and decisive battle. But the firing in the outskirts stopped soon after noon: it was announced that Marmont had capitulated. The report struck the people with stupor and fury. They had vainly been demanding arms since early morning; and even after the capitulation unsigned papers were handed about by men of the working classes, advocating further *Attack on Paris, March 30.* *Capitulation of Marmont.*

resistance.* But the people no longer knew how to follow leaders of its own. Napoleon had trained France to look only to himself: his absence left the masses, who were still eager to fight for France, helpless in the presence of the conqueror: there were enemies enough of the Government among the richer classes to make the entry of the foreigner into Paris a scene of actual joy and exultation. To such an extent had the spirit of caste and the malignant delight in Napoleon's ruin overpowered the love of France among the party of the old noblesse, that upon the entry of the allied forces into Paris on the 31st of March hundreds of aristocratic women kissed the hands, or the very boots and horses, of the leaders of the train, and cheered the Cossacks who escorted a band of French prisoners, bleeding and exhausted, through the streets.

<small>Allies enter Paris, March 31.</small>

Napoleon's reign was indeed at an end. Since the rupture of the Congress of Châtillon on the 18th of March, the Allies had determined to make his dethronement a condition of peace. As the end approached, it was seen that no successor was possible but the chief of the House of Bourbon, although Austria would perhaps have consented to the establishment of a Regency under the Empress Marie Louise, and the Czar had for a time entertained the project of placing Bernadotte at the head of the French State. Immediately after the entry into Paris it was determined to raise the exile Louis XVIII. to the throne. The politicians of the Empire who followed Talleyrand were not unwilling to unite with the

* Béranger, Biographie, ed. duod., p. 354.

conquerors, and with the small party of Royalist noblesse, in recalling the Bourbon dynasty. Alexander, who was the real master of the situation, rightly judged Talleyrand to be the man most capable of enlisting the public opinion of France on the side of the new order. He took up his abode at Talleyrand's house, and employed this dexterous statesman as the advocate both of the policy of the Allies, and of the principles of constitutional liberty, which at this time Alexander himself sincerely befriended. A Provisional Government was appointed under Talleyrand's leadership. On the 2nd of April the Senate proclaimed the dethronement of Napoleon. On the 6th it published a Constitution, and recalled the House of Bourbon.

Napoleon dethroned, April 22.

Louis XVIII. was still in England: his brother, the Count of Artois, had joined the invaders in France and assumed the title of Lieutenant of the Kingdom; but the influence of Alexander was necessary to force this obstinate and unteachable man into anything like a constitutional position. The Provisional Government invited the Count to take up the administration until the King's arrival, in virtue of a decree of the Senate. D'Artois declined to recognise the Senate's competency, and claimed the Lieutenancy of the Kingdom as his brother's representative. The Senate refusing to admit the Count's divine right, some unmeaning words were exchanged when d'Artois entered Paris; and the Provisional Government, disregarding the claims of the Royal Lieutenant, continued in the full exercise of its powers. At length the Czar insisted that d'Artois should give way. The decree of the Senate was accordingly accepted by him at the Tuileries on the 14th of April; the Provisional Government retired, and a Council of State was formed, in which Talleyrand still continued to exercise the real powers of government. In the address made by d'Artois on this occasion, he stated that although the King had not empowered him to accept the Constitution made by the Senate on the 6th of April, he entertained no doubt that the King would accept the principles embodied in that Constitution, which were those of Representative Government, of the freedom of the press, and of the responsibility of ministers. A week after d'Artois' declaration, Louis XVIII. arrived in France.

Louis XVIII., though capable of adapting himself in practice to a constitutional system, had never permitted himself to question the divine right of the House of Bourbon to sovereign power. The exiles who surrounded him were slow to understand the needs of the time. They recommended the King to reject the Constitution. Louis made an ambiguous answer when the Legislative Body met him at Compiègne and invited an expression of the royal policy. It was again necessary for the Czar to interfere, and to explain to the King that France could no longer be an absolute monarchy. Louis, however, was a better arguer than the Count of Artois. He reasoned as a man whom the sovereigns of Europe had felt it their duty to restore without any request from himself. If the Senate of

Louis XVIII. and the Czar.

Napoleon, he urged, had the right to give France a Constitution, he himself ought never to have been brought from his peaceful English home. He was willing to grant a free Constitution to his people in exercise of his own royal rights, but he could not recognise one created by the servants of an usurper. Alexander was but half satisfied with the liberal professions of Louis: he did not, however, insist on his acceptance of the Constitution drawn up by the Senate, but he informed him that until the promises made by d'Artois were confirmed by a royal proclamation, there would be no entry into Paris. The King at length signed a proclamation written by Talleyrand, and made his festal entry into the capital on the 3rd of May.

Louis XVIII. enters Paris, May 3.

The promises of Louis himself, the unbroken courtesy and friendliness shown by the Allies to Paris since their victory a month before, had almost extinguished the popular feeling of hostility towards a dynasty which owed its recall to the overthrow of French armies. The foreign leaders themselves had begun to excite a certain admiration and interest. Alexander was considered, and with good reason, as a generous enemy; the simplicity of the King of Prussia, his misfortunes, his well-remembered gallantry at the Battle of Jena, gained him general sympathy. It needed but little on the part of the returning Bourbons to convert the interest and curiosity of Paris into affection. The cortége which entered the capital with Louis XVIII. brought back, in a singular motley of obsolete and of

Feeling of Paris.

foreign costumes, the bearers of many unforgotten names. The look of the King himself, as he drove through Paris, pleased the people. The childless father of the murdered Duke of Enghien gained the pitying attention of those few who knew the face of a man twenty-five years an exile. But there was one among the members of the returning families whom every heart in Paris went out to meet. The daughter of Louis XVI., who had shared the captivity of her parents and of her brother, the sole survivor of her deeply-wronged house, now returned as Duchess of Angoulême. The uniquely mournful history of her girlhood, and her subsequent marriage with her cousin, the son of the Count of Artois, made her the natural object of a warmer sympathy than could attach to either of the brothers of Louis XVI. But adversity had imprinted its lines too deeply upon the features and the disposition of this joyless woman for a moment's light to return. Her voice and her aspect repelled the affection which thousands were eager to offer to her. Before the close of the first days of the restored monarchy, it was felt that the Bourbons had brought back no single person among them who was capable of winning the French nation's love.

The recall of the ancient line had been allowed to appear to the world as the work of France itself; Napoleon's fate could only be fixed by his conquerors. After the fall of Paris, Napoleon remained at Fontainebleau awaiting events. The soldiers and the younger officers of his army were still ready to fight for him; the marshals, however, were utterly weary,

Napoleon.

and determined that France should no longer suffer for the sake of a single man. They informed Napoleon that he must abdicate. Yielding to their pressure, Napoleon, on the 3rd of April, drew up an act of abdication in favour of his infant son, and sent it by Caulaincourt to the allied sovereigns at Paris. The document was rejected by the Allies; Caulaincourt returned with the intelligence that Napoleon must renounce the throne for himself and all his family. For a moment the Emperor thought of renewing the war; but the marshals refused their aid more resolutely than before, and, on the 6th of April, Napoleon signed an unconditional surrender of the throne for himself and his heirs. He was permitted by the Allies to retain the unmeaning title of Emperor, and to carry with him a body-guard and a considerable revenue to the island of Elba, henceforward to be his principality and his prison. The choice of this island, within easy reach of France and Italy, and too extensive to be guarded without a large fleet, was due to Alexander's ill-judged generosity towards Napoleon, and to a promise made to Marmont that the liberty of the Emperor should be respected. Alexander was not left without warning of the probable effects of his leniency. Sir Charles Stewart, military representative of Great Britain at the allied headquarters, urged both his own and the allied Governments to substitute some more distant island for Elba, if they desired to save Europe from a renewed Napoleonic war, and France from the misery of a second invasion. The Allies, though not without misgivings, adhered to their

Napoleon sent to Elba.

and determined that France should no longer suffer for the sake of a single man. They informed Napoleon that he must abdicate. Yielding to their pressure, Napoleon, on the 3rd of April, drew up an act of abdication in favour of his infant son, and sent it by Caulaincourt to the allied sovereigns at Paris. The document was rejected by the Allies; Caulaincourt returned with the intelligence that Napoleon must renounce the throne for himself and all his family. For a moment the Emperor thought of renewing the war; but the marshals refused their aid more resolutely than before, and, on the 6th of April, Napoleon signed an unconditional surrender of the throne for himself and his heirs. He was permitted by the Allies to retain the unmeaning title of Emperor, and to carry with him a body-guard and a considerable revenue to the island of Elba, henceforward to be his principality and his prison. The choice of this island, within easy reach of France and Italy, and too extensive to be guarded without a large fleet, was due to Alexander's ill-judged generosity towards Napoleon, and to a promise made to Marmont that the liberty of the Emperor should be respected. Alexander was not left without warning of the probable effects of his leniency. Sir Charles Stewart, military representative of Great Britain at the allied headquarters, urged both his own and the allied Governments to substitute some more distant island for Elba, if they desired to save Europe from a renewed Napoleonic war, and France from the misery of a second invasion. The Allies, though not without misgivings, adhered to their

Napoleon sent to Elba.

original plan, and left it to time to justify the predictions of their adviser.

It was well known what would be the terms of peace, now that Napoleon was removed from the throne. The Allies had no intention of depriving France of any of the territory that it had held before 1792 : the conclusion of a definitive Treaty was only postponed until the Constitution, which Alexander required King Louis XVIII. to grant, had been drawn up by a royal commission and approved by the King. On the 27th of May the draft of this Constitution, known as the Charta, was laid before the King, and sanctioned by him ; on the 30th, the Treaty of Paris was signed by the representatives of France and of all the great Powers.* France, surrendering all its conquests, accepted the frontier of the 1st of January, 1792, with a slight addition of territory on the side of Savoy and at points on its northern and eastern border. It paid no indemnity. It was permitted to retain all the works of art accumulated by twenty years of rapine, except the trophies carried from the Brandenburg Gate of Berlin and the spoils of the Library of Vienna. It received back nearly all the colonies which had been taken from it by Great Britain. By the clauses of the Treaty disposing of the territory that had formed the Empire and the dependencies of Napoleon, Holland was restored to the House of Orange, with the provision that its territory should be largely increased; Switzerland was declared independent; it was stipulated that

Treaty of Paris, May 30

---

* British and Foreign State Papers, 1. 151.

Italy, with the exception of the Austrian Provinces, should consist of independent States, and that Germany should remain distributed among a multitude of sovereigns, independent, but united by a Federal tie. The navigation of the Rhine was thrown open. By a special agreement with Great Britain the French Government undertook to unite its efforts to those of England in procuring the suppression of the Slave-trade by all the Powers, and pledged itself to abolish the Slave-trade among French subjects within five years at the latest. For the settlement of all European questions not included in the Treaty of Paris it was agreed that a Congress of the Powers should, within two months, assemble at Vienna. These were the public articles of the Treaty of Paris. Secret clauses provided that the Allies—that is, the Allies independently of France—should control the distributions of territory to be made at the Congress; that Austria should receive Venetia and all Northern Italy as far as the Ticino; that Genoa should be given to the King of Sardinia; and that the Southern Netherlands should be united into a single kingdom with Holland, and thus form a solid bulwark against France on the north. No mention was made of Naples, whose sovereign, Murat, had abandoned Napoleon and allied himself with Austria, but without fulfilling in good faith the engagements into which he had entered against his former master. A nominal friend of the Allies, he knew that he had played a double game, and that his sovereignty, though not yet threatened, was insecure.*

* Lord W. Bentinck, who was with Murat, warned him against the

Territorial arrangements of 1814.

Much yet remained to be settled by the Congress at Vienna, but in the Treaty of Paris two at least of the great Powers saw the objects attained for which they had struggled so persistently through all the earlier years of the war, and which at a later time had appeared to pass almost out of the range of possibility. England saw the Netherlands once more converted into a barrier against France, and Antwerp held by friendly hands. Austria reaped the full reward of its cool and well-balanced diplomacy during the crisis of 1813, in the annexation of an Italian territory that made it the real mistress of the Peninsula. Castlereagh and every other English politician felt that Europe had done itself small honour in handing Venice back to the Hapsburg; but this had been the condition exacted by Metternich at Prague before he consented to throw the sword of Austria into the trembling scale;*

probable consequences of his duplicity. Bentinck had, however, to be careful in his language, as the following shows. Murat having sent him a sword of honour, he wrote to the English Government, May 1, 1814: "It is a severe violence to my feelings to incur any degree of obligation to an individual whom I so entirely despise. But I feel it my duty not to betray any appearance of a spirit of animosity." To Murat he wrote on the same day: "The sword of a great captain is the most flattering present which a soldier can receive. It is with the highest gratitude that I accept the gift, Sire, which you have done me the honour to send."—Records: Sicily, Vol. 98.

* Treaties of Teplitz, Sept. 9, 1813. In Bianchi, Storia Documentata della Diplomazia Europea, i. 334, there is a long protest addressed by Metternich to Castlereagh on May 26, 1814, referring with great minuteness to a number of clauses in a secret Treaty signed by all the Powers at Prague on July 27, 1813, and ratified at London on August 23, giving Austria the disposal of all Italy. This protest, which has been accepted as genuine in Reuchlin's Geschichte Italiens and elsewhere, is, with the alleged secret Treaty, a forgery. My grounds for this statement are as

and the Republican traditions both of Venice and of Genoa counted for little among the statesmen of 1814, in comparison with the divine right of a Duke of Modena or a Prince of Hesse Cassel.* France itself, though stripped of the dominion won by twenty years of warfare, was permitted to retain, for the benefit of a restored line of kings, the whole of its ancient territory, and the spoil of all the galleries and museums of Western Europe. It would have been no unnatural wrong if the conquerors of 1814 had dealt with the soil of France as France had dealt with other lands; it would have been an act of bare justice to restore to its rightful owners the pillage that had been brought to Paris, and to recover from the French treasury a part of the enormous sums which Napoleon had extorted from conquered States. But the Courts were too well satisfied with their victory to enter into a strict account upon secondary matters; and a prudent regard on the part of the Allies

follows:—(1) There was no British envoy at Prague in July, 1813. (2) The private as well as the official letters of Castlereagh to Lord Cathcart of Sept. 13 and 18, and the instructions sent to Lord Aberdeen during August and September, prove that no joint Treaty existed up to that date, to which both England and Austria were parties. Records: Russia, 207, 209 A. Austria, 105. (3) Lord Aberdeen's reports of his negotiations with Metternich after this date conclusively prove that almost all Italian questions, including even the Austrian frontier, were treated as matters to be decided by the Allies in common. While Austria's right to a preponderance in upper Italy is admitted, the affairs of Rome and Naples are always treated as within the range of English policy.

* The originals of the Genoese and Milanese petitions for independence are in Records: Sicily, Vol. 98. "The Genoese universally desire the restoration of their ancient Republic. They dread above all other arrangements their annexation to Piedmont, to the inhabitants of which there has always existed a peculiar aversion."—Bentinck's Despatch, April 27, 1814, *id.*

to the prospects of the House of Bourbon saved France from experiencing what it had inflicted upon others.

The policy which now restored to France the frontier of 1792 was viewed with a very different feeling in France and in all other countries. Europe looked with a kind of wonder upon its own generosity; France forgot the unparalleled provocations which it had offered to mankind, and only remembered that Belgium and the Rhenish Provinces had formed part of the Republic and the Empire for nearly twenty years. These early conquests of the Republic, which no one had attempted to wrest from France since 1795, had undoubtedly been the equivalent for which, in the days of the Directory, Austria had been permitted to extend itself in Italy, and Prussia in Germany. In the opinion of men who sincerely condemned Napoleon's distant conquests, the territory between France and the Rhine was no more than France might legitimately demand, as a counterpoise to the vast accessions falling to one or other of the Continental Powers out of the territory of Poland, Venice, and the body of suppressed States in Germany. Poland, excluding the districts taken from it before 1792, contained a population twice as great as that of Belgium and the Rhenish Provinces together:

All the Powers except France gained territory by the war, 1792–1814. Venice carried with it, in addition to a commanding province on the Italian mainland, the Eastern Adriatic Coast as far as Ragusa. If it were true that the proportionate increase of power formed the only solid principle of European policy, France sustained a grievous injury in receiving back the limits of 1791, when every other State on the Continent was permitted to retain the territory, or an equivalent for the territory, which it had gained in the great changes that took place between 1791 and 1814. But in fact there had never been a time during the last hundred and fifty years when France, under an energetic Government, had not possessed a force threatening to all its neighbours. France, reduced to its ancient limits, was still the equal, and far more than the equal, of any of the Continental Powers, with all that they had gained during the Revolutionary War. It remained the first of European nations, though no longer, as in the eighteenth century, the one great nation of the western continent. Its efforts after universal empire had aroused other nations into life. Had the course of French conquest ceased before Napoleon grasped power, France would have retained its frontier of the Rhine, and long have exercised an unbounded influence over both Germany and Italy, through the incomparably juster and brighter social life which the Revolution, combined with all that France had inherited from the past, enabled it to display to those countries. Napoleon, in the attempt to impose his rule upon all Europe, created a power in Germany whose military future was to be not less solid than that of France itself, and left to Europe, in the accord of his enemies, a firmer security against French attack than any that the efforts of statesmen had ever framed.

The league of the older monarchies had proved stronger in the end than the genius and the ambition of a single man. But if, in the service of Napoleon, France had exhausted its wealth, sunk its fleets, and sacrificed a million lives, only that it might lose all its earlier conquests, and resume limits which it had outgrown before Napoleon held his first command, it was not thus with the work which, for or against itself, France had effected in Europe during the movements of the last twenty years. In the course of the epoch now ending the whole of the Continent up to the frontiers of Austria and Russia had gained the two fruitful ideas of nationality and political freedom. There were now two nations in Europe where before there had been but aggregates of artificial States. Germany and Italy were no longer mere geographical expressions: in both countries, though in a very unequal degree, the newly-aroused sense of nationality had brought with it the claim for unity and independence. In Germany, Prussia had set a great example, and was hereafter to reap its reward; in Italy there had been no State and no statesman to take the lead either in throwing off Napoleon's rule, or in forcing him, as the price of support, to give to his Italian kingdom a really national government. Failing to act for itself, the population of all Italy, except Naples, was parcelled out between Austria and the ancient dynasties; but the old days of passive submission to the foreigner were gone for ever, and time was to show whether those were the dreamers who thought of a united Italy, or those who thought that Metternich's statesmanship had for ever settled the fate of Venice and of Milan.

The second legacy of the Revolutionary epoch, the idea of constitutional freedom, which in 1789 had been as much wanting in Spain, where national spirit was the strongest, as in those German States where it was the weakest, had been excited in Italy by the events of 1796 and 1798, in Spain by the disappearance of the Bourbon king and the self-directed struggle of the nation against the invader: in Prussia it had been introduced by the Government itself when Stein was at the head of the State. "It is impossible," wrote Lord Castlereagh in the spring of 1814, "not to perceive a great moral change coming on in Europe, and that the principles of freedom are in full operation."* There was in fact scarcely a Court in Europe which was not now declaring its intention to frame a Constitution. The professions might be lightly made; the desire and the capacity for self-government might still be limited to a narrower class than the friends of liberty imagined; but the seed was sown, and a movement had begun which was to gather strength during the next thirty years of European history, while one revolution after another proved that Governments could no longer with safety disregard the rights of their subjects.

<small>Desire for political liberty.</small>

Lastly, in all the territory that had formed Napoleon's Empire and dependencies, and also in Prussia, legal changes had been made in the rights and relations of the different classes of society, so important as almost to create a new type of social life. Within the Empire itself the Code Napoléon,

<small>Social changes.</small>

* Castlereagh, x. 18.

conferring upon the subjects of France the benefits which the French had already won for themselves, had superseded a society resting on class-privilege, on feudal service, and on the despotism of custom, by a society resting on equality before the law, on freedom of contract, and on the unshackled ownership and enjoyment of land, whether the holder possessed an acre or a league. The principles of the French Code, if not the Code itself, had been introduced into Napoleon's kingdom of Italy, into Naples, and into almost all the German dependencies of France. In Prussia the reforms of Stein and Hardenberg had been directed, though less boldly, towards the same end; and when, after 1814, the Rhenish Provinces were annexed to Prussia by the Congress of Vienna, the Government was wise enough and liberal enough to leave these districts in the enjoyment of the laws which France had given them, and not to risk a comparison between even the best Prussian legislation and the Code Napoléon. In other territory now severed from France and restored to German or Italian princes, attempts were not wanting to obliterate the new order and to re-introduce the burdens and confusions of the old régime. But these reactions, even where unopposed for a time, were too much in conflict with the spirit of the age to gain more than a temporary and precarious success. The people had begun to know good and evil: examples of a free social order were too close at hand to render it possible for any part of the western continent to relapse for any very long period into the condition of the eighteenth century.

It was indeed within a distinct limit that the Revolutionary epoch effected its work of political and social change. Neither England nor Austria received the slightest impulse to progress. England, on the contrary, suspended almost all internal improvement during the course of the war, the domestic policy of the Austrian Court, so energetic in the reign immediately preceding the Revolution, became for the next twenty years, except where it was a policy of repression, a policy of pure vacancy and inaction. But in all other States of Western Europe the period which reached its close with Napoleon's fall left deep and lasting traces behind it. Like other great epochs of change, it bore its own peculiar character. It was not, like the Renaissance and' the Reformation, a time when new worlds of faith and knowledge transformed the whole scope and conception of human life; it was not, like our own age, a time when scientific discovery and increased means of communication silently altered the physical conditions of existence; it was a time of changes directly political in their nature, and directly effected by the political agencies of legislation and of war. In the perspective of history the Napoleonic age will take its true place among other, and perhaps greater, epochs. Its elements of mere violence and disturbance will fill less space in the eyes of mankind; its permanent creations, more. As an epoch of purely political energy, concentrating the work of generations within the compass of twenty-five years, it will perhaps scarcely find a parallel.

Limits.

PRINTED BY
CASSELL & COMPANY, LIMITED, LA BELLE SAUVAGE,
LONDON, E.C.

A SELECTED LIST

OF

CASSELL & COMPANY'S

PUBLICATIONS.

Illustrated, Fine Art, and other Volumes.

Abbeys and Churches of England and Wales, The: Descriptive, Historical, Pictorial. Series II. 21s.
A Blot of Ink. Translated by Q and PAUL FRANCKE. 5s.
Adventure, The World of. Fully Illustrated. Complete in Three Vols. 9s. each.
Africa and its Explorers, The Story of. By Dr. ROBERT BROWN, M.A., F.I.S., F.R G.S., &c. With numerous Original Illustrations. Vols. I. and II. 7s. 6d. each.
Agrarian Tenures. By the Rt. Hon. G. SHAW LEFEVRE, M.P. 10s. 6d.
Allon, Henry, D.D.: A Biographical Sketch. By the Rev. W. HARDY HARWOOD. With Sermons and Addresses. 6s.
American Life. By PAUL DE ROUSIERS. 12s. 6d.
Animal Painting in Water Colours. With Coloured Plates. 5s.
Anthea. By CÉCILE CASSAVETTI (a Russian). A Story of the Greek War of Independence. *Cheap Edition*, 5s.
Arabian Nights Entertainments (Cassell's). With about 400 Illustrations. 10s. 6d.
Architectural Drawing. By R. PHENÉ SPIERS. Illustrated. 10s. 6d.
Army, Our Home. Being a Reprint of Letters published in the *Times* in November and December, 1891. By H. O. ARNOLD-FORSTER, M.P. 1s.
Art, The Magazine of. Yearly Volume. With about 400 Illustrations, and Twelve Etchings, Photogravures, &c. 16s.
Artistic Anatomy. By Prof. M. DUVAL. *Cheap Edition*, 3s. 6d.
Astronomy, The Dawn of. A Study of the Temple Worship and Mythology of the Ancient Egyptians. By Professor J. NORMAN LOCKYER, C B., F.R S., &c. Illustrated. 21s.
Atlas, The Universal. A New and Complete General Atlas of the World, with 117 Pages of Maps, handsomely produced in Colours, and a Complete Index to about 125,000 Names. Complete in One Vol., cloth. 30s. net; or half-morocco, 35s. net.
Awkward Squads, The; and other Ulster Stories. By SHAN F. BULLOCK. 5s.
Bashkirtseff, Marie, The Journal of. Translated by MATHILDE BLIND. 7s. 6d.
Bashkirtseff, Marie, The Letters of. Translated by MARY J. SERRANO. 7s. 6d.
Beetles, Butterflies, Moths, and other Insects. By A. W. KAPPEL, F.L S., F.E.S., and W. EGMONT KIRBY. With 12 Coloured Plates. 3s. 6d.
Biographical Dictionary, Cassell's New. Containing Memoirs of the Most Eminent Men and Women of all Ages and Countries. 7s. 6d.
Birds' Nests, Eggs, and Egg-Collecting. By R. KEARTON. Illustrated with 16 Coloured Plates of Eggs. 5s.
Breechloader, The, and How to Use It. By W. W. GREENER. 2s.
British Ballads. 275 Original Illustrations. Two Vols. Cloth, 15s.
British Battles on Land and Sea. By JAMES GRANT. With about 600 Illustrations. Three Vols., 4to, £1 7s.; *Library Edition*, £1 10s.
British Battles, Recent. Illustrated. 9s. *Library Edition*, 10s.
Browning, An Introduction to the Study of. By ARTHUR SYMONS. 2s. 6d.
Butterflies and Moths, European. By W. F. KIRBY. With 61 Coloured Plates. 35s.
Canaries and Cage-Birds, The Illustrated Book of. By W. A. BLAKSTON, W. SWAYSLAND, and A. F. WIENER. With 56 Fac-simile Coloured Plates. 35s.
Capture of the "Estrella," The. A Tale of the Slave Trade. By COMMANDER CLAUD HARDING, R.N. 5s.
Carnation Manual, The. Edited and Issued by The National Carnation and Picotee Society (Southern Section). 3s. 6d.
Cassell, John. By G. HOLDEN PIKE. With Portrait. 1s.
Cassell's Family Magazine. Yearly Volume. Illustrated. 9s.
Cathedrals, Abbeys, and Churches of England and Wales. Descriptive, Historical, Pictorial. *Popular Edition*. Two Vols. 25s.
Catriona. A Sequel to "Kidnapped." By ROBERT LOUIS STEVENSON. 6s.
China Painting. By FLORENCE LEWIS. With Sixteen Coloured Plates, &c. 5s.
Chips by an Old Chum; or, Australia in the Fifties. 1s.
Choice Dishes at Small Cost. By A. G. PAYNE. *Cheap Edition*, 1s.
Christianity and Socialism, Lectures on. By BISHOP BARRY. 3s. 6d.
Chums, The Illustrated Paper for Boys. Yearly Volume. 7s. 6d.
Cities of the World. Four Vols. Illustrated. 7s. 6d. each.
Civil Service, Guide to Employment in the. *New and Enlarged Edition*, 3s. 6d.

Selections from Cassell & Company's Publications.

...ical Manuals for Practitioners and Students of Medicine. (*A List of Volumes forwarded post free on application to the Publishers.*)
...ien Club, Works published for the. (*A Complete List on application.*)
...nist's Medical Handbook, The. By E. ALFRED BARTON, M.R.C.S. 1s.
...ur. By Prof. A. H. CHURCH. *New and Enlarged Edition*, 3s. 6d.
...mbus, The Career of. By CHARLES ELTON, F.S.A. 10s. 6d.
...be, George, The Select Works of. Issued by Authority of the Combe Trustees. *Popular Edition*, 1s. each, net.
 The Constitution of Man. | Science and Religion.
 Moral Philosophy. | Discussions on Education.
   American Notes.
...mercial Botany of the Nineteenth Century. By J. R. JACKSON, A.L.S. Cloth gilt, 2s.
...ning Tower, In a. By H. O. ARNOLD-FORSTER, M.P., Author of "The Citizen Reader," &c. With Original Illustrations by W. H. OVEREND. 1s.
...quests of the Cross. Edited by EDWIN HODDER. With numerous Original Illustrations. Complete in Three Vols. 9s. each.
...kery, A Year's. By PHYLLIS BROWNE. *New and Enlarged Edition*, 3s. 6d.
...kery, Cassell's Popular. With Four Coloured Plates. Cloth gilt, 2s.
...kery, Cassell's Shilling. 110*th Thousand.* 1s.
...kery, Vegetarian. By A. G. PAYNE. 1s. 6d.
...king by Gas, The Art of. By MARIE J. SUGG. Illustrated. Cloth, 2s.
...tage Gardening, Poultry, Bees, Allotments, Food, House, Window and Town Gardens. Edited by W. ROBINSON, F.L S., Author of "The English Flower Garden." Fully Illustrated. Half-yearly Vols., I., II., and III., 2s. 6d. each.
...ntries of the World, The. By ROBERT BROWN, M.A., Ph.D., &c. Complete in Six Vols., with about 750 Illustrations. 4to, 7s. 6d. each.
...lopædia, Cassell's Concise. Brought down to the latest date. With about 600 Illustrations. *New and Cheap Edition*, 7s. 6d.
...lopædia, Cassell's Miniature. Containing 30,000 Subjects. Cloth, 2s. 6d.; half-roxburgh, 4s.
...ectable Duchy, The. Stories, Studies, and Sketches. By Q. 6s.
...k Whittington, A Modern. By JAMES PAYN. *Cheap Edition in one Vol.*, 6s.
...tionaries. (For description see alphabetical letter.) Religion, Biographical, Encyclopædic, Mechanical, Phrase and Fable, English, English History, English Literature, Domestic. (French, German, and Latin, see with *Educational Works.*)
...t and Cookery for Common Ailments. By a Fellow of the Royal College of Physicians, and PHYLLIS BROWNE. 5s.
..., Illustrated Book of the. By VERO SHAW, B.A. With 28 Coloured Plates. Cloth bevelled, 35s.; half-morocco, 45s.
...nestic Dictionary, The. An Encyclopædia for the Household. Cloth, 7s. 6d.
...é Don Quixote, The. With about 400 Illustrations by GUSTAVE DORÉ. *Cheap Edition*, bevelled boards, gilt edges, 10s. 6d.
...ré Gallery, The. With 250 Illustrations by GUSTAVE DORÉ. 4to, 42s.
...ré's Dante's Inferno. Illustrated by GUSTAVE DORÉ. *Popular Edition.* With Preface by A. J. BUTLER. Cloth gilt or buckram, 7s. 6d.
...ré's Dante's Purgatory and Paradise. Illustrated by GUSTAVE DORÉ. *Cheap Edition.* 7s. 6d.
...ré's Milton's Paradise Lost. Illustrated by GUSTAVE DORÉ. 4to, 21s.
..., Dumány's Wife. A Novel. By MAURUS JÓKAI. *Cheap Edition*, 6s.
...rth, Our, and its Story. Edited by Dr. ROBERT BROWN, F.L.S. With 36 Coloured Plates and 740 Wood Engravings. Complete in Three Vols. 9s. each.
...inburgh, Old and New, Cassell's. With 600 Illustrations. Three Vols. 9s. each; library binding, £1 10s. the set.
...ypt: Descriptive, Historical, and Picturesque. By Prof. G. EBERS. Translated by CLARA BELL, with Notes by SAMUEL BIRCH, LL.D., &c. Two Vols. 42s.
...ctricity, Practical. By Prof. W. E. AYRTON. Illustrated. Cloth, 7s. 6d.
...ctricity in the Service of Man. A Popular and Practical Treatise. With upwards of 950 Illustrations. *New and Revised Edition*, 10s. 6d.
...iployment for Boys on Leaving School, Guide to. By W. S. BEARD, F.R.G.S. 1s. 6d.
...cyclopædic Dictionary, The. Complete in Fourteen Divisional Vols., 10s. 6d. each; or Seven Vols., half-morocco, 21s. each; half-russia, 25s. each.

Selections from Cassell & Company's Publications.

England, Cassell's Illustrated History of. With 2,000 Illustrations. Ten Vols., 4to, 9s. each. *New and Revised Edition.* Vols. I. to VI., 9s. each.
English Dictionary, Cassell's. Containing Definitions of upwards of 100,000 Words and Phrases. *Cheap Edition*, 3s. 6d., *Superior Edition*, 5s.
English History, The Dictionary of. *Cheap Edition*, 10s. 6d.; roxburgh, 15s.
English Literature, Library of. By Prof. H. MORLEY. In 5 Vols. 7s. 6d. each.
English Literature, Morley's First Sketch of. *Revised Edition*, 7s. 6d.
English Literature, The Dictionary of. By W. DAVENPORT ADAMS. *Cheap Edition*, 7s. 6d.; roxburgh, 10s. 6d.
English Literature, The Story of. By ANNA BUCKLAND. 3s. 6d.
English Writers. By HENRY MORLEY. Vols. I. to X. 5s. each.
Æsop's Fables. Illustrated by ERNEST GRISET. *Cheap Edition.* Cloth, 3s. 6d.; bevelled boards, gilt edges, 5s.
Etiquette of Good Society. *New Edition.* Edited and Revised by LADY COLIN CAMPBELL. 1s.; cloth, 1s. 6d.
Europe, Cassell's Pocket Guide to. *Edition for* 1893. Leather, 6s.
Fairway Island. By HORACE HUTCHINSON. With Four Full-page Plates. *Cheap Edition*, 3s. 6d.
Faith Doctor, The. A Novel. By Dr. EDWARD EGGLESTON. *Cheap Edition*, 6s.
Family Physician. By Eminent PHYSICIANS and SURGEONS. *New and Revised Edition.* Cloth, 21s.; roxburgh, 25s.
Father Mathew: His Life and Times. By FRANK J. MATHEW. 2s. 6d.
Father Stafford. A Novel. By ANTHONY HOPE. *Cheap Edition*, 3s. 6d.
Fenn, G. Manville, Works by. Boards, 2s. each; or cloth, 2s. 6d.

> Poverty Corner. | The Parson o' Dumford.
> My Patients. | The Vicar's People. } In boards only.

Field Naturalist's Handbook, The. By Revs. J. G. WOOD and THEODORE WOOD. *Cheap Edition.* 2s. 6d.
Figuier's Popular Scientific Works. With Several Hundred Illustrations in each. 3s. 6d. each.

> The Insect World. | Reptiles and Birds. | The Vegetable World.
> The Human Race. | Mammalia. | Ocean World.
> The World before the Deluge.

Figure Painting in Water Colours. With 16 Coloured Plates. 7s. 6d.
Flora's Feast. A Masque of Flowers. Penned and Pictured by WALTER CRANE. With 40 pages in Colours. 5s.
Flower Painting, Elementary. With Eight Coloured Plates. 3s.
Flowers, and How to Paint Them. By MAUD NAFTEL. With Coloured Plates. 5s.
Football: the Rugby Union Game. Edited by Rev. F. MARSHALL. Illustrated. 7s. 6d.
Fossil Reptiles, A History of British. By Sir RICHARD OWEN, F.R.S., &c. With 268 Plates. In Four Vols. £12 12s.
Fraser, John Drummond. By PHILALETHES. A Story of Jesuit Intrigue in the Church of England. 5s.
Garden Flowers, Familiar. By SHIRLEY HIBBERD. With Coloured Plates by F. E. HULME, F.L.S. Complete in Five Series. Cloth gilt, 12s. 6d. each.
Gardening, Cassell's Popular. Illustrated. Complete in Four Vols. 5s. each.
Geometrical Drawing for Army Candidates. By H. T. LILLEY, M.A. 2s. 6d.
Geometry, First Elements of Experimental. By PAUL BERT. 1s. 6d.
Geometry, Practical Solid. By Major ROSS. 2s.
George Saxon, The Reputation of. By MORLEY ROBERTS. 5s.
Gilbert, Elizabeth, and her Work for the Blind. By FRANCES MARTIN. 2s. 6d.
Gleanings from Popular Authors. Two Vols. With Original Illustrations. 4to, 9s. each. Two Vols. in One, 15s.
Gulliver's Travels. With 88 Engravings. Cloth, 3s. 6d.; cloth gilt, 5s.
Gun and its Development, The. By W. W. GREENER. Illustrated. 10s. 6d.
Guns, Modern Shot. By W. W. GREENER. Illustrated. 5s.
Health, The Book of. By Eminent Physicians and Surgeons. Cloth, 21s.
Heavens, The Story of the. By Sir ROBERT STAWELL BALL, LL.D., F.R.S. With Coloured Plates and Wood Engravings. *Popular Edition*, 12s. 6d.
Heroes of Britain in Peace and War. With 300 Original Illustrations. *Cheap Edition.* Two Vols. 3s. 6d. each; or two vols. in one, cloth gilt, 7s. 6d.

Selections from Cassell & Company's Publications.

Hiram Golf's Religion; or, the Shoemaker by the Grace of God. 2s.
Historic Houses of the United Kingdom. With Contributions by the Rev. Professor BONNEY, F.R.S., and others. Profusely Illustrated. 10s. 6d.
History, A Footnote to. Eight Years of Trouble in Samoa. By ROBERT LOUIS STEVENSON. 6s.
Home Life of the Ancient Greeks, The. Translated by ALICE ZIMMERN. Illustrated. 7s. 6d.
Horse, The Book of the. By SAMUEL SIDNEY. Thoroughly Revised and brought up to date by JAMES SINCLAIR and W. C. A. BLEW." With 17 Full-page Collotype Plates of Celebrated Horses of the Day, and numerous other Illustrations. Cloth, 15s.
Houghton, Lord: The Life, Letters, and Friendships of Richard Monckton Milnes, First Lord Houghton. By T. WEMYSS REID. Two Vols. 32s.
Household, Cassell's Book of the. Illustrated. Complete in Four Vols. 5s each; or Four Vols. in two, half-morocco, 25s.
Hygiene and Public Health. By B. ARTHUR WHITELEGGE, M.D. Illustrated. *New and Revised Edition.* 7s. 6d.
India, Cassell's History of. By JAMES GRANT. With 400 Illustrations. Two Vols., 9s. each, or One Vol., 15s.
In-door Amusements, Card Games, and Fireside Fun, Cassell's Book of. With numerous Illustrations. *Cheap Edition.* Cloth, 2s.
Into the Unknown: a Romance of South Africa. By LAWRENCE FLETCHER. 3s. 6d.
Iron Pirate, The. A Plain Tale of Strange Happenings on the Sea. By MAX PEMBERTON. Illustrated. 5s.
Island Nights' Entertainments. By R. L. STEVENSON. Illustrated, 6s.
Italy from the Fall of Napoleon I. in 1815 to 1890. By J. W. PROBYN. 3s. 6d.
"Japanese" Library, Cassell's. Consisting of 12 Popular Works bound in Japanese style. Covers in water-colour pictures. 1s. 3d. each, net. *⁎⁎* *List post free on application.*
Joy and Health. By MARTELLIUS. Illustrated, cloth, 3s. 6d. (*Edition de Luxe,* 7s. 6d.)
Kennel Guide, Practical. By Dr. GORDON STABLES. Illustrated. *Cheap Edition,* 1s.
King's Hussar, A. Memoirs of a Troop Sergeant-Major of the 14th (King's) Hussars. Edited by HERBERT COMPTON. 6s.
"La Bella," and Others. By EGERTON CASTLE. Buckram, 6s.
Ladies' Physician, The. By a London Physician. 6s.
Lady Biddy Fane, The Admirable. By FRANK BARRETT. *New Edition.* With 12 Full-page Illustrations. 6s.
Lady's Dressing Room, The. Translated by LADY COLIN CAMPBELL. 3s. 6d.
Lake Dwellings of Europe. By ROBERT MUNRO, M.D., M.A. Cloth, 31s. 6d.
Leona. By Mrs. MOLESWORTH. 6s.
Letters, The Highway of; and its Echoes of Famous Footsteps. By THOMAS ARCHER. Illustrated, 10s. 6d.
Letts's Diaries and other Time-saving Publications are now published exclusively by CASSELL & COMPANY. (*A List sent post free on application.*)
Lisbeth. A Novel. By LESLIE KEITH. Three Vols. 31s. 6d.
List, ye Landsmen! A Romance of Incident. By W. CLARK RUSSELL. *Cheap Edition,* One Vol., 6s.
Little Minister, The. By J. M. BARRIE. *Illustrated Edition,* 6s.
Little Squire, The. A Story of Three. By Mrs. HENRY DE LA PASTURE. 3s. 6d.
Locomotive Engine, The Biography of a. By HENRY FRITH. 3s. 6d.
Loftus, Lord Augustus, P.C., G.C.B., The Diplomatic Reminiscences of. First Series. With Portrait. Two Vols. 32s. Second Series. Two Vols. 32s.
London, Greater. By EDWARD WALFORD. Two Vols. With about 400 Illustrations. 9s. each. *Library Edition.* Two Vols. £1 the set.
London, Old and New. By WALTER THORNBURY and EDWARD WALFORD. Six Vols., with about 1,200 Illustrations. Cloth, 9s. each. *Library Edition,* £3.
Lost on Du Corrig; or, 'Twixt Earth and Ocean. By STANDISH O'GRADY. With 8 Full-page Illustrations. 5s.
Man in Black, The. By STANLEY WEYMAN. With 12 full-page Illustrations. 3s. 6d.
Medical Handbook of Life Assurance. By JAMES EDWARD POLLOCK, M.D., F.R.C.P., and JAMES CHISHOLM, Fellow of the Institute of Actuaries. London. 7s. 6d.
Medicine Lady, The. By L. T. MEADE. *Cheap Edition,* One Vol., 6s.
Medicine, Manuals for Students of. (*A List forwarded post free on application.*)

Selections from Cassell & Company's Publications.

Modern Europe, A History of. By C. A. FYFFE, M.A. Complete in Three Vols., with full-page Illustrations. 7s. 6d. each.
Mount Desolation. An Australian Romance. By W. CARLTON DAWE. 3s. 6d.
Musical and Dramatic Copyright, The Law of. By EDWARD CUTLER, THOMAS EUSTACE SMITH, and FREDERIC E. WEATHERLY. 3s. 6d.
Music, Illustrated History of. By EMIL NAUMANN. Edited by the Rev. Sir F. A. GORE OUSELEY, Bart. Illustrated. Two Vols. 31s. 6d.
Napier, The Life and Letters of the Rt. Hon. Sir Joseph, Bart., LL.D., D.C.L., M.R.I.A. By ALEX. C. EWALD, F.S.A. *New and Revised Edition,* 7s. 6d.
National Library, Cassell's. In Volumes. Paper covers, 3d.; cloth, 6d. (*A Complete List of the Volumes post free on application.*)
Natural History, Cassell's Concise. By E. PERCEVAL WRIGHT, M.A., M.D., F.L.S. With several Hundred Illustrations. 7s. 6d.; also kept half-bound.
Natural History, Cassell's New. Edited by P. MARTIN DUNCAN, M.B., F.R.S., F.G.S. Complete in Six Vols. With about 2,000 Illustrations. Cloth, 9s. each.
Nature's Wonder Workers. By KATE R. LOVELL. Illustrated. 3s. 6d.
Nelson, The Life of. By ROBERT SOUTHEY. Illustrated with Eight Plates. 3s. 6d.
New England Boyhood, A. By EDWARD E. HALE. 3s. 6d.
Nursing for the Home and for the Hospital, A Handbook of. By CATHERINE J. WOOD. *Cheap Edition,* 1s. 6d.; cloth, 2s.
Nursing of Sick Children, A Handbook for the. By CATHERINE J. WOOD. 2s. 6d.
O'Driscoll's Weird, and Other Stories. By A. WERNER. Cloth, 5s.
Odyssey, The Modern. By WYNDHAM F. TUFNELL. Illustrated. 10s. 6d.
Ohio, The New. A Story of East and West. By EDWARD EVERETT HALE. 6s.
Old Dorset. Chapters in the History of the County. By H. J. MOULE, M.A. 10s. 6d.
Our Own Country. Six Vols. With 1,200 Illustrations. Cloth, 7s. 6d. each.
Out of the Jaws of Death. By FRANK BARRETT. *Cheap Edition,* One Vol., 6s.
Painting, The English School of. By ERNEST CHESNEAU. *Cheap Edition,* 3s. 6d.
Paris, Old and New. A Narrative of its History, its People, and its Places. By H. SUTHERLAND EDWARDS. Profusely Illustrated. Vol. I., 9s., or gilt edges, 10s. 6d.
Peoples of the World, The. By Dr. ROBERT BROWN. Complete in Six Vols. With Illustrations. 7s. 6d. each.
Perfect Gentleman, The. By the Rev. A. SMYTHE-PALMER, D.D. 3s. 6d.
Photography for Amateurs. By T. C. HEPWORTH. *Enlarged and Revised Edition.* Illustrated, 1s.; or cloth, 1s. 6d.
Phrase and Fable, Dictionary of. By the Rev. Dr. BREWER. *Cheap Edition, Enlarged,* cloth, 3s. 6d.; or with leather back, 4s. 6d.
Physiology for Students, Elementary. By ALFRED T. SCHOFIELD, M.D., M.R.C.S. With Two Coloured Plates and numerous Illustrations. 7s. 6d.
Picturesque America. Complete in Four Vols., with 48 Exquisite Steel Plates, and about 800 Original Wood Engravings. £2 2s. each. Vol. I. of the *Popular Edition* now ready, price 18s.
Picturesque Canada. With about 600 Original Illustrations. Two Vols. £6 6s. the set.
Picturesque Europe. Complete in Five Vols. Each containing 13 Exquisite Steel Plates, from Original Drawings, and nearly 200 Original Illustrations. £21; half-morocco, £31 10s.; morocco gilt, £52 10s. *Popular Edition.* In Five Vols. 18s. each.
Picturesque Mediterranean, The. With a Series of Magnificent Illustrations from Original Designs by leading Artists of the day. Two Vols. Cloth, £2 2s. each.
Pigeon Keeper, The Practical. By LEWIS WRIGHT. Illustrated. 3s. 6d.
Pigeons, The Book of. By ROBERT FULTON. Edited by LEWIS WRIGHT. With 50 Coloured Plates and numerous Wood Engravings. 31s. 6d.; half-morocco, £2 2s.
Pity and of Death, The Book of. By PIERRE LOTI, Member of the French Academy. Translated by T. P. O'CONNOR, M.P. Antique paper, cloth gilt, 5s.
Planet, The Story of Our. By the Rev. Prof. BONNEY, F.R.S., &c. With Coloured Plates and Maps and about 100 Illustrations. 31s. 6d.
Playthings and Parodies. Short Stories, Sketches, &c., by BARRY PAIN. 5s.
Poetry, The Nature and Elements of. By E. C. STEDMAN. 6s.
Poets, Cassell's Miniature Library of the. Price 1s. each Vol.
Polytechnic Series, The. Practical Illustrated Manuals specially prepared for Students of the Polytechnic Institute, and suitable for the Use of all Students. (*A List will be sent on application.*)
Portrait Gallery, The Cabinet. *Series I. to IV.,* each containing 36 Cabinet Photographs of Eminent Men and Women of the day. With Biographical Sketches. 15s. each.
Poultry Keeper, The Practical. By LEWIS WRIGHT. Illustrated. 3s. 6d.
Poultry, The Book of. By LEWIS WRIGHT. *Popular Edition.* Illustrated. 10s. 6d.

Selections from Cassell & Company's Publications.

Poultry, The Illustrated Book of. By LEWIS WRIGHT. With Fifty Exquisite Coloured Plates, and numerous Wood Engravings. *Revised Edition.* Cloth, 31s. 6d.
Prison Princess, A. A Romance of Millbank Penitentiary. By MAJOR ARTHUR GRIFFITHS. 6s.
Q's Works, Uniform Edition of. 5s. each.
   Dead Man's Rock.
   The Splendid Spur.
   The Blue Pavilions.
   The Astonishing History of Troy Town.
   "I Saw Three Ships," and other Winter's Tales.
   Noughts and Crosses.
Queen Summer; or, The Tourney of the Lily and the Rose. Penned and Portrayed by WALTER CRANE. With 40 pages in Colours. 6s.
Queen Victoria, The Life and Times of. By ROBERT WILSON. Complete in 2 Vols. With numerous Illustrations. 9s. each.
Quickening of Caliban, The. A Modern Story of Evolution. By J. COMPTON RICKETT. 5s.
Rabbit-Keeper, The Practical. By CUNICULUS. Illustrated. 3s. 6d.
Raffles Haw, The Doings of. By A. CONAN DOYLE. *New Edition.* 5s.
Railways, British. Their Passenger Services, Rolling Stock, Locomotives, Gradients, and Express Speeds. By J. PEARSON PATTINSON. With numerous Plates. 12s. 6d.
Railways, National. An Argument for State Purchase. By JAMES HOLE. 4s. net.
Railways, Our. Their Development, Enterprise, Incident, and Romance. By JOHN PENDLETON. Illustrated. 2 Vols., demy 8vo. 24s.
Railway Guides, Official Illustrated. With Illustrations on nearly every page. Maps, &c. Paper covers, 1s.; cloth, 2s.
   Great Eastern Railway.
   Great Northern Railway.
   Great Western Railway.
   London, Brighton, and South Coast Railway.
   London and North Western Railway.
   London and South Western Railway.
   Midland Railway.
   South Eastern Railway.
Railway Library, Cassell's. Crown 8vo, boards, 2s. each.
   Metzerott, Shoemaker. By Katharine P. Woods.
   David Todd. By David Maclure.
   Commodore Junk. By G. Manville Fenn.
   St. Cuthbert's Tower. By Florence Warden.
   The Man with a Thumb. By W. C. Hudson (Barclay North).
   By Right Not Law. By R. Sherard.
   Within Sound of the Weir. By Thomas St. E. Hake.
   Under a Strange Mask. By Frank Barrett.
   The Coombsberrow Mystery. By J. Colwall.
   A Queer Race. By W. Westall.
   Captain Trafalgar. By Westall and Laurie.
   The Phantom City. By W. Westall.
   Jack Gordon, Knight Errant. By W. C. Hudson (Barclay North).
   The Diamond Button: Whose Was It? By W. C. Hudson (Barclay North).
   Another's Crime. By Julian Hawthorne.
   The Yoke of the Thorah. By Sidney Luska.
   Who is John Noman? By C. Henry Beckett.
   The Tragedy of Brinkwater. By Martha L. Moodey.
   An American Penman. By Julian Hawthorne.
   Section 558; or, The Fatal Letter. By Julian Hawthorne.
   The Brown Stone Boy. By W. H. Bishop.
   A Tragic Mystery. By Julian Hawthorne.
   The Great Bank Robbery. By Julian Hawthorne.
Rivers of Great Britain: Descriptive, Historical, Pictorial.
   The Royal River: The Thames from Source to Sea. *Popular Edition,* 16s.
   Rivers of the East Coast. With highly-finished Engravings. *Popular Edition,* 16s.
Robinson Crusoe. *Cassell's New Fine-Art Edition.* With upwards of 100 Original Illustrations. 7s. 6d.
Romance, The World of. Illustrated. One Vol., cloth, 9s.
Ronner, Henriette, The Painter of Cat Life and Cat Character. By M. H. SPIELMANN. Containing a Series of beautiful Phototype Illustrations. *Popular Edition,* 4to, 12s.
Rovings of a Restless Boy, The. By KATHARINE B. FOOT. Illustrated. 5s.
Russo-Turkish War, Cassell's History of. With about 500 Illustrations. Two Vols., 9s. each; library binding, One Vol., 15s.
Salisbury Parliament, A Diary of the. By H. W. LUCY. Illustrated by HARRY FURNISS. Cloth, 21s.
Saturday Journal, Cassell's. Illustrated throughout. Yearly Vol., 7s. 6d.
Scarabæus. The Story of an African Beetle. By THE MARQUISE CLARA LANZA and JAMES CLARENCE HARVEY. *Cheap Edition,* 3s. 6d.
Science for All. Edited by Dr. ROBERT BROWN, M.A., F.L.S., &c. *Revised Edition.* With 1,500 Illustrations. Five Vols. 9s. each.
Shadow of a Song, The. A Novel. By CECIL HARLEY. 5s.
Shaftesbury, The Seventh Earl of, K.G., The Life and Work of. By EDWIN HODDER. Illustrated. *Cheap Edition,* 3s. 6d.
Shakespeare, Cassell's Quarto Edition. Edited by CHARLES and MARY COWDEN CLARKE, and containing about 600 Illustrations by H. C. SELOUS. Complete in Three Vols., cloth gilt, £3 3s.—Also published in Three separate Vols., in cloth, viz.:—The COMEDIES, 21s.; The HISTORICAL PLAYS, 18s. 6d.; The TRAGEDIES, 25s.

Selections from Cassell & Company's Publications.

Shakespeare, The Plays of. Edited by Prof. HENRY MORLEY. Complete in Thirteen Vols. Cloth, in box, 21s.; half-morocco, cloth sides, 42s.
Shakspere, The International. *Edition de luxe.*
    King Henry VIII. By Sir JAMES LINTON, P.R.I. (*Price on application.*
    Othello. Illustrated by FRANK DICKSEE, R.A. £3 10s.
    King Henry IV. Illustrated by Herr EDUARD GRÜTZNER. £3 10s.
    As You Like It. Illustrated by the late Mons. ÉMILE BAYARD. £3 10s.
Shakspere, The Leopold. With 400 Illustrations, and an Introduction by F. J. FURNIVALL. *Cheap Edition*, 3s. 6d. Cloth gilt, gilt edges, 5s.; roxburgh, 7s. 6d.
Shakspere, The Royal. With Exquisite Steel Plates and Wood Engravings. Three Vols. 15s. each.
Sketches, The Art of Making and Using. From the French of G. FRAIPONT. By CLARA BELL. With Fifty Illustrations. 2s. 6d.
Smuggling Days and Smuggling Ways; or, The Story of a Lost Art. By Commander the Hon. HENRY N. SHORE, R.N. Illustrated. Cloth, 7s. 6d.
Snare of the Fowler, The. By Mrs. ALEXANDER. *Cheap Edition in one Vol.*, 6s.
Social England. A Record of the Progress of the People. By various writers. Edited by H. D. TRAILL, D.C.L. Vols. I. and II., 15s. each.
Social Welfare, Subjects of. By LORD PLAYFAIR, K.C.B., &c. 7s. 6d.
Sports and Pastimes, Cassell's Complete Book of. *Cheap Edition*, 3s. 6d.
Squire, The. By MRS. PARR. *Cheap Edition in one Vol.*, 6s.
Standishs of High Acre, The. A Novel. By GILBERT SHELDON. Two Vols. 21s.
Star-Land. By Sir ROBERT STAWELL BALL, LL.D., &c. Illustrated. 6s.
Statesmen, Past and Future. 6s.
Storehouse of General Information, Cassell's. Illustrated. In Vols. 5s. each.
Story of Francis Cludde, The. A Novel. By STANLEY J. WEYMAN. 6s.
Successful Life, The. By AN ELDER BROTHER. 3s. 6d.
Sun, The Story of the. By Sir ROBERT STAWELL BALL, LL.D., F.R.S., F.R.A.S. With Eight Coloured Plates and other Illustrations. 21s.
Sunshine Series, Cassell's. Monthly Vols. 1s. each.
    The Temptation of Dulce Carruthers. By C. E. C. WEIGALL.
    Lady Lorrimer's Scheme and The Story of a Glamour. By EDITH E. CUTHELL.
    Womanlike. By FLORENCE M. KING.
    On Stronger Wings. By EDITH LISTER.
    You'l Love Me Yet. By FRANCES HAWELL; and That Little Woman. By IDA LEMON.
    A Man of the Name of John. By FLORENCE M. KING.
    Stephen Wray's Wife; or, Not all in Vain. By LAMBERT SHIELDS.
    For Erica's Sake. By MARY E SHEPHERD
    Comrades Once and A Treacherous Calm. By THOMAS KEYWORTH.
    A Step in the Dark. By KATE EYRE.
Sybil Knox; or, Home Again. A Story of To-day. By EDWARD E. HALE, Author of "East and West," &c. *Cheap Edition*, 6s.
Tenting on the Plains. By E. B. CUSTER. Illustrated. 5s.
Thackeray in America, With. By EYRE CROWE, A.R.A. Illustrated. 10s. 6d.
The "Belle Sauvage" Library. Cloth, 2s. each.

Shirley.	Adventures of Mr. Ledbury.	Old Mortality.
Coningsby.	Ivanhoe.	The Hour and the Man.
Mary Barton.	Oliver Twist.	Washington Irving's Sketch-Book.
The Antiquary.	Selections from Hood's Works.	Last Days of Palmyra.
Nicholas Nickleby. Two Vols.	Longfellow's Prose Works.	Tales of the Borders.
Jane Eyre.	Sense and Sensibility.	Pride and Prejudice.
Wuthering Heights.	Lytton's Plays.	Last of the Mohicans.
The Prairie.	Tales, Poems, and Sketches (Bret Harte).	Heart of Midlothian.
Dombey and Son. Two Vols.	The Prince of the House of David.	Last Days of Pompeii.
Night and Morning.		Yellowplush Papers.
Kenilworth.	Sheridan's Plays.	Handy Andy.
The Ingoldsby Legends.	Uncle Tom's Cabin.	Selected Plays.
Tower of London.	Deerslayer.	American Humour.
The Pioneers.	Eugene Aram.	Sketches by Boz.
Charles O'Malley.	Jack Hinton, the Guardsman.	Macaulay's Lays and Selected Essays.
Barnaby Rudge.	Rome and the Early Christians.	Harry Lorrequer.
Cakes and Ale.		Old Curiosity Shop.
The King's Own.	The Trials of Margaret Lyndsay.	Rienzi.
People I have Met.	Edgar Allan Poe. Prose and Poetry, Selections from.	The Talisman.
The Pathfinder.		Pickwick. Two Vols.
Evelina.		Scarlet Letter.
Scott's Poems.		Martin Chuzzlewit. Two Vols.
Last of the Barons.		

The Short Story Library. List of Vols. on application.
Things I have Seen and People I have Known. By G. A. SALA. 2 Vols. 21s.
Tiny Luttrell. By E. W. HORNUNG. Cloth. *Popular Edition.* 6s.

Selections from Cassell & Company's Publications.

"**Treasure Island" Series, The.** *Cheap Illustrated Edition.* Cloth, 3s. 6d. each.
"**Kidnapped."** By ROBERT LOUIS STEVENSON.
Treasure Island. By ROBERT LOUIS STEVENSON.
The Master of Ballantrae. By ROBERT LOUIS STEVENSON
The Black Arrow: A Tale of the Two Roses. By ROBERT LOUIS STEVENSON.
King Solomon's Mines. By H. RIDER HAGGARD.
Treatment, The Year-Book of, for 1894. A Critical Review for Practitioners of Medicine and Surgery. Tenth Year of Issue. 7s. 6d.
Tree Painting in Water Colours. By W. H. J. BOOT. With Eighteen Coloured Plates, and valuable instructions by the Artist. 5s.
Trees, Familiar. By Prof. G. S. BOULGER, F.L.S., F.G.S. Two Series. With Forty full-page Coloured Plates by W. H. J. BOOT. 12s. 6d. each.
"**Unicode":** The Universal Telegraphic Phrase Book. Pocket or Desk Edition. 2s. 6d. each.
United States, Cassell's History of the. By EDMUND OLLIER. With 600 Illustrations. Three Vols. 9s. each.
Universal History, Cassell's Illustrated. With nearly ONE THOUSAND ILLUSTRATIONS. Vol. I. Early and Greek History.—Vol. II. The Roman Period.—Vol. III. The Middle Ages—Vol. IV. Modern History. 9s. each.
Vaccination Vindicated. By JOHN C. MCVAIL, M.D., D.P.H. Camb. 5s.
Verses Grave and Gay. By ELLEN THORNEYCROFT FOWLER. 3s. 6d.
Vicar of Wakefield and other Works, by OLIVER GOLDSMITH. Illustrated. 3s. 6d.; cloth, gilt edges, 5s.
Vision of Saints, A. By LEWIS MORRIS. *Édition de luxe.* With 20 Full-page Illustrations. Crown 4to, extra cloth, gilt edges. 21s.
Water-Colour Painting, A Course of. With Twenty-four Coloured Plates by R. P. LEITCH, and full Instructions to the Pupil. 5s.
Wedlock, Lawful: or, How Shall I Make Sure of a Legal Marriage? By Two BARRISTERS. 1s.
Wild Birds, Familiar. By W. SWAYSLAND. Four Series. With 40 Coloured Plates in each. 12s. 6d. each.
Wild Flowers, Familiar. By F. E. HULME, F.L.S., F.S.A. Five Series. With 40 Coloured Plates in each. 12s. 6d. each.
Won at the Last Hole. A Golfing Romance. By M. A. STOBART. Illustrated. 1s. 6d.
Wood, The Life of the Rev. J. G. By his Son, the Rev. THEODORE WOOD. With Portrait. Extra crown 8vo, cloth. *Cheap Edition.* 3s. 6d.
Work. The Illustrated Journal for Mechanics. *New and Enlarged Series.* Vols. V. and VI., 4s. each.
World of Wit and Humour, The. With 400 Illustrations. Cloth, 7s. 6d.
World of Wonders, The. With 400 Illustrations. Two Vols. 7s. 6d. each.
Wrecker, The. By R. L. STEVENSON and LLOYD OSBOURNE. Illustrated. 6s.
Yule Tide. CASSELL'S CHRISTMAS ANNUAL. 1s.
Zero the Slaver. A Romance of Equatorial Africa. By LAWRENCE FLETCHER. 3s. 6d.

ILLUSTRATED MAGAZINES.

The Quiver, for *Sunday and General Reading.* Monthly, 6d.
Cassell's Family Magazine. Monthly, 7d.
"Little Folks" Magazine. Monthly, 6d.
The Magazine of Art. With Three Plates. Monthly, 1s. 4d.
Chums. The Illustrated Paper for Boys. Weekly, 1d.; Monthly, 6d.
Cassell's Saturday Journal. Weekly, 1d.; Monthly, 6d.
Work. Illustrated Journal for Mechanics. Weekly, 1d.; Monthly, 6d.
Cottage Gardening. Illustrated. Weekly, ½d.; Monthly, 4d.
*** *Full particulars of* CASSELL & COMPANY'S **Monthly Serial Publications** *will be found in* CASSELL & COMPANY'S COMPLETE CATALOGUE.

Catalogues of CASSELL & COMPANY'S PUBLICATIONS, which may be had at all Booksellers', or will be sent post free on application to the Publishers:—
CASSELL'S COMPLETE CATALOGUE, containing particulars of upwards of One Thousand Volumes.
CASSELL'S CLASSIFIED CATALOGUE, in which their Works are arranged according to price, from *Threepence to Fifty Guineas.*
CASSELL'S EDUCATIONAL CATALOGUE, containing particulars of CASSELL & COMPANY'S Educational Works and Students' Manuals.

CASSELL & COMPANY, LIMITED, *Ludgate Hill, London.*

Selections from Cassell & Company's Publications.

Bibles and Religious Works.

Bible Biographies. Illustrated. 2s. 6d. each.
　The Story of Joseph. Its Lessons for To-Day. By the Rev. GEORGE BAINTON.
　The Story of Moses and Joshua. By the Rev. J. TELFORD.
　The Story of Judges. By the Rev. J. WYCLIFFE GEDGE.
　The Story of Samuel and Saul. By the Rev. D. C. TOVEY.
　The Story of David. By the Rev. J. WILD.

　　The Story of Jesus. In Verse. By J. R. MACDUFF, D.D.

Bible, Cassell's Illustrated Family. With 900 Illustrations. Leather, gilt edges, £2 10s.; full morocco, £3 10s.

Bible, The, and the Holy Land, New Light on. By B. T. A. EVETTS, M.A. Illustrated. Cloth, 21s.

Bible Educator, The. Edited by E. H. PLUMPTRE, D.D. With Illustrations, Maps, &c. Four Vols., cloth, 6s. each.

Bible Student in the British Museum, The. By the Rev. J. G. KITCHIN, M.A. *Entirely New and Revised Edition*, 1s. 4d.

Biblewomen and Nurses. Yearly Vol., 3s.

Bunyan's Pilgrim's Progress (Cassell's Illustrated). 4to. *Cheap Edition*, 3s. 6d.

Child's Bible, The. With 200 Illustrations. Demy 4to, 830 pp. 150*th Thousand*. *Cheap Edition*, 7s. 6d. *Superior Edition*, with 6 Coloured Plates, gilt edges, 10s. 6d.

Child's Life of Christ, The. Complete in One Handsome Volume, with about 200 Original Illustrations. *Cheap Edition*, cloth, 7s. 6d.; or with 6 Coloured Plates, cloth, gilt edges, 10s. 6d. Demy 4to, gilt edges, 21s.

"Come, ye Children." By the Rev. BENJAMIN WAUGH. Illustrated. 5s.

Commentary, The New Testament, for English Readers. Edited by the Rt. Rev. C. J. ELLICOTT, D.D., Lord Bishop of Gloucester and Bristol. In Three Vols. 21s. each.
　　Vol. I.—The Four Gospels.
　　Vol. II.—The Acts, Romans, Corinthians, Galatians.
　　Vol III.—The remaining Books of the New Testament.

Commentary, The Old Testament, for English Readers. Edited by the Rt. Rev. C. J. ELLICOTT, D.D., Lord Bishop of Gloucester and Bristol. Complete in 5 Vols. 21s. each.
　Vol. I.—Genesis to Numbers.　　　　|　Vol. III.—Kings I. to Esther.
　Vol. II.—Deuteronomy to Samuel II.　|　Vol. IV.—Job to Isaiah.
　　　　Vol. V.—Jeremiah to Malachi.

Commentary, The New Testament. Edited by Bishop ELLICOTT. Handy Volume Edition. Suitable for School and General Use.

St. Matthew. 3s. 6d.	Romans. 2s. 6d.	Titus, Philemon, Hebrews, and James. 3s.
St. Mark. 3s.	Corinthians I. and II. 3s.	
St. Luke. 3s. 6d.	Galatians, Ephesians, and Philippians. 3s.	Peter, Jude, and John. 3s.
St. John. 3s. 6d.		The Revelation. 3s.
The Acts of the Apostles. 3s 6d	Colossians, Thessalonians, and Timothy. 3s	An Introduction to the New Testament. 2s. 6d.

Commentary, The Old Testament. Edited by Bishop ELLICOTT. Handy Volume Edition. Suitable for School and General Use.

Genesis. 3s. 6d.	Leviticus. 3s.	Deuteronomy. 2s. 6d.
Exodus. 3s.	Numbers. 2s. 6d.	

Dictionary of Religion, The. An Encyclopædia of Christian and other Religious Doctrines, Denominations, Sects, Heresies, Ecclesiastical Terms, History, Biography, &c. &c. By the Rev. WILLIAM BENHAM, B.D. *Cheap Edition*, 10s. 6d.

Doré Bible. With 230 Illustrations by GUSTAVE DORÉ. *Original Edition*. Two Vols., best morocco, gilt edges, £15. *Popular Edition*. With Full-page Illustrations. In One Vol. 15s. Also in leather binding. (*Price on application*.)

Early Days of Christianity, The. By the Ven. Archdeacon FARRAR, D.D., F.R.S.
　LIBRARY EDITION. Two Vols., 24s.; morocco, £2 2s.
　POPULAR EDITION. Complete in One Vol., cloth, 6s.; cloth, gilt edges, 7s. 6d.; Persian morocco, 10s. 6d.; tree-calf, 15s.

Family Prayer-Book, The. Edited by the Rev. Canon GARBETT, M.A., and the Rev. S. MARTIN. Extra crown 4to, morocco, 18s.

Gleanings after Harvest. Studies and Sketches. By the Rev. JOHN R. VERNON, M.A. Illustrated. 6s.

"Graven in the Rock;" or, the Historical Accuracy of the Bible confirmed by reference to the Assyrian and Egyptian Sculptures in the British Museum and elsewhere. By the Rev. Dr. SAMUEL KINNS, F.R.A.S., &c. &c. Illustrated. 12s. 6d.

Selections from Cassell & Company's Publications.

"Heart Chords." A Series of Works by Eminent Divines. Bound in cloth, red edges, 1s. each.

My Father. By the Right Rev. Ashton Oxenden, late Bishop of Montreal.
My Bible. By the Rt. Rev. W. Boyd Carpenter, Bishop of Ripon.
My Work for God. By the Right Rev. Bishop Cotterill.
My Object in Life. By the Ven. Archdeacon Farrar, D.D.
My Aspirations. By the Rev. G. Matheson, D.D.
My Emotional Life. By Preb. Chadwick, D.D.
My Body. By the Rev. Prof. W. G. Blaikie, D.D.
My Soul. By the Rev. P. B. Power, M.A.
My Growth in Divine Life. By the Rev. Prebendary Reynolds, M.A.
My Hereafter. By the Very Rev. Dean Bickersteth.
My Walk with God. By the Very Rev. Dean Montgomery.
My Aids to the Divine Life. By the Very Rev. Dean Boyle.
My Sources of Strength. By the Rev. E. E. Jenkins, M.A.

Helps to Belief. A Series of Helpful Manuals on the Religious Difficulties of the Day. Edited by the Rev. TEIGNMOUTH SHORE, M.A., Canon of Worcester, and Chaplain-in-Ordinary to the Queen. Cloth, 1s. each.

CREATION By the late Lord Bishop of Carlisle.
MIRACLES. By the Rev. Brownlow Maitland, M.A.
PRAYER. By the Rev. T. Teignmouth Shore, M.A.
THE MORALITY OF THE OLD TESTAMENT. By the Rev. Newman Smyth, D.D.
THE DIVINITY OF OUR LORD. By the Lord Bishop of Derry.

THE ATONEMENT. By William Connor Magee, D.D., Late Archbishop of York.

Hid Treasure. By RICHARD HARRIS HILL. 1s.
Holy Land and the Bible, The. A Book of Scripture Illustrations gathered in Palestine. By the Rev. CUNNINGHAM GEIKIE, D.D., LL.D. (Edin.). With Map. Two Vols. 24s. *Illustrated Edition.* One Vol. 21s.
Life of Christ, The. By the Ven. Archdeacon FARRAR, D.D., F.R.S., Chaplain-in-Ordinary to the Queen.
  POPULAR EDITION, New and Revised Edition, extra crown 8vo, cloth gilt, 7s. 6d.
  CHEAP ILLUSTRATED EDITION. Large 4to, cloth, 7s. 6d. Cloth, full gilt, gilt edges, 10s. 6d.
  LIBRARY EDITION. Two Vols. Cloth, 24s.; morocco, 42s.
Marriage Ring, The. By WILLIAM LANDELS, D.D. Bound in white leatherette. *New and Cheaper Edition*, 3s. 6d.
Morning and Evening Prayers for Workhouses and other Institutions. Selected by LOUISA TWINING. 2s.
Moses and Geology; or, the Harmony of the Bible with Science. By the Rev. SAMUEL KINNS, Ph.D., F.R.A.S. Illustrated. Demy 8vo, 8s. 6d.
My Comfort in Sorrow. By HUGH MACMILLAN, D.D., LL.D., &c. 1s.
New Light on the Bible and the Holy Land. By BASIL T. A. EVETTS, M.A. Illustrated. Cloth, 21s.
Old and New Testaments, Plain Introductions to the Books of the. Containing Contributions by many Eminent Divines. In Two Vols., 3s. 6d. each.
Plain Introductions to the Books of the Old Testament. 336 pages. Edited by the Right Rev. C. J. ELLICOTT, D.D., Lord Bishop of Gloucester and Bristol. 3s. 6d.
Plain Introductions to the Books of the New Testament. 304 pages. Edited by the Right Rev. C. J. ELLICOTT, D.D., Lord Bishop of Gloucester and Bristol. 3s. 6d.
Protestantism, The History of. By the Rev. J. A. WYLIE, LL.D. Containing upwards of 600 Original Illustrations. Three Vols., 27s.; *Library Edition*, 30s.
"Quiver" Yearly Volume, The. With about 600 Original Illustrations and Coloured Frontispiece. 7s. 6d. Also Monthly, 6d.
St. George for England; and other Sermons preached to Children. *Fifth Edition.* By the Rev. T. TEIGNMOUTH SHORE, M.A., Canon of Worcester. 5s.
St. Paul, The Life and Work of. By the Ven. Archdeacon FARRAR, D.D., F.R.S., Chaplain-in-Ordinary to the Queen.
  LIBRARY EDITION. Two Vols., cloth, 24s.; calf, 42s.
  ILLUSTRATED EDITION, One Vol., £1 1s.; morocco, £2 2s.
  POPULAR EDITION. One Vol., 8vo, cloth, 6s.; cloth, gilt edges, 7s. 6d.; Persian morocco, 10s. 6d.; tree-calf, 15s.
Shall We Know One Another in Heaven? By the Rt. Rev. J. C. RYLE, D.D., Bishop of Liverpool. *New and Enlarged Edition.* Paper Covers, 6d.
Shortened Church Services and Hymns, suitable for use at Children's Services. Compiled by the Rev. T. TEIGNMOUTH SHORE, M.A., Canon of Worcester. *Enlarged Edition.* 1s.
Signa Christi: Evidences of Christianity set forth in the Person and Work of Christ. By the Rev. JAMES AITCHISON. 5s.
Sunday-School Teacher's Bible Manual, The. By the Rev. ROBERT HUNTER, LL.D. Illustrated. 7s. 6d.
"Sunday:" Its Origin, History, and Present Obligation. By the Ven. Archdeacon HESSEY, D.C.L. *Fifth Edition*, 7s. 6d.
Twilight of Life, The: Words of Counsel and Comfort for the Aged. By JOHN ELLERTON, M.A. 1s. 6d.

Selections from Cassell & Company's Publications.

𝕰ducational 𝖂orks and 𝕾tudents' 𝕸anuals.

Agricultural Text-Books, Cassell's. (The "Downton" Series.) Fully Illustrated. Edited by JOHN WRIGHTSON, Professor of Agriculture. **Soils and Manures.** By J. M. H. MUNRO, D.Sc (London), F.I.C., F.C.S. 2s. 6d. **Farm Crops.** By Professor Wrightson, 2s. 6d. **Live Stock.** By Professor Wrightson, 2s. 6d.

Alphabet, Cassell's Pictorial. Mounted on Linen, with rollers. 3s. 6d.

Arithmetic:—Howard's Art of Reckoning. By C. F. HOWARD. Paper, 1s.; cloth, 2s. *Enlarged Edition,* 5s.

Arithmetics, The Modern School. By GEORGE RICKS, B.Sc. Lond. With Test Cards. (*List on application.*)

Atlas, Cassell's Popular. Containing 24 Coloured Maps. 2s. 6d.

Book-Keeping. By THEODORE JONES. FOR SCHOOLS, 2s.; or cloth, 3s. FOR THE MILLION, 2s.; or cloth, 3s. Books for Jones's System, Ruled Sets of, 2s.

British Empire Map of the World. New Map for Schools and Institutes. By G. R. PARKIN and J. G. BARTHOLOMEW, F.R.G.S. Mounted on cloth, varnished, and with Rollers 25s

Chemistry, The Public School. By J. H. ANDERSON, M.A. 2s. 6d.

Cookery for Schools. By LIZZIE HERITAGE. 6d.

Dulce Domum. Rhymes and Songs for Children. Edited by JOHN FARMER, Editor of "Gaudeamus," &c. Old Notation and Words, 5s N.B.—The Words of the Songs in "Dulce Domum" (with the Airs both in Tonic Sol-Fa and Old Notation) can be had in Two Parts, 6d. each.

English Literature, A First Sketch of, from the Earliest Period to the Present Time. By Prof. HENRY MORLEY. 7s. 6d

Euclid, Cassell's. Edited by Prof. WALLACE, M.A. 1s.

Euclid, The First Four Books of. *New Edition.* In paper, 6d.; cloth, 9d.

French, Cassell's Lessons in. *New and Revised Edition.* Parts I. and II., each, 2s. 6d.; complete, 4s. 6d. Key, 1s. 6d.

French-English and English-French Dictionary. *Entirely New and Enlarged Edition.* 1,150 pages, 8vo, cloth, 3s. 6d.

French Reader, Cassell's Public School. By GUILLAUME S. CONRAD. 2s. 6d.

Galbraith and Haughton's Scientific Manuals.
Plane Trigonometry. 2s. 6d. Euclid. Books I., II., III. 2s. 6d Books IV., V., VI. 2s. 6d. Mathematical Tables. 3s. 6d. Mechanics. 3s. 6d. Natural Philosophy. 3s. 6d Optics. 2s. 6d. Hydrostatics. 3s. 6d. Steam Engine. 3s. 6d. Algebra. Part I, cloth, 2s. 6d. Complete, 7s. 6d. Tides and Tidal Currents, with Tidal Cards, 3s.

Gaudeamus. Songs for Colleges and Schools. Edited by JOHN FARMER. 5s. Words only, paper, 6d.; cloth, 9d.

Geometry, First Elements of Experimental. By PAUL BERT. Illustrated. 1s. 6d.

Geometry, Practical Solid. By Major ROSS, R.E. 2s.

German Dictionary, Cassell's New. German-English, English-German. *Cheap Edition,* cloth, 3s. 6d.; half-roan, 4s. 6d.

German Reading, First Lessons in. By A. JÄGST. Illustrated. 1s.

Hand-and-Eye Training. By G. RICKS, B.Sc. Two Vols., with 16 Coloured Plates in each Vol. Crown 4to, 6s each.

"Hand-and-Eye Training" Cards for Class Work. Five sets in case. 1s. each.

Historical Cartoons, Cassell's Coloured. Size 45 in. × 35 in. 2s. each. Mounted on canvas and varnished, with rollers, 5s. each. (Descriptive pamphlet, 16 pp., 1d.)

Historical Course for Schools, Cassell's. Illustrated throughout. I.—Stories from English History, 1s. II.—The Simple Outline of English History, 1s. 3d. III.—The Class History of England, 2s. 6d.

Italian Lessons, with Exercises, Cassell's. In One Vol. 3s. 6d.

Latin Dictionary, Cassell's New. (Latin-English and English-Latin.) Revised by J. R. V. MARCHANT, M.A., and J. F. CHARLES, B.A. 3s. 6d.

Latin Primer, The New. By Prof. J. P. POSTGATE. 2s. 6d.

Latin Primer, The First. By Prof. POSTGATE. 1s.

Latin Prose for Lower Forms. By M. A. BAYFIELD, M.A. 2s. 6d.

Laws of Every-Day Life. For the Use of Schools. By H. O. ARNOLD-FORSTER, M.P. 1s. 6d. *Special Edition* on green paper for those with weak eyesight, 2s.

Lessons in Our Laws; or, Talks at Broadacre Farm. By H. F. LESTER, B.A. Part I.: THE MAKERS AND CARRIERS-OUT OF THE LAW. Part II.: LAW COURTS AND LOCAL RULE, etc. 1s. 6d. each.
Little Folks' History of England. By ISA CRAIG-KNOX. Illustrated. 1s. 6d.
Making of the Home, The. By Mrs. SAMUEL A. BARNETT. 1s. 6d.
Marlborough Books:—Arithmetic Examples. 3s. French Exercises. 3s. 6d. French Grammar. 2s. 6d. German Grammar. 3s. 6d.
Mechanics for Young Beginners, A First Book of. By the Rev. J. G. EASTON, M.A. 4s. 6d.
Mechanics and Machine Design, Numerical Examples in Practical. By R. G. BLAINE, M.E. *New Edition, Revised and Enlarged.* With 79 Illustrations. Cloth, 2s. 6d.
Natural History Coloured Wall Sheets, Cassell's New. Consisting of 18 subjects. Size, 39 by 31 in. Mounted on rollers and varnished. 3s. each.
Object Lessons from Nature. By Prof. L. C. MIALL, F.L.S., F.G.S. Fully Illustrated. *New and Enlarged Edition.* Two Vols. 1s. 6d. each.
Physiology for Schools. By ALFRED T. SCHOFIELD, M.D., M.R.C.S., &c. Illustrated. 1s. 9d. Three Parts, paper covers, 5d. each; or cloth limp, 6d. each.
Poetry Readers, Cassell's New. Illustrated. 12 Books. 1d. each. Cloth, 1s. 6d.
Popular Educator, Cassell's New. With Revised Text, New Maps, New Coloured Plates, New Type, &c. Complete in Eight Vols., 5s. each; or Eight Vols. in Four, half-morocco, 50s.
Reader, The Citizen. By H. O. ARNOLD-FORSTER, M.P. Cloth, 1s. 6d.; also a Scottish Edition, Cloth, 1s. 6d.
Reader, The Temperance. By Rev. J. DENNIS HIRD. 1s. 6d.
Readers, Cassell's "Higher Class." (*List on application.*)
Readers, Cassell's Readable. Illustrated. (*List on application.*)
Readers for Infant Schools, Coloured. Three Books. 4d. each.
Readers, The Modern Geographical. Illustrated throughout. (*List on application.*)
Readers, The Modern School. Illustrated. (*List on application.*)
Reading and Spelling Book, Cassell's Illustrated. 1s.
Round the Empire. By G. R. PARKIN. With a Preface by the Rt. Hon. the Earl of Rosebery, K.G. Fully Illustrated. 1s. 6d.
School Certificates, Cassell's. Three Colours, 6⅛ × 4¾ in., 1d.; Five Colours, 11⅞ × 9¼ in., 3d.; Seven Colours and Gold, 9⅜ × 6⅞ in., 3d.
Science Applied to Work. By J. A. BOWER. Illustrated. 1s.
Science of Every-Day Life. By J. A. BOWER. Illustrated. 1s.
Sculpture, A Primer of. By E. ROSCOE MULLINS. Illustrated. 2s. 6d.
Shade from Models, Common Objects, and Casts of Ornament, How to. By W. E. SPARKES. With 25 Plates by the Author. 3s.
Shakspere's Plays for School Use. Illustrated. 9 Books. 6d. each.
Spelling, A Complete Manual of. By J. D. MORELL, LL.D. 1s.
Technical Educator, Cassell's New. An entirely New Cyclopædia of Technical Education, with Coloured Plates and Engravings. In Vols., 5s. each.
Technical Manuals, Cassell's. Illustrated throughout. 16 Vols., from 2s. to 4s. 6d. (*List free on application.*)
Technology, Manuals of. Edited by Prof. AYRTON, F.R.S., and RICHARD WORMELL, D.Sc., M.A. Illustrated throughout.

The Dyeing of Textile Fabrics. By Prof. Hummel. 5s.	Design in Textile Fabrics. By T. R. Ashenhurst. 4s. 6d.
Watch and Clock Making. By D. Glasgow, Vice-President of the British Horological Institute. 4s. 6d.	Spinning Woollen and Worsted. By W. S. McLaren, M.P. 4s. 6d.
	Practical Mechanics. By Prof. Perry, M.E. 3s. 6d.
Steel and Iron. By Prof. W. H. Greenwood, F.C.S., M.I.C.E., &c. 5s.	Cutting Tools Worked by Hand and Machine. By Prof. Smith. 3s. 6d.

Things New and Old; or, Stories from English History. By H. O. ARNOLD-FORSTER, M.P. Fully Illustrated. Strongly bound in Cloth. Standards I. and II., 9d. each; Standard III., 1s.; Standard IV., 1s. 3d.; Standards V., VI., and VII., 1s. 6d. each.
World of Ours, This. By H. O. ARNOLD-FORSTER, M.P. Fully Illustrated. 3s. 6d.

Selections from Cassell & Company's Publications.

Books for Young People.

"**Little Folks**" **Half-Yearly Volume.** Containing 432 pages of Letterpress, with Pictures on nearly every page, together with Two Full-page Plates printed in Colours and Four Tinted Plates. Coloured boards, 3s. 6d. ; or cloth gilt, gilt edges, 5s.

Bo-Peep. A Book for the Little Ones. With Original Stories and Verses. Illustrated with beautiful Pictures on nearly every page, and Coloured Frontispiece. Yearly Vol. Elegant picture boards, 2s. 6d. ; cloth, 3s. 6d.

Beyond the Blue Mountains. By L. T. MEADE. Illustrated. 5s.

The Peep of Day. Cassell's Illustrated Edition. 2s. 6d.

Maggie Steele's Diary. By E. A. DILLWYN. 2s. 6d.

A Sunday Story-Book. By MAGGIE BROWNE, SAM BROWNE, and AUNT ETHEL. Illustrated 3s. 6d.

A Bundle of Tales. By MAGGIE BROWNE, SAM BROWNE, & AUNT ETHEL. 3s. 6d.

Story Poems for Young and Old. By E. DAVENPORT. 3s. 6d.

Pleasant Work for Busy Fingers. By MAGGIE BROWNE. Illustrated. 5s.

Born a King. By FRANCES and MARY ARNOLD-FORSTER. Illustrated. 1s.

Magic at Home. By Prof. HOFFMAN. Fully Illustrated. A Series of easy and startling Conjuring Tricks for Beginners. Cloth gilt, 3s. 6d.

Schoolroom and Home Theatricals. By ARTHUR WAUGH. With Illustrations by H. A. J. MILES. Cloth, 2s. 6d.

Little Mother Bunch. By Mrs. MOLESWORTH. Illustrated. Cloth, 3s. 6d.

Heroes of Every-Day Life. By LAURA LANE. With about 20 Full-page Illustrations. 256 pages, crown 8vo, cloth, 2s. 6d.

Ships, Sailors, and the Sea. By R. J. CORNEWALL-JONES. Illustrated throughout, and containing a Coloured Plate of Naval Flags. *Cheap Edition*, 2s. 6d.

Gift Books for Young People. By Popular Authors. With Four Original Illustrations in each. Cloth gilt, 1s 6d. each.

- The Boy Hunters of Kentucky. By Edward S. Ellis.
- Red Feather: a Tale of the American Frontier. By Edward S Ellis.
- Fritters; or, "It's a Long Lane that has no Turning."
- Trixy; or, "Those who Live in Glass Houses shouldn't throw Stones."
- The Two Hardcastles.
- Seeking a City.
- Rhoda's Reward.
- Jack Marston's Anchor.
- Frank's Life-Battle.
- Major Monk's Motto; or, "Look Before you Leap."
- Tim Thomson's Trial; or, "All is not Gold that Glitters."
- Ursula's Stumbling-Block.
- Ruth's Life-Work; or, "No Pains, no Gains."
- Rags and Rainbows.
- Uncle William's Charge.
- Pretty Pink's Purpose.

"**Golden Mottoes**" **Series, The.** Each Book containing 208 pages, with Four full-page Original Illustrations. Crown 8vo, cloth gilt, 2s. each.

- "Nil Desperandum." By the Rev. F. Langbridge, M.A.
- "Bear and Forbear." By Sarah Pitt.
- "Foremost if I Can." By Helen Atteridge.
- "Honour is my Guide." By Jessie Hering (Mrs. Adams-Acton).
- "Aim at a Sure End." By Emily Searchfield.
- "He Conquers who Endures." By the Author of "May Cunningham's Trial," &c.

"**Cross and Crown**" **Series, The.** With Four Illustrations in each Book. Crown 8vo, 256 pages, 2s. 6d. each.

- Heroes of the Indian Empire; or, Stories of Valour and Victory. By Ernest Foster.
- Through Trial to Triumph; or, "The Royal Way." By Madeline Bonavia Hunt.
- In Letters of Flame: A Story of the Waldenses. By C. L. Matéaux.
- Strong to Suffer: A Story of the Jews. By E. Wynne.
- By Fire and Sword: A Story of the Huguenots. By Thomas Archer.
- Adam Hepburn's Vow: A Tale of Kirk and Covenant. By Annie S. Swan.
- No. XIII.; or, The Story of the Lost Vestal. A Tale of Early Christian Days. By Emma Marshall.
- Freedom's Sword: A Story of the Days of Wallace and Bruce. By Annie S. Swan.

Albums for Children. Price 3s. 6d. each.

- The Chit-Chat Album. Illustrated.
- The Album for Home, School, and Play. Set in bold type, and illustrated throughout.
- My Own Album of Animals. Illustrated.
- Picture Album of All Sorts. Illustrated.

"**Wanted—a King**" **Series.** *Cheap Edition.* Illustrated. 2s. 6d. each.

- Robin's Ride. By Ellinor Davenport Adams.
- Great-Grandmamma. By Georgina M. Synge.
- Fairy Tales in Other Lands. By Julia Goddard.
- Wanted—a King; or, How Merle set the Nursery Rhymes to Rights. By Maggie Browne.

Selections from Cassell & Company's Publications.

Crown 8vo Library. Cheap Editions. 2s. 6d. each.

- Rambles Round London. By C. L. Matéaux. Illustrated.
- Around and About Old England. By C. L. Matéaux. Illustrated.
- Paws and Claws. By one of the Authors of "Poems Written for a Child." Illustrated.
- Decisive Events in History. By Thomas Archer. With Original Illustrations.
- The True Robinson Crusoes. Cloth gilt.
- Peeps Abroad for Folks at Home. Illustrated throughout.
- Wild Adventures in Wild Places. By Dr. Gordon Stables, R.N. Illustrated.
- Modern Explorers. By Thomas Frost. Illustrated. *New and Cheaper Edition.*
- Early Explorers. By Thomas Frost.
- Home Chat with our Young Folks. Illustrated throughout.
- Jungle, Peak, and Plain. Illustrated throughout.
- The England of Shakespeare. By E. Goadby. With Full-page Illustrations.

Three-and-Sixpenny Books for Young People. With Original Illustrations. Cloth gilt, 3s. 6d. each.

- Bashful Fifteen. By L. T. Meade.
- The King's Command. A Story for Girls. By Maggie Symington.
- † A Sweet Girl Graduate. By L. T. Meade.
- † The White House at Inch Gow. By Sarah Pitt.
- Lost in Samoa. A Tale of Adventure in the Navigator Islands. By E. S. Ellis.
- Tad; or, "Getting Even" with Him. By E. S. Ellis.
- † Polly. By L. T. Meade.
- † The Palace Beautiful. By L. T. Meade.
- "Follow my Leader."
- For Fortune and Glory.
- † The Cost of a Mistake. By Sarah Pitt.
- Lost among White Africans.
- † A World of Girls. By L. T. Meade.

Books marked thus † can also be had in extra cloth gilt, gilt edges, 5s. each.

Books by Edward S. Ellis. Illustrated. Cloth, 2s. 6d. each.

- The Hunters of the Ozark.
- The Camp in the Mountains.
- Ned in the Woods. A Tale of Early Days in the West.
- Down the Mississippi.
- The Last War Trail.
- Ned on the River. A Tale of Indian River Warfare.
- Footprints in the Forest.
- Up the Tapajos.
- Ned in the Block House. A Story of Pioneer Life in Kentucky.
- The Lost Trail.
- Camp-Fire and Wigwam.
- Lost in the Wilds.

Sixpenny Story Books. By well-known Writers. All Illustrated.

- The Smuggler's Cave.
- Little Lizzie.
- The Boat Club.
- Luke Barnicott.
- Little Bird.
- Little Pickles.
- The Elchester College Boys.
- My First Cruise.
- The Little Peacemaker.
- The Delft Jug.

Cassell's Picture Story Books. Each containing 60 pages. 6d. each.

- Little Talks.
- Bright Stars.
- Nursery Joys.
- Pet's Posy.
- Tiny Tales.
- Daisy's Story Book.
- Dot's Story Book.
- A Nest of Stories.
- Good Night Stories.
- Chats for Small Chatterers.
- Auntie's Stories.
- Birdie's Story Book.
- Little Chimes.
- A Sheaf of Tales.
- Dewdrop Stories.

Illustrated Books for the Little Ones. Containing interesting Stories. All Illustrated. 1s. each; or cloth gilt, 1s. 6d.

- Tales Told for Sunday.
- Sunday Stories for Small People.
- Stories and Pictures for Sunday.
- Bible Pictures for Boys and Girls.
- Firelight Stories.
- Sunlight and Shade.
- Rub-a-dub Tales.
- Fine Feathers and Fluffy Fur.
- Scrambles and Scrapes.
- Tittle Tattle Tales.
- Dumb Friends.
- Indoors and Out.
- Some Farm Friends.
- Those Golden Sands.
- Little Mothers and their Children.
- Our Pretty Pets.
- Our Schoolday Hours.
- Creatures Tame.
- Creatures Wild.
- Up and Down the Garden.
- All Sorts of Adventures.
- Our Sunday Stories.
- Our Holiday Hours.
- Wandering Ways.

Shilling Story Books. All Illustrated, and containing Interesting Stories.

- Seventeen Cats.
- Bunty and the Boys.
- The Heir of Elmdale.
- The Mystery at Shoncliff School.
- Claimed at Last, and Roy's Reward.
- Thorns and Tangles.
- The Cuckoo in the Robin's Nest.
- John's Mistake.
- Diamonds in the Sand.
- Surly Bob.
- The History of Five Little Pitchers.
- The Giant's Cradle.
- Shag and Doll.
- Aunt Lucia's Locket.
- The Magic Mirror.
- The Cost of Revenge.
- Clever Frank.
- Among the Redskins.
- The Ferryman of Brill.
- Harry Maxwell.
- A Banished Monarch.

Eighteenpenny Story Books. All Illustrated throughout.

- Wee Willie Winkie.
- Ups and Downs of a Donkey's Life.
- Three Wee Ulster Lassies.
- Up the Ladder.
- Dick's Hero; & other Stories.
- The Chip Boy.
- Raggles, Baggles, and the Emperor.
- Roses from Thorns.
- Faith's Father.
- By Land and Sea.
- The Young Berringtons.
- Jeff and Leff.
- Tom Morris's Error.
- Worth more than Gold.
- "Through Flood—Through Fire."
- The Girl with the Golden Locks.
- Stories of the Olden Time.

Selections from Cassell & Company's Publications.

"Little Folks" Painting Books. With Text, and Outline Illustrations for Water-Colour Painting. 1s. each.

Fruits and Blossoms for "Little Folks" to Paint.

The "Little Folks" Proverb Painting Book. Cloth only, 2s.

The "Little Folks" Illuminating Book.

Library of Wonders. Illustrated Gift-books for Boys. Cloth, 1s. 6d.

Wonderful Adventures.
Wonderful Escapes.
Wonders of Animal Instinct.
Wonderful Balloon Ascents.
Wonders of Bodily Strength and Skill.

The "World in Pictures" Series. Illustrated throughout. 2s. 6d. each.

A Ramble Round France.
All the Russias.
Chats about Germany.
The Land of the Pyramids (Egypt).
Peeps into China.
The Eastern Wonderland (Japan).
Glimpses of South America.
Round Africa.
The Land of Temples (India).
The Isles of the Pacific.

Cheap Editions of Popular Volumes for Young People. Illustrated. 2s. 6d. each.

In Quest of Gold; or, Under the Whanga Falls.
On Board the *Esmeralda*; or, Martin Leigh's Log.
The Romance of Invention: Vignettes from the Annals of Industry and Science.
Esther West.
Three Homes.
For Queen and King.
Working to Win.
Perils Afloat and Brigands Ashore.

Two-Shilling Story Books. All Illustrated.

Stories of the Tower.
Mr. Burke's Nieces.
May Cunningham's Trial.
The Top of the Ladder: How to Reach it.
Little Flotsam.
Madge and her Friends.
The Children of the Court.
Maid Marjory.
The Four Cats of the Tippertons.
Marion's Two Homes.
Little Folks' Sunday Book.
Two Fourpenny Bits.
Poor Nelly.
Tom Heriot.
Aunt Tabitha's Waifs.
In Mischief Again.
Through Peril to Fortune.
Peggy, and other Tales.

Half-Crown Story Books.

Margaret's Enemy.
Pen's Perplexities.
Notable Shipwrecks.
Wonders of Common Things
At the South Pole.
Truth will Out.
Pictures of School Life and Boyhood.
The Young Man in the Battle of Life. By the Rev. Dr Landels
Soldier and Patriot (George Washington).

Cassell's Pictorial Scrap Book. In Six Sectional Volumes. Paper boards, cloth back, 3s. 6d. per Vol.

Our Scrap Book.
The Seaside Scrap Book.
The Little Folks' Scrap Book.
The Magpie Scrap Book.
The Lion Scrap Book.
The Elephant Scrap Book.

Books for the Little Ones. Fully Illustrated.

Rhymes for the Young Folk. By William Allingham. Beautifully Illustrated. 3s. 6d.
The Sunday Scrap Book. With Several Hundred Illustrations. Boards, 3s. 6d.; cloth, gilt edges, 5s.
The History Scrap Book. With nearly 1,000 Engravings. Cloth, 7s. 6d.
Cassell's Robinson Crusoe. With 100 Illustrations. Cloth, 3s. 6d.; gilt edges, 5s.
The Old Fairy Tales. With Original Illustrations. Boards, 1s.; cloth, 1s. 6d.
My Diary. With Twelve Coloured Plates and 366 Woodcuts. 1s.
Cassell's Swiss Family Robinson. Illustrated. Cloth, 3s. 6d.; gilt edges, 5s.

The World's Workers. A Series of New and Original Volumes by Popular Authors. With Portraits printed on a tint as Frontispiece. 1s. each.

John Cassell. By G. Holden Pike.
Charles Haddon Spurgeon. By G. Holden Pike.
Dr. Arnold of Rugby. By Rose E. Selfe.
The Earl of Shaftesbury.
Sarah Robinson, Agnes Weston, and Mrs. Meredith.
Thomas A. Edison and Samuel F. B. Morse.
Mrs. Somerville and Mary Carpenter.
General Gordon.
Charles Dickens.
Florence Nightingale, Catherine Marsh, Frances Ridley Havergal, Mrs. Ranyard ("L. N. R.").
Dr. Guthrie, Father Mathew, Elihu Burritt, Joseph Livesey.
Sir Henry Havelock and Colin Campbell Lord Clyde.
Abraham Lincoln.
David Livingstone.
George Müller and Andrew Reed.
Richard Cobden.
Benjamin Franklin.
Handel.
Turner the Artist.
George and Robert Stephenson.
Sir Titus Salt and George Moore.

*** *The above Works can also be had Three in One Vol., cloth, gilt edges, 3s.*

CASSELL & COMPANY, Limited, *Ludgate Hill, London;*
Paris & Melbourne.

www.ingramcontent.com/pod-product-compliance
Lightning Source LLC
Chambersburg PA
CBHW031933290426
44108CB00011B/539